AUSTRALIAN CULTURAL STUDIES: A READER

Edited by
John Frow and Meaghan Morris

University of Illinois Press
Urbana and Chicago

© 1993 by John Frow and Meaghan Morris

Manufactured in Singapore

1 2 3 4 5 C P 5 4 3 2 1

This book is printed on acid-free paper.

Library of Congress Cataloging-in-Publication Data

Australian cultural studies : a reader / edited by John Frow and
Meaghan Morris.
p. cm.
Includes bibliographical references.
ISBN 0-252-02059-6.—ISBN 0-252-06353-8 (pbk.)
1. Australia—Civilization. 2. Australia—Popular culture—
History. 3. Australia—Cultural policy. I. Frow, John, 1948- .
II. Morris, Meaghan.
DU107.A899 1993
994—dc20   93-9639
                                                    CIP

Contents

Acknowledgements

We wish to thank the editors of the following journals for permission to reprint: *Southern Review, Textual Practice, Art and Text* and the Estate of Eric Michaels, *Intervention, Meanjin, Metro Magazine, Australian Journal of Communication, Cultural Studies, On the Beach*, and Local Consumption Publications. Full publication details are given on the first page of each article.

Many people helped us with the planning and production of this book. Our special thanks to Adrian Martin and Stephen Muecke for help with the bibliographies; to Noel King for advice and encouragement throughout the whole process of editing; to Graeme Turner for collegial sympathy and support; and to Rhonda Black and the team of editors at Allen and Unwin for their generosity and their professionalism.

Introduction
JOHN FROW AND MEAGHAN MORRIS

During the past few years the word 'culture' has come to be used by Australians in a sense that seems far removed from anything to do with artistic and literary texts. When Australian Labor Party Senator Stephen Loosley declares that 'resetting industrial policy is really a matter of reshaping cultural attitudes', he is not defining culture as a domain of aesthetic pleasure, as a set of masterpieces, or even as an expression of national identity. Nor is he speaking in economic terms of culture as a major industry which (the Sydney *Daily Telegraph Mirror* assures us) 'fills Aussie tills'.[1] He is referring to a complex of social customs, values and expectations which affect our ways of working. So, too, was Rupert Murdoch in an interview screened on ABC-TV in 1990. Just as the worst company crashes in Australian history ended an era of financial mismanagement and entrepreneurial crime, the Melbourne host of the ABC current affairs program *7.30 Report* asked Mr Murdoch what 'we' should do to save our economy. Mr Murdoch replied perfunctorily, 'Oh, you know: change the culture'.

Unlike Senator Loosley, Murdoch expected us to 'know' that he was quoting a formula of the neo-liberal rhetoric now broadly shared in Australia (as elsewhere) by bureaucrats, politicians, economists, journalists and financiers as well as union and corporate leaders, namely: economic problems need 'cultural' solutions. Culture in this sense is not just a topic for specialised debate by an esoteric caste of interpreters ('critics'). On the contrary: 'changing the culture' is a shorthand but *expansive* way of challenging the conduct of other people's everyday working lives—whether within the framework of a single company ('changing the culture is not a quick process in something as old and as large as ARC', says a chief executive of Australia's main producer of concrete reinforcing steel); of an industry (a marketing expert offers a paper on 'Changing culture for service: how to effect a change to the service culture in shopping centres'); or an entire national economy ('Professor Hughes said Australians had relied on the "lucky country" attitude for too long. . ."We have got to cultivate an export culture" ').[2]

In other words, culture itself is imagined as a plastic medium which politically powerful social elites may rework and remould at will. For these economic critics of Australian life, changing the culture primarily means that 'fewer workers must produce more for less'. But this program has social implications. It means changing the minutiae of behaviour ('work practices') at the workplace, and thus the texture and organisation of home and family life; it means inducing workers to invest more actively in the corporate ethos; it can mean improving race and gender relations in the interests of achieving an 'international outlook'; it means sharpening class consciousness by making competitiveness, 'inequality of outcomes' and, therefore, poverty, more acceptable to Australians.

Aesthetic implications follow. 'Changing the culture' means questioning the value of some of the canonical myths of modern Australian history—egalitarianism, mateship, upward mobility for 'all'—along with the ethical images of pleasure, personal development and social worth that circulate in our society. Despite appearances, the neoliberal critique of culture cannot neatly be disentangled from 'artistic and literary' concerns. By the end of the 1980s it had even prompted a media debate about Australian national identity: 'We are', said Peter Robinson, 'nearly all of us, bludgers. That is the reason the country is in a mess and it will not get out of that mess until the national bludging culture has been reversed.'[3]

Shorn of its subordination of all other goals to that of economic productivity, and without the *moralism* that characterises neo-liberal rhetoric, this usage turns out to be strikingly close to one dimension of the way the word is used in contemporary Australian cultural studies. In this context, too, culture is thought of as directly bound up with work and its organisation; with relations of power and gender in the workplace and the home; with the pleasures and the pressures of consumption; with the complex relations of class and kith and kin through which a sense of self is formed; and with the fantasies and desires through which social relations are carried and actively shaped. In short, 'culture' is a term that can designate, in Raymond Williams' phrase, the 'whole way of life' of a social group as it is structured by representation and by power.[4] It is not a detached domain for playing games of social distinction and 'good' taste. It is a network of representations—texts, images, talk, codes of behaviour, and the narrative structures organising these—which shapes every aspect of social life.

II

But to say that the concept of culture refers to the existence of social groups—their formation, their maintenance, their definition against other groups, the constant process of their re-formation—is to raise difficult questions about the kinds of unity that groups lay claim to. At what level, we must ask, does the concept of culture operate—that of the nation-state and/or of a 'national' culture? That of class, gender, race, sexuality, age, ethnicity? The answer is that it may operate at any of these levels, and that they do not slot neatly into each other.

Australian cultural studies, it seems to us, has been acutely aware of the danger of positing imaginary social unities as the explanatory basis for its accounts of cultural texts. Its constant impetus is to think of cultures as processes which divide as much as they bring together, and to be suspicious of those totalising notions of culture which assume that there is always, at the end of cultural processes, the achievement of a whole and coherent 'society' or 'community'.

One reason for this may be that Australia moved very rapidly in the late 1960s and early 1970s from attributing to itself a unitary culture and tradition, and indeed conceiving these as directly based in its cultural and even racial inheritance from Britain, to a recognition at the level of official government policy of the diversity of its ethnic make-up (based to a substantial degree on massive postwar migration from southern Europe and elsewhere); the new policy of multi-culturalism sought to recognise cultural diversity within, and as the basis of, a more differentiated mode of national cohesion.[5] At roughly the same time Australia moved—again, for good and for bad, at the level of official government doctrine—away from its assimilationist and paternalist policies towards Aboriginal people.[6] What followed was in many ways of little practical difference, as both state and federal governments failed to legislate land rights and self-government for Aborigines. The symbolic step nevertheless had its own force. It defined Aboriginal people rather than government institutions as the ones to decide on their future, and it thereby created its own demand for political empowerment.

The policy of multiculturalism is a compromise formation, and it works well in part because the centrifugal pressures on Australian national unity are relatively weak (there is no profound linguistic split, as there is in Canada for instance, and white settler culture is still comfortably installed as the dominant and unmarked term). The policy is imperfect in both its political and its philosophical dimensions: it is always possible for the category of culture with which it operates to remain at the decorative level of folkloric ethnic markers detached from substructures of real and agonistic difference; conversely, it tends to reproduce imaginary identities at the level of the ethnic 'community' and thereby to screen differentiations and contradictions *within* the community (those of class and gender, for example); it depends upon covering over an asymmetry between migrant and indigenous groups (as though both could have the same historical and structural relation to settler society); and it depends, above all, on a final moment of absorption of difference back into unity at the level of language and national identity.

Within its limits, nevertheless, multiculturalism in Australia has been a relatively successful policy, acting as a working model for a conception of culture ideally based on difference and the recognition of otherness, rather than on cultural and social identity. This history of 'policy' forms part of the context for the essays in Section I of this book, 'Representation Wars', all of which explore the *consequences* of assuming a concept of social identity as mobile, differential and provisional (that is, identity as figure rather than as essence)—and all of which work critically on problems defining the *limits* of multiculturalism as a doctrine of conflict management.

Sneja Gunew's essay on ' "Wongar's " *Walg*', for example, considers the unnegotiable status (for this doctrine) of a novel 'authored' by an immigrant Serbian man under an Aboriginal name, and fictively narrated by an Aboriginal woman. Here, the ideology of authorial identity creates a problem of inauthentic difference which can only be resolved by an (impossible) interdiction that seeks to erase the text: ' "Wongar" may neither speak nor write'. Conversely, Eric Michaels discusses the elaborate *'mise en discours'* by which Aboriginal Australian art was promoted in the speculative global market (and the postmodernism boom) of the late 1980s. Suggesting that contemporary Warlpiri 'creative and authorial practices' render fraudulent any aesthetic of the Warlpiri 'product'—which raises issues of cultural *authority*, not authenticity, and which derives its value from conditions of struggle with colonialism and racism—Michaels demands that Warlpiri paintings be judged in terms of their complex processes of production and circulation: 'the contradictions of this system resist resolution'.

Vijay Mishra and Bob Hodge argue that aesthetic postmodernism in fact works broadly to mask an 'unmanageable' plethora of asymmetries between settler and non-settler, white and non-white, colonies. As a 'justifying' discourse that incorporates settler cultures in the temporal framework of a unified 'postcolonialism', it reduces the postcolonial to a 'liberal Australian version of multiculturalism'. In her essay on the high-level diplomatic dispute between Australia and Malaysia over the ABC-TV series *Embassy*, Suvendrini Perera examines an instance of crisis in such postmodern conflict-masking. While specifying her own concerns with issues of authority in a 'mesh of cultural economies', Perera's essay also makes explicit the *regional*-historical context (and the flagrant contradictions) in which multiculturalism tries to 'manage' racism in Australia without risking the political legitimacy of White settler concepts of nationhood, challenging the cultural security of the ethnic ('Anglo-Celtic') status quo[7]—or endangering the governmental economic aim of furthering trade with other Asian–Pacific countries.

III

The essays in the opening section are not theoretically congruent, or politically continuous, with each other, nor with the other essays in the book; there are incompatibilities, divergences and edges of dis-agreement as well as resonances between them (compare, for example, Perera on *Embassy* with Stuart Cunningham on Australian mini-series; Mishra and Hodge on postcolonial literatures with John Hartley on 'invisible fictions' of audience, and global regimes of TV pleasure; Michaels with Adrian Martin on aesthetics; Noel Sanders with Ross Gibson on the cultural construction of landscape; or Tony Bennett with Meaghan Morris on locality tourism). We have, however, used this first section to *frame* as well as to introduce the Reader, because we think that the pressingly political questions of differential repres-entation raised by these essays have strongly inflected most Australian work in cultural studies. Perera's essay lends its title to the section ('Representation Wars') because her analysis of the fears, desires, and conflicts provoked as well as expressed by *Embassy*'s 'charged', fantasmatic Orientalism also helps to clarify two crucial aspects of the context in which, we would argue, Australian work is carried out.

Both aspects 'mesh', in complicated ways, with multiculturalism as well as with each other. One can briefly be described by noting a by-product of policy debates about the social and cultural dimensions of Australia's increasing economic integration with Japan (our major trading partner) and other east Asian countries: the wide circulation in the media of competing narratives—whether dreams or nightmares, fantasies or fears—about 'becoming part of "Asia"'.[8] After the 1970s, it became commonplace for proponents of *economic* 'Asianisation' publicly to criticise those features of our cultural life (xenophobia and parochialism for some, 'free speech' for others), political organisation (the monarchy for some, 'union power' for others) and historical tradition (racism for some, human rights and 'individualism' for others) which can be held to act as obstacles to promoting Australian interests, and 'credibility', with governments and business in the region. In this period, too, articulated racist hostility to 'Asian immigration' moved from the mainstream to the still vociferous margins of policy debate; 'business migration from Asia' became a governmental object of de-sire, and militant Social Darwinism gave way to a flexible Orientalism in foreign affairs.

Again, this shift away from an ideology of purity and identity (and from a 'closed' to an 'open' economy) has been rapid; only in 1965 were the words 'White Australia' removed from the Australian Labor Party platform. One of its effects has been to undermine the rhetorical force of older nationalist appeals to 'authenticity' and 'tradition' in the field of *public* debate; powerful sectors of both the state and capital in Australia have good reasons to fund their own critiques of 'essen-tialism'.[9] Another has been to make available an official discourse of 'nationality' which openly promotes a constructive, not an organic, concept of Australian culture, and a pragmatic, even enterprising approach to the uses of historical representation; for this discourse, both 'culture' and 'history' can be valued more as practices responsible for shaping a prosperous national future than as ways of conserving a 'heritage' from the past. When Prime Minister Keating declared in 1992 that the Pacific War and the Kokoda Track are more appropriate than World War I and Gallipoli as a myth of origins for contemporary Australia, what semioticians call the 'productivity' of discourse was officially taken for granted—and the practice of history *formally* defined as a powerful adjunct to trade.

This may be one reason why Australian work in cultural studies has generally been less concerned to debate the pros and cons of 'essentialism' as a philosophical stance than to examine the *political* conflicts at stake, in concrete contexts and for particular groups of people, between differing stories of community or nation, and to articulate the *historical* struggles occurring in the gaps between competing narrative programs (of 'prosperity', for example), and the complex social experiences that these aspire to organise. A geo-economic insistence on *location* ('becoming part of Asia') is not, in itself, a new development in the public rhetoric of Australian cultural life, and in this volume the essays by Perera, Mishra and Hodge, Turner, Gibson, Morris, Sanders and Stern explore ways in which old colonial genres and 'structures of feeling' (in Raymond Williams' phrase[10]) continue to shape the social meanings of events in the landscapes produced by economic internationalisation.

At the same time, some writers suggest, Australia may well be caught up in a long-term historical process of 'becoming a nation' in these conditions of ethnic diversity, state multiculturalism and economic internationalism: if so, this is a process in which critical intellectuals perhaps inevitably take part. Dating the current phase of 'nationing' to the 1960s (the period in which Donald Horne published *The Lucky Country*, and another time of lively talk about Australia's 'Asian' location), Tony Bennett explores some of the strategies currently deployed in the formation of a national past; Graeme Turner observes the use of an anti-colonial rhetoric to obscure the responsibility of a series of national governments for the social and environmental effects of nuclear testing; while Stuart Cunningham values the historical miniseries that flourished on TV in the 1980s for taking seriously 'the radical historiographical dictum that "the past is only interesting politically because of something which touches us in the present"'— praising the agenda-setting pedagogy of *Cowra Breakout* and *Vietnam* for their 'multiperspectival', elliptical dramaturgy of major events in Australian history.

The importance of the media in shaping debates about location and nationality in Australia highlights the second contextual feature of cultural studies that we want to emphasise. If 'representation wars' are occurring everywhere in part because of the social uptake of communications technology,[11] many Australians are now receiving a plethora of differing local, regional, 'global' and, for the first time, *national* representations of their own and others' lives. In an important essay published elsewhere, Tom O'Regan argues that it was not until the 1980s—with the introduction of satellite networking and complex changes in federal government broadcasting regulations as well as in media markets—that a 'space-binding', 'nationalising' emphasis could fully emerge in the once strongly state-oriented Australian media system. Paradoxically, he suggests, this emphasis favours 'decontextualised' ways of thinking about self, politics and identity while simultaneously fostering a more national *and* international 'mind-set', confirming as well as disconfirming state boundaries and regional autonomies, and 'encouraging the further development of corridors of information'.[12]

The pressure of these contradictory movements may help to explain the remarkable explicitness of public debate in Australia about power, propriety and representation (who has, and who should have, the power to represent whom; how; and under which conditions). If new national frames of reference are, in fact, emerging just as local, regional and global flows of information are redrawing cultural and political boundaries, then the complex issue of *control* over image production, circulation and consumption becomes enmeshed (as Perera points out) in a whole range of political, economic, legal and diplomatic concerns. At the same time, the technological and geo-economic conditions forcing the question of 'what is involved in the representation of another culture, especially when it is seen by members of that culture' on to the government and thence the *media* agenda are precisely those conditions which make it impossible for 'control' to be fully assured from any given point in the system—or for every dispute to be 'managed' within the national framework of Australian democratic multiculturalism.

Moreover, Australia also has a long history of colonial sensitivity about 'the Australian image' abroad, and a solid record of using public resources to shape the representation of our history and ways of life through state-funded image production. In an article on the furore created by the British-produced ABC-TV series *Sylvania Waters* in 1992, Graeme Turner has pointed out that the reception of this 'documentary' about the everyday lives of the Donaher family was a lot like the outrage which greeted *The Adventures of Barry McKenzie* in 1972 and, to a lesser extent, *Crocodile Dundee* in 1986.[13] Like the 'ocker' films of twenty years ago, *Sylvania Waters* provoked heated ethical debates about aesthetic responsibility, genre, and Australian social reality: are many of us *really* like that? are the Donahers' values widely shared? what will people overseas think? should 'ordinary Australians' be allowed to express their racism and homophobia on TV? are British producers entitled to sensationalise the lives of real Australians to flatter British consumers? was the portrayal of Noeline sexist? or class-prejudiced? should soap opera be promoted as 'reality television'? is 'reality TV' ever *real*? Like *Crocodile Dundee*, *Sylvania Waters* also aroused economic anxiety about its impact in Australia (is it a bad sign that most viewers admired the poorest members of the family?) and in other countries (what effect will this have on tourism? immigration? foreign trade?).

The intertwining of ethical and 'image' concerns with political conflicts in a vulnerable *tourist* economy is a recurring theme of this book; as tourism has vastly expanded in scale and in importance to the Australian economy, so public debate has intensified about the social costs and environmental effects of tourist culture.[14] An important influence on Australian discussions of the politics of representation, however, has come from the work of Aboriginal people directly *confronting* these costs and effects. Historically used as targets for the technological practices, 'nationing' experiments and ethnocidal image campaigns of White Australian society,[15] Aboriginal groups have recently used the media to wage a 'war' of their own to protect their languages and ways of life; to increase their economic independence by developing their own artistic and tourist ventures; to bring political pressure to bear on federal and state governments sensitive to embarrassment and reactive to 'credibility'; to educate public opinion in Australia; to demand positive, informed coverage of Aboriginal activities, and more control over Aboriginal images; and, by these means, to further their political struggle for self-determination.[16]

While there is always controversy about the practical results of this kind of 'symbolic' politics, Aboriginal media practices have at the very least challenged (and, we would argue, altered) the terms on which issues of race, colonialism, cultural value, national identity and history, land ownership and environmental ethics are publicly discussed in Australia—which is to say, they have powerfully affected our political and intellectual life. So have feminist campaigns around images of women, and so, too, have the efforts of migrant groups to change the representational 'norm' of an Anglo-Celtic Australia. In this context, it is not simply a conceit of cultural studies to claim that people can contest and transform the meanings circulated by the culture industries of a media society. On the contrary, the fact that people actually *do* this is a given of contemporary politics, and one determinant of the social context in which cultural studies is practised.

In our view, the most innovative Australian work has therefore been more interested in developing the *implications* of particular forms of symbolic action, and the *consequences* of particular moments of cultural practice, than in proving the case for doing so against older theories of culture. It is not that Australian cultural studies (as we see it) is in any way hostile to 'theory'; theoretical work can also be considered a form of cultural practice. It is merely that the doctrinal disputes which have marked and perhaps enabled the emergence of cultural studies elsewhere—disputes between humanism and formalism, formalism and Marxism, Frankfurt School Marxism and post-structuralism, deconstruction and new historicism, 'textualism' and ethnography—have not long remained the *focus* of debate in Australia, where they are often resolved in practice by a kind of rigorous *mixing* (see the essays by Helen Grace, Virginia Nightingale and Tom O'Regan).

There are many complex institutional reasons for this: the humanities academy is small, state funded, and relatively poor; the publishing industry is embattled; many academics can and do engage in several spheres of public life; few of the theoretical traditions so hotly debated internationally in recent years have played a strong or an inhibiting role in Australian intellectual history.[17] The point here, however, is simply that Australian cultural studies has not only been a *response* to the political and social movements of the past three decades (this much can be said of cultural studies as a project in general), but has also derived many of its themes, its research priorities, its polemics and, in some ways, its theoretical emphases and privileged working methods, from an *engagement* with those movements—and the 'worldly, historical frames' (to borrow a phrase from Said and Perera) in which they operate.

IV

The first set of determinations that we want to posit as acting on Australian cultural studies, then, has to do with its involvement in and its confrontation with the intensities of a 'national' culture and a 'national' politics. A second set of determinations—although this separation is no more than a conceptual artifice—has to do with the emergent logic of the discipline (or the antidiscipline) of cultural studies itself, as it struggles to define its object, the *form* of its relation to its object, and the theoretical stakes of its practice.

At the beginning of his essay on the gift, Marcel Mauss writes:

> In these 'early' societies, social phenomena are not discrete; each phenomenon contains all the threads of which the social fabric is composed. In these total social phenomena, as we propose to call them, all kinds of institutions find simultaneous expression: religious, legal, moral, and economic. In addition, the phenomena have their aesthetic aspect and they reveal morphological types.[18]

For cultural studies, we suggest, a similar concentration of social relations is thought to occur in the pressure points of complex modern societies, but without the microcosmic expressiveness that Mauss finds in 'archaic' social structures; rather, social relations are dispersed through these points, composing their complexity but permitting no read-off of a social totality. Instead of the 'total social phenomenon', the corresponding concept for cultural studies is perhaps that of the 'site' (the point of intersection and of negotiation of radically different kinds of determination and semiosis), while 'expression' is displaced by the concept of 'event' (a moment of practice that crystallises diverse temporal and social trajectories).

Thus a shopping mall—to take a banal but central example—offers no quintessential insight into the organisation of an epoch or a culture (it is not an emblem or an essence of the postmodern condition or of consumer capitalism); it is a place where many different things happen, and where many different kinds of social relations are played out. It is, of course, the end point of numerous chains of production and transportation of goods, as well as of the marketing systems that channel them to consumers (and of the financial structures that underlie all this). These chains belong to regional and national as well as to global circuits (the 'gourmet' aisle in the supermarket or the shelves of a delicatessen make visible the global nature of the capitalist marketplace, and may evoke something of the history of its formation, while the produce section may—or may not—be quite local in its reach. In each case the forms of packaging and presentation—'exotic' or 'fresh', for example—will carry particular ideologies and particular aesthetic strategies). In another of its dimensions, the mall is an architectural construct, designed in accordance with an international format (anchored strategically by one or two large stores, with a particular disposition of parking and pedestrian traffic, a particular mix of boutiques, of services, of facilities . . .); it constructs (or perhaps fails to construct) a particular existence and image of community, and works in calculated ways to display the rewards and pleasures that follow upon work (or, again, that fail to). It sets up a normative distinction between men's and women's interactions with this space, and between adults', children's, and teenagers' uses. It distinguishes sharply, of course, between its affluent clientele (the proper subjects of its community) and those who are less welcome—some of them, like schoolkids, it may tolerate; others, like vagrants and drunks, it will not. The aesthetic organisation of the mall has to do with the gratification of desire and the organisation of bodies in space; it's a sensual, subtly coercive kind of space.

But it is also a space that is put to use, that is diverted to ends other than those foreseen by its architects and managers and guards. This is perhaps the most familiar lesson of cultural studies: that structures are always structures-in-use, and that uses cannot be contained in advance. The semiotic space of the shopping mall is a conflictual space, where meanings are negotiated and projected through quite different formations of fantasy and need. This is to suggest a certain freedom, a function perhaps merely of the complexity of these interactions; but, knowing how readily the appearance of freedom can itself be a ruse of power, a cultural studies critic is likely to be wary of positing any transcendental value for this ability to use public space.

In order to get at these disparate structures that meet in and flow through a complex site like a shopping mall, the theorist (because this is never simply a *descriptive* activity) will have of necessity to draw upon, and to cross, the discourses of a number of different disciplines (and again, this cross-disciplinary perspective is characteristic of the working methods of cultural studies). These might include:

- several rather different forms of economic discourse: some relatively technical ways of discussing mall management, commodity supply and demand, and regional patterns of employment; and

xvi

a more theoretical discourse about commodity production and circulation;

- an aesthetic discourse, relating particularly to architecture, but also to advertising and display; a discourse of musicology, or socio-musicology, to talk about the workings of Muzak or of live performance; and a higher level discourse to deal with the interrelation between aesthetics and economics;
- a discourse of politics, both of the 'mundane' kind that refers to zoning permits and struggles over property values, and a micrological discourse concerned with the politics of bodies in space; the first of these might draw in turn upon the discourses of the law and of town planning; the latter upon a Foucauldian account of corporeal discipline, or upon symbolic interactionism or ethnomethodology, or upon urban geography;
- a discourse about gender (itself necessarily a mixed discourse) to analyse the organisation of gender relations by a mythologised spatial structure, by the gender-specific targeting of consumer desire, by the structure of employment, by childcare provision or its absence, and so on;
- an ethnographic discourse, to get at the particularity of responses to and uses of the mall, to understand it as lived experience (or lived textuality, to use a more precise phrase);
- a discourse of history, capable of talking about changes in the organisation of consumption, perhaps in terms of the 'postmodern' or 'post-Fordist' centrality of consumption to a reorganised capitalist system; and of theorising the changing modes of organisation of community and of the public sphere;
- a discourse perhaps more specific to cultural studies that understands the mall as an intricate textual construct, and understands shopping as a form of popular culture directly interrelated with other cultural forms and with an economy of representations and practices that make up a 'way of life';
- possibly governing the use of some of these other discourses, a policy discourse, serving either the managers of and investors in shopping malls, or local government, or perhaps community groups with an interest in reshaping the forms of community structured by the mall;
- finally some mix of sociology, semiotics, and philosophy which one might draw on to talk about the position(s) from which such an analysis can be enunciated: to come to terms with the odd duality that splits the critic into participant and observer, practitioner and reflexive intellectual, on the basis of the privilege given by the possession of cultural capital and a relation of some kind to the institutions of knowledge that make such reflexivity possible.

It is perhaps this 'self-situating' and *limiting* moment of analysis that most clearly distinguishes work in cultural studies from some other modes of analysis on which its practitioners may draw. Unlike much empirical work in positivist social science, cultural studies tends to incorporate in its object of study a critical account of its own motivating questions—and thus of the institutional frameworks and disciplinary rules by which its research imperatives are formed. At the same time, cultural studies is not a form of that 'multi'-disciplinarity which dreams of producing an exhaustive knowledge map, and it does not posit (unlike some totalising forms of Marxism) a transcendental space from which knowledges could be synthesised and a 'general' theory achieved.[19]

On the contrary, work in cultural studies accepts its partiality, in both senses of the term: it is openly incomplete, and it is partisan in its insistence on the political dimensions of knowledge. For this reason, the 'splitting' of critical practice between diverse and often conflicting social functions does not give rise, in cultural studies, to a discourse of intellectual *alienation*. While there is no consensus about the politics of intellectual work among the critics represented in this book (still less for cultural studies imagined 'as a whole'), the intellectual project of cultural studies is always at some level marked, we would argue, by a discourse of social *involvement*.

v

The point of this discussion of an imaginary object, the shopping mall, is to give a sense not only of the working methods of cultural studies but of their rationale. Cultural studies often operates in what looks like an eccentric way, starting with the particular, the detail, the scrap of ordinary or banal existence, and then working to unpack the density of relations and of intersecting social domains that inform it. Rather than being interested in television or architecture or pinball machines in themselves—as industrial or aesthetic structures—it tends to be interested in the way such apparatuses work as points of concentration of social meaning, as 'media' (literally), the carriers of all the complex and conflictual practices of sociality.

To say that the shopping mall is organised by a range of diverse and overlapping systems (economic, aesthetic, demographic, regulatory, spatial . . .) and can be the object of very different discourses, none of which has a privileged relation to its object, is to say that it is subject to very different kinds of *reading*, and that there is no principle of totality that can bring these readings into a coherent complementarity. To cast it in terms of reading is then to suggest a relation between the specialised readings of the various disciplines of knowledge and the 'folk' readings performed by the users of the site (readings which are bound up with the 'things to do' in shopping centres rather than being detached analytic exercises—but which are also themselves, however, pleasurable and interesting 'things to do'). This, too, is a characteristic move in cultural studies: a relativising and democratising move which seeks to ensure that talk about an object is not closed off on the assumption that we know everything there is to know about it; and to ensure that the relationality of any discourse to the full range of others is kept constantly in view.

Another way of talking about all this might be to say that it has to do with the way we understand the concept of *genre*. The mixing of discourses and genres in much work in cultural studies has to do with its methodological impurity, perhaps with a certain fruitful insecurity about its legitimacy as a discipline, but perhaps too with the way it conceives its object as being relational (a network of connections) rather than substantial. Anne Freadman puts it this way:

> With the professionalisation of the social sciences and of the humanities, we put ourselves at risk of writing and reading with carefully administered 'methods' that can only be called mono-generic . . . if I am right, that the conditions of sociality are best described as the occupation of, and enablement by, heterogeneous ranges of generic practices, then mono-generic strategies of interpretation will always miss the mark.[20]

The concept of 'sociality' here carries that active, processual sense that cultural studies gives to the concept of culture, and the two are directly related: both have to do with the *practice* (rather than the implementation) of structures of meaning—genres or codes, for example—and with the construction of social space out of the weaving together, the crisscrossing, of such practices (there are clear analogies with the way ethnomethodology understands the construction and maintenance of the social).

There is a precise sense in which cultural studies uses the concept of *text* as its fundamental model. However, in the working out of this metaphor (at its most abstract, that of the marking or tracing of pure relationality), the concept of text undergoes a mutation. Rather than designating a place where meanings are constructed in a single level of inscription (writing, speech, film, dress . . .), it works as an interleaving of 'levels'. If a shopping mall is conceived on the model of textuality, then this 'text' involves practices, institutional structures and the complex forms of agency they entail, legal, political, and financial conditions of existence, and particular flows of power and knowledge, as well as a particular multilayered semantic organisation; it is an ontologically mixed entity, and one for which there can be no privileged or 'correct' form of reading. It is this, more than anything else, that forces cultural studies' attention to the diversity of audiences for or users of the structures of textuality it analyses—that is, to the open-ended social life of texts— and that forces it, thereby, to question the authority or finality of its own readings.

At the same time, this 'text' exists only within a network of *intertextual* relations (the textual networks of commodity culture, let's say, of architecture, of formations of community, of postmodern spatiality). The concept of text in cultural studies is more rich, more complex, more differentiated, and altogether more tricky than it is in the traditional interpretive disciplines (which is not to say that some of these disciplines may not in practice work with a similar conception of textuality). Thus when Tony Bennett writes about the development for tourism of The Rocks in Sydney, the textual object he reads is not, or not only, a physical place but the sets of local struggles and of clashing representations that go to make up the complex temporality of this site, and that link it both to other such sites of historical recuperation, and to a history of discourses about the national past. Similarly, the object of Noel Sanders' reading of the Azaria Chamberlain case is not the 'facts' of the matter (whatever they might have been) but the gossip, jokes, folk etymologies, journalistic innuendo, narrative patterns, and the various official discourses, through all of which 'the Azaria affair' in its full mythological richness was formed.

VI

The conception of culture that, we argue, increasingly informs the discipline of cultural studies—culture not as organic expression of a community, nor as an autonomous sphere of aesthetic forms, but as a contested and conflictual set of practices of representation bound up with the processes of formation and re-formation of social groups—depends upon a theoretical paradox, since it necessarily presupposes an opposition (between culture and society, between representations and reality) which is the condition of its existence but which it must constantly work to undo. Both the undoing of these oppositions, and the failure ever completely to resolve the tension between them, are constitutive of work in cultural studies. If representations are dissolved into the real (if they are thought only to reflect or to re-present, in a secondary way and either more or less accurately, a reality which has an autonomous existence and against which the representation can thus be measured) then the sense of the ways in which the real is textually constructed (as story, as desire, as repetition) gets lost. Conversely, if the real is nothing more than the sum of its representations ('nothing but texts' as the caricature goes) then the sense of *urgency* to the cultural studies project gets lost.

The concerns of this project are not epistemological, however, but have to do with the social processes by which the categories of the real and of group existence are formed. (The word 'social' here means at once semiotic and political, in the sense of involving relations of power. Foucault's concept of power/knowledge is one influential way of thinking this intertwining of meaning and social relationality; the linguistic concept of enunciation is another.[21]) When Ross Gibson and Lesley Stern, in this volume, meditate upon the mode of being of an Australian landscape or cityscape, they apprehend it, as a matter of principle, by means of its constitution through particular apparatuses of signification. There is no brute reality prior to this process of constitution (which is always, however, both a multi-layered and dispersed process, and one which happens in time—which is to say, in history). Landscape—a term that can so quickly become metaphysical—is understood as a social practice of place.

The concept of culture is an important one for many other disciplines, notably perhaps for cultural anthropology and the sociology of culture. What, we might ask, is special or different about its use in cultural studies? One answer may be—nothing; and it may be, too, that cultural studies shouldn't be described as a 'discipline'. (It's perhaps too young and unformed to have the strong sense of boundaries required of a discipline; it's also shaped—although this is a different issue—by its rebellion against disciplinarity itself.) Nevertheless, those who work in cultural studies tend to have strong opinions about what distinguishes their work from other fields of enquiry, and it might be useful briefly to explore both the differences and the overlap with these other fields.

The most obvious difference is in the object of study. Whereas anthropology is defined by its relation to an 'allochronic' Other[22]—an Other defined as such by its sociocultural difference within a quite different structure of time, and especially by what's understood as a qualitative difference in social organisation—cultural studies takes as its object the ordinary culture (two very loaded words, but let them stand for the moment) of its own society. Certainly there are movements towards such an orientation in contemporary anthropology, but often—for example, in ethnographic studies of rural or working-class communities or of the homeless—this continues to reproduce the same structure of otherness (of an exoticism now caught within the home society). Cultural studies is sometimes caught in this trap too—treating subcultures, for example, as an exotic or subversive other within the dominant culture—but its *impulse* is towards studying the diverse forms of cultural organisation without recourse to such exoticisation.

There are also differences in methodological orientation. Although cultural studies has adopted (often naively) many of the techniques of fieldwork observation and description developed by ethnography (see Virginia Nightingale's essay in this volume), its focus on complex industrialised societies means that other methodologies may in many instances be more appropriate: in particular because vast archives of written and electronic texts are available to it—because, that is, information about cultural codes and practices can be obtained in many other forms than discussion with an informant and participant observation; and because the writer is a member of the culture that is being studied. Cultural studies tends, as a consequence, to make much greater use of techniques of textual analysis; to make use of a greater diversity of sources; to make a more eclectic use of methodologies; and, once again, to work with a more complex problematic of the relation between the writer and the culture being studied (that is, with an *intensification* of the anthropological problem of the tension

xxi

between personal and political distance and personal and political involvement).

In relation to the sociology of culture, cultural studies has certainly learned from its use of statistical survey techniques. The interest of cultural studies, however, tends to lie much more in the lived effects and formations of culture, and questions of the distribution of competency, preference and access are usually made secondary to this concern. But the difference between the two disciplines is more likely one of focus than of kind; and the same holds true of the overlapping relationship between cultural studies and social history.[23] One can observe, finally, an overlap with literary studies to the (limited) extent that the latter has retheorised its object in recent years to cover the analysis of social relations of textuality rather than texts or textual systems in themselves. It's worth noting (since our selection includes several essays that deal with 'high' cultural texts) that cultural studies is not restricted to the study of popular culture, and certainly has little in common with folkloric studies (including the 'folkloric' orientation to mass media studies). Rather, as Grossberg, Nelson and Treichler write:

> Cultural studies does not require us to repudiate elite cultural forms—or simply to acknowledge, with Bourdieu, that distinctions between elite and popular cultural forms are themselves the products of relations of power. Rather, cultural studies requires us to identify the operation of specific practices, of how they continuously reinscribe the line between legitimate and popular culture, and of what they accomplish in specific contexts.[24]

The concern of cultural studies is with the constitution and working of systems of relations rather than with the domains formed by these processes. Hence a further characteristic concern of cultural studies (one it shares with much post-structuralist thought): a concern with boundaries and limits, and especially with the fuzziness of such edges and the consequent impurity of genres and disciplines. For example, John Hartley suggests, in his study of broadcast TV as a 'paedocratic' regime, that it is possible 'to see in impurities not a problem but a fundamental criterion for cultural studies', and he defends an inter-national television criticism on the grounds that 'neither television nor nations can be understood . . . except in relational terms'; Tom O'Regan rearticulates the vexed question of the relationship between cultural criticism and cultural policy by considering both as 'porous systems'; and Helen Grace examines the increasingly fluid relations between value and utility, art and commerce, aesthetics and logic, 'play' and 'war', now being produced in the 'serious business' of con-temporary management culture.

The effect of this concern is not to dissolve analysis into an all-encompassing description ('cultural studies' as 'studying culture'), but rather to foreground the question of the relation *between* the de-scription of textual/cultural networks and the position of enunciation from which that description is possible. This question is, again, at once *semiotic* (it has to do with the organisation and enablement of textuality by structures of genre) and *political* (it has to do with the social relations of textuality: that is, with the relative positioning of speakers and their discursive construction as the carriers of a certain social identity and authority). It follows that an interest in the concrete conditions and particular instances in which conflicts of authority and problems of authorship are negotiated (or not negotiated), and settled (or unsettled), is not confined to studies which are explicitly concerned with cross-cultural conflict and postcolonial struggle. Here, it is also crucial to McKenzie Wark's study of the cultural politics practised in Australia by Midnight Oil, to Adrian Martin's reflections on the uses of the 'name' of popular culture, and to the essays by Virginia Nightingale, Meaghan Morris and Tom O'Regan on the disciplinary metaphors underpinning cultural studies.

VII

Genealogies are as misleading for intellectual work as they are for studying personal behaviour: they can tell us nothing about where we are going, or should go, or might want to go. The standard genealogy for Australian cultural studies is British: rather than looking, say, to the North American work of Harold Innis and James Carey on space and communication, or to the 'suburbia' debate amongst Australian social critics in the 1960s,[25] a filiation is set up with the influential enterprise of 'British Cultural Studies' that took shape in the late 1950s as a challenge to hierarchical distinctions between the public and the private, the major and the minor, the 'great' and the 'everyday', as these regulated the field of culture (and the discipline of English) in Britain.

According to the usual narrative, British Cultural Studies begins with the so-called 'scholarship' generation of scholars formed, as Graeme Turner elsewhere explains, by 'the expansion of educational opportunities within Britain after the war, and the spread of adult education as a means of postwar reconstruction as well as an arm of the welfare state'.[26] Children of the working class like Richard Hoggart and Raymond Williams saw their task as one of validating the culture of the common people over and against the canonical values of British high cultural elitism, pitting the study of 'culture and society' (the title of Williams' most famous book) against Matthew Arnold's defence of 'culture and civilization'. Where the latter had fostered a nostalgia for pre-industrial English *folk* culture, the new intellectuals examined and affirmed the 'authentic' *popular* culture of the industrial working class. But, as Turner points out, this phase of educational modernisation also corresponded to the postwar expansion of 'industrial' *mass* culture—often North American in source or inspiration. Early critical responses to this 'inauthentic' development (and to working-class enthusiasm for it) were ambiguous, or negative: wedged between the 'folk' and the 'mass', the 'popular' became an increasingly unstable and contested object of study. Some echoes can be traced between British cultural studies in this period, and the nationally inflected but often ambivalent work on Australian popular culture by such diverse critics as AA Phillips, Ian Turner and Russell Ward.

Cultural studies emerges as a program in Britain with the work of the Birmingham Centre for Contemporary Cultural Studies (founded in 1964). During the 1970s and early 1980s, and under the influence of younger scholars who had grown up at home in mass-mediated popular culture, the study of working-class life evolved into 'subcultures' theory, with its interests in pop music, fashion and television on the one hand, and in the politics of race and (a little less so) gender on the other.[27] In this phase, too, there was an acceptance, even a celebration of the Americanisation of Britain as a further way of contesting English 'high' (now also, for some, 'white male') cultural hegemony. In Australia, some of John Docker's work on cultural elites shares the assumptions of this strand of cultural studies.[28]

In theoretical terms, these developments correspond to an increasing insistence on notions of agency in cultural theory. This means studying not how people *are* in a passively inherited culture ('tradition') but what we *do* with the cultural commodities that we encounter and use in daily life ('practice') and thus what we *make* as 'culture'. Inflected by post-structuralist theories of reading as well as by empirical audience research, this shift enabled a redefinition of popular culture not as a stratum (the 'low' one) of aesthetic practice but as a social 'zone of contestation', in Stuart Hall's famous phrase[29]—the ground in and over which different interests struggle for hegemony. *Myths of Oz* by John Fiske, Bob Hodge and Graeme Turner applies this principle to the study of Australian life.[30] It can be argued, however, that later work was more concerned to struggle over popular culture in universities than to explore its constitutive conflicts. In the mid to late 1980s, theories of consumption (defined as an appropriation of cultural meanings rather than the acquisition of goods) came to dominate the field at the height of the economic boom. In the recent work of John Fiske, popular culture is celebrated as a utopian principle of unlimited pleasure production.[31]

Looking back at the Birmingham project, Hall has said that 'there is no doubt in my mind that we were trying to find an institutional practice in cultural studies that might produce an organic intellectual'.[32] Derived from the work of Antonio Gramsci, the notion of an organic (as opposed to traditional) intellectual is now widely used to describe those able to express the knowledges, needs and interests of an emergent class or 'historic movement', in Hall's terms. Instead of representing the interests of socially dominant forces in the name of a mythical 'general public', the organic intellectual will, as McKenzie Wark puts it with reference to Peter Garrett, '[use] his position in a particular set of social relations . . . in order to give voice to his constituency'. For Hall as for Gramsci, organic intellectuals work on two

xxiv

fronts: they must be at the forefront of current theoretical work (they need to 'know more' than traditional intellectuals do), but they must also find ways to share their knowledge with people who are not professional intellectuals.

This model of cultural studies has been criticised on several grounds. Hall himself notes that Gramsci expected the organic intellectual's work to be 'clinched' by a revolutionary party; since there was no such party in 1970s Britain, the organic model defined a 'hope'. Tony Bennett then argues that the whole idea involves a misrecognition of cultural studies' relations to its real conditions of existence, which were and continue to be primarily academic.[33]

Perhaps an extreme form of this misrecognition occurs in work declaring that popular cultural pleasure has socially 'critical' effects. A focus on the active uses made of cultural texts can beg the question of whose uses are being taken as exemplary, and even the laudable attempt to bracket the analyst's theoretically informed criteria of valuation in favour of an ethnographic reconstruction of the value system of a particular group has the consequence that in some sense the analyst's own values are being disavowed and are therefore partly *uncontrolled*. This may mean, to be more precise, that the values of that group—always an analytic construct—may act as a kind of alibi, a fiction into which the analyst's own values are projected in a screened form; and this possibility raises that whole complex set of political issues to do with the propensity of intellectuals to speak 'on behalf of' those who lack a voice in cultural and social debate.[34]

In Australian conditions, however, Bennett's judgment may be too harsh. Wark's essay on Midnight Oil suggests that the organic model may still usefully be applied to non-academic forms of intellectual cultural work. Furthermore, the modest notion of constituency can obviate the need for conjuring up those phantom 'emergent' subjects of history and encourage us to pay more attention to the actual practices developed by real intellectuals in Australia—that is, in a small society with relatively limited institutional resources and with flexible traditions (not to mention mateship networks) allowing a good deal of mobility between institutions. We suspect that a history of cultural studies in Australia would find that the 1960s and 1970s adult education influence (notably in the Workers' Educational Association) both nourished and perpetuated a strong but informal intellectual culture of autodidactic and amateur practice which shaped the values of many who later became, with the expansion of the educational system, professional intellectuals.[35] Our own first encounters with a 'culture and society' approach in the late 1960s came not from reading Raymond Williams but from attending WEA summer schools on film run at Newport Beach in Sydney by John Flaus.

Flaus works as a teacher in university and adult education contexts, as a critic who uses radio as fluently as he writes for magazines, and as an actor in a variety of media from experimental film to TV drama and commercials. If we substitute Wark's notion of constituency for the grand Marxist dream of historic force, we can say that Flaus (like Sylvia Lawson) helped to create a constituency for the project of cultural studies as well as to train a generation of film and media critics. Yet his work, along with the socially mixed but intensely familial urban subculture and the small journal networks[36] which sustained it (both of which were historically deep-rooted in the inner-city life of Sydney and Melbourne) has been erased from those Australian accounts of cultural studies which take their bearings from the British tradition— and then pose problems of application.

Coinciding with the belated professionalisation of media studies in Australia in the late 1970s as well as with the arrival of British cultural studies as a serious academic force, this erasure introduces a distortion, in our view, into current debates. It is one thing to argue that British cultural studies always was primarily academic. It is quite another to assume that if an Australian practice wasn't or isn't primarily academic then it can't be cultural studies—or that it fails to understand what its real situation would have been if it were British. To do this is to ignore the conditions in which Australians have actually worked. This in turn renders invisible the social basis of the partly academic but primarily constituency-oriented work of journalist-critics like Philip Brophy, Ross Gibson, Sylvia Lawson, Adrian Martin and McKenzie Wark,[37] or indeed of policy-oriented intellectuals like Elizabeth Jacka.[38] As the essays in this volume by Stuart Cunningham and Adrian Martin may suggest, the popular media in Australia should perhaps also be thought of as forming a 'porous system' (in Tom O'Regan's phrase)— open on occasion (and to good or bad effect) to exchanging ideas, rhetoric and research images, as well as personnel, with cultural criticism and public policy.

Other genealogies and other kinds of intellectual practice, we suggest, have been at least as important to the development of cultural studies in Australia as the official line of descent. We have no space here for a detailed account, but let us briefly mention Foucault's work. Two texts have been particularly influential: the theoretical model developed in *The Archaeology of Knowledge* opened the way to a more extended and institutionally anchored model of discursivity than was available in other, language- and text-centred notions of discourse; and the first volume of *The History of Sexuality* seemed to offer a much more complex micro-sociological mapping of social power than did other intellectual traditions such as Marxism, as well as overlapping with the rather different ways of conceptualising the construction of sexuality that were prevalent in feminism (especially the psychoanalytic model).

We should also mention the strong influence of Baudrillard, especially for art and media debates, in the early 1980s: his work seemed, for a while, to offer an understanding of the transformations in the structure of 'reality' brought about by the industrialisation, and thus the massive proliferation, of sign-production;[39] and, as Eric Michaels notes, his theory of simulation was read as promising a way to rethink

xxvi

'the contradictions of colonialism and creativity' in an 'import' economy increasingly geared towards generating cultural images and events for tourist consumption (see the essays by Bennett, Gibson, Morris and Stern). More recently, the writings of Henri Lefebvre and Michel de Certeau have begun to feed into the way cultural studies theorises the structure and practice of everyday life; and Bourdieu's sociology of culture has begun to provide a strong counter-tradition to the culture-and-society line that descends from Raymond Willams.[40]

The list of inputs into this emerging discipline could be extended almost indefinitely; it is perhaps the mark of the newness of a discipline that, lacking an established methodology and even a well-defined object, it draws eclectically and energetically upon a variety of theoretical sources as it seeks to define its own specificity. The influence of phenomenology and ethnomethodology can certainly be traced in its refusal to privilege the interpretations of 'expert' readers and its concern with the experiential dimension of everyday life. The understanding of culture as a site of contestation, which had its roots in Gramscian and post-Gramscian theories of hegemony,[41] has been more recently inflected by postcolonial theory, which gives a more ambivalent and complex account both of the flow of power and of the projective identifications and identities of actors in situations of cultural struggle.

Perhaps more fundamental and more lasting than any other single intellectual influence has been feminism and the feminist understanding of the politics of the everyday and of 'personal' life. In Australia as elsewhere, a critique of culture (and of theories of culture) was already crucial to the 'second wave' movement of Women's Liberation in the early 1970s, and this was reflected in such publications as *Mejane* and *Refractory Girl*. While it would be difficult to try to characterise either the 'effects' on cultural studies of such a complex and diverse social movement, or the affinities (and disjunctions) between work in cultural studies and the now vast literatures of women's studies, gay and lesbian studies, and feminist theory, we can point to two of the *consequences* that have followed for Australian cultural studies from the influence of particular currents in Australian feminism.

One is a tendency to think of 'the self' as a site of *social* creativity, rather than simply as a medium of individual expression. Many Australian feminists have always taken the slogan 'the personal is political' to mean that the resources of the state must be captured and used in the interests of transforming women's lives by increasing their access to social equity and power ('changing the culture'). As a result, work on cultural policy is now able to refer for a precedent (though it does not always do so) to a record of significant achievement by Australian feminist bureaucrats.[42] The other consequence is a tendency to assume that a politics of the everyday and of personal life will always involve a confrontation with the workings of class, racism, and colonialism in Australia as well as with sex and gender—and hence a labour of *historical* understanding. Ann Curthoys argued in 1970 that we 'must analyze why public life has been considered to be the focus of history, and why public life has been so thoroughly occupied by men';[43] if cultural studies continues this line of questioning in an expanded framework today, it finds a precedent in the work of Australian feminist historians.

VIII

We have put together this anthology because we believe that there has been a rich and varied tradition of Australian writing in cultural studies over the last ten or fifteen years. We have not tried to give a representative selection of all of this work, however. Instead, we have chosen to make our selection tendentiously, emphasising the kinds of writing that we value and leaving out certain kinds of work that we find less challenging.

At the same time, we have organised the Reader into sections corresponding to some of the recurring themes and problems broadly addressed in cultural studies: the politics of representation in Australia today; the uncertain boundaries of 'art' and 'everyday life' in mediated societies; the multiple ways in which 'popular culture' informs the practices, and shapes the dreams, of modern citizenship; the impact of institutional knowledges and desires on their objects of study; and the intricate, charged relations between stories and spaces, events and sites, 'making history' and 'taking place', in contemporary cultural economies.

This list does not claim to cover all the *major* topics discussed in recent years, and its divisions are somewhat arbitrary; most essays connect or overlap with others in ways which we have not tried to describe, and the sections simply work as a way of framing some basic areas of concern. Some texts also refer in detail to wider debates, and to other writers, not otherwise included here: we hope that the critical essays on literary postcolonialism (Mishra and Hodge), ethnographic audience research (Nightingale), cultural policy studies (O'Regan) and popular consumption (Morris) will be taken as further reading guides, rather than as writing the last word on their subjects.

Inevitably, we have had to omit some writers of whose work we think highly. We wanted, but were unable, to include some of Ian Hunter's recent work on the ethical technologies of 'forming the self', and some of Anne Freadman's writings on the semiotics of genre and enunciation. Had we had more space (the anthologist's despairing cry) we would have included one of Stephen Muecke's essays in 'ficto-criticism', and Noel King and Tim Rowse's piece on media constructions of the national-popular; we would have expanded the material on postcolonial theory with essays by Simon During and Dipesh Chakrabarty; we would have used Jon Stratton's long essay on the Northern Territory as a way of challenging the limited geographical imagination of most of the work that comes out of Melbourne or

Sydney; we would have given more representation to the policy debate that has produced much heat and less light in the last couple of years; we would have included more work on the media—perhaps one of Elizabeth Jacka's essays on the film industry, or some of Bob Hodge's influential work on television. And we would have given space to Sylvia Lawson, who did so much to open the way for cultural studies in Australia. This list of omissions already has the scope of a phantom second volume; we hope you will use the Further Reading list as a way of exploring some of its table of contents.

NOTES

1 Stephen Loosley, 'Step Towards Real Changes', (Sydney) *Sunday Telegraph*, 17 March 1991; 'Culture Fills Aussie Tills', (Sydney) *Daily Telegraph Mirror*, 11 October 1990.
2 'Swan Steels ARC for Competition', *Sunday Telegraph* 26 November, 1989; Advertisement, Shopping Centres Conference, *Australian Financial Review*, 13 August 1992; 'Poor Performance "Shooting Aust in the Head"', *Australian Financial Review*, 26 October 1989.
3 Peter Robinson, 'Fair Go, We're All Bludgers', *Sun Herald* 18 June, 1989.
4 Raymond Williams, *The Long Revolution*, Chatto & Windus, London, 1961.
5 On the history of this policy, see Stephen Castles, Mary Kalantzis, Bill Cope & Michael Morrissey, *Mistaken Identity: Multiculturalism and the Demise of Nationalism in Australia*, Pluto Press, Sydney, 1988.
6 See Roberta B Sykes, *Black Majority*, Hudson Publishing, Hawthorn, 1989.
7 See Ghassan Hage, 'Racism, Multiculturalism and the Gulf War', *Arena* 96 (1991), pp. 8–13.
8 See MT Daly & MI Logan, *The Brittle Rim: Finance, Business and the Pacific Region*, Penguin Books, Ringwood, 1989; Abe David and Ted Wheelwright, *The Third Wave: Australia and Asian Capitalism*, Left Book Club Co-operative Ltd, Sutherland, 1989.
9 On Australian cultural nationalist formations, see Graeme Turner, '"It Works for Me": British Cultural Studies, Australian Cultural Studies, Australian Film' in eds Lawrence Grossberg, Cary Nelson & Paula Treichler (eds), *Cultural Studies*, Routledge, New York and London, 1992, pp. 640–53; cf *National Fictions: Literature, Film and the Construction of Australian Narrative*, Allen & Unwin, Sydney, 1986.
10 See Raymond Williams, *Politics and Letters*, New Left Books, London, 1979.
11 For a theory of this phenomenon in the US context, see Joseph Meyrowitz, *No Sense of Place: The Impact of Electronic Media on Social Behavior*, Oxford University Press, New York and Oxford, 1985.
12 Tom O'Regan, 'Towards a High Communication Policy', *Continuum* 2, 1 (1988/89), pp. 135–58; cf the revised version of this article in *Media Information Australia* 58 (1990), pp. 111–24.
13 Graeme Turner 'Suburbia Vérité', *Australian Left Review* 144 (October 1992), pp. 37–9.
14 See Jennifer Craik, *Resorting to Tourism: Cultural Policies for Tourist Development in Australia*, Allen & Unwin, Sydney, 1991.
15 For an account of a recent image campaign against Aboriginal people, see Steve Mickler, 'Visions of Disorder: Aboriginal people and youth crime

reporting'; *Cultural Studies* 6, 3 (1992), pp. 322–36; cf *Gambling on the First Race: A Comment on Racism and Talk-Back Radio—6PR, the TAB and the WA Government*, report commissioned and published by the Louis St John Memorial Trust Fund, Centre for Research in Culture and Communication, Murdoch University, Perth 1992.

16   On these issues, see *Artlink* 10, 1/2 (1990) [*Contemporary Australian Aboriginal Art*]; *Continuum* 3, 2 (1990) [*Communication & Tradition: Essays After Eric Michaels*]; Sue Cramer (ed), *Postmodernism: A Consideration of the Appropriation of Aboriginal Imagery*, Institute of Modern Art, Brisbane, 1989; Henrietta Fourmile, 'Aboriginal Heritage Legislation and Self-Determination', *Australian–Canadian Studies* 7, 1–2 (1989) pp. 45–61; Adrian Marrie, 'Museums and Aborigines: A Case Study in Internal Colonialism', *Australian–Canadian Studies* 7, 1–2 (1989), pp 63–80; Eric Michaels, *The Aboriginal Invention of Television in Central Australia 1982–1986*, Australian Institute of Aboriginal Studies, 1986; Eric Michaels, *For A Cultural Future: Francis Jupurrurla Makes TV at Yuendumu*, Artspace, Sydney, 1987; John Mundine, 'Aboriginal Art in Australia Today', *Third Text* 6 (1989); 'Aboriginal Art in the Public Eye', special supplement to *Art Monthly Australia*, 56 (1992–93), pp. 3–48.

17   On the problems that 'importing' these debates can create in Australian conditions, see Graeme Turner, 'Dilemmas of a cultural critic: Australian cultural studies today', *Australian Journal of Communication* 16 (1989), pp. 1–12.

18   Marcel Mauss, *The Gift: Forms and Functions of Exchange in Archaic Societies*, trans Ian Cunnison, Cohen & West, London, 1970, p. 1.

19   On this debate, see Meaghan Morris, 'The Man in the Mirror: David Harvey's "Condition" of Postmodernity', in Mike Featherstone (ed), *Cultural Theory and Cultural Change*, Sage Publications, London, 1992; reprinted in *Continental Shift: Globalisation and Culture*, ed Elizabeth Jacka, Local Consumption Publications, Sydney (forthcoming 1993).

20   Anne Freadman, 'The Vagabond Arts', in *In the Place of French: Essays in and around French Studies in Honour of Michael Spencer*, Boombana Publications, Mt Nebo, 1992, p. 280.

21   On Foucault, see Graeme Burchell, Colin Gordon & Peter Miller, *The Foucault Effect: Studies in Governmentality*, Harvester Wheatsheaf, London and Sydney, 1991; John Frow, 'Some Versions of Foucault', *Meanjin* 47, 1 (1988), pp. 144–56, and *Meanjin* 47, 2 (1988), pp. 353–65; Meaghan Morris & Paul Patton (eds), *Michel Foucault: Power, Truth, Strategy*, Feral Publications, Sydney, 1979.

On enunciation, see Ross Chambers, *Room for Maneuver: Reading Oppositional Narrative*, University of Chicago Press, Chicago and London, 1991; Anne Freadman & Meaghan Morris, 'Import Rhetoric: "Semiotics in/and Australia"' in *The Foreign Bodies Papers*, eds Peter Botsman, Chris Burns & Peter Hutchings, Local Consumption Publications, Sydney, 1981; Sneja Gunew, Anne Freadman & Meaghan Morris, 'Forum: Feminism and Interpretation Theory', *Southern Review*, 6, I (March 1983), pp. 149–73; Tom O'Regan, 'Some Reflections on the "Policy Moment"', *Meanjin* 51, 3 (1992), pp. 517–32.

22   See Johannes Fabian, *Time and the Other: How Anthropology Makes Its Object*, Columbia University Press, New York, 1983.

23   See Julian Thomas, 'History With and Without Film', *Meanjin* 48, 2 (1989), pp. 419–27; Tony Bennett, Colin Mercer, Pat Buckridge & David Carter (eds), *Celebration of a Nation*, Allen & Unwin, Sydney, 1992.

24 Lawrence Grossberg, Cary Nelson & Paula Treichler, 'Introduction', *Cultural Studies*, op cit (note 9), p. 13.
25 On North America, see James Carey, *Communication As Culture: Essays on Media and Society*, Unwin Hyman, London and Sydney, 1989; and Arthur Kroker, *Technology and the Canadian Mind: Innis, McLuhan, Grant*, New World Perspectives, Montreal, 1984.
    For Australia, see Robin Boyd, *The Australian Ugliness*, Penguin Books, Ringwood, 1963; Ronald Conway, *The Great Australian Stupor: An Interpretation of the Australian Way of Life*, Sun Books, Melbourne, 1971; Donald Horne, *The Lucky Country*, Penguin Books, Ringwood, 1964; Craig McGregor, *Profile of Australia*, Hodder and Stoughton, London, 1966 and *People, Politics and Pop*, Ure Smith, Sydney, 1968.
26 Graeme Turner, *British Cultural Studies: An Introduction*, Unwin Hyman, Boston and Sydney, 1990, p. 44.
27 See, for example, Stuart Hall & Tony Jefferson, *Resistance Through Rituals: Youth Subcultures in Post-War Britain*, Hutchinson, London, 1976; Angela McRobbie, 'Settling Accounts with Subcultures: A Feminist Critique' in *Culture, Ideology and Social Process: A Reader*, eds T Bennett, G Martin, C Mercer & J Woollacott, Batsford Academic and Education Ltd, London, 1981, pp. 113–23; Paul Gilroy, *There Ain't No Black in the Union Jack: The Cultural Politics of Race and Nation*, Hutchinson, London, 1987.
28 John Docker, 'Popular Culture versus the State: An Argument against Australian Content Regulations for Television', *Media Information Australia* 59 (February 1991), pp. 7–26; cf *Australian Cultural Elites: Intellectual Traditions in Sydney and Melbourne*, Angus & Robertson, Sydney, 1974.
29 Stuart Hall, 'Notes on Deconstructing "the popular"', in Raphael Samuel (ed), *People's History and Socialist Theory*, Routledge & Kegan Paul, London, 1981.
30 John Fiske, Bob Hodge & Graeme Turner, *Myths of Oz: Reading Australian Popular Culture*, Allen & Unwin, Sydney, 1987.
31 John Fiske, *Reading the Popular* and *Understanding Popular Culture*, Unwin Hyman, Boston and Sydney, 1989. See also John Frow, 'The Concept of the Popular', *New Formations* 18 (1992), pp. 25–38.
32 Stuart Hall, 'Cultural Studies and its Theoretical Legacies', in Grossberg, Nelson & Treichler, *Cultural Studies*, op cit (note 9), p. 281.
33 Tony Bennett, 'Putting Policy into Cultural Studies', in Grossberg, Nelson & Treichler, *Cultural Studies*, op cit (note 9), p. 34.
34 On these issues, see John Frow, 'Michel de Certeau and the Practice of Representation', *Cultural Studies* 5, 1 (1991), pp. 52–60, and Meaghan Morris, 'Banality in Cultural Studies' in Patricia Mellencamp (ed), *Logics of Television*, Indiana University Press, Bloomington, 1990, pp. 14–43.
35 On 'amateurism' and/or small journal culture in Australia, see George Alexander, 'Introduction: On Editorial Strategies' in *Language, Sexuality & Subversion*, eds Paul Foss & Meaghan Morris, Feral Publications, Sydney 1978; John Forbes, 'Aspects of Contemporary Australian Poetry' in *The Foreign Bodies Papers*, eds Peter Botsman, Chris Burns & Peter Hutchings, Local Consumption Publications, Sydney, 1981'; Adrian Martin, 'S.O.S.', *Continuum* 5, 2 (1992).
36 Many small journals and magazines have published work in cultural studies since the 1970s. Alongside regular outlets like *Continuum*, *Meanjin* and the *Local Consumption* series, we would include the following (not all of which are extant): *Age Monthly Review*, *Agenda*, *ALR* [*Australian Left Review*], *Antithesis*, *Arena*, *Art & Text*, *Australian Feminist Studies*, *Australian*

Cultural History, Australian Journal of Communication, Australian Journal of Cultural Studies, Binocular, Cinema Papers, Culture and Policy, Filmnews, Frogger, GLP, Hecate, Intervention, Island Magazine, Media Information Australia, Metro, NMA [New Music Articles], *On The Beach, Paper Burns, Praxis M, Photofile, Social Analysis, Social Semiotics, Southern Review, STUFF, STUFFING, Tension, The Third Degree, Transition, Typereader, The Virgin Press, West, Westerly, Working Papers in Sex, Science and Culture* [later *Working Papers*].

37 See Ross Gibson, *South of the West: Postcolonialism and the Narrative Construction of Australia*, Indiana University Press, Bloomington, 1992; Adrian Martin, *Phantasms*, McPhee Gribble, Melbourne (forthcoming 1993); McKenzie Wark, *Logic Bombs: Living with Global Media Events*, Indiana University Press, Bloomington (forthcoming 1994). For reprints of Philip Brophy's magazine work, see *Restuff 1: Horror-Gore-Exploitation* (1988), *2: Rock & Pop Culture* (1988), *3: Media-Theory-Technology* (1991), Stuff Publications, Northcote.

An influential account of the importance of journalism to Australian cultural history is Sylvia Lawson, *The Archibald Paradox: A Strange Case of Authorship*, Allen Lane/Penguin Books, London and Ringwood, 1983; cf Lawson's 'Pieces of a Cultural Geography', *The Age Monthly Review*, February 1987, pp. 10–13.

38 See Stuart Cunningham & Elizabeth Jacka, 'Cultural Studies in the Light of the Policy Process: A Curate's Egg?', in *Australian Cultural Studies Conference 1990: Proceedings*, eds Deborah Chambers & Hart Cohen, Faculty of Humanities and Social Sciences, University of Western Sydney, 1991, pp. 26–56.

39 See André Frankovits ed, *Seduced and Abandoned: The Baudrillard Scene*, Stonemoss Publications, Sydney, 1984.

40 For an early use of Bourdieu to analyse Australian culture, see Tim Rowse, *Australian Liberalism and National Character*, Kibble Books, Malmsbury, 1978; cf Rowse's *Arguing the Arts: The Funding of the Arts in Australia*, Penguin, Ringwood, 1985. See also John Frow, 'Accounting for Tastes: Some Problems in Bourdieu's Sociology of Culture', *Cultural Studies* 1, 1 (1987), pp. 59–73.

41 See Tony Bennett, 'Introduction: Popular Culture and "The Turn to Gramsci"' in *Popular Culture and Social Relations*, eds Tony Bennett, Colin Mercer & Janet Woollacott, Open University Press, Milton Keynes, 1986, pp. xi–xix.

42 See Hester Eisenstein, *Gender Shock: Practising Feminism on Two Continents*, Allen & Unwin, Sydney, 1991; Suzanne Franzway, Dianne Court & RW Connell, *Staking A Claim: Feminism, Bureaucracy and the State*, Allen & Unwin, Sydney, 1989; Marian Sawer, *Sisters in Suits: Women in Public Policy*, Allen & Unwin, Sydney, 1990; Sophie Watson ed, *Playing the State: Australian Feminist Interventions*, Allen & Unwin, Sydney, 1990; Anna Yeatman, *Bureaucrats, Technocrats, Femocrats: Essays on the Contemporary Australian State*, Allen & Unwin, Sydney, 1990.

43 Ann Curthoys, 'Women's Liberation and the Writing of History' in *For and Against Feminism*, Allen & Unwin, Sydney, 1988, p. 4.

PART I
Representation wars

1

Culture, gender and the author-function: 'Wongar's' *Walg*

SNEJA GUNEW

'Banumbir Wongar' is known overseas as one of our most prolific Aboriginal writers.[1] The name translates roughly as 'messenger from the spirit world'. As someone said to me, how can you take seriously as an Aboriginal writer someone who calls themselves 'God'?; it is tantamount to sacrilege. One way of answering this, I suppose, is to reply that all writers of fiction play out or perform a god-function at some level, but of course there is also a much more complicated answer which has to do with the concept of the author in relation to cultural and, more specifically within the Australian context, multi-cultural politics. Because Banumbir Wongar is also Sreten Bozic, a Serbian immigrant who appears to have some interest in anthropology.[2]

To begin unravelling these complications it might be useful to consider part of the history of the reception of 'Wongar's' texts, and here we must distinguish at the outset between the reception in Australia and their reception overseas. Published outside Australia in the first instance, the books return to us here with the endorsement of *Les Temps Modernes* (in which early work appeared), and the dustcover of *Walg* carries the specific approbation of Simone de Beauvoir, linking the novel's themes with the issue of French nuclear tests in the Pacific. Another collection of stories, *The Track to Bralgu*,[3] includes a Foreword by the South African writer Alan Paton. The German version of *Walg* (translated by Annemarie Böll) appears in a series entitled 'Third World Dialogue' and includes an Epilogue, not found in the English edition, in which the author sets out a brief history of white colonial oppression of the Aboriginal peoples. It incorporates the Maralinga tests and more recent campaigns by the mining lobby against Land Rights. In

---

* This essay was first published in *Southern Review* 20 (November 1987).

short, Wongar's books overseas are contextualised by the writings of those groups who have been oppressed in various ways by Western imperialism.

Reviews of *Walg* in the US link it to Rousseauist romanticising of the noble savage and see it as an allegory detailing modern man's destruction of the environment. So much is clear from Colin Walter's review in the *Washington Times Magazine*.[4] Ironically, the same reviewer commenting on the second book of the trilogy, *Karan*, takes issue with the reference to genetic engineering as an unpardonable distortion and exaggeration, albeit fictional. Suddenly and paradoxically the allegorical mode is taken to task for its deviation from codes of verisimilitude.[5] That the trilogy is centrally concerned with radioactive pollution as the logical culmination of uranium mining and with the exploitation of the Aborigines is possibly a relevant factor for producing such reviewing logic. In general terms, overseas, 'Wongar's' texts appear to be received as the voice of Aboriginal Australia.

Within Australia one barely sees any reviews of the texts[6] and instead there is a widespread obsession with 'Wongar's' biographical credentials.[7] Here I refer you to the two biographical résumés, one from *The Oxford Companion to Australian Literature*,[8] the other, purportedly an authorised one, from Robert Drewe's 1981 article in the *Bulletin*. It is not a question as to whether one or the other is 'true' but why this discourse should be generated around this body of writing to the extent that it eclipses any consideration of the fictional texts as part of Australian writing. Underlying much of it is a variety of moral indictments ranging from Elizabeth Perkins's contention that this is 'simply another form of white usurpation', to a vein (familiar in Australian cultural politics) that all artists are charlatans, who con the public.[9]

We are confronted then with the question of distinguishing between our readings of 'Wongar' and our reading of the texts which bear his proper name. Among the many issues and contradictions abounding in multicultural Australia is the practice of bracketing Aboriginal writing in English with so-called ethnic writing. Here surely is a prime illustration of the fact that dominant discourses on Australian culture operate with an unmarked monocultural norm of Anglo Australia and measure against this the 'others', the ethnic groups, the prevailing logic being that the Anglo-Celts do not participate in 'ethnicity'. That the Aborigines should be classed with the minority others is surely one of the more outrageous of the dispossessions they have suffered as a colonised people.

The question of what exactly constitutes Aboriginal writing echoes earlier ones such as: what constitutes women's writing or migrant writing? The way such questions are posed already obscures some crucial elements, one of which is the issue of homogenisation. Thus we are referred to 'the' woman writer and 'the' Aboriginal writer. Behind all these variations on the same question lurk such issues as

4

who is posing them (the hegemonic groups) and the whole terrain of the constitution of the subject which in turn becomes attached to notions of authenticity and authority.[10] When we are dealing with writing which emanates from a politically and historically oppressed group it is very difficult to set aside the problem of phonocentrism— the privileging of speech over writing which, in another context, Gayatri Spivak has termed the problem of the 'native informant'.[11] The object of knowledge supposedly speaks authentically and unproblematically as unified subject on behalf of the groups she or he represents. The question of irony, for example, does not arise. In the drive towards universalism one cannot afford to admit that those oppressed others whom we hear as speaking authentic experience might be playing textual games.[12] Their authenticity is grounded, as it so often still is in the example of women, in biological essentialism. Thus the ridiculous debates, for instance, over the extent to which Aboriginal writers have, or have not, a major percentage of Aboriginal blood. Jack Davis resolved this by saying that the important factor is whether or not one 'lives as an Aboriginal'.[13] But, even so, who legitimates whom in this regard?

The issue of authenticity with respect to minority writers returns to centre stage the figure of the author, a figure who in most recent critical debates had been well and truly decentred; either killed off by the reader in Roland Barthes's version, or dispersed across discursive formations in Foucault's account. And it may be as well to remind ourselves at this point of the classic (and very different) statements on this topic produced by Barthes and Foucault.[14] In Barthes's essay 'The Death of the Author', there is a sentence which in this context bristles with significance: '. . . in ethnographic societies the responsibility for a narrative is never assumed by a person, but by a mediator, shaman or relator whose "performance"—the mastery of the narrative code— may possibly be admired but never his "genius."'[15] Without (I hope) doing too much violence through summarising, traditional Aboriginal storytelling might be described as group narratives which tell the country, expressing ownership and custodial responsibilities through this storytelling. For non-Aboriginal Australians these stories have all been mediated by anthropologists who have translated them not only into other languages but also into other narrative structures. In collections of Australian poetry these translations function as a mark of authenticity, as the country speaking, as an appropriation of historical continuity in ways akin to the inclusion of Old Norse in anthologies of English Literature.[16] Thus we have Ur-texts, but translated ones, and translation, as Paul de Man points out, 'reveals the death of the original'.[17] In this instance there is more at stake, as Gayatri Spivak points out:

> When, however, the violence of imperialism straddles a subject-language, translation can become a species of violation. . .What is at play there is a phenomenon that can be called 'sanctioned ignorance'.[18]

5

But to return to Barthes. Should 'Wongar' then be read as mediating shaman who has mastered a narrative code? Should he be applauded for acting as an Aborigine? Acting for whom? In the introduction to *Aboriginal Myths*, Sreten Bozic refers to his source as Mulluk who entertains the white tourists at Mandorah and Mika Beach not only to demonstrate his culture to them, but also to keep 'the cultural heritage of his race alive'.[19] In the Australian reception of 'Wongar's' texts the concentration on the non-authenticity of the author constitutes a refusal of these texts. Is their subject matter irrelevant in this context, an indictment of white Australian atrocities against the Aboriginal people? Does this explain the concentration on the author's authority—a right to speak rather than to write? Thus, not a refusal of the author as God in Barthes's sense ('to refuse to fix meaning is, in the end, to refuse God and his hypostases—reason, science, law')[20] but, rather, that the author is reinforced as *false* god. The text becomes fixed, in Barthes's term, by the improper name of the author and is declared illegitimate by a series of displacements: 'Wongar', Bozic, 'Merry Xmas'. Thus Margaret Jones in the article cited earlier:

> *Karan* is certainly topical, following almost immediately after the findings of the royal commission into nuclear testing in Australia but it may be hard to induce Australian reviewers to take it too seriously, especially, as seems likely, if this tragic tale of poisoned oranges and Aboriginal/dingo crosses was written by a Yugoslav called Merry Christmas. (p. 5)

Foucault's essay 'What Is an Author?' is more detailed about the concept of the author as a limitation imposed on the text, 'the principle of thrift in the proliferation of meaning'.[21] Foucault transforms the author into the author-function and again we are back with theology. Writing, he maintains, either refers to the theological notion of a hidden meaning which requires deciphering (thus a question of hermeneutics) or to an aesthetic unity which guarantees the writer's immortality and generates commentary (textual offsprings).[22] With the development of the concept of property the author too must now own up to her/his texts so that they may be policed, and trangressions may be recorded. In the case of 'Wongar' it is the name itself which apparently constitutes the trangression:

> Since literary anonymity is not tolerable, we can accept it only in the guise of an enigma . . . Nevertheless, these aspects of an individual which we designate as making him an author are only a projection, in more or less psychologizing terms, of the operations that we force texts to undergo, the connections that we make, the traits that we establish as pertinent, the continuities that we recognize, or the exclusions that we practice. All these operations vary according to periods and types of discourse. (Foucault, p. 150)

Foucault compares these textual operations to Christian exegesis which proves the value of a text by displaying the saintliness of its author. Again, in the case of 'Wongar', we have not the hagiography so much as its reverse—demonology. Referring back to Foucault's definition of

6

the 'author-function' as being 'characteristic of the mode of existence, circulation, and functioning of certain discourses within a society' (p. 148), one might note that the discourses circulating around the name of 'Wongar' displace the texts written under this name. Why this should be so is surely worth pursuing.

It represents an example of how a cluster of questions concerning authority linked with authenticity resonate within cultural politics: who has the right to speak, on behalf of whom and, just as crucially, who reads and from where? Let me reiterate at this point that I am emphatically not eliminating the author here but rather raising questions as to what one should do with the author. In a post-colonial phase we cannot plead ignorance of the apparatus of literary histories, which determine whose texts get published, circulated and endorsed. At the same time our reference point is a post-structuralism which refuses authenticity in the terms of a humanist unified subject. At the end of his essay, Barthes affirms not origins but destinations, the death of the author and the birth of a reader:

> [T]he reader is without history, biography, psychology; he is simply that *someone* who holds together in a single field all the traces by which the written text is constituted. (Barthes, p. 148)

I agree that the reader 'cannot any longer be personal' but affirm nevertheless that reading acts are grounded in history, gender, culture and class. Thus we come now to such a reading act and to *Walg*.

In general discussion *Walg* has been condemned not only because the author transgresses cultural authenticity but also because he is transgressing gender authenticity.[23] Not only is he acting as an Aborigine but as an Aboriginal woman. Precisely! To 'act as' is quite different from 'speaking as'; thus we encounter here instances of bad or blind reading, further examples of a refusal to acknowledge that the writings which purportedly emanate from marginal groups also command recognition of textuality, have a command of textual conventions. In other words, that 'Wongar' may only speak, and falsely, and that he may not write.

In *Walg* the first-person narrator is an Aboriginal woman: she functions as a naive narrator but is not a foil for a more knowing implied author, the kind of example traced by John Frow in Keneally's *The Chant of Jimmie Blacksmith*:

> The collusion between implied author and reader against a character who is necessarily ignorant of the metaphors controlling his existence works as a kind of well-mannered dig in the ribs.[24]

Nonetheless, can a case be made at all for calling this simply 'another form of white usurpation'?[25] To begin with, the genre of the novel scarcely signals traditional Aboriginal storytelling, as Mudrooroo (formerly Colin Johnson) pointed out at a conference on Aboriginal writing when he called his talk on the novel 'White Forms, Aboriginal Content'.[26] Thus, at best, we have here a white form being utilised by someone who may, or may not, have lived as an Aborigine. Does *Walg* signal any overt or covert claims for authenticity of this kind? The dust jacket represents a black woman's face brooding over a parched Australian landscape. The title means 'Womb'—and so we are confronted by the traditional figurative merging of the country and the feminine, signifying in this case that doubly oppressed black women are the last hope for a new life. The back cover carries a lengthy passage by Simone de Beauvoir linking *Walg*'s narrator to her Polynesian sisters. Inside the book are a series of prefatory epigraphs. The first, to Djumala, is the protagonist's name and is also the author's tribal wife (as we discover from the Preface). This particular frame therefore, situating the narrative exchange,[27] functions as a posthumous tribute. The second epigraph is a translation of a fertility chant from Arnhem Land.

Sacred young girls of the northern tribes,
the evening sky smeared with menstrual flow
—the blood from a speared kangaroo,
from *walg*, the sacred uterus. (*Walg*, p. vii)

Aboriginal chants, even in translation, do not feature in the text, so that this reminder might be seen to function as a Derridean supplement, or, in the terms of the previous discussion, as a translation which signals the death of the original. In other words, this does not pretend to be a traditional Aboriginal tale.

The third epigraph is a simple statement that the book is fiction and that only a handful of the five hundred and fifty tribes and six hundred Aboriginal languages now survive. It is inserted into a community of readers where the prevailing belief is still that Aborigines and their cultures are more or less extinct. One way of dealing with the legacy of imperialism is to assert the elegaic mode which signals that the problem no longer exists. A fourth epigraph reminds readers outside Australia that 'the land is an extension of man's body and soul'. This is followed by a glossary of Aboriginal words, and we are reminded again of Spivak's comments regarding the 'sanctioned ignorance' of imperialism. Those who are serious about de-privileging themselves, who seriously wish to challenge the constituent elements of their privilege, need to learn the language of the oppressed. At the same time one notes that the author has presumably embarked on this de-privileging process, that he *has* participated in the learning of this language, however elementary this may be.

The preface, written in the first person, which is not the first person of the novel proper, tells a bizarre little story of how the author was trapped in a police van in the middle of Arnhem Land without any water but with an Aboriginal companion, and how consequently 'my survival depended solely on the virtues of tribal poetry' (p. xv). The Aboriginal companion sings a chant which brings rain. On the next page there is the following:

For much of my understanding of tribal poetry, I am indebted to my late tribal wife, Djumala, through whom I was able to learn about the wide application of oral verses. In the reserve and the nearby area we lived from the bush as most of the economically independent tribal groups did at that time. The poetry was very much alive then; it was there, as so many generations ago, in order to show man how to live with his land and from the land. (p. xvi)

Very clearly the implied author, with the authority of a first-person perspective, signals the artifice of the book and his own status as tribal outsider. What follows in the novel proper is clearly an imaginative impersonation. *Walg* does not purport to be an unmediated first-person narrative, the unproblematic account of a native informant. In ways already set out by the signifier of the dust cover the female black narrator functions as a vehicle for an allegory about black–white relations in Australia. The further structural features, also not classic realist, borrow from the detective novel. The narrator stumbles across clues which lead her to uncover the extent of white plotting against the Aborigines, both in the past and in the present. Her ignorance is a plausible mediation device for the indefensible ignorance of white readers:

The rocks are partly covered with soot, but it does not look so dark inside. A large opening in one of the walls lets in the daylight; even the sun finds a way in, throwing the shape of the large gap through which it has come onto one wall. The cave looks a good shelter . . . no! On the dusty ground near the entrance, partly sunk in dust, lies a woman's waist belt made of human hair and cockatoo feathers. Near it are several empty cartridges. The metal has long lost its shine and is covered with green spots. Two skeletons are resting up against the wall. Each has a chain attached to a wrist and the metal, long gone reddish in colour, has been rubbed against the rock leaving marks . . . and . . . one link has been half filed off, but something must have run out, either time or human strength. Another skeleton, a smaller one of a woman, lies beside the dead fire, bits of long hair trailing through the ashes. Her face must have been stamped into the fire. The jaws are wide open and look as though they are chewing lumps of charcoal. A step away, a young woman hugs her child. A patch of sun falls on the bones of a tiny hand stretching towards the mother's breast, light it up for a moment, and then the shadows return. Not far from the fire, one of the women must have lifted a stick but fallen before she had time to swing it. Above her, a dog with a large hole in its head is caught among the rocks. Something unknown, perhaps a dying yell, must have tossed the animal against the cave wall. (pp. 100–1)

This episode from the past is inserted into the present conspiracy in which the mysterious and dying Dr Cross, an ex-missionary, is engaged in a program of eugenics executed on the tribal survivors and aided by a group of white men who have all been implicated by their participation in an earlier atrocity of rape and murder which is referred to throughout as the incident at 'Gin Downs'. Dr Cross and his son Ranger infiltrate the narrator's tribe and are initiated into its secrets. Ranger abducts the narrator after illegally initiating her at the ritual defloration ceremony and drags her in chains across the country while he collects his uranium samples. The narrator is rescued by her tribesmen but in the present time of the narrative they have all been murdered or captured and caged in an artificial compound where Dr Cross attempts to recreate the tribal fertility rites while, outside, the uranium mining consortium bulldozes the sacred sites.

Djumala's discovery of these facts and the fate of her tribe, learnt as she escapes back to her country, are juxtaposed with the recurrent motif of a female white television reporter whose interpretations act as ironic counterpoint to the narrator's reading of the events. The reporter functions as brutal apologist for the white community who are attempting to wrest the land away from its traditional owners. Dr Cross's breeding of a new race is, in part, meant to undermine the rights of the traditional owners. Thus the issue of what constitutes Aboriginality in relation to land ownerships is very much at the core of the novel.[28]

So much then for the case of acting as, or imaginatively impersonating, an Aborigine. What about the issue of gender impersonation? Although the novel is undoubtedly a very sympathetic political allegory which forms part of the anti-colonialist project in this country it is, nonetheless, a male intervention. As stated earlier, the frames for the terms of reference of this narrative exchange signal an imaginative recreation but it is with the covert emphases and exclusions as they relate to gender that I am now concerned.

The depiction of an Aboriginal woman's world is somewhat different from the one constructed in Diane Bell's *Daughters of the Dreaming*. Djumala is led back to her country by male ancestral spirits but is also constantly advised by her mother and grandmother in particular, both of whom speak to her through dreams or bird incarnation. They advise her concerning her own reproductive cycle but leave things out so that it is the male guides who complete the process. At the same time there are disarming references to misplaced male hubris:

> It might not be so: in the old time the women were the bosses of our world, but the fellows prefer to keep quiet about that now. The Wawalag sisters made spears, built huts, organized the first ceremonies and later, much later, they journeyed to Bralgu to ask Djanbuwal to come to *nara* and bring the monsoon rain with him. From Bralgu, the sisters brought back *badi* ('dilly bag') with magic power to bring plants and animals to life—the same one Marngit carries now. (p. 141)

And later:

> I am not sure if you should believe all the men say; the Wawalags had no husbands to care for and listen to, yet they bred children and made all the ceremonies. They even made rain. I am not saying the elders are wrong, but men are made differently and like to feel they are the boss—black and white alike. (p. 157)

Throughout the novel, signalled initially by the second of the epigraphs, there is the figurative leitmotif of blood as a regenerative force. But whereas the quoted chant refers to menstrual blood, the novel stresses the blood of defloration. The phrase 'being made' or 'becoming a woman' refers to defloration rather than the onset of menstruation (pp. 65; 143). There are hints that the former takes place when the first menses occur but this is not made explicit. In other words, the perspective does not appear to be from a woman's point of view but seems overlaid with male emphases. There are also no references to the kinds of female solidarity which Bell describes, for example, the *yilpinji* and *yawalyu* rituals:

> For women I found that it was not the role of child bearer *per se* that was being celebrated. Rather, women were casting themselves as the nurturers of emotions, of country, and of people . . . Within their own ritual domain women exercise complete autonomy and totally exclude men.[29]

I should add that in the German epilogue there is mention of a similar set of ideas where the women are described as being in charge of social harmony and reference is again made to the ritual importance of menstrual blood.[30] Thus we are talking here of a matter of emphasis rather than misrepresentation through exclusion. In other words, one might argue that the female mask slips a little—as in *Walg*, pp. 65–66: in this passage who speaks is distinct from who sees and the former appears to offer a male perspective.

To return to the question of how these texts circulate within Australia. In an interview 'Wongar' is quoted as saying, 'My origins are not important compared to the tribes I write about' and going on to state that he felt that his work had been suppressed because of a photographic exhibition concerning the impact of mining on Arnhem Land Aborigines which he had organised in 1974 and which had been mysteriously cancelled.[31] One could therefore speculate on whether a concern with origins, the paternity of a text, may well in this case have been invoked in order to curtail potentially embarrassing political meanings.

As a politically committed writer who has attempted to learn Aboriginal languages and cultures, 'Wongar' fuses these elements with a tradition of Middle European political allegory in order to produce his texts. The genres and modes he uses are as reminiscent of Kafka and Brecht (or Lem or Gogol) as of what we think of as traditional Aboriginal storytelling. The issue of who gets published and circulated informs but is separate from how one reads. In *Aboriginal Writing Today* Bruce McGuiness stresses that Aboriginal writing should emanate from the Aboriginal community who should control the publishing and circulation process. That is one way of seeing it and could fall prey to the kind of essentialism referred to at the opening of this paper.[32] When we are dealing, patently, with white forms, in this case a novel, the proliferation of meaning is traversed by various reading positions which are constructed through history, culture, gender and class and include histories of reading—intertextuality. To foreclose these by spurious references to theology—the god author—means that one is refusing textuality in terms either of interpretation or of the processes whereby meanings become constructed. In this case it both refuses the overt political meanings of this text and refuses to acknowledge the ways in which these meanings are consistently denied. 'Wongar' may neither speak nor write.[33]

NOTES

1 B Wongar, *Walg: A Novel of Australia*, Dodd, Mead & Co, NY, 1983. Bahumir Wongar, *Der Schoss*, Lamuv Verlag, Bornheim-Merlen, 1983. *Walg* is the first book of a 'nuclear trilogy' of which the second volume is *Karan*, Dodd, Mead & Co, NY, 1985 and the third is *Gabo Djara: A Novel*, Dodd, Mead & Co 1987. This trilogy has now also been published by Macmillan Australia.

2 For a brief biography see *A Bibliography of Australian Multicultural Writers*, compiled by Sneja Gunew, Loló Houbein, Alexandra Karakostas-Seda and Jan Mahyuddin, Centre for Studies in Literary Education, Deakin University, Geelong, Victoria, 1992.

3 B Wongar, *The Track to Bralgu*, Little, Brown & Co, Boston, 1978.

4 C Walters, 'The Case for Natural Man', *Washington Times Magazine*, 27 December 1983.

5 C Walters, 'Atomic Age Hits Outback', *Washington Times Magazine*, 11 November 1985.

6 An exception is M Jurgensen's enthusiastic review of *Barbaru* in *Outrider* 1, 1, 1984, pp. 175–7.

7 My first encounter with 'Wongar' was through Robert Drewe's article, 'Solved: the Great B Wongar Mystery', *Bulletin Literary Supplement*, 21 April 1981, pp. 2–7 to which my attention was drawn by Ian Reid. Subsequent references to this article will appear in the text.

8 WH Wilde, J Hooton, B Andrews (eds), *The Oxford Companion to Australian Literature*, Oxford University Press, Melbourne, 1985, p. 753.

9 E Perkins, Review of B Wongar's *Bilma*, *Outrider* 2, 1, 1985, p. 239. M Jones, 'B Wongar Publishes a Ferocious Fable, Collects $25 000', *Good Weekend*, 17–19 January 1986, pp. 4–5. The reference in the latter is to a senior writer's grant from the Literature Board.

10 For an extended analysis of 'authenticity' in relation to minority writings see my paper, 'Authenticity and the Writing Cure: Reading Some Migrant Women's Writing', in *Grafts: Feminist Cultural Criticism*, ed S Sheridan, Verso, 1989, pp. 111–24.

11 GC Spivak & S Gunew, 'Questions of Multi-Culturalism' in *Alien and Critical: Women Writers in Exile*, eds ML Broe & A Ingram, University of North Carolina Press, Chapel Hill, 1989, pp. 412–20; and in GC Spivak, *The Post-Colonial Critic: Interviews, Strategies, Dialogues*, ed S Harasym, Routledge, New York, 1990 (pp. 59–66).

12 On the problem of universalism, see Roland Barthes in 'The Great Family of Man', *Mythologies*, Paladin, 1972, pp. 100–2. See also my article 'Ania Walwicz and Antigone Kefala: Varieties of Migrant Dreaming', *Poetry and Gender*, eds B & D Brooks, University of Queensland Press, St Lucia, 1989,

pp. 205–19. That minority writers are also readers is rarely part of the picture.

13 J Davis, 'Aboriginal Writing: A Personal View', in *Aboriginal Writing Today*, eds J Davis and B Hodge, Australian Institute of Aboriginal Studies, Canberra, 1985, pp. 16–17

14 The distinction between the two positions is usefully summarised by D Williamson, 'Authorship and Criticism', Local Consumption, Occasional Paper No 7, 1986, Sydney, p. 15:

> Foucault does not criticise author-centred practices for being based on an ideological illusion of the plenitude of a constitutive subject. From this point of view, the idea that the author is a discursive function can be contrasted with the idea that the author is an ideological fiction, a purely mythical origin. The main outcome of Foucault's account is not to embrace some radical textual practice which is supposedly waiting in the wings of authorial practice and which is already truer to the process-without-origin of language. It is, rather, to show the kinds of discursive and institutional relations which any attempt to alter author-centred practice needs to take into account.

15 R Barthes, 'The Death of the Author', *Image-Music-Text*, trans S Heath, Fontana/Collins, Glasgow, 1979, p. 148.

16 For example, L Murray (ed), *The New Oxford Book of Australian Verse*, Oxford, Melbourne, 1986.

17 P de Man, '"Conclusions" on Walter Benjamin's "The Task of the Translator"', *Yale French Studies* 69, 1985, p. 38.

18 G Spivak, 'Imperialism and Sexual Difference', *Oxford Literary Review* 8, 1–2, 1986, pp. 234–5.

19 S Bozic & A Marshall, *Aboriginal Myths*, Gold Star, Melbourne, 1972, p. 11.

20 Barthes, op. cit., p. 147.

21 M Foucault, 'What is an Author?', in *Textual Strategies*, ed J Harari, Methuen, London, 1970, p. 159.

22 Ibid, pp. 144–5.

23 An exception is Faith Bandler's review for *First Edition*, ABC Radio National, 20 June 1985.

24 J Frow, 'The Chant of Thomas Keneally', *Australian Literary Studies* 10, 3, May 1982, p. 295.

25 E Perkins (see note 9). I should point out that the review in which this comment appeared was of *Bilma*, a collection of poems and that Perkins is referring to the promulgation of Wongar's work as being Aboriginal.

26 C Johnson, 'White Forms, Aboriginal Content' in *Aboriginal Writing Today* (see note 13), p. 31.

27 I am referring here to R Chambers, *Story and Situation: Narrative Seduction and the Power of Fiction*, University of Minnesota Press, Minneapolis, 1985.

28 That this is not entirely a fanciful exaggeration was shown in a newspaper article in which a so-called part-Aboriginal was quoted as saying, 'What they ought to do is castrate all the men and then breed the Abo out of the women.' M Gawenda, 'This is Albert Namatjira Junior: It's 1986. So What has Changed?' *Age*, 27 September 1986.

29 D Bell, 'Central Australian Aboriginal Women's Love Rituals', in *Religion in Aboriginal Australia*, eds M Charlesworth et al, University of Queensland Press, St Lucia, 1984, pp. 348–9. 'Yawalyu' refers to these general social rituals whereas 'yilpinji' refers specifically to love rituals. See also D Bell, *Daughters of the Dreaming*, McPhee Gribble, Melbourne, 1983,

pp. 160–2. The female solidarity groups which Bell describes are specific to desert tribes and not so much to Arnhem Land where the novel is set.

30 *Der Schoss*, op. cit., p. 255. The German edition also includes passages where the rape of Aboriginal women is more explicitly linked to the rape of the land so that, for example, Ranger's penis metamorphoses into a mining drill.

31 K Kizilos, 'Shadowy Literary Figure', *Age*, 23 February 1985.

32 As pointed out in a review of *Aboriginal Writing Today*: S Muecke, 'On not comparing', *Age Monthly Review*, November 1985, p. 8.

33 Recent publications continue the preoccupation with 'Wongar's' life and his 'right' to write but at least these are tempered a little more by some considerations of his texts. See Larry Schwartz, 'White Writer, Black Heart', *Sunday Age*, 19 April 1992, p. 7 and an interview with Wongar in *Speaking Volumes: Australian Writers and Their Work*, Ray Willbanks, Penguin, Melbourne, 1992, pp. 201–14.

2
Representation wars: Malaysia, *Embassy*, and Australia's *Corps Diplomatique*

SUVENDRINI PERERA

At the 1991 Commonwealth Summit the Prime Ministers of Australia and Malaysia signed into existence a pact now known as 'the Harare agreement', a document legitimising representation as an item of formal diplomatic concern.[1] In a statement which incorporated many of the questions currently circulating in the debates around postmodernism, postcolonialism and representation, the then Australian Prime Minister acknowledged the cause of the dispute as the Australian Broadcasting Corporation's television series *Embassy*:

> Mr Hawke said yesterday that it was clear, based on internal evidence, that although *Embassy* was fictional 'the Malaysians were entitled to draw the conclusion that Malaysia was being referred to' [in that production].
> (*Australian*, 19 October 1991)

This essay situates the high-level diplomatic attempt to negotiate issues of referentiality, textuality and the crisis of meaning, of authenticity and simulacra, of national and popular subjectivities, within a mesh of cultural economies. At the same time it examines how a television show such as *Embassy* can have come to figure so prominently—so publicly to be privileged and canvassed over a year or more—in the transactions over security, environmental policy, trade

* This paper was first delivered at the symposium 'Practising Postmodernism', held at the University of Newcastle in November 1991, at which time I was the recipient of a University of Newcastle research fellowship. I am grateful to several students and colleagues who contributed to my thinking during this period; for valuable comments on the spoken version of this paper I am especially grateful to Mary Anne Hughes, Meaghan Morris, and Stephen Muecke. This essay is dedicated to Edward Said in recognition of a continuing intellectual debt.

and, above all, regional hegemony that are clearly at stake in current relations between the governments of Australia and Malaysia.[2]

As Bob Hawke's comments bear out, the entire exchange is distinctly postmodernist in its engagement with both the mechanisms and the principles of representational power. More than any other, representation figures as *the* issue in this international dispute: whatever disguised anxieties and aggressions patrol the border fence, representation seems to have been agreed upon by both parties as the ground of contestation. How does Australia represent Malaysia? Whether in Prime Ministerial denunciations—for example, Hawke's much-reported description of Malaysia as 'barbaric' for imposing the death penalty on two Australians convicted for drug smuggling—or in what both sides characterise as Australia's free press, are these representations acceptable?[3] In turn, how do the Australian media represent this dispute over representation? What are the relations between these representations and official Australian rhetoric? What are the relations between these representations and Australian political *practice*? How are these in turn re-represented in Australian media?

In posing these questions this essay is concerned also with another set of questions that have come up repeatedly in the aftermath of decolonisation and will, I suspect, come up with increasing frequency during the next few years: what is involved in the representation of another culture, when interaction between the cultures concerned has been structured at every level by colonial and imperialist histories? This question has been raised most often as a diplomatic issue in the context of the Middle East—the Saudi reaction to the BBC screening of the film *Death of a Princess* in the late 1970s, the representations of Iran and Islam on US television throughout the 1980s and, most recently, the widespread and even more widely publicised furore over the publication of Salman Rushdie's *The Satanic Verses*. Regionally, however, the question of representation continues to be staged as a local dispute between Australia and Malaysia, and as one that can be adequately explained at the level of anecdote and autobiography—the Malaysian Premier's 'sulks' or his resentment over his unhappy college years in Australia—or as so much diplomatic byplay, a smokescreen for really important concerns like trade and security.[4] To historicise the diplomatic wrangle over *Embassy*, I want to begin by outlining Australia's complicated contemporary positioning within contradictory regional and cultural economies.

PRECARIOUS POSTURES I: THE DIPLOMATIC POSITION

The claim authoritatively to represent, and therefore to *know* Malaysia cannot be separated from the various kinds of authority that are combined in orientalism, the cluster of knowledges about 'oriental' cultures that has underwritten Western colonialism and imperialism. In Australia recent recognitions of—and celebratory explorations into—a newfound 'postcolonial' condition often pass over the problems posed by an older national self-image of Australia as regional heir to the coloniser's discarded mantle. This history positions Australia in an unequal and uneasy triangle with Europe (and especially Britain) at one end, and 'Asia' on the other—a relationship perceived as a set of continuing hierarchical rearrangements based on current conditions of military, economic and cultural (which also at times includes 'racial') superiority.

This heritage of anxiety about place has produced its own complement of orientalist texts in Australia, representations examined in detail by Alison Broinowski in a highly publicised recent study, *The Yellow Lady*. Written by a career diplomat and launched by Governor-General Bill Hayden (who used the occasion to make a speech widely perceived as pro-republican and therefore 'anti-British'), Broinowski's book has been acclaimed for its contribution to regional understanding and the promotion of closer ties with Asia. Like *Embassy*, *The Yellow Lady* produces (and is a product of) Australian knowledge about Asia; for this reason it needs serious consideration as a text which at once critiques and reinscribes Australian orientalism (a process already enacted in its title). In spite of its careful cataloguing of orientalist representations of Asia by Australians, Broinowski's text simultaneously participates in the long history of cultural and economic panic over relations with Asia. The Foreword (by Professor James Mackie) warns ominously:

> Soon, very soon, we will have to be capable of meeting them [Asians] on their terms . . . If we continue to turn our backs on them . . . we are doomed to isolation and insignificance as a nation.[5]

Mackie represents the threat of 'Asia' as an overturning of given hierarchies, an anxiety couched in the language of an inversion of physical and spatial relations of dominance.

Similar anxieties about location and place also underlie a somewhat different group of texts, those popular cultural productions that rewrite Australian–Asian relations within an already available cultural and geographical scheme. This group includes the novel and film versions of *The Year of Living Dangerously*, the recent *Turtle Beach* and, of course, *Embassy*. In these texts South-East Asia is produced as a surrogate Middle East of Islam, despotism, violence, oil and sex, a storehouse where young boys as well as women circulate as endlessly accessible objects of desire and of destruction. Such a localising of wider international tensions is reproduced at yet another level in recent attempts to construct Malaysian Prime Minister Mahathir Mohamad as a new Saddam Hussein, a construction evident, for example, in a cartoon in the *Australian* portraying Mahathir as a swaggering bully-boy in boxing gloves while an Australia-shaped punching bag hangs limply in the background.[6]

Increasingly, however, such representations are contested. The evolving power relations between Australia and the region that CJ

Koch (in *The Year of Living Dangerously*) calls Australia's Middle East, but which we might perhaps describe as Australia's Orient—South-East Asia and the Pacific—mean that these nations can now officially challenge their own orientalisation, for reasons that include not only decolonisation and its aftermath, but also the whole complex of specific outcomes that make up what Andrew Milner has detailed so persuasively as 'Australia's own distinctively postmodern condition':

> So Australia has been catapulted towards post-industrialism at a speed possible only in a society that had never fully industrialized; towards consumerism in a fashion barely imaginable in historically less affluent and egalitarian societies . . . towards an integration into multinational capitalism easily facilitated by longstanding, pre-existing patterns of economic dependence; towards a sense of 'being after', and of being post-European, entirely apposite to a colony of European settlement suddenly set adrift, in intellectually and imaginatively unchartered Asian waters . . . Postcolonialism —or better, perhaps, post-imperialism—is . . . Australia's own distinctively postmodern condition.[7]

As Australian economic and cultural assurance drains, nations like Malaysia and Indonesia, no longer subjected or voiceless in regional or international affairs, can—and do—actively contest representations of primitivism, barbarity and underdevelopment.[8] While on the one hand the sense of post-imperial malaise is only highlighted by the increasingly desperate ring of official assertions of republicanism and regional affiliation, on the other, the energy expended in sustaining an older self-representation of regional dominance and racial superiority is correspondingly increased.

Embassy provides a charged instance for articulating this complicated cultural positioning, inflected as it is by a range of historical experience. The *Sydney Morning Herald*'s recent banner headline of 29 July 1991, 'Malaysia renews attack' is only the most obvious in a series of news reports to represent Malaysian–Australian relations as a battleground where bilateral negotiation and the language of diplomatic interchange are figured as absolute victories and absolute surrenders. In July 1991, when Foreign Minister Gareth Evans visited Malaysia and made some rather awkward efforts to distance himself from *Embassy* after more than a year of strained relations, Richard Ackland, ABC Radio National's coyly unctuous announcer on the current affairs program *Daybreak*, repeatedly described Evans's behaviour as 'grovelling'. This is a term that draws on a set of long-established associations to achieve a startling consciousness of reversal: in the archive of orientalism it is the orientals who grovel. Of course Australia, as a former colony, also possesses a historical memory of 'grovelling' to its colonial overlords, a memory that resonated in Prime Minister Paul Keating's denunciations of 'forelock-tugging' during Queen Elizabeth II's last visit. This complicated triangular relationship between Britain, Australia and an increasingly powerful 'Asia', I would argue, only intensifies the emotional impact produced by the rhetoric of physical mastery and dominance.[9]

In an article in the *Australian* that plays throughout on images of physical submission and humiliation—complemented by the cartoonist Löbbecke's bizarre illustration of Evans attempting to polish a sandalled (presumably Malaysian) foot with the Australian flag—Tony Parkinson wrote even more pointedly that Evans had approached the Malaysian government 'on bended knee' and warned, 'Evans is in danger of going down as the foreign minister who rolled over for Mahathir'.[10] Next to the illustration, the *Australian* printed a quotation from Evans that said: 'Diplomacy should be conducted not on one's back or belly but on one's two feet . . . I think I know, and I think the majority of Australians know, which is the more dignified posture.' Drawing on the same set of associations evoked by the representation of Australia as Mahathir's punching bag, the grotesque absurdity of this illustration of Evans can be unpacked as a range of echoes of verbal and physical abasement. Images of boot licking, the adult man transformed into a shoeshine *boy*, the grovelling and prostration imagery provocatively invoked in Parkinson's characterisation of 'the foreign minister who rolled over for Mahathir', combine with the iconography of the cramped and constricted body (even Evans's face is contorted and twisted) as it fits itself into a new posture of deference. Against the detail of Evans's representation—hairy legs in sagging socks, the paraphernalia of brush, stool, and flag-rag—the smooth, sandalled foot metonymically invoking Malaysia is curiously disembodied. The sandal, the one obvious clue to the foot's identity, makes nonsense of the shoeshine analogy: we are left with a representation of cultural accommodation that is at once violent, incomplete, and absurd.

In the public interchange between Australia and Malaysia on recognition, reciprocity and representation, all signalled in the struggle for proper posture, *Embassy* functions, then, at once as agent and object. But having placed the series locally, so to speak, in a regional-historical frame, there emerge some implicit, but I think inescapable, questions about cultural status and authority that need to be rearticulated within a number of global discursive fields. These intersect with and sustain one another in uneven and uncertain ways: I will isolate them here by labelling them, quite arbitrarily and inconsistently, the Gulf War, the Rushdie Affair, and postmodernism.

This selection calls for immediate explanation in its lumping together of the Gulf War and the Rushdie affair, distinct if complex public events, with something as murky and indeterminate as postmodernism. I can explain myself most directly by saying that all three seem to restate questions of nationalism and ethnicity in particularly troublesome ways. They generate an anxiety, at very different political and ideological positions, about affirmations of cultural or ethnic identity and about assertions of nationhood, either by privileging unstable and variable subjectivities or, as in the Gulf War, by a universalist insistence on a common human condition.

If 'the new world order' and 'the end of history', perhaps the most characteristic locutions of the Reagan–Bush years leading up to the Gulf War, frighteningly foreshadow the dangers to locally based and localised forms of resistance, in the course of the Rushdie Affair the once liberatory properties of nationalism and culturalism often appeared to be dispersed or to be remobilised in the service of fundamentalism and essentialism. The story of the opposition to *The Satanic Verses* is much more complicated than this allows for, but that is not the story I want to tell here; my reason for introducing it is only to suggest how the Rushdie Affair might be available to be read as a confrontation between the master narratives of nationalism or cultural identity, on the one hand, and postmodernism on the other. In this version of the story, Rushdie, as literary lion of the West, could be seen as a key supplier of the sceptical, problematised metafictions of empire so highly prized by postmodernist theorists like Linda Hutcheon, while on the other side, mobs of intractable and incurably literal cultural nationalists shout, equally reprehensibly, for just representation and for blood.[11] This is not to trivialise even for a moment the enormity of the imposition made on Rushdie; rather, I am asking about two divergent strategies—those of *The Satanic Verses* and those of its opponents—for inscribing cultural identity and difference within a global culture that unfailingly produces for every media bogey of a Khomeini or Qaddafi, its Le Pen or Kahane; for each new world order, its Saddam Hussein.

Where the Gulf War held out a scenario that was simultaneously a threat and a bribe in its proposed new world order, postmodernism seems to put forth, for some of us at least, no less expansive or exhaustive a program. To quote from Kumkum Sangari's influential essay of 1987:

> On the one hand the world contracts into the West . . . a 'specialized' skepticism is carried everywhere as cultural paraphernalia and epistemological apparatus . . . and the postmodern problematic becomes the frame through which the cultural products of the rest of the world are seen. On the other hand, the West expands into the world; late capitalism muffles the globe and homogenizes (or threatens to) all cultural production—this, for some reason, is one 'master narrative' that is seldom dismantled . . . The writing that emerges from this position, however critical it may be of colonial discourses, gloomily disempowers the 'nation' as an enabling idea and relocates the impulses for change as everywhere and nowhere.[12]

While the postmodernist suspicion of nationalism and ethnicity has been valuable in helping us break out of the conceptual prisonhouses of authenticity and essence, that same scepticism is often unable to distinguish between a strategic and shifting *process* of identity and difference among peoples and what Christopher Miller describes as the 'Western myth of tribalism, a metaphysical, essentialized means of segmentation'.[13] Before dismantling and demystifying concepts like nationalism and ethnicity, the specific histories which continually constitute and reconstitute these modes of resistance in their changing, even contradictory, configurations need to be acknowledged and examined. This is *not* to reinstall nation, 'race' or ethnicity as absolute, unified and given categories, but to see them as strategic and provisional responses produced at both international and local levels by a range of needs and practices.

If poststructuralism and postmodernist theory have promoted a number of concepts such as alterity, deferral, difference and the non-unified subject that have refined and extended our thinking of national and cultural identity, they have at the same time foreclosed *other* ways of thinking these constructs—those ways, for instance, that locate them within *worldly*, historical frames. It is possible then to identify two complementary moves: on the one hand a celebration and even fetishisation of difference at the levels of language, narrative and representation; on the other, a failure to engage with disturbingly challenging, uncompromisingly oppositional expressions of difference by colonised and post-colonised peoples whose languages and self-representations are either dismissed as naively referential or delegitimised, and even demonised, by being labelled essentialist, totalising or plain fanatic.

PRECARIOUS POSTURES II: *THE CORPS DIPLOMATIQUE*

This section examines an episode of *Embassy* drawing on a strategy suggested by Rey Chow in *Woman and Chinese Modernity*.[14] Chow's starting point is the question I raised before: '[W]hat is involved in the representation of another culture, especially when that representation is seen by members of that culture[?]' (p. 19). What is important in such an instance, Chow argues, is not the correction or revision of a particular text by a set of competing 'facts' authorised by a different history; what matters rather is how this (often occluded or denied) history 'should be reintroduced materially as a specific way of reading —not . . . 'reality' . . . but cultural artifacts such as films and narratives. The task involves not only the formalist analysis of the *producing* apparatus. It also involves rematerialising such formalist analysis with a pregazing . . . that has always already begun.' 'Pregazing' then is Chow's term for the historical understanding brought to a film; to rematerialise this pregazing, she continues, 'we need to shift our attention away from the moment of production to the moment of reception' (p. 19).

Extending the insights of feminist film theory developed by Laura Mulvey, Kaja Silverman and Teresa de Lauretis, Chow examines Bernardo Bertolucci's film *The Last Emperor* and its effects on viewers produced as 'Chinese' by 'rearguing the relationship between image and spectator and by foregrounding the cultural components that are specific to an *imaged spectatorship*' (p. 23). Examining a film like *The Last Emperor* at its point of reception by viewers interpellated by specific cultural processes, for Chow, turns what she calls ethnic spectatorship into 'a site of productive relations' (p. 23).

In what follows I consider a particular episode of *Embassy* from one possible site of ethnic or ethnicised spectatorship before going on to ask some questions about representation, particularly the role of representation in oppositional assertions of ethnicity and cultural difference.

In 'White Panic',[15] her lecture on the recent Australian backlash against multiculturalism, Meaghan Morris discusses Ella Shohat's concept of the ethnically embarrassed text:[16] in recent Hollywood-style productions, Shohat and Morris propose, ethnicity is epidermically ubiquitous on the screen although as a question it is usually textually submerged. In a curious way, *Embassy* participates in this verbal avoidance of difference although its intertexts also evidently include the older, more imperially assured narratives of Kipling, Conrad and Maugham. In its anxiety at once to invite and evade the spectre of referentiality, the series conjures an Orient simultaneously anonymous and exhaustive, contemporary yet effectively unchanged in its implied relations of domination, where questions of racism, imperialism and power are both always present and almost always unasked.

Filmed in Pacific locations from Melbourne to Fiji, with its shifting cast of non-white actors (all the main regulars are Anglo-Australians) spanning the spectrum of visible Asian ethnicities and speaking interchangeably in the less familiar regional languages, *Embassy* recalls in some ways that mad project of cartography described by Baudrillard of an ideal coextensivity between colonisers' map and colonised territory; or is it a perfect simulacrum, 'the generation by models of a real without origins or reality: a hyperreal'?;[17] is it both? Indubitably, *Embassy* is an assemblage of orientalism's most familiar constructs and practices. If, as Edward Said puts it, 'the Orient is the stage on which the whole East is confined',[18] *Embassy* tries hard to pack the whole Orient into the few seconds of its opening montage alone. From palm trees to black-chadored women, from minarets to sinister armed guards, the paraphernalia of orientalism clutter the screen, the found objects of old and new adventures; quickly and efficiently, these define a familiar border and survey the affective landscape of what is to follow.

The episode I discuss is titled 'Hanky Panky' and deals with a classic situation: in a characteristic inversion of the sexual relations of imperialism, an Australian diplomat, Michael, lets himself succumb to a seductive Asian 'housegirl' named Katut, the mistress of another Australian who is just leaving the country. The seduction is figured coyly as a massage scene; Michael, tired and vulnerable after a day of negotiating an international trade deal and arguing with Canberra over staff cuts, yields to Katut's entreaties to let her make him feel better. His friend, already halfway to the door, invites Michael to become Katut's next employer, assuring him, 'She's a Christian; no problem about the religious laws.'

The sequence brings into play two discourses that are understated but pivotal throughout this episode and in the series as a whole: firstly, what is always constructed as a characteristic Australian discourse of mateship, unionism and (masculine) solidarity and—intersecting that in a somewhat ambiguous and contradictory way—the discourse of national interest and national security, figured in what is referred to throughout the series as 'the trade deal'. One of *Embassy*'s ongoing interests is the fiction that this fictional Muslim country, Ragaan, possesses its own oil deposits and that the fictional Australians are interested in ensuring a stable government in the region—even if it means supporting an antidemocratic General as ruler—so that access to the oil is regulated in a way acceptable to Australia. The 'trade deal' is put at risk when the episode of 'hankee pankee', as Katut has learned to call it, becomes a public issue; talk show hosts and tabloids all over Australia pick up the story when Katut's parents, predictably, discover her pregnancy and turn up at the embassy accusing the innocent Michael of being responsible. Since Michael cannot, of course, tell on his mate, his promising diplomatic future also hangs in the balance . . .

I will return to the discourse of mateship in this episode, but first I want to consider the seduction/rape sequence in which Katut beguiles the reluctant Michael into submitting to her handmaidenly ministrations. Katut occupies here the role of what has been positioned traditionally as a source of local knowledge for different kinds of Western (male) observers in a range of orientalist narratives: as the 'housegirl' she is the domesticated, sexually available and faithful native informant. But, Katut, as Michael discovers later when he hires her to work as a 'cleaning lady' at the embassy, is also simultaneously the unreliable informant and the unfaithful native; she has a police record as a petty thief and might be a security risk, a potential spy, in the all-important trade deal; even worse, we discover by the end, she is *sexually* unreliable, having worked as 'housegirl' for a number of Western diplomats: she had been steadily 'working her way through the diplomatic corps' when his mate handed her over to Michael. And the worst thing of all: she might even have been lying when she said she was pregnant—or she may have had a secret abortion.

The indecipherability, unknowability and the sheer *energy* that accumulates around the figure of Katut is in striking contrast to Michael's positioning in relation to her. If, in the *Australian* article cited earlier, Foreign Minister Evans's seeming accommodation of the Malaysian objections to *Embassy* was represented as rolling over for Mahathir, *Embassy* itself represents this scene of Australian diplomatic capitulation as at once an assault and a seduction. The diplomatic body is revealed once more as vulnerable and quiescent, succumbing, first anxiously, then with increasing pleasure, to the knowing and sinuous manipulations of the oriental mistress/servant. I need hardly remark on the significance of casting Katut as the seductress not only of Michael but of the entire diplomatic corps: the body of the oriental woman becomes the means at once of unifying and objectifying, as well as of potentially rupturing or splitting apart, the diplomatic body.

If *Embassy*, as I suggested earlier, replaces the older spies and sailors of Conrad and Kipling with the figure of the diplomat, diplomacy is in many ways a perfect reimagining of colonial contact in the neo- or post-colonial world. It allows questions of cultural conflict, power and imperialism to be managed and negotiated between West and non-West within a postmodernity characterised by cosmopolitanism and a spurious equality among nations. Like Kipling's Kim, the postcolonial diplomat inhabits two unequal cultures, enacting through work the complicated state of being at home and not at home—though in a world now more uneasy than Kipling's about the need for national belonging. In *Embassy* the demands of national interest often come into conflict with the humane instincts of the diplomats themselves; in one episode Belinda, the young Australian secretary, is threatened with recall to Canberra because in a moment of sympathy she gives her used clothes to her cleaning woman. These are meagre contacts, confined to a benevolent third worldism or to the kind of sexual adventuring indulged in by Michael, but cultural accommodation of any kind also puts the diplomatic body at risk, exposing it to the overflow of national and ethnic excess.

In this episode ethnic excess is represented by Katut's non-English-speaking parents. When the charges against Michael become public and he is in danger of losing his position at the embassy, Belinda persuades the other Australian staff into threatening mass resignations if he is sent home; then she decides to appeal to Katut herself. The redeployment of mateship as a discourse of Australian solidarity here—and the consequent containment of gender as a function of difference within the diplomatic body itself—is accomplished by making Belinda, the youngest and institutionally the least powerful woman at the embassy, the one who puts mateship into action. When 'good old Belinda' later takes matters even more firmly into her own hands and decides to meet Katut face to face, Belinda and Katut become jointly responsible for 'saving' Michael from being sent back to Canberra.

Belinda's confrontation with Katut and her parents is the emotional high point of the episode; I want to discuss briefly my own sense of being positioned and ethnicised by that scene in a very specific way. In watching that scene I was suddenly made intensely conscious of how language is used here both in the words that are spoken by the actors and in the subtitles that begin to appear on the screen. The parallel use of language works here to construct ethnicity as at once an interruption and a hysteria. Throughout the episode Katut's mother, who tries frantically to prevent her daughter leaving the house with Belinda, is represented as the irrational, frantic and *impenetrable* native, in contrast to her daughter who has learned the skills of manipulation of and collaboration with the West. When Katut's mother speaks in this scene, the subtitles no longer translate what she says; instead they comment or paraphrase. A long passionate outburst, for example, is subtitled 'speaks angrily'. When I played this episode to my students at the University of Technology, Sydney, last year, the entire class

24

broke out in laughter during this scene. The students' assumption was a perfectly legitimate and appropriate one within the codes of production through which they were understanding the scene: for them the woman spoke gibberish which the subtitles tried to reproduce as words.

Any Sinhala speakers in the ABC's viewing audience, however, would have realised that the mother was not, in fact, speaking nonsense; she was speaking a real, living language, a language that I as a Sri Lankan spectator instantly understood. Like the class, I too laughed aloud at the scene, but *my* laugh was one of recognition and pleasure to hear profanities from the back streets of Colombo, a speech I haven't heard in over ten years, transmitted to me over the ABC. This is not to suggest mine was a unique experience; instead I want to point out the shifts by which intelligibility is first procured here—presumably with some effort—by having an actress speak perfectly appropriate lines (though admittedly in one of the least recognisable languages in Asia), then repressed in the subtitles which are supposed to render meaning legible.

There is also a second, more crucial, repressing: the mother is the only one who makes a spoken accusation, in words, of Michael and by extension the other diplomatic masters Katut has worked for. (Katut herself comes to blame her parents rather than any of her lovers.) Yet the mother's protests and resentment are not available, in words, to anyone except the ethnicised spectator who, like myself, is directly interpellated by her speech (but who remains, in the context of *Embassy*'s codes of production, a *mis*interpreter and misreader).[19]

Two complementary constructions of cultural difference, then, are identifiable here: The first is an *accommodation* of difference—it includes not only the alliance between Belinda and Katut but also Katut's manoeuvres and manipulations within the compound, hybridised space provided by Western presence. This could perhaps be described as the text of ethnic embarrassment. The second, an unforgiving, hysterical and uncompromising ethnicity is available only in the mother's anger, though it recalls other frantic representations permanently available in Western cultural memory: the scenes recreated and endlessly recycled as the materiality of the Gulf War and the Rushdie Affair, for instance. This is the text of ethnic excess. It is incomplete, violent, untranslatable, represented only metonymically as fragments of gesticulating bodies, upraised arms, veiled heads; or in scraps of chants and indecipherable text: half slogans, bits of flaming effigies waved frantically in the wind.

PRECARIOUS POSTURES III: THE POSTCOLONIAL SUBJECT

'[I]t may well be', Stephen Slemon hopefully concludes his essay in *Past the Last Post*, an Australian–Canadian anthology on postmodernism and postcolonialism, 'that the postmodernist debate can become one of the key sites upon which the Anglo-American West, if it is to unravel its own moment of cognitive and cultural aporia, finds itself *forced* to take the representational claims of the post-colonial world seriously'.[20] Leaving aside the issue of whether moments of aporia are, indeed, 'unravellable', and even the somewhat questionable division of labour implied by Slemon in his positioning of 'the post-colonial world' as, once again, the potential salvation of the 'Anglo-American West', the last section of this essay examines the orthodoxies of institutionalised 'postcolonial criticism' and its preoccupation with issues of representation.

To return for a moment to Chow's reading of *The Last Emperor*: Chow cites her mother's reaction to Bertolucci's film to suggest how the polarised opposition between 'truth' on the one hand and 'illusion' or 'lies' on the other is sometimes inadequate in understanding the positioning of the ethnicised spectator in relation to the orientalist text. Chow's mother responded to the many-Oscared *Last Emperor* by saying, 'It is remarkable that a foreign devil should be able to make a film like this about China. I'd say he did a good job!' (24). For Chow, this remark encompasses her mother's experience of the Japanese atrocities committed in China with the collaboration of Emperor Pu Yi, and her (the mother's) historically informed suspicion of Bertolucci as a westerner and foreigner, *as well* as her intense absorption, as an exile, in the visual pleasure and nostalgia so expertly produced by the film. The unexamined, or as Chow calls it, the academic, orientalist reading of *The Last Emperor* would write off her mother's response as 'simplistic' or 'manipulated', thus failing to take into account specific histories within the Chinese diaspora. 'The ethnic[ized] spectator,' Chow concludes, 'occupies an impossible space that almost predetermines its dismissal from a theoretical reading that is intent on exposing the "ideologically suspect" technicalities of production alone' (24).

Chow's reading demands that we do not discount or avoid her mother's implication, as a viewer, in the undeniably orientalist structures of Bertolucci's film. Entangled in orientalist discourse, the mother responds by redeploying it ('in spite of being a foreign devil he did a good job') rather than with an outright rejection or unqualified approval.

I will conclude by introducing a piece of text that can be put next to the *Embassy* episode representing Katut 'working her way through the diplomatic corps'. The quotation is from a brochure designed by the Malaysian government to attract technologically advanced industries into that country's Free Trade Zone. These zones, everyone knows, offer the appeal of cheap labour combined with no taxes and almost non-existent union regulation; the brochure promises in addition one other very specialised local product as part of its multiple attractions:

> The manual dexterity of the oriental female is famous the world over. Her hands are small and she works fast with extreme care. Who, therefore, could be better qualified by nature and inheritance to contribute to the efficiency of a bench assembly production line than the oriental girl?[21]

As Gayatri Spivak has pointed out, 'for reasons of collusion between pre-existing structures of patriarchy and transnational capitalism, it is the urban sub-proletarian female who is the paradigmatic subject of the current configuration of the International Division of Labor.'[22] The structure of that collusion is evident here: the celebration of 'manual dexterity' by the FTZ authorities refers not only to the industrial skills publicly advertised in the brochure; it also alludes, carefully and knowingly, to the massage parlors of Bangkok and Manila. The 'oriental girl' invoked here as the handmaiden of hi-tech and heroine of the bench assembly production line has her more familiar counterparts in whole generations of Singapore Girls, and in many similar constructions, as well as in *Embassy*'s Katut.

In citing the brochure here, I want to do more than simply suggest that oriental femininity is produced and reproduced as a national commodity in texts as different as *Embassy* and a Malaysian trade publication. I want to show how the circulation of such representations is regulated and managed as part of official Malaysian policy in its exchanges with post-colonising or imperialist nations. In this instance the brochure, primarily designed to attract foreign investment from industrialised Western Europe and North America, manipulates and repackages orientalist discourses for its own ends. I select this example to demonstrate how, in an instance like this, the repackaging of colonial constructs confirms in the most damaging way the post-colonised state's official collusion in the orientalising and mass-marketing of its women. But there is also a different point that it is very important to make here: whereas what Slemon calls 'the representational claims of the post-colonial world' have appeared in recent instances as unintelligible or untranslatable excesses of hysteria and fanaticism, a more careful examination might reveal a programmatic logic at work, a logic that redeploys orientalist constructs to its own ends. These, I need hardly add, are not always unimpeachable. The official cultural production of the post-colonised state does not spring new-made from the void but is shaped by its own long history of de-formation.[23]

I have already discussed how the postmodernist delegitimation or dispersal of categories like nation and ethnicity work to disempower the strategic and oppositional functioning of these categories; but the answer, as Chow points out, is not to register the 'representational claims' of the post-colonised in a polarised relation of 'truth and illusion' or referentiality and representation. To recognise and permit the thinking of difference in a way that neither dissipates and disallows it nor distorts, literally, beyond interpretation, calls for attention to local stories and local conditions and a careful examination of how these intersect and are intersected by global discourses. Then, to cite a recent article by Said, individual 'cultures may . . . be represented as zones of control or of abandonment, of recollection and of forgetting, of force or of dependence, of exclusiveness or of sharing, all taking place in the global history that is our element'.[24]

NOTES

1 The *Sydney Morning Herald* (26 February 1992) reported that the agreement 'commits both Governments to dissociating themselves from inaccurate and distorted media reports about each other's affairs', and was first invoked by Australian Foreign Affairs Minister Gareth Evans in his condemnation of the film *Turtle Beach*.

2 The struggle for regional hegemony, evident in the conflict over a number of issues including the Commonwealth Games, relations with Fiji, and UN candidates, is detailed in an article by Greg Sheridan revealingly titled 'One Perfect Whipping-Boy for Malaysia'. Reinforcing the *Australian's* preoccupation with postures of physical subjection and sadomasochism, the article attributes a number of reasons for the direction of Malaysia's foreign policy, ranging from personal snubs to a general sense that Australia is an outsider in the Pacific (6 November 1991).

3 Although the Malaysian government has argued that the ABC's official status suggests implicit government sanction of *Embassy*, Hawke and Evans have insisted on the ABC's freedom from governmental pressure. This assurance is complicated by the government's highly visible attempt to direct ABC content during the Gulf War. An official inquiry was recently announced into the ABC's bias in featuring supposedly 'pro-Iraq' commentators like Dr Robert Springborg during the war. Springborg's fitness to appear as an impartial Middle East 'expert', (or 'orientalist' as they are still called in some circles) was formally challenged by the federal government. So the ABC's attempt, in that particular instance, to represent an alternative and less demonised—a less *orientalised*—Middle East, did in fact lead to public intervention by members of the Hawke government.

4 See Greg Sheridan, 'One Perfect Whipping Boy', *Australian*, 6 November 1991.

5 Alison Broinowski, *The Yellow Lady*, Oxford University Press, Melbourne, 1992, p. v.

6 Löbbecke, *Australian*, 6 November 1991. (The cartoon accompanied Greg Sheridan's article—see note 4.) This is not to evade the valid criticisms of Mahathir's regime that have emerged from a range of Malaysian and non-Malaysian sources. I am interested here only in how such critiques tend to be posed and reposed in orientalist terms in Australian media. A similar problem was apparent during the Gulf War, when the Western peace movement deployed an older rhetoric of 'oriental despotism' in its denunciations of the anti-democratic rule of the Emir of Kuwait. My focus is on the continuing availability of the cultural lexicon of orientalism for mobilisation in any kind of political criticism of the region.

7 Andrew Milner, 'Postmodernism and Popular Culture', *Meanjin* 49/1 (1990), pp. 35–42 at p. 39.

8 The anthropologist Johannes Fabian has described the peculiar cultural relativism and the denial he calls 'allochronism'—the differentiation between so-called 'traditional' or 'primitive' societies on the one hand and 'developed' or 'modern' societies on the other, in a way that denies coevalness or co-temporality between them. As power relations change, the observers and observed in these exercises have begun to face each other across the same time, in positions of co-temporality and contemporaneousness. See Fabian, *Time and the Other*, Columbia University Press, New York, 1983.

9   I am grateful to Meaghan Morris and Joseph Pugliese for discussing this point with me.
10 Tony Parkinson, 'Gareth's Malaise', *Weekend Australian*, 3–4 August 1991, p. 25.
11 In his article 'Cosmopolitans and Celebrities' (published before *The Satanic Verses*) Tim Brennan remarks on the political ambiguity of the proliferating figure of the 'Third World Cosmopolitan Celebrity': 'Propelled and defined by media and market, cosmopolitanism today involves not so much an elite *at home*, as it does spokespersons for a kind of perennial immigration, valorised by a rhetoric of wandering, and rife with allusions to the all-seeing eye of nomadic sensibility.' Brennan, 'Cosmopolitans and Celebrities', *Race and Class* 31, 1 (1989), pp. 1–19 at p. 2.
12 Kumkum Sangari, 'The Politics of the Possible', *Cultural Critique* 7(1987), pp. 157–86 at pp. 183–4.
13 Christopher Miller, *Theories of Africans*, University of Chicago Press, Chicago, 1990, p. 34.
14 Rey Chow, *Woman and Chinese Modernity*, University of Minnesota Press, Minnesota, 1991. Further page references appear in the text in parentheses.
15 Meaghan Morris, 'White Panic or *Max* and the Sublime (The Costs of Multiculturalism)', Mari Kuttna Lecture on Film, University of Sydney, 17 September 1991 [publication forthcoming, The Power Institute, University of Sydney, 1993].
16 Ella Shohat, 'Ethnicities in Relation: Toward a Multicultural Reading of American Cinema', in *Unspeakable Images: Ethnicity and the American Cinema*, ed Lester D Friedman, University of Illinois Press, Chicago, 1991, pp. 215–50.
17 Jean Baudrillard, 'Simulacra and Simulations', in *Selected Writings* (ed Mark Poster), Polity Press, Cambridge, 1988, p. 166.
18 Edward Said, *Orientalism*, Vintage, New York, 1978, p. 63.
19 I thank John Frow for making this last point.
20 Stephen Slemon, 'Modernism's Last Post', in *Past the Last Post*, eds Ian Adam & Helen Tiffin, Harvester, Hempstead, 1991, pp. 1–11 at p. 9.
21 This is quoted in A Sivanandan, 'Imperialism and Disorganic Development in the Silicon Age', *Race and Class* 21, 2 (1979), pp. 111–26 at p. 122.
22 Gayatri Spivak, *In Other Worlds*, Methuen, New York, 1987, p. 218.
23 cf Spivak's suggestion that the Indian government's staging of its early campaign against *The Satanic Verses* was influenced by the need to manage the political damage to the Muslim vote following the Shahbano trial: in Afsaneh Najmabadi, 'Interview with Gayatri Spivak', *Social Text* 28, pp. 122–34 at pp. 133–4.
24 Edward Said, 'Representing the Colonized: Anthropology's Interlocutors', *Critical Inquiry* 15, 2 (Winter 1989), pp. 205–25 at p. 225.

3
What is post(-)colonialism?
VIJAY MISHRA AND BOB HODGE

As the British Empire broke up and attempted to sustain an illusion of unity under the euphemistic title of 'Commonwealth', a new object appeared on the margins of departments of English Literature: 'Commonwealth literature'. The ambiguous politics of the term was inscribed in the field that it called into being. 'Commonwealth literature' did not include the literature of the centre, which acted as the impossible absent standard by which it should be judged. The term also occluded the crucial differences between the 'old' and the 'new' Commonwealth, between White settler colonies and Black nations that typically had a very different and more difficult route into a different kind of independence.

The struggling enterprise of 'Commonwealth literature' was jeopardised from the start by the heavily ideological overtones of its name. Now a new term has gained currency to designate the field: 'post-colonial'. Post-colonial(ism) has many advantages over the former term. It foregrounds a politics of opposition and struggle, and problematises the key relationship between centre and periphery. It has helped to destabilise the barriers around 'English literature' that protected the primacy of the canon and the self-evidence of its standards. But in order to consolidate its place in the curriculum it needed a good, teachable text. With the publication of *The Empire Writes Back*[1] (hereafter abbreviated to *EWB*) that need is now met. *EWB* is a lucid, judicious and representative text which is destined to play a decisive role in this emerging field. That importance is good reason for subjecting it to close critical scrutiny, as we propose to do.

The word post-colonialism (hyphenated) is not given an independent entry in the *OED* (1989). It is still a compound in which the 'post-'

* This essay is reprinted from *Textual Practice* 5, 3 (1991).

is a prefix which governs the subsequent element. 'Post-colonial' thus becomes something which is 'post' or after colonial. In the *OED* the compound exists alongside other compounds such as post-adolescent, post-cognitive, post-coital and so on. The first entry for the word is dated 12 December 1959: 'It was probably inevitable that India, in the full flush of post-colonial sensitivity, should fear that association with the America of that period might involve her necessarily in troubles which were little to do with Asia'. Subsequent entries (1969; 1974) carry this meaning of post-colonial as something which happened after colonisation. Edward Said writes about a 'postcolonial field'[2] to which modern anthropologists can no longer return with their erstwhile certitudes. Here too 'post-colonial' is used in the sense in which the *OED* defines the term.

EWB takes up as its central theme the relationship of the periphery to the metropolitan centre in the context of post-colonial literature. Some of the problems that it faces in positioning itself in relation to this theme can be seen in some ambiguities in the title of the book itself, which makes connections with two seemingly divergent moments in modern culture. The first is the intertext that the title echoes, *The Empire Strikes Back*, the second film in the Star Wars Trilogy in which the father and the Empire are momentarily on the ascendant as Darth Vader all but incapacitates his son (Luke Skywalker) and the counter-insurgence of the guerrillas is checked by the might of the Empire.

The second intertext is not so much a narrative as a personality around whom a bizarre postmodern fiction has been constructed. The title is a quotation from Salman Rushdie who, writing from within the centre as a critic of it, now finds himself denounced for complicity with the values of the coloniser, the imperialist. Saladin the 'chamcha' becomes Rushdie the 'chamcha' who, in Rushdie's own definition, is someone who 'sucks up to powerful people, a yes-man, a sycophant'. 'The Empire', adds Rushdie, 'would not have lasted a week without such collaborators among the colonized people.'[3] The condemnation of Rushdie by the Islamic post-colonial world raises interesting questions about the category of the post-colonial itself and whether one can ever totally remove the stains of complicity with the Empire that come with the 'profession' of post-colonial writer. For the Islamic post-colonial world the moral is clear and succinct: to write in the language of the coloniser is to write from within death itself. As a result of all this, the title of *EWB* begins to sound like a Freudian slip, announcing the inevitable triumph of the Empire's counter-attack as the slogan for a book that celebrates post-colonial subversion.

The Rushdie case is a parable that challenges the notion of post-colonial writing as defined by Ashcroft, Griffiths and Tiffin. In the final analysis post-colonial writers who write in the language of the Empire are marked off as traitors to the cause of a reconstructive post-colonialism. The authors of *EWB* seem to be conscious of this paradox, the paradox that the 'post' in 'post-colonialism' may well imply 'business as usual, only *more so*'.[4] Consequently, they point to the dangers of writing in English (spelt with a lower case whenever non-British English is being referred to) and they know that the post-colonial writers compose in the shadow of 'death'. Many years ago Frantz Fanon anticipated this paradox when he wrote that the colonised is either doomed to be a mere reflection of his master (located in the Imaginary) or he must fight his master through active struggle (so as to enter into the realm of the Symbolic).[5] The withholding of legitimate consciousness, I-ness or selfhood, the impossibility on the part of the colonised even to qualify for the thingness of things (thingword), produces a radical politics in which violence is embraced. But as the ANC's own struggle for self-legitimation demonstrates, the coloniser never completely withholds 'I-ness' or 'selfhood' since to do so would make the colonised worthless. Thus there is always, in the colonial regime, a tantalising offer of subjectivity and its withdrawal which, for the colonised, momentarily confirms their entry into the world of the coloniser only to be rejected by it. The colonised never know when the colonisers consider them for what they are, humans in full possession of a self, or merely objects.

In Fanon's version of the conditions under which the radical post-colonial might come into being, the colonial world must be strategically rendered as Manichean in its *effects*, since the system reduces the colonised to the status of permanent bondage. Consequently, it is in the nature of the Manichean world order that violence should be seen as a cleansing force. This is a severe indictment of the imperialist since the withdrawal of subjectivity hits at the very core of the enlightenment project, the civilising values of modernity which the colonised (a VS Naipaul for instance) sees as imperialism's positive, reconstructive, and basically humane face. The complexity of this essentially Hegelian problematic, the centrality of action in a retheorisation of history as class struggle, is transformed by the authors of *EWB* into a broader, somewhat depoliticised category, the 'counter-discourse'. Political insurgency is replaced by discursive radicalism, for which the West Indian example is offered as paradigmatic.

The danger here is that the post-colonial is reduced to a purely textual phenomenon, as if power is simply a matter of discourse and it is only through discourse that counter-claims might be made. This move is clearly aimed at making the diverse forms of the post-colonial available as a single object on the curriculum of the centre. Since a *grand récit* is not available equally to the varieties of post-colonialism that *EWB* addresses, it is hardly surprising that the dominant tone in the book is the tolerant pluralism of liberal humanism. Difference is recognised but contained within a single pattern, the coexistence of two kinds of relationship to the language and culture of the centre: 'abrogation' or refusal, and 'appropriation'. The latter gathers under a single term a large and diverse set of strategies involving both accommodation and compromise, whose political meaning is highly dependent on specific historical circumstances.

POST-ORIENTALISM AND COUNTER-DISCURSIVITY

A grand theory of post-colonialism inevitably throws up comparisons with another totalising form of scholarship, orientalism. This is not to say that *EWB* duplicates orientalism's political strategy or, more significantly, is unaware of its redemptive as well as damning characteristics. What *EWB*, however, ends up doing is something which is endemic to a project in which particularities are homogenised, perhaps unconsciously, into a more or less unproblematic theory of the Other. One remembers Edward Said's well-known warning that even with the best of intentions one might, and sometimes does, give the impression that through one's own discourses the Other is now representable without due regard to its bewildering complexity. Perhaps it is in the very nature of any totalising enterprise that simplifications which are avoided elsewhere (as in individual articles by Ashcroft, Griffiths and Tiffin) make their way into the body of the text.

The paradox that surfaces—a paradox that we would call post-orientalism—is part of an historical process that grew out of Europe's reading of the Other. Orientalism's heavily skewed and ideologically marked discourses—the enterprise was never totally homogeneous, and often contradictory—haunts the post-colonial in ways that makes, in places, the post-colonial itself post-oriental. Depending upon one's point of view, this might be a positive acknowledgement of a larger continuity. At the same time a more sophisticated orientalism (as post-orientalism) would take us back to Warren Hastings's astute observation in his panegyric on Charles Wilkins's path-breaking translation of the *Bhagavadgita* (1785):

> But such instances can only be obtained in their [the Hindus'] writings: and these will survive when the British dominion in India shall have long ceased to exist, and when the sources which it once yielded of wealth and power are lost to remembrance.[6]

What Hastings is anticipating here are the different forms of pre-english literatures which will have a very different relationship with the emergent literatures in English. When the power of the British is 'lost to remembrance', as is increasingly becoming evident in the new Indian *Lebenswelt* for instance, indigenous literatures would again begin to show a resurgence and self-confidence which would question the self-evident primacy of a literature written in English. In jettisoning the almost auratic status given to the English language, the new reckoning with an imperial language both changes the form of the language itself and marginalises it politically: the Shiv Sena uses Marathi, the Sikh militants Punjabi, and so on.

In this instance, a post-colonial theory becomes a radical form of orientalism (or post-orientalism) which insinuates, at every point, a dialectical process now under way between literature in English, and those written and oral non-english discourses which, in Hastings's words, 'will survive'. Where the early version of orientalism effectively reduced this multiplicity of languages and ideologies into a homogenised European discourse—E Trump gave up his translation of the *Adi Granth* (1877) because it lacked a grand epic narrative—the *EWB* strategy, for very different reasons, can't hear the almost carnivalesque sounds of the non-english unconscious either. It is a price that *EWB*, like any other enterprise with totalising ambitions, must inevitably pay. The failure to position author(s) into a culture so as to 'mediate between discrepant worlds of meaning'[7] led the orientalists back into the essentially European reconstructions of the Other. The authors of *EWB* do make a conscious attempt at this mediation, and bring together some of the best insights into post-orientalism of most contemporary theorists of the subject. However, there are intrinsic problems with any proposal to account, within a unitary scheme, for the unmanageable plethora of 'discrepant worlds of meaning' in contemporary post-colonial societies. *EWB* proposes the category of 'context' as the crucial source for the construction of meaning, but this solution has its own difficulties.

The scope of the 'context' that they mobilise in analysis is necessarily a closed frame, not an open-ended plenitude of meanings connecting unpredictability with other meanings and texts. For the authors of *EWB*, once the context of a text is understood, there is nothing terribly difficult about a Sanskrit compound or a hidden cultural text which might require specialised knowledge to identify. Thus if one were to read the song of Gibreel in Rushdie's *The Satanic Verses*[8] through *EWB*, its effect within the context is all that would really matter to the reader. The fact that beneath the song is an entire text of Bombay cinema which, to the bilingual reader, would recall, more specifically, Raj Kapoor's *Shree 420* (1955) is knowledge that *EWB* must either ignore or relegate to the level of spurious or unnecessary footnote. This supplementarity, however, even in terms of *EWB*'s own design is counter-discursive in a radically different fashion. The supplement, the anecdotal invasion or culture-specific power, is, however, a form of intervention that questions, as supplements always do, the very adequacy of a theory of the centre and its periphery. At the very moment that the narrative is invaded by an intertext from a different centre—the centre and centrality of the Bombay commercial cinema, India's pre-eminent contemporary cultural form—the focus shifts from a fixed centre and its satellite system to a multiplicity of centres in the culture itself.

There is an intractable problem here for the syncretic enterprise of *EWB*. Actually to explore every 'pre-english' literature is clearly beyond its scope, but their mere existence, acknowledged or otherwise, makes the unitary post-colonial itself extremely problematic. Should one, therefore, acknowledge the impossibility of a comprehensive post-colonial literary theory without encroaching upon a multiplicity of other theories and disciplines? Can the post-colonial be anything other than a celebration of a specious unity rather than a critique? The political danger here is not that post-colonial literary theory might

34

become post-oriental without orientalism's philosophical strengths; rather it might become not unlike the project of the raj historians of the 1960s who were totally bereft of any culture-specific know-how and effectively lost the chance to develop the study of Indian culture in universities.

With these other forms of knowledge ruled out as unnecessary because they are too difficult, a comprehensive theory of an un-canonised genre such as the novel is all that one needs to interpret post-colonial literature. Beneath the strategies of *EWB* is the dialogism of Bakhtin; and beneath post-colonial literature lies the might of the novel form. Absence of cultural specificity leads to cultural collapse, and cultural collapse takes us to the modern genre *par excellence*, the novel. The European bourgeois novel comes with a pre-existent philo-sophical apparatus that implicitly questions the representation of history to the extent that any counter-historical move must begin with a reading of the capacities of the novelistic genre itself. The extreme extension of this theory is that the post-colonial as a dupli-cation of Bakhtin's essentially polyphonic reading of the novel form makes the post-colonial redundant. It is important that we meet this hypothesis halfway, accept that a European epic narrative mediated through the European bourgeois model was an available discourse to the post-colonial writer, and then fill out the other half of the equation with those very precise, historically and culturally specific distinctions that mark off post-colonial difference without constructing, in turn, a post-colonial homogeneity that cancels out its own oppositions and fractures.

Those writers who use forms of 'appropriation' recognise that col-onial discourse itself is a complex, contradictory mode of represen-tation which implicates both the coloniser and the colonised. Nowhere is this more evident than in VS Naipaul, who is so very conscious of writing from within the shadow of an English master like Conrad, whose personal contact with England as a Polish émigré he finds echoes his own journey back to the centre. Years before, Romesh Dutt had translated sections from the *Ramayana* and *Mahabharata* in octametric lines. It is therefore not totally true that the post-colonial precursor discourse, the colonial, existed only in the hands of the coloniser. The Aboriginal writer Mudrooroo Narogin Nyoongah cer-tainly recognises the paradox of his writing in the language of the master, for the master, in novels and criticism that nevertheless insist upon the category of 'Aboriginality' as a defining feature of the Ab-original post-colonial.[9]

Into this colonial discourse, into a discourse which has been identificatory, constructing the colonised as a fixed reality, the post-colonial makes its dramatic entry. But the post-colonial is neverthe-less lumbered by the discourse of the colonised and is inexorably fissured. And it is not only fissured. It has also a political agenda that requires it to deconstruct an 'alien' subjectivity (a subjectivity growing out of a Hegelian master–slave relationship) but still hold on to the dominant genre through which it had been initially constituted, realism, and that leads to the crossing over of post-colonialism into postmodernism.

THE POSTMODERN CONNECTION

Linda Hutcheon, whose reading of postmodernism as parody has been taken up by so many post-colonial writers, gets her own discussion of the two (postmodernism and post-colonialism) under way by emphasising their distinct political agendas. Implicit in the diverging political agendas is the question of the definition of the *subject*. If for postmodernism the object of analysis is the subject as defined by humanism, with its essentialism and mistaken historical verities, its unities and transcendental presence, then for post-colonialism the object is the imperialist subject, the colonised as formed by the processes of imperialism. Hutcheon's warning is salutary and should be quoted in full:

> The current post-structuralist/postmodern challenges to the coherent, autonomous subject have to be put on hold in feminist and post-colonial discourses, for both must work first to assert and affirm a denied or alienated subjectivity: those radical postmodern challenges are in many ways the luxury of the dominant order which can afford to challenge that which it securely possesses.[10]

In spite of Linda Hutcheon's warning—one which she herself later in the same essay seems to forget in proclaiming the ambiguous post-colonialism of Canadian culture—the project of *EWB* is essentially postmodern. Admittedly, there is a whole section in *EWB* where postmodernism is treated agonistically, and earlier Tiffin had subtly accused postmodernism of hegemonic tendencies driven by a European desire to dominate the field of post-colonialism as well,[11] but *EWB*'s version of post-colonialism, it seems to us, cannot, as a unified field, function without it. The central problematic arises out of the status of settler cultures, and their place in this unified field.

The 'justifying' discourse which allows this settler incorporation into post-colonialism is clearly postmodernism. In someone as astute as Stephen Slemon the strategies of modernism/postmodernism arise out of a European assimilation of the heterogeneous colonial Other into its own social and discursive practices.[12] It is this reading of post-colonialism as already present in European thought, as well as, by extension, in colonial culture, which allows Slemon to shift gear and move into Canadian settler culture forthwith. He speaks of Canada and the other White dominions as second-world societies in which the post-colonial is an anti-colonial discourse, a kind of counter-discursive energy. Through this counter-discursivity the settler colony acquires a political agenda which demonstrates its reaction against an imperial homogenising tendency. How this happens, in Slemon's subtle argument, is clearly based upon a 'complicity' theory

36

of post-colonialism. Though Slemon does not make it explicit, in the complicity theory the literature of settler colonies, which did not have to go through a prolonged independence struggle, still has post-colonial tendencies embedded within it. In the age of the postmodern, the settler colonies' counter-discursive energy can now speak with greater assurance.

Like the authors of *EWB*, Slemon is at pains to avoid the collapse of the post-colonial and the postmodern. He must therefore insist upon the political strategy of post-colonialism, and argue that all post-colonial literatures demonstrate the recuperative work going on in marginalised societies. But it is salutary that the argument is developed not through, say, Patrick White's *A Fringe of Leaves* but through Salman Rushdie's *Midnight's Children*. For postmodernism, Rushdie's questioning of historical certainties is exemplary of its own project; for the post-colonial what is important is the way in which another, lost master-narrative recalled through the creative power of *maya*, of illusion, is used to free the colonised. The narrative energy of Rushdie is to be found in the magical narratives of the *Mahabharata* and the *Kathasaritasagara*. Whereas a postmodern reading of *Midnight's Children* would emphasise play and deferral, a fully post-colonial reading will locate the meaning of the untranslated words and the special, culture-specific resonances of the text. It might even offer a radical reshaping or rethinking of what Habermas has called our 'communicative rationality'. The post-colonial text persuades us to think through logical categories which may be quite alien to our own. For a text to suggest even as much is to start the long overdue process of dismantling classical orientalism.

But the positions outlined above are not mutually exclusive. Precolonial Indian narratives too are all about deferral, and play; they are open-ended where meaning is constantly displaced.[13] That is, a post-colonial text in this case can draw on an indigenous precursor tradition that has some of the features of postmodernism. In Mammata's theory and poetics (which he borrowed from the *Dhvanyaloka* of Anandavardhana), *dhvani* theory is really a theory of the signifier where meaning is constantly deferred. *Dhvani* clearly stipulates that the referent is not available, only the suggested meanings are. Thus writes Mammata:

> This [the poem] is best when the suggested meaning far excels the expressed sense; it is called *dhvani* by the learned.[14]

Rushdie's *The Satanic Verses* is a case in point, since it has been (and can be) defended on aesthetic/postmodern grounds. Thus for John McLaren *The Satanic Verses* offers the possibilities of alternative histories to the reader, since Rushdie cannot accept any history as fixed, especially through the *ipsissima verba*, God's exact words.[15] Similarly Helen Watson-Williams bypasses the political arguments completely by a universalist move: the text explores 'truth' and may be explained rationally.[16] Fantasy is simply a metaphor which can be reduced to its realist origins. As it becomes clear in Amin Malak's reading,[17] *The Satanic Verses* is defensible on postmodern grounds, where everything is subjected to subversive parody, but this kind of reading is highly dangerous politically. And here is the crux of the matter. The moment the dominant culture itself begins to draw generic lines (fiction, history, politics and postmodern play), the text gets transformed into distinct objects, with distinct effects and meanings. In political terms *The Satanic Verses* ceases to be post-colonial and becomes postmodern. Srinivas Aravamudan's suggestive essay shows how *The Satanic Verses* can be both postmodern and post-colonial at the same time.[18] In it, pastiche, parody and history as unstable discourse, in short all the root-metaphors of postmodernism, are juxtaposed alongside culture-specific knowledges (the '*420*' reference requires no research for the Indian reader), the privileged position of the native reader, the absence of orientalist glossary and those obvious stylistic nuances which mark the text's post-coloniality.

By seeming to transform the post-colonial into an object of knowledge that might be critiqued through a postmodern/novelistic critical discourse, what *EWB* has done is to remove the post-colonial as a radical political act of self-legitimation and self-respect locked into practices which antedate the arrival of the coloniser, and bracket it with postmodern practices generally. It is not surprising, therefore, that the trope of metonymy becomes so decisive for the authors of *EWB*. Since metonymy bypasses the laws of censorship (Lacan called it the trope of the Unconscious), it enables the return of the repressed, the articulation of that which has become taboo in a colonised world. Thus in an example taken from Nkosi it is the power of the book, the pen, which is advanced: since writing is power, the pen, metonymically, is the displaced colonial phallus seeking a fulfilment of desire in its relationship with the absent Other. Occasionally, as in Chapter 3, where Nkosi is examined at some length, the political argument comes across decisively: 'only by denying the authenticity of the line [the apartheid line] and taking control of the means of communication can the post-colonial text overcome this silence' (p. 87).

FORMS OF POST-COLONIALISM

What emerges, especially past Chapter 4 of *EWB*, is the fact that we are really talking about not one 'post-colonialism' but many postcolonialisms. When we drop the hyphen, and effectively use 'postcolonialism' as an always present tendency in any literature of subjugation marked by a systematic process of cultural domination through the imposition of imperial structures of power, we can begin to see those aspects of the argument of *EWB* which could be profitably extended. This form of 'postcolonialism' is not 'post-' something or other but is already implicit in the discourses of colonialism themselves. We would then want to distinguish sharply between two kinds of postcolonialism, viewed as ideological orientations rather than as a historical stage. The first, and more readily recognisable, is what we call oppositional postcolonialism, which is found in its most overt form in post-independent colonies at the historical phase of 'post-colonialism' (with a hyphen). This usage corresponds to the *OED's* definition of the 'post-colonial'. The second form, equally a product of the processes that constituted colonialism but with a different inflection, is a 'complicit postcolonialism', which has much in common with Lyotard's unhyphenated 'postmodernism': an always present 'underside' within colonisation itself.[19] Thus Charles Harpur, Marcus Clarke, Christopher Brennan as well as VS Naipaul and Bibhutibhushan Banerji are postcolonial in this sense.

It would follow, therefore, that other theories such as feminism which are also predicated upon some definition of oppression would find points of contact with postcolonialism. Significant terms used by the authors of *EWB* such as 'other', 'subversion', 'marginalized' and 'linguistic difference' are all replicated in feminist discourses. But the analogy also gives rise to a problem within postcolonial women's writing which would require a different order of theorising, since postcolonial women are like a fragment, an oppositional system, within an overall colonised framework. Women therefore function here as burdened by a twice-disabling discourse: the disabling master discourse of colonialism is then redirected against women in an exact duplication of the coloniser's own use of that discourse *vis à vis* the colonised in the first instance.

One finds a reaction against this twice-disabling discourse even in the context of someone who writes, essentially, within the *riti* ('love') and *bhakti* ('devotional') poetics of India.[20] In Mahadevi Varma's *chhayavad* poetry the metaphysical domains of both *riti* and *bhakti* are replaced by a search for an ennobling humanism, the discriminatory desire of a woman herself as she seeks fulfilment in love. Into the hegemonic world of traditional Sanskrit genres and discourses, Mahadevi Varma inserts the female body, its sensations and its self-identity as woman. In the 1920s and 1930s Mahadevi Varma, as a woman, was grasping the nettle of a poetics which had produced the great patriarchal figures of Nanak and Tulsidasa.

The homogenising drive of *EWB* leads it to seek to establish a dominant field and not a set of heterogeneous 'moments' arising from very different historical processes. As we have said, it is especially important to recognise the different histories of the White settler colonies which, as fragments of the metropolitan centre, were treated very differently by Britain, which, in turn, for these settler colonies, was not the imperial centre but the Mother Country. What an undifferentiated concept of postcolonialism overlooks are the very radical differences in response and the unbridgeable chasms that existed between White and non-White colonies.

A difficult category which is in need of theorising is, of course, *race*. The decisive role that race has played in all forms of colonial society over the past five hundred years (and perhaps even before that) cannot be overestimated. At the same time since racial categories interweave with social classes at every point, they become much more complex in their uses and effects. There is certainly no essentialist meaning of race itself. It is what one does with the category and, more importantly, how it impinges upon power relations in the colonial/post-colonial world that is of concern to the cultural theorist. It is here that the concept itself, in a non-essential fashion, nevertheless needs a level of specificity which would identify its function as a category of analysis. Race is not part of an unproblematic continuum alongside discursive categories such as linguistic rupture, syncreticism, hybridity and so on. In all kinds of oppositional postcolonialism (within settler countries themselves and without) race was part of a larger struggle for self-respect. The post-colonial is the single most important phenomenon in which it played such a decisive role.

These difficulties disrupt the smooth and seamless surface of *EWB*'s definition of the 'post-colonial':

> We use the term 'post-colonial', however, to cover all the culture affected by the imperial process from the moment of colonization to the present day. This is because there is a continuity of preoccupations throughout the historical process initiated by European imperial aggression. (p. 2)

What is this 'continuity of preoccupations'? Is it purely aesthetic? What is the material basis of this aesthetic? How is the 'post-colonial experience' reconstructed? How does it become 'rich' and 'incisive' (p. 91) if we can't relativise this image of discursive wealth through some understanding of social conditions? The annual per capita income of an Indian, for instance, is around $150, that of an African is around $300. In the West Indies it is probably not much more. And social security is non-existent. An average Australian worker (though not an unemployed Aborigine) earns above these levels in a week. Perhaps it is only in the Indian diaspora of Britain, the US and Canada that the 'historical process initiated by European imperialist aggression' can be placed upon a uniform material footing. Without an adequate materialist theory of postcolonialism, *EWB*'s theory of 'post-coloniality' is a general hypothesis applicable to any text which dismantles power relations existing in an 'anterior' text. The problematic, extended and reformulated, finds centre and periphery in social structures as diverse as race, class, women's rights and so on.

In practice, therefore, for the authors of *EWB*, the postcolonial is a hermeneutic which is vindicated by the conditions in non-settler colonies, but is then used unchanged to apply to settler colonies, thus making strategic moves of these settler colonies towards greater political and economic autonomy within a capitalist world economy appear as heroic and revolutionary ruptures. 'The Empire strikes back' indeed, under the cover yet again of its loyal White colonies. From the base of this elision, the construction of meaning in these non-settler colonies takes up a highly postmodern resonance. Meaning resides in the 'slippage' of language; meaning is constantly deferred; meaning grows out of a dialectical process of a relationship between the margins and the centre (meaning arises out of a discourse of marginality); meanings are not culture-specific and in postcolonial texts are constructed metonymically, not metaphorically. Since metonymy defers meaning, it is repetitive, and returns to haunt us in a replay of a version of the Gothic. Not surprisingly, then, the postcolonial text is 'always a complex and hybridised formation' (p. 10).

The more we probe statements such as these, the more conscious we become of a model for the construction of meaning which advances metonymy over metaphor, hybridity over purity, syncretism over difference, pluralism over essentialism or pan-textualism, and diglossia over monoglossia. The paradigmatic postcolonial text is the West Indian novel which is elevated, implicitly, to the position of pre-eminence: all postcolonial literatures aspire to the condition of the West Indian, and the achievements of West Indian writers are read back into the settler traditions. But the West Indian paradigm is just not applicable to a country like Australia for instance, either historically or linguistically. Australian English is an almost exact duplication of Received Standard English and Australian colloquialisms (its most obvious anti-language) follow exactly the rules by which the language of the British underground comes into being. That crucial fracturing of the deep structure of a language found in non-settler 'englishes' just does not occur in Australia, a country which, historically, has always seen itself as part of the Empire, ever ready to follow, uncritically, in the footsteps of the Mother Country. Gallipoli, the Australian colonisation of the Pacific, the White Australia Policy, Prime Minister Menzies's recitation of love-poetry for the departing Queen Elizabeth in 1953, may be explained simply in terms of a country which saw itself as an integral part of the White British Empire. The settler colonies provided the manpower, the support systems for colonialism to flourish.

At the heart of the oppositional post-colonial are three fundamental principles—principles which are as much points of difference between White settler colonies and the rest—which may be summarised as (a) racism, (b) a second language, (c) political struggle. For the category of the post-colonial to work in any other fashion it must become a 'complicit post-colonialism' and therefore effectively postmodern. It is the uneasy manner in which these three principles may be discussed with reference to the settler colonies which, to our minds, explains the pan-textualist bias within an otherwise mutually exclusive pluralist enterprise. Thus where subversion, for instance, is emphasised, this is done in largely non-political and non-racial terms. In short subversion becomes a kind of an anti-language (the authors call it an inter-language) which largely defines the postcolonial experience. What is

41

worrying is that the category of subversion applies without change to literary tendencies within the canon itself (Donne, Sterne, Mary Shelley, etc) rather than specifying those material conditions which give rise to post-colonial difference.

An uncritical adulation of pluralism, which leads, finally, to post-colonialism becoming the liberal Australian version of multiculturalism, then produces concepts such as 'hybridity' and 'syncretism' as the theoretical 'dominants' of post-colonial society. In doing so the authors then implicitly argue that the post-colonial rejects a monocentric view of human experience: assimilation (monocentrism) is out, hybridity (multiculturalism) is in. John Lennon sings 'Imagine all the people . . .' Theories of syncretism/hybridisation are essentially pluralistic, as they maintain a pluralism which encourages freedom and independence. Their parallel, as we have said, is to be found in Australian multiculturalism, a utopian view of the world which is so very recent in origin and reflects as much global economic policies as any concerted effort on the part of Anglo-Celtic Australian society to change itself.

The emphasis on hybridisation leads to an uneasiness with social and racial theories of post-colonial literature. Though Sanskrit theories are given an extended gloss, their interest for the authors of *EWB* lies, it seems to us, in their affirmation, finally, of an ahistorical aesthetic. Sanskrit theories of reception (*rasa*) and suggestiveness (*dhvani*) after all keep the primacy of the literary object intact. Sanskrit theories are still individual-oriented and easier for a pluralist to handle than theories of negritude (Aimé Césaire, Leopold Senghor, Fanon) or Aboriginality (Narogin). The authors of *EWB* tend to use the word 'essentialism' for any mode of criticism that claims indigeneity and avoids pluralism without in fact conceding that pluralism itself might be yet another version of what Achebe called 'colonialist criticism' (p. 127).

Furthermore, a related question may now be posed. Does the post-colonial exist only in English? The emphasis on language and 'englishes' in *EWB* seems to say so. But why are Premchand, Bannerjee (of *Pather Panchali* fame) and Satyajit Ray, and Raj Kapoor and Guru Dutt (the last three film-makers) not postcolonial? And what about the writings of the Indian diaspora not written in English, such as the Mauritian Abhimanyu Anat's *Lal Pasina* ('Blood and Sweat')?

For the authors of *EWB* it is syncretism ('syncretism is the condition within which post-colonial societies operate' [p. 180]) and hybridity ('hybridity . . . is the primary characteristic of all post-colonial texts' [p. 185]) which are the hallmarks of postcolonial writing. As a consequence post-colonial literatures are 'constituted in counter-discursive rather than homologous practices' (p. 196). In the process, as we have argued, the post-colonial has adopted almost every conceivable postmodern theory as well as a number of propositions which are absolutely central to the rise of the bourgeois novel in Europe.

WHAT IS POST(-)COLONIALISM?

The work of Bill Ashcroft, Gareth Griffiths and Helen Tiffin is a timely contribution to the post-colonial debate. The strategic moves they adopt in their unenviable task for a comprehensive post-colonial theory have paved the way for our own critique. What follows is, we hope, an extension, albeit in a slightly different form, of their own intrinsically difficult project. Firstly, there is, we feel, a need to make a stronger distinction between the postcolonialism of settler and non-settler countries. But within each of these there is a need to see greater continuities between the colonial and the post-colonial. In some ways the postcolonial is really a splinter in the side of the colonial itself and the kinds of rebellion that we find in the postcolonial are not unlike the reactions of the child against the law of the father.[21] Because of the indeterminacy of the fused postcolonial (in which oppositional and complicit forms coexist) theorisation about it inevitably pushes us towards postmodernism. If we catalogue the crucial features of postcolonialism as advanced by *EWB*—fracture, interlanguage, polyglossia, subversion, and so on—we find that we are drawn, via the defining qualities of postmodernism, to propose a counter-literary history functioning as the underside of the dominant literary history. The postcolonial (unhyphenated) is a ghost that stalks the parent literary history just as vernacular literatures of Europe in Rome's former colonies challenged Latin, and Hindi-Urdu literature challenged Sanskrit/Persian. From this point of view it is then possible to claim that the postcolonial as a category subsumes the postmodern.

As the memory of independence struggles recedes, global capitalism in its latest avatar dominates our lives, and Hastings's prophecy is no longer simply a future hope but a living if still partial reality, we believe that postcolonialism, in its unhyphenated variety, will become the dominant 'post-colonial' practice. Though it seems highly unlikely that the difference between settler and non-settler countries will cease to exist—they will in fact become more marked—it is, nevertheless, possible to construct a theory which predicts the inevitable triumph of various complicit forms of postcolonialism in all late post-colonial societies. In order to explore the ramifications of this claim we would need further research into the nature of colonialism itself and the ways in which the struggle towards self-determination found expression. In doing so we should be able to acknowledge the quite radical differences in the 'colonial' relationship between the imperial centre and the colonised in the various parts of the former empires. It appears that the experience of colonialisation was more similar across all the White settler colonies than in the non-settler colonies. In the Indian subcontinent the colonial experience seems to have affected the cities only, in Africa it worked hand in hand with evangelical Christianity, in South-East Asia the use of migrant labour—notably Chinese and Indian—mediated between the British and the

Malays. In the West Indies slave labour, and later indentured Indian labour, again made the relationship less combative and more accommodating. To use a non-literary marker, cricket triumphed in the British settler countries, on the Indian subcontinent and in the West Indies but not in non-settler Africa, the Middle East or South-East Asia. Smaller *récits* must replace the *grand récit* of postcolonialism in all these instances so that we can know the historical background better. In these smaller *récits* it may well be that the term 'postcolonial' is never used.

Beyond that, in the present late stage of world capitalism, the complicit postcolonial is on the way to becoming the literary dominant of 'post-colonialism'. In this situation it is important to recognise its complex relationship with postmodernism, neither collapsing the two categories nor positing an absolute distinction. The postmodern has made some features of the postcolonial visible or speakable for the colonisers, reassuringly strange and safely subversive, just as orientalism did in an earlier stage of colonial ideology. In return, postcolonialism draws attention to the occluded politics and forgotten precursors of postmodernism.

Postcolonialism, we have stressed, is not a homogeneous category either across all postcolonial societies or even within a single one. Rather it refers to a typical configuration which is always in the process of change, never consistent with itself. In settler countries like Australia, for instance, writers such as Harpur, Brennan, Richardson and Patrick White can be read as aspirants to the canon, extending but not challenging the standards of the imperial centre. But even while this was going on, the indigenous peoples whom the settlers had silenced could not be ignored, and their ghosts began to invade the texts of the dominant tradition. The kind of parasitism found in the original settler literature *vis à vis* the Mother Country is at first a prominent feature of the emerging writings of the Australian Aborigine, the New Zealand Maori and the Canadian Indian. Then a distinctive form of the postcolonial arises, as defiant as oppositional postcolonialism but without political independence or autonomy ever becoming a realistic option. This symbiotic postcolonial formation has many of the same features as the more exciting postcolonialism of the non-settler countries as they establish their national identity. From here it begins to affect the form of writing of the settlers themselves, leading to a shift of balance within a type of the fused postcolonial.

In the age of the postmodern, then, there is a double trend towards the complicit postcolonial: an increasing alliance with the postmodern at the level of theory, and an increasing predominance in political life. The echoes of guilty partnership in an illicit affair are set off by the word 'complicit', and these overtones hold back the difficult task of defining the 'new' postcolonialism which would take us beyond the oppositional postcolonialism of non-settler colonies that pivots around the moment of independence. It must be possible to acknowledge difference and insist on a strongly theorised oppositional postcolonialism as crucial to the debate, without claiming that this form is or has been everywhere the same wherever a coloniser's feet have trod. We can trace the creative process of cultural syncretism and its collapse of distinctions without having to overlook the contradictions and oppositions which still survive, and without disavowing the sometimes violent nature of colonial struggles in non-settler countries before and after independence. It is precisely if we acknowledge the pervasiveness but not universality of complicit forms of the postcolonial that we can trace the connections that go back to the settler experience and beyond, and forward to the new postcolonialism. Theory must be flexible and prudent enough to say: the post-colonial is dead; long live postcolonialism.

NOTES

1   Bill Ashcroft, Gareth Griffiths & Helen Tiffin, *The Empire Writes Back: Theory and Practice in Post-colonial Literature*, Routledge, London, 1989. All quotations from this text are cited parenthetically.
2   Edward W Said, 'Representing the Colonized: Anthropology's Interlocutors', *Critical Inquiry* 15, 2 (Winter 1989), p. 209.
3   Salman Rushdie, 'The Empire Writes Back with a Vengeance', *The Times*, 3 July 1980, p. 8.
4   Terry Eagleton, *The Ideology of the Aesthetic*, Basil Blackwell, Oxford, 1990, p. 381.
5   Frantz Fanon, *The Wretched of the Earth,* Penguin Books, Harmondsworth, 1961. See also Frantz Fanon, *Black Skin White Masks*, Grove Press, New York, 1967.
6   Charles Wilkins (trans.), *The Bhagvat-Geeta or Dialogues of Kreeshna and Arjoon*, C Nourse, 1785, London, p. 13.
7   James Clifford, *The Predicament of Culture: Twentieth-Century Ethnography, Literature and Art*, Harvard University Press, Cambridge Mass, 1988, p. 113.
8   Salman Rushdie, *The Satanic Verses*, Viking, 1988, London, p. 5.
9   Mudrooroo Narogin, *Writing from the Fringe: A Study of Modern Aboriginal Literature*, Hyland House, Melbourne, 1990.
10 Linda Hutcheon, 'Circling the Downspout of Empire: Post-Colonialism and Postmodernism', *Ariel* 20, 4 (October 1989), p. 151.
11 Helen Tiffin, 'Post-Colonialism, Post-Modernism and the Rehabilitation of Post-colonial History', *Journal of Commonwealth Literature* 21, 1 (1988), pp. 169–81.
12 Stephen Slemon, 'Modernism's Last Post' *Ariel* 20, 4 (October 1989), pp. 3–17.
13 Vijay Mishra, 'The Centre Cannot Hold: Bailey, Indian Culture and the Sublime', *South Asia*, n.s., 12, 1 (June 1989), pp. 103–14.
14 Mammata, *Kavyaprakasha*, ed Acharya Vishveshvar, Jñanamandala, Varanasi, 1960, IV, 39, 24, p. 91.
15 John McLaren, 'The Power of the Word: Salman Rushdie and *The Satanic Verses*', *Westerly* 1 (March 1990), pp. 61–5.

16 Helen Watson-Williams, 'Finding a Father: A Reading of Salman Rushdie's *The Satanic Verses*', *Westerly* 1 (March 1990), pp. 66–71.

17 Amin Malak, 'Reading the Crisis: The Polemics of Salman Rushdie's *The Satanic Verses*', *Ariel* 20, 4 (October 1989), pp. 176–86.

18 S Aravamudan, 'Salman Rushdie's *The Satanic Verses*', *Diacritics* 19, 2 (Summer 1989), pp. 3–20.

19 See Jean-François Lyotard, *The Postmodern Condition*, Manchester University Press, Manchester, 1986.

20 See Karine Schomer, *Mahadevi Varma and the Chhayavad Age of Modern Hindi Poetry*, University of California Press, Berkeley, 1983.

21 See Bob Hodge & Vijay Mishra, *The Dark Side of the Dream: Australian Literature and the Postcolonial Mind*, Allen & Unwin, Sydney, 1991.

4

Bad Aboriginal art

ERIC MICHAELS

During 1987 the Australian press reported frequently that Aboriginal art, especially Western Desert[1] acrylic 'dot paintings', had become flavour of the month in New York, Paris and Munich. Flavour of the month is an odd descriptor Australians overuse to resolve the incompatibility of such reports of Australian success overseas with a cherished and characteristic myth of the second rate, sometimes labelled cultural cringe. Indeed, Australia now has a suspiciously elaborate terminology for identifying the contradictions of colonialism and creativity. The notion of radical unoriginality is claimed to privilege this discourse, so that Sydney for example now asserts itself as the most dislocated, imitative, unoriginal, and therefore *postmodern* city (which only goes to show that Sydneysiders never make it north to Brisbane).[2] What Australia (and postmodernism) may not have a vocabulary to deal with so readily is the unwelcome appearance of any possible claims to authentic creativity, as with our own indigenous art.

In this essay I want to consider examples of the *mise en discours* by which Aboriginal Australian paintings are positioned for sale in contemporary markets, in order to ask what chance exists for the work to command serious prices, and to note some peculiar difficulties of evaluating it. I want to consider the curious fact that almost nothing of this work is ever designated 'bad'—a lacuna which would not seem to make it easy to sell anything as especially good, either. There are exceptions (including a vulgar judgment that all primitive art is bad),

* This text is an edited version of a paper given at the Department of Anthropology, University of Sydney, 29 October 1987. I wish to thank John von Sturmer for his close reading and suggestions. [Reproduced here from *Art & Text* 28 (1988) and from Eric Michaels, *Bad Aboriginal Art and Other Essays*, University of Minnesota Press, Minneapolis, 1993.]

and I will feature some as examples here. But my main purpose in this essay is to advance a critical perspective on some contemporary Aboriginal painting practices in what I believe must be uncharacteristically contemporary terms: to identify how particular 'primitive' painting traditions can articulate what have been identified as issues in the postmodern debate, and to describe why such painting might be of particular interest (and value) right now. Considering Aboriginal art practices as problems in contemporary discourse—of production, circulation and exchange—may indicate that something about world economics and ideology also is centrally involved here.

Neo-Kantianism asserts more than just the end of determinate concepts and, therefore, of any consensus in aesthetic taste.[3] That we no longer think it odd that a commodity comes onto the market whose uncertainty of value seems itself part of that value, is arguably itself a consequence of this aesthetic dilemma. As the auction traffic of the 1980s at Parke Bernet and Christie's has shown, the creations of value now can come quite late in the production game, to the point of challenging the approved methodologies of materialist analysis. Part of what makes Fine Art particularly attractive to the investment market obviously must be this negotiability of worth based on cultural, rather than material, calculations. But material constraints also underpin the contemporary art market's evaluations: these include a concern for the identity and scarcity of the resource. Art history links these calculations to certain conventions of authorship and assumptions of creativity.

Jean Baudrillard has traced these conventions to a history which pre-dates the industrial revolution in an account of how it has become established that the individual artist/author/identity now constitutes the domain of value: 'The painting is a signed object as much as it is a painted surface.'[4] It is not a given artwork but named individual artists who, with respect to their oeuvre, are judged better or worse; from that assessment, when it is approved in any critically designated moment, flows the assignment of market value to particular signed works. The signature in this system does literally sign the commodity and constitute its value. A 'bad' Picasso will probably cost more than a 'good' Sidney Nolan, assuming that we still have critics willing to risk discriminating between particular works of individual artists (on grounds other than typicality to an oeuvre).

One attraction of this system, at least to the present machinations of the speculative art market, is that the artist's oeuvre provides a manageable limitation on the availability of the resource, which is the number of paintings produced in a given individual creative lifetime. Here the importance of an artist's death is related to the closing of the series, that essential limitation which allows a far more definitive post-mortem valuation of the work than is possible while the artist is alive and continues to produce.

In all of these terms, 'primitive' art (particularly Aboriginal Australian paintings, and specifically Warlpiri acrylics, with which I am most familiar) poses certain intrinsic problems of valuation and even evaluation, because it involves very different creative and authorial practices:

1 The modes and relations of production from which many Aboriginal forms arise do not emphasise original creative individuals or assign them responsibility as author. Instead of an ideology of creative authority, there is an ideology of reproduction. The artist is *counter-interpolated to* the tradition so that the art masks inventiveness and authorial intent.

2 In the example of Warlpiri artists, the body of work is predetermined; one earns rights to paint certain pre-existing designs, not so much to introduce new ones. Death has no purchase here. Rights to an oeuvre are inherited so that one's son, daughter-in-law or some other (usually explicitly prescribed) individual continues producing the same designs. The details of this system are complex.

3 Consequently, plagiarism is impossible in Western Desert painting. What is feared, instead, is thievery—the unauthorised appropriation of a design, as well as the potential for such stolen designs to convey rights and authority to the thief. A forgery adequately executed, when circulated, may be no forgery.

4 Everyone in traditional society is effectively entitled to paint certain designs, not from particular notions of skill or talent (ie personal predispositions) but as a result of certain negotiated positions within systems of inherited rights and obligations. These design traditions are considered to originate in a collective past, and project towards an infinite, impersonal future. By necessity, the authority of this system would be compromised by an ideology of invention which singled out individual producers.

Because my focus here is on issues of practice and exchange, the above list does not pursue the observation that Western Desert symbology resonates with contents privileged in contemporary international painting. For example, I do not consider a recent argument by George Alexander: 'Today images are read as texts and texts are read as images. Something strangely calligrammatic is afoot.'[5] Rather, I am concerned with contrasts of the sort Baudrillard has identified between modern art and some apparently historically-prior, pre-industrial, practice in which artistic creativity also is not emphasised:

> In a world that is the reflection of an order (that of God, of nature or, more simply, of discourse) in which all things are representation, endowed with meaning and transparent to the language that describes them, artistic 'creation' proposes only to describe ... The oeuvre wishes to be the perpetual commentary of a given text, and all copies which take their inspiration from it are justified as the multiplied reflection of an order whose original is in any case transcendent. In other words, the question of authenticity does not arise ...[6]

This actually refers to something more than a contrast between modern, and an unspecified 'traditional', practice. Unlike Lévi-Strauss (who covers some similar territory in *La Pensée sauvage* with his notion of 'le bricoleur'), Baudrillard is not really interested in defining primitive art, but in anticipating a postmodern critique of originality in the 'age of reproduction'. For him, these questions of authorship, ownership, and signature within a radical reproductive practice seem to be at the core of postmodernist activity. Not only do we now have a genealogy of unabashed reproducers and imitators (from Duchamp to Warhol to Sherrie Levine), but also the great forgers of both recent and distant past (Rrose Sélavy, Dali, and maybe da Vinci) are re-evaluated in a more positive light. Practices of a once merely ethnographic interest, ascribed to pre-industrial culture (but obscured when marketing so-called primitive art), now resonate with modern or postmodern aesthetics and obviously affect the manner of inserting 'traditional' works into the contemporary market.

A full, academic treatment here of the subject would require a review of the critical literature on Australian Aboriginal Art, necessarily focusing on the anthropological contribution given the paucity of any other. Recent articles by Howard Morphy and Vincent Megaw,[7] for example, take up the question of the intrusion of European history and aesthetics into 'traditional' Aboriginal painting practices—a question whose significance the Berndts identified in their pioneering work on Arnhem Land barks.[8] This work may be set against the more familiar taxonomic pedantries that characterise Rock Art studies,[9] which offer a less problematic invocation of an unsullied tradition. The collection by Loveday and Cook of 'applied essays' on the market are helpful.[10] But in none of this literature is there really anything other than an ethnographic standard promoted for evaluating particular works: aesthetic judgments of value are avoided. This would be the expected consequence of Australian academic positivism, which required until recently (when the funding ran out) an 'objective' separation of commerce from scholarship. The result masks what in fact may be an implicit standard of 'traditionalism' and 'authenticity' which, by avoiding definition, seeks to avoid aesthetic controversy and suppress possible alternative 'non-expert' judgments. But if Baudrillard is right, then traditionalism and authenticity are now completely false judgments to assign to Aboriginal painting practices, which is borne out by contemporary ethnography and material history. The situation I worked in at Yuendumu demonstrated unequivocally that the Warlpiri painting I saw, even if it accepts the label 'traditional' as a marketing strategy, in fact arises out of conditions of historical struggle and expresses the contradictions of its production. This is really where its value and interest as 'serious' fine art lies; furthermore, it may also be the source of its social legitimacy. To make any other claims is to cheat this work of its position in the modernist tradition as well as to misappropriate it and misunderstand its context.

THIS ACRYLIC LASSETER'S REEF

Consider a recent article in the *Weekend Australian* (8–9 August, 1987) that describes an intriguing expedition to the Warlpiri at Yuendumu: some anthropologists from the South Australian Museum, a French ethnographer studying at the Australian National University, an 'important' art curator (from an unfamiliar, but nonetheless, New York gallery), and, by implication, the journalist. These clever sorts managed to discover a whole tribe of Picassos in the desert, presumably a mysterious result of spontaneous cultural combustion. We're told of the curator's astonishment at finding more painters per capita of population than in Manhattan's Soho! The tedious description of painting as the desert's new crop is trucked out again, as if for the first time. Here we have any number of the current discourses on 'aboriginality', art, and cultural cringe personified:

• a pair of authorised Australian academic experts properly institutionally affiliated, assisting in the location of this hidden treasure—this acrylic Lasseter's Reef—in the distant outback (Burke & Wills? Spencer & Gillen? Lone Ranger & Tonto?—why do men always go amongst the natives in pairs, and why, incidentally, do women go alone?)
• an anthropological student who speaks this complex Australian language absolutely fluently (as only the French can!), and proves to be intimate with the natives (she is shown fondling a baby in a six-inch photo)
• and the requisite overseas valuer ready to pronounce the work 'first class, export quality,' or at least worth a full page in the *Weekend Australian*.

As proof of the value of the art, with New York and Paris both represented, who could ask for anything more? But I find it telling that no historical perspective is offered in this article. It's as if Nancy Munn had not described Yuendumu graphic traditions, and some of the very same artists, a quarter century ago.[11] As if the half-dozen canvasses hanging in the Australian National Gallery ceased to exist, as well as a number of current private shows in Sydney, Melbourne and Perth (implying that this art is too valuable, or difficult, for the Australian public to see and appreciate). As if a book describing examples of this work hadn't been launched a few weeks previously and wasn't concurrently being reviewed in the national press . . .[12] We never discover that the community has been engaging in five years of difficult arts organising and marketing, resulting in dozens of shows and hundreds of thousands of dollars of sales in the last two years. There is no mention of what is, for the artists, the very important if somewhat seedy history of art advisers, marketing schemes and attempts at state intervention that resulted in an all too typical history of missing profits, receipts, and paintings. All or any of that would obviously compromise the myth being manufactured, and thus their stake in the promotion of the art. The material circumstances that produced these paintings are obscured by such fantastic reports.

The overseas expert did, however, raise an issue of interest to us here—his astonishment at Central Australia's demography of creativity. Given so many painters, what is the limitation on the body of Aboriginal art that closes the series, identifies the degree of uniqueness of artwork, and assures its rarity value? We may be in some difficulty when admitting that each of the 50 000 Aborigines classed as 'tribal,' and (arguably) each of the 250 000 urban and rural 'non-tribals' as well, is entitled to claim the signature 'Aboriginal' for nearly any product. The facile reduction of contemporary Aboriginal painting to a cash crop is certainly encouraged by such a situation.

Is an assertion of authorship the only marketing solution for Aboriginal art to be classed as Fine? Do painters need to succumb, and assign a personal signature to their work to solve the problem? Andrew Crocker has argued in the catalogue for a recent solo show that it is a necessary precondition for any serious critical attention.[13] I disagree. Postmodern debates offer some very interesting alternatives to individual authorship, into which Warlpiri production practices may be fitted comfortably at the same time as advancing these debates. Even so, one finally must admit sympathy for the arts advisers and tourist shop proprietors who fall back on the old crafts-pricing criterion of so much neatness per square inch. Under what other political or aesthetic circumstances would anybody be willing to identify anything as bad Aboriginal art? In fact, some recent reports of the 'desecration' of desert paintings may imply just this sort of judgment.

THE CASE OF BAD ROCK ART

I began with a search for bad art, but so far have mostly discussed bad talk. Tangible examples of bad Aboriginal art may not be so rare as implied; some are close at hand. The most startling case concerns the recent 'restoration' of certain Western Australian cave paintings (the 'Wandjinas') by unemployed Aboriginal youths from Derby, producing a result claimed by some to be rather more like tea-towel kitsch than original 5000 year-old designs. The circumstances, as reported by the popular press and television, involve Mr Lorin Bishop, owner of Mt Barnett cattle station in the Kimberleys, and his concern that the designs painted on a cave rock face situated on the property were deteriorating. He contacted the Federal Minister for Aboriginal Affairs, seeking advice. The result was a $110 000 Commonwealth Employment Program grant, administered through the Wanang Ngari Cultural Corporation in Derby, 310 kilometres east of the site. The young workers were brought out from Derby with video, and still-cameras. After recording the site, Bishop charged, they painted it out with 'housepaint, aquadhere, wood glue and plastic' (*West Australian*, 8 August 1987, p. 3). It was then repainted from the photographic record, according to a subsequent lead story on *60 Minutes*.

One can study the example as a typical tragic case of bureaucrat-isation of Aboriginal processes that ensures the defeat of the culture. Why did Bishop write to a Federal Minister instead of just heading down the creek to talk with the local Aboriginal stockmen, who were either Ngarinyin owners responsible for the cave and its paintings (according to the *West Australian*) or would know who was?[14] Why did Canberra in turn contact Derby rather than the locals? These were the pivotal questions raised at a later meeting between the concerned parties and Bishop, recorded on video by the Wanang Ngari organis-ation—presumably with the same, offending camera as was purchased for the project.

Reasons for such disrespect may be self-evident to anyone familiar with Aboriginal affairs in Australia, but would require hundreds of pages of sociology and historical analysis to begin to explain to anyone else. A brief gloss would say: colonial Australian administration has always refused to recognise that there is no one Aboriginal culture but hundreds of them, as there are hundreds of distinct languages, all insistently autonomous. Local political systems promoted no 'leader' to be taken to, a problem that apparently stymied Captain Cook and has plagued 200 years of subsequent race relations. The overarching class 'Aboriginal' is a wholly European fantasy, a class which comes into existence as a consequence of colonial domination and not be-fore (although many Aborigines will make concessions to this fantasy, seeing possibilities thereby for political and economic power). But my point here is not to explore the political background or criticise the bureaucracy. I'm not convinced it was the government that made the art bad.

The evaluations which resulted from the 'restoration' were repres-ented in the media in headlines like 'Priceless Art Desecrated, Grant Cancelled' (*Australian*, 11 September, p. 1). That such matters should command front page banners in the national press itself must be noted. Later issues provide us with some more thoughtful features ('Coming to Grips with a Living Culture', by Alex Harris, *West Aus-tralian*, 18 August) or offer the editors opportunities for some quite startling agenda-hijacking editorials ('How Sacred?,' *West Australian*, 15 June). It remained for *60 Minutes*, that uniquely Americanised news and features format, to raise the alarm to a more general public. *60 Minutes* reported the story using the following cast of characters: Lorin Bishop, the station owner/protagonist; Michael Robinson, sites officer from the West Australian Museum (the bureaucrat officially responsible for Aboriginal sites and paintings); David Mowarljarlai, Aboriginal elder and chairman of Wanang Ngari who organised and administered the grant and oversaw the restoration; the requisite 'anthropological ex-pert' (one who seems suspiciously to emerge only on TV, and whose credentials were properly questioned later by Mowarljarlai); and the old men whose cave it was said to be and whose responsibility these paintings presumably are, along with some of their young descendants. This entire cast, excepting Mowarljarlai, claimed the effort was a

53

disaster, one of the remarkably rare examples of a consensus which defines a work of Aboriginal art as bad. But Mowarljarlai's defence of the outcome was more interesting than it was allowed to appear. Certainly, he would want to deny accusations of having participated in sacrilege and desecration. In this account he does seem to have been operating well beyond any local basis for authority (although he might well be able to claim some traditional association with the area of the cave; none of the reports discussed this, which, from the juridical perspective, is the critical point). Although the rhetoric of the program resists empathising with Mowarljarlai, he is allowed to raise some telling points: for example, he privileges the pedagogic function of these paintings, arguing that, although perhaps 5000 years old, these paintings would have been cyclically renewed on ritual occasions in which young initiates would probably play a part not entirely different from the one that the young fellows from Derby played (the point taken up in Alex Harris's feature). It would have been fair to ask why the local owners had let the paintings deteriorate, or whether this was entirely in the perception of the station owner—who, we only discover later, runs a tourist business on the property. But one has to look elsewhere for such pertinent facts, or to find Bishop's more blatant statements which may help to explain his motives—such as 'the safeguarding of these relics is too important to be left to Aborigines' (Harris). The question of authority is pivotal, but can't be resolved with the data made available through these reports, which are contradictory. Certainly, Mowarljarlai believed that the designs were in bad shape and that he rescued them. The other grounds for objection seem related to the technology: materials (permanent acrylics rather than soluble ochres—the actual mediums are variously reported in the different accounts), the accuracy of reproduction (one report has shorts painted on an 'Aboriginal God'), and perhaps the use of camera images as authorities instead of Aboriginal elders. Mowarljarlai was allowed one great line. When the reporter asked why they couldn't have practised first on another rock, he said: 'Aborigines don't practise'.

Mowarljarlai may be denying any possibility of a traditionalist aesthetic judgment of art products, or at least of Wandjinas such as these, privileging their process and practice instead. He refuses the notion that the cruder, less detailed, more graphicised acrylic version is less valid, less 'good' than any original. Even when such an evaluation is imposed on him, he resists it, challenging in turn the prerogative of others to make these judgments.

The episode of the Wandjinas is ripe, perhaps overripe, with such cross-cultural discourses; but I leave it to others to analyse the full implications. I am more interested here in how the critical consensus manufactured by the mass media—an apparently clear, determinate judgment of Bad Aboriginal Art—dissolves instead into a dispute requiring a historico-political analysis more than an explicitly aesthetic one. We cannot rule out circumstances in which legitimate Aboriginal owners might have made the same 'mistake'. If that were so, then we would have a less convincing instance of such bureaucratic offences, providing a particularly difficult case study in the politics of Aboriginal aesthetics. Therefore, this episode is not the best illustration of my thesis. I believe I can provide a better example, one with which I am more familiar: the Yuendumu Doors.

A TELLING SECRET

Yuendumu Doors is a series of 30 to 40 'traditional dot' paintings on the doors of the primary school buildings at Yuendumu Community. (To call these paintings traditional requires qualification: for example, translators had a difficult time finding a Warlpiri language equivalent for 'door' to use in the bilingual documentation.) Yuendumu is a settlement of about 1000 Warlpiri people, the product of a government induced movement from the desert regions, west and northwest of the present location, mostly during the 1940s. The community can be a strange and anomalous sight. It retains the skeletons of several discourses applied to it over the years: Baptist Missionary, government assimilationist, self-determination, and lately, Country–Liberal Party 'Tidy Town.' Whatever one makes of the jumble of abandoned buildings, new demountables, white painted rocks, satellite receiving dish, graffitied walls, it is soon clear that the residents view all this with eyes quite different from what Europeans first imagine. The Education Department is the major landholder and most visible presence in the community. Commissioning the doors in 1984 was intended to make the school look 'more indigenous'. A number of senior men, mostly connected to the school already as cleaners and yardmen, were enlisted, supplied with acrylic poster paints, and promised $5 per door.

The result is fully documented.[15] But that process—the recognition not just of the doors, but of a painting oeuvre which came to be dubbed the 'Yuendumu Style'—provides an interesting history. For the original pronouncement by designated valuators was that the paintings weren't very good. When the official experts of the Inada Holdings Pty Ltd (an Aboriginal Affairs operation then engaged in attempting a monopoly on all non-urban Aboriginal art marketing) first saw these early paintings, they suggested that the artists might wish to spend some time at Papunya settlement to learn their craft and improve their technique—and that federal funds might be found for such training.

Papunya is the motherlode of the Western Desert Painting movement. In 1971 a sympathetic and innovative art school teacher, Geoff Bardon, bucked the assimilationist policy of the Education Department and recognised in the old men's wall paintings something eminently worth encouraging. After muralising the Papunya school, the men moved onto boards and canvasses, forming an artists' cooperative and, by the late 1970s, attracting considerable interest amongst cognoscenti in Sydney and Melbourne. At least some of this interest concerned the appearance of old forms in new, marketable mediums.

Bardon describes how he exercised, though hesitantly, some selective pressures in his role as art adviser,[16] an unavoidable consequence of such bi-directional mediation between artists and markets. When he commented on some representational animal forms appearing alongside the abstract Western Desert iconographs in an early painting, the artists painted them out.[17] Bardon presumes, but doesn't bother substantiating, that such representationalism implies modern influences. Even so, he denies any justification for imposing his own aesthetics ('I was always conscious that I must not intrude my own opinions about colours, methods or subject matter'); but such contradictory evidence of an enforcement of 'traditionalism' is striking. The same contradictions can be detected in nearly all arts advisers' confessions—they are built into the project. What may differ is how they are managed and, then, how they are admitted.

The earliest Papunya paintings look similar in many respects to the first generation of Yuendumu canvasses produced a decade later. The communities are nearby (150 kilometres), they are closely related by kin, ceremony and language, and share rights to many of the same designs. By the late 1970s, with land rights and the end of restricted movement, the frequent traffic desired by residents between the two communities became possible. Despite ten years lag between market painting at Papunya and Yuendumu, the logistics of using the new mediums (acrylics, rectangular portable surfaces) combined with the overlap of local graphic traditions in such a way that the early work from the two sites is strikingly alike. This seems to support Bardon's claims to non-intervention. But within a year or so of the introduction of acrylics, something already remarkably different had begun to happen with Papunya painting, imparting its characteristic look which deserves a hypothetical reconstruction here. For as the painters interacted more and more with Australian, and then overseas markets, attracting sophisticated brokers, critics and patrons along the way, the 'Papunya Style' began to interact with certain issues in 1960s and 1970s international painting, especially the extreme schematisations of New York minimalism.

Arts advisers can deny influencing indigenous art until they are mauve in the face. But even if they never commented on a painting in progress or completed, by word or look or gesture or price, in Central Australia at least one irreducible source of influence persists: materials. Unlike Arnhem Land, where local bark and pigments are still collected, marketable painting in the Centre requires a supply of canvas and acrylics, and the painters consider this to be the advisers' first responsibility. As Papunya art became recognised, it obviously received advice on materials justified by arguments of durability and suitability for the museum/collector market it was attracting. Canvas boards and school poster-paints would no longer do. What evolved was the use of raw linen, and thinned acrylics. This produced a comparatively flat, stained surface. There must have been some restriction on paint colours during the late 1970s, emphasising an

56

'authentic' earth palette: red, yellow and white ochres, browns and pinks (what Brisbane upholsterers call 'autumn tonings').

A set of conventions seems to have arisen at Papunya—at least partly, as an articulation of these modern materials which favour the precision, placement and colouration of the 'fill' dots. This resulted, I suspect, in the curiously schematic, minimal, Jules Olitski/Agnes Martinesque technique, as much as the ensuing critical and market approval. The look was muted, cerebral, and undeniably tasteful in exactly the way that tourist Aboriginal art—black, red and yellow cartoons (also the product of an invented palette)—was not. By 1980 there had arisen an unerringly recognisable Papunya Style. Not all painters adhered to the style and some truly original works were produced that don't at all fit this description. But to the extent that an industry came into being (by now promoted and fought over at the national level by the Australia Council, the Aboriginal Development Corporation, and marketing units within the Department of Aboriginal Affairs, as well as museum/university staffs), it produced that redundant, recognisable, brand-name product: *Papunya Tula*.

Desert Aboriginal ground, body, implement or rock art employs earth pigments, animal products, plants and feathers. Each material, in a manner Lévi-Strauss associates with 'bricolage', retains its association with its source, origin and locale, and brings these into the work as elements of its meaning.[18] Even the words for the elements used may signify all of these associations: red ochre from Karrku Mountain is called *karrku*, which may signify 'red' generally. Thus, colour is only one basis for identifying, choosing, and then 'reading' a medium. But with acrylics, colour is the only basis for differentiation. This radical difference in the semiology of materials can take some getting used to, but in the end may free the artist in another sense, presenting new choices unavailable to the bricoleur. My argument is that there is nothing that can be called 'traditional colours', as the concept is quite alien in this context. Never mind the evidence that pre-contact palettes in fact contained green oxides, pink and blue flowers, and other shades now judged non-traditional. The very idea of choices based solely on colour is itself a result of contemporary conditions and materials.

Were the Papunya painters totally passive while their art advisers conspired with the market to invent Papunya Tula aesthetics, to define both the 'good' and the 'tasteful,' and to construct the painters' authenticities in the process? The invention of such traditions was possible only because what mattered to the painters about the art was usually quite different from what mattered to Europeans. Specifically, acrylic colours offered all sorts of decorative possibilities, but were conceptually so unlike traditional media that these painters probably regarded colour as incidental. Likewise dotting, which came to be the strongest visual element of the Papunya Tula style, was generally background, mere fill, inconsequential, and often omitted in the ground and body paintings on which these canvasses were based.[19] This technique, which privileges pattern and grid, tends to play down the iconographic figures. The mythological text remained hidden and obscure, which was fine with the painters who at first had great difficulty (according to Bardon) in keeping secret designs out of the canvasses and off the market.

It is too bad that Nancy Munn did not take an active role as art adviser during her field studies of Warlpiri iconography in the 1960s.[20] Imagine if she had. Given her interest in Warlpiri proto-writing, wouldn't she have encouraged, even unconsciously, a technique which resisted this tendency to foreground the semantically empty dots at the expense of iconic forms, and preserved the centrality of the figure against the ground? The example is not entirely hypothetical. My own researches twenty-five years later, not unlike Munn's, concerned issues of semiotics and communication in which Warlpiri iconography was of considerable interest. I began working with the old men on their painting as a respite from my researches and the more politically confrontative video work with the younger men (I intended only to satisfy my own creative interests in a setting that I might find less emotionally demanding, less painfully contradictory). In short, I saw my involvement with the painting studio as an indulgence. I was aware that the old men, frustrated by my refusal to become involved in ceremony (atypical for most anthropologists), considered my participation in the painting activities as a means of not merely teaching me, but of establishing my accountability to them, a lacuna that had persisted rather too long at this point in my fieldwork. Whatever the motives, those lovely days spent sitting around, priming canvas, getting water, fetching tea, assisting where and when requested, were among the most pleasant I spent at Yuendumu. If painting subsequently proved the basis for many surprising insights and actions, I still thought of myself as on holiday from my formal research and free of any scholarly agenda. But good ethnographic questions are not always imposed; some may only emerge from the fieldwork itself. The differences between Yuendumu and Papunya painting posed a contrast with considerable implications.

If Papunya Tula seeks to distance itself from tourist art, then what does Yuendumu art oppose and engage? Two possible solutions may be developed. First, the Yuendumu style seeks to distinguish itself from Papunya Tula, partly as a marketing strategy and partly on the basis of an implicit criticism of the legitimacy of certain technical choices generally regarded as externally, and perhaps unnecessarily, influenced. However and by whomever they were made, certain formal choices employed in Yuendumu painting contrast dramatically with those made at Papunya. As adviser and in-house critic at Yuendumu, I at least gave no encouragement to neatness or limited palettes; nor did Peter Toyne, then an adult educator, or Mark Abbot, the first Warlukurlangu art adviser. We all favoured the 'sloppy' style that first appeared on the doors, where I imagined I found confirmation that neatness was not a preferred criterion for the painters themselves. Yuendumu painting during this time was bold, bright, colourful, and messy—perhaps 'gestural'. It turned out that the symbolism assumed a fully central place in the image, which meant that the contemporary preference for 'something strangely calligrammatic' was also engaged. Consequently, the shift in Western Desert painting styles closely imitates what occurred in the international art world during approximately the same time (say, in very general terms, the apparent shift from minimalism to neo-expressionism). Thus the Yuendumu product might well look at home in any contemporary New York gallery, without even so much as a program note to describe its Aboriginal sources—a hypothetical and wildly subjective criterion I sometimes applied in my personal evaluations. Here, an anecdote might confirm that such a phenomenon is only possible when the painting practices are freed from Papunya tastefulness.

One of Yuendumu's more prolific and accomplished painters had been spending considerable time with close relations at Papunya. While there, he joined in on a painting work (not at all an unusual reciprocal cultural exchange). On his return, he joined a group of four to six men attempting an especially large canvas—a Milky Way Dreaming. The preference at Yuendumu for collective painting is preserved, especially on larger canvasses. To describe these relations of production requires a full treatment of Warlpiri kinship and social organisation too detailed to attempt here, except to say that our painter did not have primary responsibility for this dreaming nor this project. The senior man who did was noted for his expansive performances at such times when he was in authority, and in this case he defined and took up a position at the head of the canvas which was rolled out on the ground (Yuendumu also preserves this association with sand painting). Work proceeded over several days.

Midway in the process I noted that the painter who had just returned from Papunya had brought the dotting style back with him: orderly rows of contrasting dots in the characteristic palette. This imparted a very unwieldy look to that corner of the painting, the rest of which, by hue and design, appeared stylistically wholly different. Sometimes such differences work and create appealing textures which articulate the social complexity of the painting collective. In any case, one is hesitant (as Bardon said) to offer any explicit critique. Usually, things work out.[21] But now I was getting nervous, as this large canvas represented a major investment in labour and materials. It was one of those occasions which screamed 'major project'. The men were already talking about a sizable return for this one. So, I intervened.

I casually asked the senior painter (not the offender) 'what he thought' about the dots. Were they part of the Dreaming/Story (jukurrpa/jimi)? No, of course not. He went over the story again, tracing the large dark figures centrally placed in this canvas. Sometime later, I remarked that it was hard to see the story in the Papunya-looking section: there were so many colours, the dots looked like *jukurrpa* (text). Europeans might get confused looking at the picture. I held my breath.

Everything stopped. With the grand gestures I associated with the senior painter, a pronouncement was made. My Warlpiri is not good enough to follow the specifics, but a full ten minutes was spent discussing the matter which resulted in a paintbrush being applied to some of the offending section, producing a more consistent and less defined area of fill. The painting subsequently set a new record for Yuendumu prices and now hangs in the Australian National Gallery— whatever that tells us about our example, and whatever questions it raises about interventions.

The choice of dots as background or foreground is one of the contradictions of intervention which tends to occupy the thoughts of most Central Australian arts advisers I've discussed it with. Dots label and authenticate desert acrylics for the European viewer, but may be inconsequential to the painters, for whom dotting might be likened to stripping in wallpaper. Dotting may be treated as a chore, assigned to junior painters. What if it should actually be discovered that a European was responsible for applying these dots? (At the instruction of an Aboriginal painter, of course.) Wouldn't this disqualify the painting from the discourses of authenticity, of spontaneous, untainted production which are still employed in its marketing, thus raising scandalous assessments of the adviser's professionalism and judgment? Or could we mount a myth based on the practices of classical and contemporary masters who employ others to do the backgrounds, draperies, clouds, etc. This situation is not mere conjecture. There are 'Aboriginal' paintings hanging in major collections which include large areas filled in by Europeans. My argument so far leads me to accept that this is perfectly valid, and that any notions of authenticity which are compromised by such practices are false criteria in the first place. The matter may be illustrated even better with a more peculiar, inverse example.

Earlier on, I wondered to what extent the brushes we provided, and the consistency of the paint itself, were affecting the dots as well as the difficulty of application (some of the older men tired easily). We were painting in an Education Department house in which I was also camping. One day, after the painters had all left, I took off a halfmetre of canvas and attempted my own painting. I invented a 'dreaming' based on a favourite locale from home, spent a few hours painting, and made some useful discoveries about technique. Later, I rolled up the half-done canvas (which, I thought, failed to look at all Warlpiri) and promptly forgot about it. Several months later, I discovered my painting exhibited at the community store. Not only was nobody particularly fussed by the fact that this dreaming, and its author, were unidentified, even unidentifiable, but the painting had been completed —the dotting filled in—by some old men in my absence!

Let me propose a partial response to what I take to be something of a challenge to our usual ways of thinking about art authorship and sales (but also authenticity and tradition) represented by this case. I earlier asked the question: What does Warlpiri art oppose itself to? The evidence suggests that the opposition to Papunya Style which I detected and encouraged may have mattered to Europeans, but had little relevance to what the painters themselves were concerned with. The history of the Yuendumu Doors again may provide clues.

BAD TO PAINT ON THE SCHOOL?

One of the intentions of painting the Yuendumu Doors was to prevent the children from messing up the school with graffiti as had often occurred. At least some of the old men rail against this graffiti at great length. They go so far as to question the value of literacy, when its only visible result is said to be these scrawls on public places. It was an open question whether the kids would subsequently respect the doors and keep away from them. As it happened they did not (although some doors have been overpainted and graffitied more than others, and some study could be made to see if there is any semiotic calculation at work here, though I doubt it). Indeed, in all my years of visual recording at Yuendumu, in what I intended to be a respectful manner, the only time I disputed a prohibitory judgment was when taking pictures of the children's graffiti. This alone was judged by the elders to be a subject unworthy of reproduction under any circumstances. This suggests to me that what Warlpiri painting also opposes itself to may be graffiti. What is (and will probably remain) less clear is whether this opposition has its sources in a discourse learned from Europeans—tidy towns and church sewing circles. Or are there sources in Warlpiri tradition which need to be accounted for as well?[22]

What is graffiti? It is of course writing on walls or other appropriated surfaces, and involves something of the calligrammatic which initiated this study of Warlpiri iconography. Then, is cave painting and rock art graffiti? The discrimination may have more to do with contexts of authorisation than any inherent property of the text. Graffiti is unauthorised images—images where they should not be, or images by those unauthorised to make them. This recalls the *60 Minutes* Wandjinas case and suggests that its confused reporting of it may have been more expressive of actual contradictions than it first appeared.

The way that Warlpiri people talk about paintings and designs revolves around these very questions of authority. Who owns the design? Who is authorised to paint (reproduce) it? Who may see it? The anthropological literature locates these considerations in an ethnographic past, but the story of the Wandjinas demonstrates that exactly the same issues prevail today.[23] Whether the result of these restorations is precious art or worthless graffiti is very much a current concern. When there is a dispute, it will likely be discussed by contrasting European ('official') with Aboriginal ('traditional') terms of authority. It cannot be so very far-fetched to imagine that this is at least part of what is on the Warlpiri painters' minds when they make paintings for the market: a concern to be seen as the proper authorities to value the art, untainted not by the *inauthentic* but by the *unauthorised*.

The intrusion of the art adviser may not be considered as such when responsibilities and accountabilities are understood. The intervention described here in the assessment of authenticity would mostly be seen as inconsequential in terms of Aboriginal authority: dots, refinements of colour, etc. At the same time, advisers are themselves authorities, specialists, people who are supposed to understand Western taste and economics and who will offer that expertise to the painters. It is mostly the European discourse which concerns itself with the possibility that the contribution of these advisers taints the art, renders it inauthentic, and so compromises its value, as if some intact arcane authority can be transferred directly from Aboriginal elders onto canvasses, which can then be purchased, owned and hung in European lounges and corporate boardrooms.

Examined in this light, all the possible discourses that distinguish Aboriginal art from graffiti turn out to be nonsense when judged by the proposition with which our discussion began: no such 'determinate concepts' can ever be the basis of a 'stable consensus' in matters of taste.

The failure to make discriminations of value about a painting style cannot be ascribed solely to racism, or claimed for Australian art alone. Problematics of aesthetic discrimination are now universal. Lyotard and Rogozinski, in repudiating a certain Neo-Kantianism in contemporary criticism, contrast it with their own reading of Kant:

> —[I]n matters of taste, though it is not possible to *dispute*, ie, demonstrate 'by means of *determinate* concepts,' and hence arrive at a stable consensus, it is still possible to *discuss*, to appeal to the assent of the other, without ever being certain of convincing. In fact, in this type of judgment our power to judge is not *determinate*, but *reflective*. It is not based on a category or some pre-given, universally applicable principle, but on the necessity, when dealt an odd hand, an unexpected case, of judging without rules in order to establish the rules. The activity resulting from the reflective type of judgment is that of the artist, the critical philosopher, 'republican' politics—an inventive step which, on the path of the unknown, of the unacceptable, breaks with constituted norms, shatters consensus, and revives the meaning of the *différend*.[24]

In practice it is probably easier, and more common, to identify a work of art as bad than to explain why another is good. Current criticism certainly does a better job ruling out possibilities than specifying the 'rule beyond rules' fantasised by Lyotard and Rogozinski. In arriving at such a rejection again and again, the critic always risks confronting chaos, staring directly down the maw of the primordial dark. We seek strategies to plug that gap, to obscure that sight with various critical inventions: the Sublime or divine, rules beyond rules, Benjamin's 'aura'. Doing so, criticism seeks to supersede art itself.

Pre-modern art (from primitive to classical) always was aligned with order against chaos. This is what beauty claimed of itself: a statement of order, a meta-ordering device, a means to illuminate the inchoate void. This too is the function anthropological reconstruction attributes to traditional Aboriginal rock, body, and ground designs—an ordering of the social and natural universe.

Yuendumu and Papunya acrylics, indeed all painting coming to the market today as Aboriginal, tempt us to accept this proposition we would reject in any other context. Because these designs claim sources in a religious iconography, a 'cult ritual' (satisfying Benjamin's defini- tion of 'aura'), it may somehow be imagined that they carry intact from the primitive (Dreamtime) some exemption from the modern/ postmodern condition and its unbearable (if oblique) view of chaos. But such claims require also an exemption from recognising the re- lations and conditions of their production, and their own historical (not pre-historical) construction. But this asserts that dangerous fantasy of authenticity which all our other critical terms resist. I have argued the opposite: that these works are to be judged first and foremost in terms of the social practices which produce and circulate them— practices which promote issues of authority, not authenticity. From this analysis, their history can be appreciated as expressing precisely the extreme contradictions of colonialism and racism in which they are generated and sold.

But I have not presented any criteria which can be used to judge the art object itself. I have failed to define bad Aboriginal art, or pose any scheme for evaluating the good as my title seems to promise. This is intentional. It should be clear that the work itself does not support such assertions or evaluation. It is the product of too many discourses: the painters' attempts to have their designs (and themselves) ac- knowledged seriously in the contemporary market, the market's re- quirements for exchange-value fodder, and the consumer/collector's interests which may well include the desire to be associated with auras of authenticity as well as investment speculation. The contradic- tions of this system resist resolution.

The result is a *stochastic* system, neither determinate nor indeter- minate, but one which nonetheless seeks description and deserves judgment (ie the processes of production and circulation, but not the product). Good Aboriginal art, as well as its criticism, must indeed 'appeal to the assent of the other' and does not seek to convince. Judgments of the product must always—ultimately—be exposed as fraud.

NOTES

1 Whether to classify Warlpiri people and their art as coming from the Western or Central Desert is somewhat more our problem than theirs. Because I am drawing some comparisons to work from the Kimberleys,

and because I wish to imply some continuity of techniques, I will class the Warlpiri as 'Western' here. In fact, there were once probably extensive continuities of some painting techniques throughout Australia. Certainly, that is the situation today: acrylic 'dot paintings' are being produced in inner Sydney suburbs, north Queensland workshops, Singapore towelling mills, Japanese printing houses . . . perhaps everywhere.

2 Susan Dermody made this claim at the Power Institute's forum on the debate between postmodernism and cultural studies ['(What to do) When the Going Gets Tough', in *Streetwise Flash Art*, Power Institute of Fine Arts Occasional Paper No 6, Sydney, 1987]. Overseas guest Dick Hebdige would only admit that the debates on the subject were very advanced in Sydney. See Meaghan Morris's adroit management of this contradiction of displacement in her reading of *Crocodile Dundee*, *Art & Text* 25 (June–August 1987), pp. 36–69.

3 Cf J-F Lyotard & J Rogozinzki, 'The Thought Police,' *Art & Text* 26 (September–November 1987).

4 Jean Baudrillard, 'Gesture and Signature: Semiurgy in Contemporary Art', in *For a Critique of the Political Economy of the Sign*, trans. C Levin, Telos, St Louis, 1981.

5 G Alexander, 'Slipzones: Text and Art', *Art & Text* 26 (September–November 1987), pp. 42–57, at p. 43; but see also my examination of the 'reading and writing' of Warlpiri symbolic context in E Michaels, 'Hollywood Iconography, a Warlpiri Reading', in P Drummond and R Patterson (eds) *Television and Its Audience: International Research Perspectives*, BFI, London, 1987.

6 Baudrillard, op. cit., p. 103.

7 H Morphy, 'Now You Understand: An Analysis of the Way Yolngu Have Used Sacred Knowledge to Attach Their Autonomy,' in *Aborigines, Land and Land Rights*, eds N Peterson & M Laughton, Australian Institute of Aboriginal Studies, Canberra, 1987; V Megaw, 'Contemporary Aboriginal Art—Dreamtime Discipline or Alien Adulteration,' in *Dot and Circle*, 1987.

8 RM & CH Berndt, 'Secular Figures of Northern Arnhem Land, *American Anthropologist* 19/2 (1949); 'Aboriginal Art in Central-Western Northern Territory,' *Meanjin* 9/3 (1950).

9 P Ucko (ed), *Form in Indigenous Art: Schematisation in the Art of Aboriginal Australia and Pre-Historic Europe*, Australian Institute of Aboriginal Studies, Canberra, 1977.

10 P Loveday & P Cook (eds), *Aboriginal Arts and Crafts and the Market*, North Australian Research Unit, Australian National University, Darwin, 1983.

11 N Munn, *Warlpiri Iconography*, Cornell University Press, Ithaca, 1973.

12 Warlkurlangu Artists Association, *Kuruwarri Yuendumu Doors*, Australian Institute of Aboriginal Studies, Canberra, 1987.

13 A Crocker, 'An Appreciation of the Work of the Pintubi Painter Charlie Tjaruru Tjungurrayi', in *Charlie Tjaruru Tjungurrayi—A Retrospective*, Orange City Council, 1987.

14 The *Northern Territory News* (12 September, 1987) quotes Wanang Ngari administrator Mr Leighton Leitch as saying that the two responsible elders were in Derby at the time and in fact were consulted from the beginning. Elsewhere, Mowjarlai (cf. note 23) implies they were on site supervising the work.

15 Walkurlangu Artists Association, op. cit.

16 G Bardon, *Aboriginal Art of the Western Desert*, Rigby, Adelaide, 1979, p. 15.

17 Ibid, p. 14.
18 E Michaels, 'Western Desert Sandpainting and Postmodernism,' in Warlukurlangu Artists Association, op. cit.
19 Bardon (op. cit.) describes dots as having meaning, and diagrams one painting by Johnny Warrangula Tjaparula (p. 26) to indicate how differing dots contrast the signified topologies: sandgrass, sandhills, bush tucker. It is a beautiful painting and the dotting technique is extremely effective; I have seen something similar in perhaps no more than a dozen other paintings. It may well be a specific convention which applies to a certain style. But it is in no way universal. I argue that, more generally, the dots are background and therefore may be manipulated for various effects without affecting the correctness of the painting from the painter's point of view.
20 Mann., op. cit.
21 At Yuendumu, we had a number of unscrupulous Europeans living there who sought to acquire personal collections—or fortunes—by offering immediate cash and other inducements (always a small fraction of what any canvas would eventually command), thus aborting the marketing process and depleting the local collective's supplies. Some painters resisted, but others needed money and this was a familiar mode of local exchange; after all, the paintings have to be considered each artist's property. But it was discovered that the tastes of these collectors were entirely predictable: kitsch on the one hand, and the most neat, Papunya-looking examples on the other. We realised these sales represented a kind of weeding-out process resulting in a welcome petty cash flow, and no direct action was taken. Eventually, such characters tend to leave the community, often chased by the law for other reasons, as happened here. Thus, what came to market tended to be the more 'Yuendumu' of the canvasses. (Anyone who has worked in a contemporary Aboriginal settlement will recognise this kind of story, and logic.)
22 The commercial 'Christian' printers who set the colour plates for the Yuendumu Doors book objected to some of the graffiti included in the photographs and agreed to print the pictures only after airbrushing them out. Nobody has even noted this curious revision or argued, as I might, that a desecration, perhaps equal to a mutilation of the Mona Lisa has occurred.
23 D Mowaljarlai & C Peck, 'Ngarinyin Cultural Continuity: A Project to Teach the Young People the Culture, Including the Repainting of Wandjina Rock Art Sites', *Australian Aboriginal Studies*, 1987.
24 Lyotard & Rogozinski, op. cit., p. 30. See also E Michaels, *The Aboriginal Invention of Television*, Australian Institute of Aboriginal Studies Press, Canberra, 1986.

PART II
Aesthetics and everyday life

5

A house of games: Serious business and the aesthetics of logic

HELEN GRACE

Metaphors, symptoms, signs, representations: it is always through replacement that values are created. Replacing what is forbidden, what is lacking, what is hidden or lost, what is damaged, in short, replacing with something equivalent what is not itself, in person, presentable . . .

Jean-Joseph Goux, *Symbolic Economies*[1]

This essay is concerned with two key terms, value and utility, which haunt daily life wherever it is lived. These terms act to focus anxieties about the nature of activities, particularly in the public sector and in higher education, the value and use of which were formerly taken for granted and are now subject to an unprecedented degree of scrutiny. My focus will not, however, be the public but the private sector, and my concern is with the development of some of its logic and philosophies. This is a descriptive account, in many respects, and is the beginning of a line of research which might be regarded as empirical (without apology), involving both a search for ideas in places where it is assumed they do not exist, and an exploration of discarded theories. The general concern of the speculations here is with the relation between aesthetics and economics; crudely put, we might say that aesthetics is more concerned with value than utility, while economics is more concerned with questions of utility than value. It is immediately obvious, however, that this categorisation doesn't fit—economics has always been fundamentally about value, and aesthetic value might also be thought of as a utility in a certain sense, so that there exists between aesthetics and economics what Barbara Herrnstein Smith has

*   This is a reworked version of a paper presented at the Australian Cultural Studies Conference held at the University of Western Sydney, Nepean in December 1990.

called a double discourse of value.[2] I do not have the space to discuss in greater detail the way in which the terms value and utility are currently changing places, but a discussion of the ways in which modern management increasingly depends upon attitudes formerly associated with aesthetic rather than economic fields will illustrate the process.

■

Is management an art or a science? Management textbooks commonly pose the question, in the context of attempts to construct, on the one hand, a scientific framework for discussing management theory and practice (the need for logic), and, on the other, an acknowledgement of the social dimensions of management, reduced to questions of 'interpersonal communication', 'human resource management' etc (the need for rhetoric). The question is also posed as an issue of disciplinarity within the development of the institutional claims being made for the practices in their attempts to establish the validity and authority of the knowledge which they produce. Practices which need to pose such a question cannot properly be regarded as sciences, or rather, their scientific claims tend to limit them to what have traditionally been regarded as the 'low sciences' (such as alchemy, geology, astrology, medicine). The low sciences are distinguished from the high sciences (optics, astronomy, mechanics) by their inability to demonstrate their laws; they thus deal with *opinio* rather than *scientia*, which derives from the demonstrability of propositions.[3] The question, art or science—or to put it in the language of philosophical categories, aesthetics or logic—is also clearly limited in that it suggests a false dichotomy between the two categories, while also excluding other possible categories (in particular, ethics, to continue with a usefully simple description of philosophy's divisions). Before considering management theory's claims to scientificity, some of the artistic possibilities can be noted in passing. The attempt to locate management theory in the field of aesthetics might be seen to reflect an ambivalence about the practice and its legitimacy as well as a concern about the limitations of a location solely within the field of logic. A management textbook presents one view in this way:

> Henry M. Boettinger, a corporate executive and management lecturer, argues . . . that management is an art, 'an imposition of order on chaos'. In his view, painting or poetry (or any other fine or literary art) requires three components: the artist's vision, knowledge of craft, and successful communication. In these respects management is an art, because it requires the same components. And therefore, just as artistic skill can be developed through training, so can managerial skills be developed in ways similar to those used in training artists.[4]

The argument indicates something of the anxiety behind management's problem of where to place itself. There is a recognition, in the effort to locate itself as an art, that the claims to scientificity are strained. At the same time, the well-established social legitimacy of artistic practice provides a model to which management attempts to attach itself, in order to achieve a kind of flow-on effect of legitimacy, on which its authority may be built, while its scientific claims are being assessed. There is something of this search for legitimacy behind the highly publicised incursions into the art market by well-known entrepreneurs. But of course paying extremely high prices for artworks is also a play at increasing credit ratings. To consume conspicuously is to declare the extent of one's resources; it is intended to convince banks rather than artlovers; it is also a visible attempt to acquire assets to support efforts towards increased borrowings. In the absence of gold standards, art, more than any other commodity, provides legitimacy—as well as being more susceptible to market forces than most other commodities because of its scarcity.

Then there are those entrepreneurs, dissatisfied with regarding business as merely being *like* art, who make the shift from metaphor to metonymy, so that their practice itself becomes art, resembling a late 1960s art school environment:

> I don't do it for the money. I've got enough, much more than I'll ever need, I do it to do it. Deals are my art form. Other people paint beautifully on canvas or write wonderful poetry. I like making deals, preferably big deals. That's how I get my kicks.
> Most people are surprised by the way I work. I play it very loose. I don't carry a briefcase. I try not to schedule too many meetings. I leave my door open. You can't be imaginative or entrepreneurial if you've got too much structure. I prefer to come to work each day and just see what develops.[5]

The continuity of art and life is further extended by the commissioning of art by, for example, mining companies, for whom artistic vision is seen to parallel the vision of the geologist, the two visions being linked by the power of Mind:

> The great leaps of human achievement stem from the uniquely human act of creative imagination. It is this common factor which links art with business and with science transcending the artificial barrier which our education often places between them. Only the human mind can see an old view of a familiar landscape in a new way. Only the human mind can envisage the orebody, which lies unknown and hidden from sight; the new technology, which will create work and wealth; the new medical science, which will prolong life and relieve suffering. Artists and explorers both share this ability to exercise creative imagination.[6]

The attempt to appropriate art in order to aestheticise the activities of business is one aspect of logic's dependence on aesthetics. The ways in which logic's own language can be seen as a form of aesthetics is of even more interest.

The language of business and management's techniques is in a fundamental sense a language of desire, a statement of belief and commitment to impossible dreams of neatly controlled and ordered social and political environments (stability) alongside uncontrolled markets and unlimited wealth. At a visual level, we are encouraged to see the business or corporation in terms of the interrelationship of positions and functions on the organisational chart, beautifully arranged in a neat hierarchy of order. Flow charts are images of desire, utopian visions, statements of faith in the possibility that things will work according to the model. In one sense they belong to what Foucault has called—in his description of the mutation in forms of knowing at the end of the eighteenth century—the classical episteme,[7] a science of order in which knowledge can be presented in tabular form; at the same time, the flow chart equally belongs within the category which Foucault opposes to the classical—the modern episteme, characterised by discontinuous organic structures. The very descriptive term of the structure—*flow* chart—underlines this latter possibility. But in many ways, the table has largely disappeared from the representation of knowledge in this area. The table is a textual or, perhaps more appropriately, *linguistic* figure. It needs to be *read* in order to be understood. Reading is a slower, more contemplative, more classical way of acquiring knowledge; the table presents data which needs to be analysed by the reader, in order to decide the significance of its contents. The modern businessman no longer has this time. Even travel time between appointments is no longer available for contemplation, since the mobile phone has eliminated this lost time. A traffic jam is now no longer downtime, but a time when calls can be made to clients and appointments rescheduled, as Telecom Mobilenet billboard advertisements on main traffic routes advise those who pause to read them. Decisions have to be made on the run, we are told: the businessman must think on his feet and with his eyes. Knowledge must be acquired at a glance, it must be pictorially presented, so that the significance of the image can immediately penetrate. This is one reason the question of whether management is an art or a science arises: its claims to art are founded precisely at this moment of *perception* of the image, this moment of unconscious or, more accurately, *preconscious* awareness of a visual impression, a pattern of colours, lines, shapes. There is no time for conscious, *rational* analysis—and a feature of these developments is the extent to which rationality is increasingly seen as a problem, something which takes time, slowing down the necessary speed of change. *Man*, in a sense, gets in the way of things. The analysis which the businessman might once have done himself is now done by a computer, which converts the table and then presents to him neat *pictures*—graphs, charts—in a few of his own key strokes, so that he has the sense of having produced the analysis himself. Presentation software allows the production of rhetorical devices which are no longer figures of language but abstract patterns of colour. Their promise remains, however, at the level of language, in the proper names used to identify them: Excel, Powerpoint, MORE etc. All promise to present information fast and to give power to the user, at the very point that he* is becoming redundant.

Certain very simple aesthetic principles apply in this field. For example, the pursuit of happiness is figured in lines always rising to infinity, especially in advertisements of all kinds. The promise of unlimited growth is only countered by the excitement of dramatic change in indices, which is emphasised by the use of non-zero baselines. A crude colour theory operates; there shall only be blue skies; blue (and black) is good, red is bad, green means go, yellow may mean lack of courage. Using this logic the value of entire national economies can then be charted in the terms of a most breathtaking simplicity. Dangers can be understood, not in terms of moral issues and their ethical dimensions—the need to solve problems for the general good—but simply in terms of where opportunities might be found for investment (though concepts of 'the general good' may be mobilised in support of investment decisions). A totemic structure characterises the moods of the market: the bear and the bull represent the lows and highs of activity. Art and commerce, which are ostensibly opposed, have considerable overlap in that the manner in which knowledge about economics and business is produced and circulated is largely through aesthetic means and artistic devices—a company is said to have a *shape*, to be in good or bad shape; its structure is represented by the organisational chart; considerable effort is made in the presentation of products, particularly fictional ones—ie those in development—so that a projection, an *imago*, is made of an ideal object before a product exists. Expensive advertising campaigns can be mounted around products which exist only as prototypes or as computer-simulated models; glossy advertising brochures fetishise the object even before it is 'real'. (This relation between the image and the real, though not yet existent, object obviously has parallels with the mirror phase in Lacan's account of the development of subjectivity.)

Through the use of line, colour, shape—basic artistic tools, basic aesthetic values—representational devices are employed as the principal means of circulating knowledge in this area, even though the basis of that knowledge may belong to another order, that of logic (mathematics etc). The assumed communicative function of art is appropriated as a means of imparting 'knowledge' (or a knowledge-effect), particularly to the non-expert (shareholders, customers, the taxation department).

Of further interest is the productive application of the play/seriousness opposition in the increasing use of simulation games in modern management, a tendency which considerably blurs the lines of utility as they are understood in classical economics.

---

* I use the masculine form deliberately, since this is, properly speaking, a problem of *man*, and computer advertising is generally directed at men. Women can of course participate, but it feels very often that we are merely onlookers in this process—a new, strange position of voyeurism.

Before looking at the development of mathematical games theory in more detail, it will be useful to consider a theory of game analysis from a more sociological perspective. Huizinga's and, more particularly, Caillois's[8] approaches are noteworthy because of the philosophical framework within which each is presented. Huizinga's approach is based on a notion that play forms the basis of civilisation, or rather that a play instinct exists, a notion which is derived from Schiller:

> There shall be a communion between the formal impulse and the material impulse—that is, there shall be a play instinct—because it is only in the unity of reality with the form, of the accidental with the necessary, of the passive state with freedom, that the conception of humanity is completed.[9]

Huizinga then defines play in this way:

> [W]e might call [play] a free activity standing quite consciously outside 'ordinary' life as being 'not serious', but at the same time absorbing the player intensely and utterly. It is an activity connected with no material interest, and no profit can be gained by it. It proceeds within its own proper boundaries of time and space according to fixed rules and in an orderly manner. It promotes the formation of social groupings which tend to surround themselves with secrecy and to stress their difference from the common world by disguise or other means.[10]

The common dualism of play and seriousness evoked here is conventionally Cartesian and belongs within a long history of representation in which seriousness becomes the privileged term, particularly within materialism. Thus play, being decidedly 'not serious', has no material value, and hence no real value. As Sartre puts it:

> It is not by chance that materialism is serious; it is not by chance that it is found at all times and places as the favourite doctrine of the revolutionary. This is because revolutionaries are serious. They come to know themselves first in terms of the world which oppresses them, and they wish to change this world . . . The serious man is 'of the world' and has no resource in himself. He does not even imagine any longer the possibility of getting out of the world.[11]

For the materialist, then, anything other than the purely material has no real existence, or exists solely in the world of the Idea or of idealism (hence the portrayal of aesthetics as nothing more than ideology). Out of this dualism of play and seriousness arises some of the Left's paralysed moralism. The debate around some of these questions is beyond the scope of this essay, except to suggest that part of the problem concerning 'the aesthetic' comes about because of a too great emphasis on eighteenth-century philosophy. I'd like to go back even further, before Descartes even, and suggest that in the development of mathematics, particularly in the area of logarithms (explored by John Napier between 1595 and 1614) and symbolic algebra, the problems of truth—philosophy's concerns—are sidestepped by the acceptance of a model (let's call it a metaphor, to draw out the parallel with qualitative knowledge and contemporary criticism) which does not necessarily involve a commitment to absolute truth, or to universals of any kind; it merely makes it possible to proceed on a kind of 'let us pretend . . .' conditional basis. (We will sidestep the subjectivism of this knowledge for the moment . . .)

Symbolic algebra's history is an interesting one, worth mentioning in passing and at precisely this moment in history. Most of contemporary theory concerns itself with the European tradition and particularly that moment in which Descartes becomes the Creator of the world. It is certainly true that Descartes said there ought to be a general science of numbers, forms, shapes, sounds and other objects, with the task of explaining all there is to be known about order and measure, and that this science would be mathematics. (Compare this statement of the necessity for a general science of mathematics with Saussure's statement of the necessity for another general science of signs to be called semiology, nearly three hundred years later. We might trace out a loose connection—and disconnection—between the two, beginning with Thomas Sieni's work on 'semiotics' in 1664,[12] less than a generation after *The Discourse on Method* [1637], through Lavater's physiognomic theory of types in the eighteenth century:[13] all doomed attempts to found 'general theories' of signs.) It was not possible for a claim like this to be made, however, until what has been called the 'marriage' of Hindu algebra and Greek geometry had taken place.[14] Rather than referring to a simple line of descent which made this possible, and in order to avoid what George Canguilhem has called 'the virus of the precursor' and the 'epidemic of the accident',[15] it is necessary to acknowledge that the process which brought the two together was a very diffuse one which took hundreds of years. In 773 (a mere 900 years before *The Discourse on Method* was published), the year 156 of the Hijra, a man skilled in the calculus of the stars and knowing how to solve equations complicated enough to predict eclipses came from India to Baghdad and the court of Caliph al Mansur. The book in which this knowledge was contained was translated into Arabic and various editions of it went into circulation. Of course it was no mere pursuit of truth, as the history of science might suggest, which made all this possible. Already Baghdad had been constituted as a centre of civilisation by a political process which made it natural that an Indian would be drawn there. Persia had been conquered in the seventh century, which brought the Arabs in contact with India in the same way that the Greeks had had contact a thousand years earlier. The nineteenth-century Orientalist accounts of Islamic science tend to minimise its importance by suggesting that nothing new was really added to the Ptolemaic system—although it is acknowledged that many of the texts were lost.[16] (Perhaps the Crusades destroyed them—it needs to be remembered that there was never in Islamic civilisation the same persecution of those who attempted to overthrow the dominant cosmology as there had been in Christianity. Knowledge, however heretical, was sought; its implications were not feared as they had been in the Middle Ages in Europe. We could conjecture that the Arabs might have discovered half a millennium earlier a great deal of what Europe had to reinvent in the seventeenth century: this remains conjectural, but there is political value in imagining the possibility at present.)

Against Cartesian seriousness and the desire for a general theory of meaning, there is the resistance to it in the desire for suspending rationality in the excess of some forms of game. In this regard, Caillois emphasises the distinction between the regularity of the everyday and 'the ferment of the festival' with its sacrifices and excess.[17] Caillois is critical of Huizinga's account, especially because of its tendency to regard play as devoid of material interest. Caillois's approach has the benefit of operating outside the structure of rigid dualism which Huizinga applies. As a result of this he is able to see a continuity between the logic of the game and life itself—although he maintains an assumption of separateness to the extent that he also views play as being 'essentially a separate occupation, carefully isolated from the rest of life, and generally engaged in with precise limits of time and place'.[18] The continuity which Caillois sees exists at the level of metaphor to the extent that his aim is to analyse the structure of games within which parallels with life become noticeable. Huizinga's account might be regarded as an essentialist one, whereas Caillois's might be said to be structuralist.

Caillois identifies four classes of games; firstly, games which involve competition, for example chess, he calls *agôn*. Other accounts place chess, with Monopoly and business games, as games of war. *Agôn* involves individualism, the player is entirely self-reliant; as Caillois points out, the point of the game is for the player to have his/her superior skill recognised.[19] Winning does not necessarily involve serious injury for the rival (although this may happen); rather it involves the demonstration of the winner's superiority. *Agôn* reaches its purest form in the demonstration of prowess; Caillois gives the examples of hunting, mountain-climbing, crossword puzzles, chess. One might add here all those outdoor games of endurance and adventure which have become a part of management training, especially in Japan and in Japanese-style business training, in which businessmen go off on survival camps to discover their true leadership potential.

Secondly, Caillois classifies games of chance such as roulette as *alea*, which is the Latin word for the game of dice. *Alea* is the opposite of *agôn*; it involves luck and the submission to destiny, and includes all games based on a decision which is independent of the player,[20] on an outcome over which she/he has no control, or in which winning is the result of chance rather than the defeat of an opponent by the player's own efforts. In the case of *alea*, the player does not depend on his/her skill or intelligence; work, experience, qualifications are negated. *Alea* and *agôn* involve opposite but complementary qualities and exist together in, for example, card games which involve a degree of luck-of-the-draw as well as a degree of skill. *Agôn* involves the vindication of personal responsibility—the player is dependent entirely on him or herself—whereas *alea* involves dependence on everything else but the self and on everything which is external to the self—anything might be taken as an omen or a sign. Playing the stockmarket might be said to involve elements of both *alea* and *agôn*; although *agôn* should predominate, a certain amount of risk-taking is involved: a gamble is taken (*alea*) but at the same time, the risk has to be a calculated one (*agôn*). It might be suggested that in a bull market, too much *alea* is involved, while in a bear or stable market *agôn* is dominant.[21] In games theory, Monte Carlo methods might also be categorised as an instance of *alea*.

Thirdly, Caillois lists *mimicry*, which involves simulation and role playing. It is for this work that his ideas are probably best known, since Lacan has drawn on an earlier account of the significance of mimicry (an account which Caillois himself repudiates in *Man, Play and Games*).[22] Homi Bhabha also draws indirectly on Caillois in his quotation of Lacan's use of mimicry in describing the experience of colonialism.[23] For Caillois, mimicry applies as much to the response of the spectator in a game as to the participant; and in describing as mimicry the process whereby spectators identify with the champion at sporting events, some parallels might be said to exist between *mimicry* and what has been called *suture* in film theory's description of the identification process in the cinematic experience.

Caillois's fourth category is called *ilinx*, after the Greek term for whirlpool from which the Greek word for vertigo (*ilingos*) is derived, and includes games involving vertigo, such as riding a merry-go-round. The purpose of games of this kind is deliberately but momentarily to destroy the stability of perception, so that the otherwise lucid mind is temporarily in a state of panic. Caillois cites the example of the Mexican *voladores*, who climb to the top of sixty to a hundred foot masts where, disguised as eagles with false wings attached to their wrists and a rope attached to their waists, they begin a head-first descent with arms outstretched. This perverse pleasure has a number of contemporary manifestations, such as bungy-jumping—which has been described as 'glue-sniffing for yuppies'. Drunkenness and recreational drug-taking might also be seen to be games involving *ilinx*— and, to push the category, one might also add here the frenzied and dizzying activity of the crazed broker, the screen jockey, addicted through modem-link to the constantly changing prices of international stockmarkets on the screen of the PC. More appropriately, the pleasure of speed belongs in this category. Caillois has noted that:

> In order to give this kind of sensation the intensity and brutality capable of shocking adults, powerful machines have had to be invented. Thus it is not surprising that the Industrial Revolution had to take place before vertigo could really become a kind of game.[24]

In cinema the special effects industry takes over where the amusement park leaves off in providing this experience, combining the effects of both mimicry (simulation) and ilinx (vertigo). The development of virtual reality in computer games extends this link even further.

Caillois notes that games of vertigo and games of chance have not been analysed by sociologists; he further suggests that they've in fact been boycotted.[25] The study of vertigo is left to physicians and explained in terms of the operations of the semicircular canals of the inner ear (which Caillois denies is an adequate explanation of the powers of panic which people choose to experience in play). The study of games of chance is left to mathematicians; Caillois again regards a calculus of probability as no substitute for a sociology of gambling, which is clearly absent from the mathematical approach, with its elimination of the psychological. Although ruse and bluff are part of the calculations which might be made, ruse is simply regarded as being 'the perspicacity of a player in predicting his adversaries' behaviour', and bluff is the response to this ruse, or the art of disguising the information. It is true that psychology is minimised in the mathematical approach but this is also because the psychological is itself constructed as quantitative through the techniques of behaviourism. At any rate, mathematical theories, as far as Caillois is concerned, ultimately do not promote the spirit of the game, but rather destroy its reason for being:

> Mathematical analysis either ends in certainty, and the game loses interest, or it establishes a coefficient of probability which merely leads to a more rational appreciation of the risks . . .[26]

Be that as it may, the development of games theory probably owes more to the tradition of Descartes and the pursuit of an obscure object of desire (ie, certainty) than it does to Caillois's theory of the mystery of pleasure in uncertainty—although we need to keep in mind precisely this theory as part of a tradition of resistance to rationalism and which is the other side of the supposed instinct for order said to be natural in 'man'.

It isn't altogether the case that game theorists like von Neumann and Morgenstern are so committed to rationalism either. The question of rationalism is identified as 'the problem of rational behaviour',[27] which is to be understood not in qualitative terms but in terms of quantitative relationships which, they want to believe, is the only way to take into consideration all the elements of a qualitative description.

Around the poker tables of Princeton in the 1930s, mathematicians working on probability theory began to develop the field which has come to be called games theory. Initially evolved by von Neumann and Morgenstern, applications of the theory have been most widely used in the simulation of war, especially during the Cold War, when it was no longer possible to play for real. A US admiral has claimed that all the battles of the Second World War had already been gamed in Naval training colleges before the war began.[28] More recently, the main applications have been in the area of economics[29] and it is perhaps no surprise that one of the original researchers in the field should reappear as the co-author of a text on the predictability of stock market prices.[30]

Games theory is a method of predicting outcomes of strategic situations, bypassing the ethical dilemmas involved by an emphasis on logic. Shubik refers to the need for a 'calculus of plausibility'[31] whereby, through the use of propositional calculus, it then becomes possible to speak lightly of situations which most people would regard as apocalyptic. Shubik refers to 'on the beach' phenomena, a reference to the Neville Shute novel:

> [A]berrant behaviour caused by a firm belief that there will be no tomorrow is a rarity. In some gaming exercises a group of officers may have been given a special assignment to participate in a war game for a week. On Friday afternoon of the last day of their assignment they find that at 3.00 p.m. they are still playing. This leaves them scarcely an hour in which to blow up the world so that they can get over to the officers' club for Friday afternoon 'happy hour' and make it home for the weekend.[32]

More recently, games theory has been used in some US universities and colleges to teach about politics and political strategy. Within an approach using games theory, truth is regarded not as an unreachable absolute, as it is ultimately seen to be in most ethical frameworks, but as a variable. Students will be taught that any means justifies the end; you can lie, in certain circumstances, depending on the game (or life) environment in which you are playing. There are strategic rules for playing, firstly, in a long-term game with stable power relationships, one which calls for consistency in honesty and/or dishonesty rather than honesty or dishonesty itself; secondly, in a long-term game or series of games with unstable power relationships, where extremely high levels of honesty and dependability are called for; or thirdly, a short game, where thoroughly dishonest behaviour and telling lies will be useful. In a short-term game environment, for example, you can lie to achieve your ends, because you won't see the other players again. If, however, you have to do business with them again, then lying would be bad business because integrity, or the appearance of it, is important. You can also lie to and cheat those who have less power than you, provided the game is a short one, or a one-off; in a repeat situation, they might be in a different position of power and will be able to get even.[33]

War gaming was probably born in Prussia in the late nineteenth century, but business and management gaming is generally regarded as having emerged in the US.[34] Beginning as a means of predicting the outcome of games of strategy, in a recreational situation, games theory developed to the stage where it provided the language for a description of conscious decision-making processes between individuals, corporations, armies, nations.[35]

What is most interesting, however, in plunging into the density of

Theory of Games and Economic Behaviour, is that the authors set out to make claims for mathematics as a general science which are reminiscent of Descartes. They admit that, because of the problem of rational behaviour and other complications in the nature of economic theory, mathematics has not yet achieved its full impact or potential in the area of economics. However, given time, they remain confident that all will be revealed as being reducible to a set of mathematical formulae which will effect a long overdue Copernican revolution in the area of economics. To illustrate the possibilities of the quantitative they use the example of the theory of heat:

> [B]efore the development of the mathematical theory the possibilities of quantitative measurements were less favourable there than they are now in economics. The precise measurements of the quantity and quality of heat (energy and temperature) were the outcome and not the antecedents of the mathematical theory.[36]

They remind us that the quantitative is already present in economic theory, with quantitative conceptions of prices, money and rates of interest having been developed for centuries. They conclude that the problem with the mathematical treatment of economic theory is that economic theory itself offers not proofs but mere assertions 'which are really no better than the same assertions given in literary form'.[37] We might readily agree with them as we watch the current account and balance of payments figures reaching fantastic heights because economic-rationalist Treasury officials have been permitted to write their fictions upon the economy.

Von Neumann and Morgenstern's work, which first appeared in 1944, received relatively little attention within the empirical sciences, although it is highly relevant within sociology and wherever issues of conflicts of interest arise. The principles of game theory, the notion of utility, the minimax theorem, the theory of zero-sum two-person to n-person games, the theory of non-zero-sum games and of the implications of all this in bargaining are now well established in economic theory, although it was in the areas of logistics, submarine search and air defence that much of this work first found applications.

In the 1960s and 1970s, the spectre of something called the military-industrial complex was identified as a principal evil to be opposed. But by this stage it was already too late to intervene and, besides, much of the pure research done in the name of strategic planning was useless for that purpose, in spite of the fears and conspiracy theories of those opposed to it. The uselessness of this research is freely admitted in the literature:

> Yet, even at an establishment such as the US Naval War College, where hundreds of games have been played over many years the degree of accumulation of knowledge appears to be slight.[38]

Much of the pure research in these areas has since found applications in computers and new technology, so that the games which were played fifty years ago have come to have their uses *now*, firstly as computer games in the simplest sense (*Star Wars* arrived as a game before it became a reality, with Space Invaders in every milkbar and corner shop before the Strategic Defence Initiative became an issue for the US Congress). Other more intellectual versions, such as 'Balance of Power', became available for the more privatised personal computers. Games of this form, however, remain relatively crude; they are the games of the foot soldiers rather than the generals drawing upon decision theory in war-room planning.

Anti-militarism is an easy position to take, but it is altogether too late for it, since the logic of war-room planning is no longer restricted to the war room, but has invaded every aspect of strategic thinking and planning; it is an industry standard in manufacturing; PERT and CPM methods and variations on them form the basis of planning production most particularly in the car industry and in construction.[39] These methods were first devised to plan munitions production in the First World War; they also made the space age possible, and CPM was used to develop the Polaris submarine program.

Of course, in the age of the personal computer anyone can do it—project management computer programs, such as MacProject, are based on these techniques, employing the same charts, task orientation, milestones, allocation of time, Gantt charts, time-lines and case-flow tables originally used for munitions programs and now available to organise conferences and home renovations.

In business and economics the methods of games theory have their application in the simulation techniques used in training; this has been the main area of growth of these techniques in the twenty years since the Cold War. Throughout the 1960s, game theorists were devising models to represent the economies of third-world countries which allowed those economies and their political structures to be controlled by the West (less developed countries—'LDCs'—were produced by games theory). The real utopians were not those people dreaming of a possible future of human liberation, but those who stayed at business school throughout the period, thinking and working towards the very different sort of future which has now arrived, one in which fantasies of post-scarcity anarchism no longer have a place.

Although the scenarios of games theory may seem to have little relevance to us, their importance emerges in the language which business economics columnists use:

> For decades, Australian governments misappropriated our economic growth and distributed it on the basis of political clout. Now, not only has economic growth stopped, it is contracting. Furthermore, not even the most optimistic of forecasts can see domestic demand growing between now and the next election. In other words the nation as a whole faces at best a *zero sum game* where one person can only lift his/her standard of living at the expense of somebody else. In fact it is going to be a *sub-zero sum game* where one person can only maintain his standard of living if somebody

else's falls further than the average. This is the problem confronting the Government. Living standards will be cut back in order to bring stability to our current account and foreign debt exposure. Either the Government spreads the pain as equitably as possible or the markets impose brutal and inequitable outcomes.[40] (my emphasis)

If all this proves anything, it is that there is something to be said for planning, whatever methods you use. Another conclusion which might be drawn from this state of play is that there really are no differences between business and war, or between war and peace.

But I want to finish with another aspect of games research and of defence research in general. Clearly, billions of dollars have been spent in the last fifty years on pure research, the applications of which are only now being discovered, and a large part, if not the majority, of the outcome of this work has civilian rather than military application. New technological and electronic applications are being exploited by thousands of companies who will reap the profits of that work. But the pure research which makes it all possible has already been paid for by taxpayers in various countries in defence spending. Companies simply don't have to do the preliminary research—and they didn't even enter the picture at all until the 1950s and 1960s, when much of this work had already been going on for twenty or thirty years. Computer games themselves give us some indication of the sort of time-lag that is involved here, and a recently-released game called *Synchronicity*[41] serves as a useful example in this regard. Marketed as 'the intuitive decision-making tool', on the surface you might think that we have a post-feminist weapon, which, in its intuitiveness, transcends a certain phallogocentrism. When you play *Synchronicity*, you achieve (so it is promised) mental clarity, skillful detachment, focused energy, stimulation of the intuition, relaxation and pleasure, and the answers ring true. The game promotes a certain ethical quality, not in terms of moralism or of total chance, but rather in terms of an Eastern holism, which views the world as part of a grand order of things—another general theory. At one level the game might seem to be fashionably postmodern in its dependence on chance and arbitrariness, being itself an instance of synchronicity by virtue of its affinities with current chaos theory. However, the game is actually based on a late 1960s phenomenon (in the West at least), the *I Ching* or *Book of Changes*, and on Jung's *Treatise on Synchronicity*. It has taken twenty years for the ideas to seep into the consciousness of an ethically committed, probably ex-hippy programmer, and the game arrives as a gentle solution to the problem of decision making, a solution which in its harmless pleasures engages with the same sorts of problems with which game theory in general concerns itself. Central to these concerns is the problem of subjectivity and how to do away with it. Here it should be remembered that this was the same problem Descartes attempted to deal with, in a different kind of way, and it is also the problem which von Neumann and Morgenstern face. In decision theory generally, the problem of subjectivity is being bypassed because of the limitations of rationalism and rationality.[42] So it is not only feminist theory which has discovered these limitations, and its explanation in terms of phallogocentrism is only one of a number of explanations that might be elaborated. As even a conservative Harvard professor of public policy has noted, 'the mind of man, for all its marvels, is a limited instrument'.[43]

NOTES

1 Jean-Joseph Goux, *Symbolic Economies: After Freud and Marx*, Cornell University Press, Ithaca, 1990, p. 9.
2 Barbara Herrnstein Smith, *Contingencies of Value: Alternative Perspectives for Critical Theory*, Harvard University Press, Cambridge, Mass., 1988, p. 127.
3 For a good discussion of the value of the low sciences in the emergence of probability see Ian Hacking, *The Emergence of Probability: A Philosophical Study of Early Ideas about Probability, Induction, and Statistical Inference*, Cambridge University Press, Cambridge, 1975, particularly Chapters 3 and 4 on Opinion and Evidence.
4 James AF Stoner, Roger R Collins, Philip W Yetton, *Management in Australia*, Prentice-Hall, 1985, p. 26. The full Boettinger citation: Henry M Boettinger, 'Is Management Really an Art?', *Harvard Business Review* 53, 1 (Jan–Feb 1975) pp. 54–64.
5 Donald J Trump with Tony Schwartz, *Trump: The Art of the Deal*, Random House, New York, 1987, p. 3.
6 Sir Rod Carnegie (Chairman, CRA Limited) in the Preface to: *Fred Williams: The Pilbara Series, 1979–1981*, Text by Patrick McCaughey, CRA Limited, 1983. For a more extensive and critical discussion of the aesthetics of geology, see Allan Sekula, 'Photography Between Labour and Capital' in Benjamin Buchloh and Robert Wilkie (eds), *Mining Photographs and Other Pictures, 1948–1968: Photographs by Leslie Shedden*, Nova Scotia School of Art and Design and University College of Cape Breton Press, 1983.
7 M Foucault, *The Order of Things: An Archaeology of the Human Sciences*, Vintage Books, New York, 1973.
8 Johan Huizinga, *Homo Ludens*, 1938 (English translation, Roy Publishers, New York, 1950); Roger Caillois, *Les jeux et les hommes* 1958 (English translation, *Man, Play and Games*, Thames and Hudson, London, 1962).
9 Schiller, Letter XV from *Essays and Letters Vol VIII*, quoted in H Grace, 'The Mysteries of Manhood', *Intervention* 21/22 (1988), p. 77.
10 Huizinga, op. cit. (note 9), p. 13.
11 Cited in Grace op. cit. (note 9), p. 77.
12 Thomas Sieni, *Philosophi ac Medici praestantissimi, Semiotica, sive et signis medicis*, Lugduni, 1664.
13 Lavater: *Essai sur la Physiognomie Destiné A faire Connoître l'Homme et à le Faire Aimer*, Le Havre, 1786. Lavater's theory informs the development of phrenology and the illustrations of particular medical signs and symptoms in the book set out the poses which Charcot would reproduce, using photography to illustrate the *attitude passionelle* of hysteria. Lavater also refers to the 'colours of writing', an idea which might be read as a precursor to symbolist aesthetics.
14 H Butterfield, *The Origins of Modern Science*, Bell and Sons, London, 1968, p. 90.

15 Cited in M Shortland, 'Introduction to Georges Canguilhem' *Radical Philosophy* (Autumn 1981).

16 JLE Dreyer, *History of the Planetary Systems from Thales to Kepler*, Dover Publications, New York, 1953, pp. 245ff.

17 R Caillois, 'Festival' in D Hollier, *The College of Sociology 1937–39*, University of Minnesota Press, Minneapolis, 1988, p. 281.

18 Caillois op. cit. (note 9), p. 6. This position on play as being confined within precise limits of time and place is a much milder view than his position twenty years earlier, in which the emphasis would have been on excess and the suspension of marked time. Play, as a limited activity, corresponds more with the sense of *vacation*, which Caillois, in the late 1930s, viewed as an emasculated form.

19 Ibid, p. 15.

20 Ibid, p. 17.

21 Granger and O Morgenstern's *Predictability of Stock Market Prices*, Heath Lexington Books, 1970, might be seen as an attempt to ensure the predominance of *agôn*, although Caillois would regard it as a wasted attempt. This application of Caillois's categories to an analysis of the stockmarket as a game environment is mine. Strictly speaking, Caillois is concerned with the analysis of games in formal terms only; 'real-life' scenarios, like the stockmarket—however much they follow game scenarios like the race track, for example—are not the kind of games, which are analysed within Caillois's approach, although, unlike Huizinga, he does make a point of including an economic dimension—but again, mainly as an element of a game (ie gambling).

22 Of this work, 'Mimétisme et Psychasténie', which originally appeared in *Le Mythe et L'Homme* (Paris, 1938), Caillois writes: 'Unfortunately, this study treats the problem with a perspective that today seems fantastic to me. Indeed I no longer view mimetism as a disturbance of space perception and a tendency to return to the inanimate, but rather, as herein proposed, as the insect equivalent of human games and simulation.' *Man, Play and Games*, p. 178.

23 Homi Bhabha, 'Of Mimicry and Man: The Ambivalence of Colonial Discourse', *October* 28 (Spring 1984). The passage from Lacan which is quoted by Bhabha here comes from Lacan, 'Of the Gaze as Objet Petit a: The Line and Light' in *The Four Fundamental Concepts of Psycho-analysis*, Penguin, Harmondsworth, 1979.

24 Caillois, op. cit. (note 9), p. 25.

25 Ibid, p. 170.

26 Ibid, p. 175.

27 J von Neumann and O Morgenstern, *Theory of Games and Economic Behaviour*, Princeton University Press, Princeton, NJ, 1944, p. 8.

28 Martin Shubik, *Games for Society, Business and War: Towards a Theory of Gaming*, Elsevier Scientific Publishing Co, Amsterdam, 1976, p. 296.

29 EP Holland and RW Gillespie, *Experiments on a Simulated Underdeveloped Economy: Development Plans and Balance of Payments Policies*, MIT Press, Cambridge, Mass., 1963; M Shubik, 'Simulation of Socioeconomic Systems, Part 2: An Aggregative Socioeconomic Simulation of a Latin American Country', *General Systems* XII, (1967). For a more recent presentation of the theory for use in bargaining and multilateral trade, see JC Harsanyi and R Selten; *A General Theory of Equilibrium Selection in Games*, MIT Press, Cambridge, Mass., 1988.

30 Granger and Morgenstern, op. cit. (note 22).

31 Shubik p. 15: 'We need a "calculus of plausibility" which enables us to evaluate the truth content of "cry wolf" or other statements where there is no guarantee that the statement can be interpreted as a precommitment to action.'

32 Ibid.

33 Russel G Brooker, 'Truth as a Variable: Teaching Political Strategy with Simulation Games', *Simulation & Games* 19, 1 (March 1988) pp. 43–58.

34 Although it is tempting to view business and management gaming as being essentially capitalist, it is worth noting that a variety of simulation gaming was employed in the Soviet Union in the 1930s in attempts to improve industrial efficiency and productivity. (See JH Gagnon, 'Mary M Birshtein: The Mother of Soviet Simulation Gaming', *Simulation & Games* 18, 1 (March 1987).

35 Shubik, op. cit. (note 28), p. 14.

36 Ibid, p. 3.

37 Ibid, p. 5.

38 Ibid, p. 294.

39 PERT—Program Evaluation and Review Technique; CPM—Critical Path Method.

40 Max Walsh, 'Grey Power May Take Over From Green', *Sydney Morning Herald*, 19 November 1990, p. 15.

41 ™Visionary Software Inc, Portland, Oregon.

42 See JD Steinbruner, *The Cybernetic Theory of Decision: New Dimensions of Political Analysis*, Princeton University Press, Princeton, NJ, 1974.

43 Ibid, p. 13.

6

Azaria Chamberlain and popular culture

NOEL SANDERS

Two prints from Goya's *Los Caprichos* alternately show an innocent, cherubic child torn apart by clerics or lawyers, and a raging semi-domestic beast which someone (who?—the people?) is trying to bring under control. But these scenes are enigmatic; forms are violently juxtaposed against an undefinable, desert background. Rules of perspective fail to apply, and, as both Gombrich and Foucault have observed, while Goya's work appears to represent a stage in a continuous narrative, the narrative itself is obscure. The images are neither of a 'genre', nor do they 'represent' anything.[1] They are not illustrations 'of any known subject, either biblical, historical or genre'.[2] The forms themselves appear cast without meaning onto a scene which itself does not exist; they are 'born out of nothing'.[3] At best, we are linked with 'an old world of enchantments and fantastic rides, of witches perched on the branches of dead trees'.[4] The timeless world of oral narrative is invoked, but the figures themselves seem to have become as silent as the landscape without contours on which they have been thrown. In the absence of a readable topology, a logic of forms and spaces cannot arise. The only way the forms connect is in unspeakable acts of violence—infanticide, parricide, massacres of innocents. The participants themselves become monsters, and lack of a visual causation allows human motives and 'animal instincts' free interchange. In Goya's scenes, 'nothing can assign them their origin, nature or limit'.[5]

The silent theatre of *the Azaria disappearance* has taken place in Australia against just such backgrounds, with the narrative emerging only in dislocated episodes, as new evidence was brought to light and was reported in newspapers and on TV. The scene and images may be there, but as in Goya, there is no return to the 'natal scene' or terrain.

---

* This essay was first published in *Intervention* 1982.

86

Yet for the television and print media public that watched the *Azaria Chamberlain* matter unfold, both the natal terrain and the theatre of death, the silent and contourless centre of the continent, were transformed and known via a series of metaphors that filled the unspoken areas with new signs and meanings, filling the silence of the unconscious landscape with an unauthorised speech (gossip, jokes, laughter) and with speculation that exceeded the official discourses of forensic experts and the coroner's findings on Azaria's disappearance—an incontinent, excessive discourse that subverted the official attempts at closure. Similarly, the emptiness of the interior, hitherto only known to many from the discourses of tourism which emphasised lack of habitation (by whites), primalness and 'rugged beauty' (which Michael Chamberlain's camera relentlessly captured, in the fashion known to other Australian tourist shutter-bugs), became populated by *dramatis personae* with a range of speaking parts that were not merely those of the Chamberlains or the coroner, Denis Barritt.

DEATH AND SPECTACLE

'Serialised news' and Azaria Chamberlain were made for each other. From the opening of the inquiry into Azaria's death in October 1980 to the televised findings of the coroner's inquest on 21 February 1981, Eyewitness News on Channel 10, in Sydney, presented daily revelations alongside serialised snippets on how to make the home safe for children and how to control home finances. Against the dramatic unfolding of crisis within the Chamberlain family and the daily revelation of new evidence were set the minutiae of the perils of suburban living and the instability of family life, the threats being both *technical* and *social* (accident insurance problems or marital breakdown).

At the same time, we got the dramatic televisual revelation of the centre of the continent, its dangers, the dangers of tourism, the failure of conservation and the ungratefulness of the centre's trustee inhabitants (dingoes, Aborigines). As an unfolding TV spectacle, the Azaria case provided daily dramatisation and documentarisation of the Dead Centre. Only the conquest of another 'feminine' upside-down world—the moon landing of the late 1960s—had attracted as large an audience (two million) as watched Denis Barritt engaged in perhaps the most boring 45 minutes of anticlimax in Australian TV history. The closure of his discourse ('I am satisfied . . . I am satisfied . . . I am satisfied') seemed, however, to contain the 'sense of discovery' and the adventurousness of the TV audience only for a while: Barritt relied on the backdrop of the Rock and its remoteness, together with the picturesque cast of dingoes and Aborigines, to provide a decent acceptable narrative of the eyewitness sort, but perhaps these elements in combination had set in motion wider narratives—epic, mythical—so much the stock in trade of an emergent film industry, rather than the cosy soap opera in exotic surroundings (an outback *Holiday Island*) that showed up on TV.

On television in Australia, non-urban settings are sought in which to place anything from margarine ads to long-running serial dramas—and for a predominantly urban TV audience. Rolling highlands provided the backdrop for one of the most successful ads of the late 1970s, ad agency Mojo's Amoco ad, and 'pastoral' scenes continue to construct an ideology of mobility (for the young adult audience), and (for women buying food) family stability in the down-home mode,

with a healthy family fed (paradoxically) on fresh, unprocessed fodder. On the other hand, these displaced urban scenarios are also deathly and threatening—as, for instance in the 1981 Project Australia ads, in which a voice over aerial shots of endless arcadian beaches tells both of the beach as representative of Australian values such as egalitarianism, and as the place of threat in a country without land borders over which an enemy might invade. The outback itself is variously known. The Leyland Brothers go there as mates, conquering the land by turning it into TV; Bill Peach goes there, and, via TV, tells you how you can go there; Harry Butler, on the other hand, was there already and alternately horrifies you by rising above its violence and desolation, and engages your sympathies with his respect for the 'little fellas' he finds there.

Ayers Rock—'the Rock', as it is consistently known in the media coverage—is known not only through tourist advertising and travel docos, but also through arts. Its monumentality appears both as valuable sculpture (a good risk) and as something uplifted, altar-like, a navel that is all that remains after the umbilical cord with the rest of the world has been severed. (It appears with Phar Lap as the only non-human 'redhead' that appears on Australian Redhead brand match covers, along with other famous redheads like Elizabeth I, Churchill and Van Gogh). The fact of the Rock already having become aestheticised and symbolised in this way is certainly taken up in Barritt's findings where he exploits the Rock's existence as a 'found object', a principal 'subject' for amateur art/tourist photographers: 'Pastor Chamberlain, a keen photographer, photographed the effect of sunrise on Ayers Rock, took other photographs and returned at 8 a.m. Thereafter the family breakfasted and went sightseeing around the northern side of the Rock . . . they then went to Maggie Springs in that area, including the fertility caves, where *they* observed a dingo watching *them*'.[6] (My emphases: the camera angles, high up in the rocks in Peter Weir's *Picnic at Hanging Rock* also suggests that visitors to remote, picturesque spots not only see, but are seen, sometimes by malevolent eyes). Similarly, dingoes themselves are rendered painterly and photogenic in Lindy Chamberlain's account: 'I dropped the beans. I could see the dingo quite clearly. It was a beautiful gold colour with sharp pointed ears and it was having trouble getting through the gap because of a bundle in its teeth'.[7]

Ayers Rock in particular signifies the immemorial and also the immortal—the permanence and security that transcend the social and historical (as in the insurance ads). For instance, an article in the *National Times* (10 May 1981) notes: 'Tourism's blue rinse brigade makes way for adventure seekers . . . besides the lure of spaciousness, this country offers two other "s's"—safety and political stability'. A photo of Ayers Rock accompanies the article, which is captioned: 'They like Australia's safety and stability'. But further than this, the role of 'rock'—of 'the' Rock, here—is to signify immortality and permanence in distinctive opposition to other elements—as quite the opposite of what Azaria herself signifies (having the distinctive features of human, vulnerable, soft and small against the Rock's masculine, hard, impenetrable magnitudinousness). Plants, such as the ones that left traces of Azaria's clothing, also appear in this system of signs; in a treeless landscape, they, apart from the Aborigines and dingoes, are the only animate terms, but like both Aborigines and dingoes, they appear as witnesses, accomplices and perpetrators of the crime, mediating between the other two signs, and ultimately subject to scientific scrutiny, bound to forensic biological, botanical and anthropological discourses in a way that the Rock and Azaria are to aesthetic discourses (say, Barritt's contention on ABC TV, 20 February 1981, that 'whoever removed Azaria Chamberlain's body must have had some knowledge of botany, but again it is speculation', versus Lindy Chamberlain's 'Azaria was a beautiful dream', her reminiscence that Michael Chamberlain had been 'quite passionate about dingoes [on a former holiday to Cape York] and said what good-looking dogs they were',[8] or Michael's assertion after the inquest findings that, as God's creations, 'dingoes are beautiful creatures').

The Rock, then, although it is 'known' previously in other ways (its redness, its role as a symbol of Australian fortitude and strength in isolation), signifies somewhat differently as part of the triad Rock–plant–Azaria. For instance, Lévi-Strauss notes in *The Raw and the Cooked* that in myth sign systems, 'stone or rock appears, then, as the symmetrical opposite of human flesh'. Elsewhere, he elaborates: 'Myth enlists three calls to which the hero (TV viewer?) must reply or keep still . . . these are the calls of rock (immortality/human flesh), hard wood (animal flesh), and rotten wood (cultivated plants)'. Although it is not intended that this distinction be wholly carried through to the present discussion, Lévi-Strauss's conclusion is useful in providing evidence for an 'appeal' to a media audience based on a knowledge, or perceived knowledge, of the scenario the media-reading public might be able to decode. Each of the elements in the scenario issue, out of their muteness, a call which is both visual (scopic) and aural ('invocatory', in Lacan's term[9]), which asks the reading/viewing subject to recognise something, whether it is the 'self-evidence' of the family set-up and the role that a young baby plays in it, or the grandeur and permanence of the Rock. Yet, while the visual evidences are there, the voices (Azaria's cries, Lindy's shouts on the one hand, the voice of a confessor—dingoes are, after all, voiceless dogs—on the other) are absent. Lévi-Strauss has this to say about the arrangement of mythic elements in the myth he studies:

> These things that emit sounds (calls, silent appeals, here) . . . must be chosen in such a way that they also possess other sensory connotations. They are operators which make it possible to convey the isomorphic character of all binary systems of contrasts connected with the senses, and therefore to express as a totality, a set of equivalences connecting life and death . . . silence and noise.[10]

It was to these absent voices that viewers answered. Sometimes it was in the terms indicated by Lindy Chamberlain and Denis Barritt, filling in the absent voices with their own affirmations. More often, however, it was in a negative way, replacing the words in the cartoon bubbles with subversive calls and answers, challenging the closure of the Chamberlains' and Denis Barritt's narratives through jokes and gossip and conjecture, releasing the libido of media texts and official findings, and simultaneously recognising the repressed of these texts (infanticide, as well as otherwise unspeakable forms of family violence) and allowing an approach to the death drives to be made, in the direction of *jouissance*, but at the expense of a 'pleasurable' reading.[11] The myths of the *continent*, its stability, safety, but, paradoxically also, violence, had become rather *incontinent*, excessive (through jokes especially), and messy. Perhaps the 'overflow' that popular cultural forms such as jokes and rumour enact on the contained nature of the official narratives is summarised by a dingo joke of the time which goes: 'How do you bring up a baby?' 'You stick your finger down a dingo's throat'.

AZARIA AND THE AUSTRALIAN FILM INDUSTRY

Big media events like the Azaria Chamberlain affair set into operation reading and decoding practices that are both synchronic and diachronic. From a synchronic point of vantage, they are set alongside other media events which require the same type of reading practices, rhetorics and media literacies to understand them. They also require the recognition and operation of the same sorts of 'self-evidence', such as common mythology, common recognition of the necessity for a political status quo, the integralness of the family to social life and an appeal to the avoidance of violence (except one's own) at all costs. In its synchronous aspect, the Azaria Chamberlain inquest and its coverage occurred at the same time as the hunger strike in Northern Ireland by Bobby Sands, and his subsequent death. During this, the media turned their attention from highlighting the militancy of the IRA to Sands's non-violent, self-sacrificial act, whilst converting prevailing ideologies about self-sacrifice (good if it's within the guidelines of Project Australia) into negative images of aggression. At the same time, however, against Thatcher's intransigence, Sands's approach could be seen as adding to the possibility of British victory. And, into the bargain, the inherently violent nature of confrontation in Northern Ireland could be temporarily circumvented: news reports switched from reporting the day-to-day struggle to medical reports on the increasing deterioration of Sands's body. (At the same time, the arrest of the Yorkshire Ripper also focused attention on the how rather than the why of Sutcliffe's murders.) For one reader of the *Sydney Morning Herald* (Letters, 8 May 1981), 'when people, such as Sands, are willing to give their life in protest against what they regard as a serious social injustice *in place of* [my emphasis] violence against their enemies, they do something very profound for the whole of humanity. They show that even in the face of the most appalling injustices in the world, one does not have to do violence to others'. Only to oneself, then: violence is precluded by images of self-sacrifice, which is certainly as Project Australia would also have it.

It was perhaps in the context of this sort of hypocrisy (and also in the failure to recognise Sutcliffe's female victims also as, at some level, sacrifices to the preservation of heterosexual responses to monogamous marital self-sufficiency) that the media's representation of the Azaria affair fell short. It was not able to pull off, on home territory, a reportage of the Azaria affair that did not in some ways also include the possibility of a sacrifice. The idea that both sacrifice and self-sacrifice are appropriate concepts in the decoding repertoire has been built up in many forms in Australia in the last century or so, bridging the sacrifice made by soldiers in wartime, to the sacrifices made by women in all forms of work, to the sacrifices we all must make to keep the country from anarchy. Metaphorical sacrifice and self-sacrifice and actual sacrifice resulting in death become interchangeable. And this is especially so when a set of reading and decoding practices must be used on diverse material which should be given individual treatment: it all comes to look as if it's a multimedia event—different responses, but somehow all supposably attainable with everyone using the same tools for getting at it. (Lindy Chamberlain herself, in an interview for TV said to have been given five days after Azaria's disappearance, is reported [in the *Sunday Telegraph*, 7 February 1982] to have said: 'We have agreed to the media coverage because we felt that there was a reason for her death, and that somebody needed this to bring them back to God. But God must allow this to happen for people to realize that his way is the best way and that he has the last say'.)

The reading practices involved in understanding the Azaria affair in relation to other 'hot' news items involves the media in the business of crossing thematic elements and intertwining levels of discourse at some points, and keeping them separate at others (as it has in more recent times, keeping up its Australian union-bashing activities on the one hand, while pulling out the stops for Solidarity pluck). However, there is a diachronic dimension in which it is not so much immediately contemporaneous 'stories' that are relevant for understanding how things are read (or how further meanings, not necessarily legitimised, are made available), but rather texts/issues/events that have gone before that are important. For instance, in a paradigm of 'disappearance stories' in Australia, the Azaria affair takes its place alongside others (also involving females or juveniles or both) from 'the lady of the swamp', through the Beaumont children, to Juanita Nielson.

In some writings, this addition to the repertoire has been called 'intertextuality' and it roughly covers the instance of reading in which more than one text is actually being 'read' where only one appears to be on the screen or page that a person is actually looking at at a particular time.[12] Within the category of such 'intertexts' overlaid on the Azaria texts, and which at least partially determine the way in which the latter are read are some of the key Australian movies of the last decade. Some of these movies, for instance, use a similar backdrop of outback emptiness, filled with threatening quasi-animistic 'presences', as for instance in *Picnic at Hanging Rock*. Here a group of young women goes on an expedition in a remote colonial time to a rocky uplifted place, split with passes through which the visitors go. One of the party dies—but neither the death nor the body is seen. The responsibility for the murder/disappearance is on the one hand animist: causation for the death of the young woman is located outside of society, and outside history—in (super) natural forces or extra-human animacies. At the same time, a contradictory reading presents itself: throughout the movie, the camera has tracked the girls and put them under surveillance, looking down at them from particular watchful points of vantages in the rocks above, so that the intervention of a murderous human agency must also be read into the film's 'meaning'. The same sort of contradictory readings of the Azaria texts seem in part to result from an overlay with *Picnic at Hanging Rock*: for instance, while Barritt 'found' that a dingo has abducted Azaria, and that she had, by an appeal to the 'unknown life' of Aborigines, been disposed of by 'persons unknown' (read: Aborigines), contradictory readings were produced through the implication of white intervention at some level: 'On the probabilities, I find that at Ayers Rock a scissors would be a tool used by a white person rather than an Aborigine'.

Another intertext that overlays and intertwines with the Azaria text is another Peter Weir movie, *The Last Wave*. Here also, there are unidentified causations which propel and enigmatise the film's narrative, and here also these are aligned with Aborigines—driven underground and, apparently, living in the sewers of Sydney. The disasters in the film involve catastrophes to skyscrapers and rains of mud. The elaboration of the myth of Aborigines as the possessors of the power both to up-end white social life and at the same time to 'preserve' and resymbolise it in the form of white capitalist society is at much at work here as it is in the text of Barritt's findings that imply that Aborigines may fit the bill for the 'person or persons unknown' who disposed of Azaria's body (*Daily Telegraph* 23 February 1981).

Ideologies of how city folk are alienated socially have often been constructed in Australian films in terms of a displacement to non-urban spaces—an inversion of ideologies of colonial isolation, where instead of a new innocent speech there comes the recognition of solidarity that follows on the confession of a crime (whether as convicts, women or Aborigines). In the bush, the alienation of/from urban white, male society takes its voice from, and in, a discourse of confession, and following on that, the declaration of war fought for (two common) goals. This goes as much for films such as *Eliza Frazer* and *Journey Among Women* as for *Mad Max* (1 and 2). The possibility of the bush or the outback as a setting for voicing the alienation of city life was fully realised in both the official discourses on Azaria's disappearance and the excessive gossip/rumour/joke discourses that 'exceeded' the former. But here the alienation that might have resulted in confession and declaration were precluded by another discourse—equally one of alienation and exclusion—namely, that of tourism.

SYMPATHY FOR THE DINGO

Tourism in Australia constitutes a range of practices, not least of which are reading and viewing practices. The TV ads mentioned above that use rural and outback settings to sell goods, as well as the 'nationalist' army and Project Australia ads, all depend on the assumption that Australians are as much tourists in their own country as are overseas visitors and are equally attuned to 'stability' and to the potential aggressors who/which might threaten this. In identifying a dingo as the culprit in the Azaria affair, Denis Barritt was as much identifying a tourist hazard (and a barrier to the continuing 'innocence' of nature and the land) as a potential killer. But further, this identification itself functioned as a displacement of *threat* inasmuch as the placing of the

Chamberlain affair functioned as a displacement of urban family stability and its problems into the outback.

Animals as threatening of the social fabric have long been imaged as both individual in their cunning and collective in their overwhelming, plague-like force. To take only two examples, from the 1920s: a rat scare in 1920 had occasioned an item in the *Sydney Morning Herald* that read:

> ... (if the Minister of Health and Motherhood) wishes to find an all-pervading evil waiting to be eradicated, let him tackle the rats which have grown in numbers to a most alarming extent of late. Perhaps the overcrowding of houses by human residents is pushing out the rats which cannot now find house-room in their former haunts, or perhaps a strike is on amongst the rodents, who have stopped work, and can find time to stroll about the city streets.[13]

The rat scare provided DH Lawrence with a resolution for the discussion between Calcott and Somers on the threats to Australian 'integrity':

> It was a period when Sydney was again suffering from a bubonic plague scare: a very mild scare ... But the town was placarded with notices 'Keep your town clean', and there was a stall in Martin Place where you could write your name down and become a member of the cleanliness league, or something to that effect ... The battle was against rats and fleas, and dirt. The plague affects rats first, said the notices, then fleas, and then man. All citizens were urged to wage war with the vermin mentioned.[14]

Between this and Denis Barritt's findings on dingoes have come the rabbit menace and fruit-fly campaigns of the early 1950s (all couched in Movietone newsreels in similar vein) and the mid-1970s-rats-eating-Australia campaigns that characterised the Packer-inspired anti-inflation campaigns. Barritt's findings in the Azaria case take these displacements a stage further, but in the same direction. Here the enemy is the dingo, and those—such as conservationists—who would protect it:

> In a territory whose economy is based, in part, on tourism, it is strange that [there are not representations from] the body that is responsible, if not liable, for the overall conservation policy of the Uluru National Park. In an area where advanced planning is in hand to meet the accommodation requirements of upwards of 6000 people a night, a policy of conservation seems to have been activated that has as its primary aim the intermingling of tourists with an ever-increasing number of dingoes, desert death adders, desert brown and king brown snakes. The dingo is dangerous and known to be dangerous. Prior to 17 August, 1980 the conservation authorities had received several instances of dingoes attacking children. The significance of the dingoes' range and territory was known to rangers ... and known to be an area where children might be exploring in the many areas of interest around the Rock. The conduct of dingoes around the campsites together with their propensity to enter tents was known, or ought to have been known. The propensity of a dingo, reared by *homo sapiens*, and treated

in a domestic environment to violently attack children was known, yet in the face of this knowledge dingoes have been retained and allowed virtually to infest the area as a tourist attraction. I would hope that the moral responsibility to protect children visiting the National Park appears to have been avoided in the past, [and that] the legal consequences of any such action in the future should lead to *the elimination of any species dangerous to man* from such parks, or at least any such areas frequented by tourists. Every person in our community is under an obligation to conserve human life, and those charged with the added task of conserving life in the National Parks ought to remember and apply the *primary tenet of our land*. If those charged with the protection of wild life in the National Parks would rely on laws forbidding the destruction of such creatures, then they ought to be made to publicize the dangers that exist and are permitted to exist within such parks . . . Such publicity should be included in any tourist promotion to fulfil the requirements of fair advertising. The case clearly shows that *a choice has to be made between dingoes and deadly snakes on the one hand, and tourism on the other*. The two should not be allowed to co-exist, *providing traps for decent people where formerly our forebears set traps for deadly creatures.*

Dingoes are not and never have been an endangered species; despite efforts by man they have retained their position as the most dangerous carnivore of the canine species on this continent. Tourists in National Parks should be allowed to examine fauna in its natural state, *but, I maintain, only at a safe distance . . . All animals dangerous to man [should be] safely enclosed or eliminated.*

(All emphases are my own; this portion of the text of Denis Barritt's findings were excluded from the most comprehensive transcript, *SMH*, 21 February 1981, but can be found in TV recordings of the inquest findings.)

To offset the popular notion that Azaria was somehow herself a sacrifice (acknowledged by Barritt himself in his assertion that 'the name Azaria does not mean, and has never meant "sacrifice in the wilderness" '), a scapegoat, a more visual sacrifice, was enacted. Twenty-seven dingoes died in an act of scientific self-appeasement. Azaria's death was a 'mystery' and could not be *seen*, but the death of the dingoes could; so could the sacrificed goat in the Adelaide Zoo experiment. This televisual sacrifice in the name of forensic science seems, at first sight, to be an externalisation of the sacrifice that is made by scapegoats in general, but also perhaps of the sacrifice that oneself is supposed to be making—in other words, the visual realisation of sacrifice and self-sacrifice promoted by such outfits as Project Australia.

George Bataille has interesting comments to make about the relationship between sacrifice and spectacle of sacrifice that may illuminate the huge public support for the underdog (the dingo) that was perhaps the real focus of discourses on sacrifice in the period leading up to the handing down of Barritt's findings. Of sacrifice in general, he notes that:

For people to be finally revealed to themselves, they would have to die, but they would have to do so while living—while watching themselves cease to be.

This however is impossible—the sacrifice of self is unimaginable because the act itself cannot be made visual. So, argues Bataille, the sacrifice or scapegoating of an animal arises as a solution, even though sympathy with (through identification with) the animal will also be a strong dynamic of this sacrifice:

> In principle, death reveals to people their own natural, animal being, but the revelation never takes place. For once the animal being that has supported them has ceased to exist . . . In sacrifice the sacrificer identifies with the animal struck by death.

A circle is in motion: on the one hand, the human sacrifice is an unspeakable proposition, a narrative that turns back on, and destroys itself, identifying with Lindy Chamberlain's assertion (*Woman's Day*, 1 October 1981) that:

> They're making up all sorts of dreadful stories because of Michael's religious connection. That Azaria was a sacrifice. That her name meant Bearer of Sin. That we dressed her in black. Can you imagine that? Always dressed her in black?

However, the identification with the other sacrifice, the animal one, is also untenable in that the 'identification with the animal struck by death' is also precluded on the grounds that this is not just any animal, but the dingo, represented on no coat of arms, and with strong ties with other underdogs in popular mythology.

Like the coyote of California, the dingo stands in a mediating category, between the wild and domestic. In a taxonomy of Australian animals, dingoes occupy the same space as, say, the fox in English folk narratives or the coyote in North American tales. Dingoes, foxes and coyotes in these stories have in common that they try on big things, hatch big plans, but always muck them up. They get the blame, but it is for a crime that they themselves never actually benefit from, despite the devastating punishments they incur in the process. All of them perhaps occupy the 'neighbour' category prescribed for 'fox' in Edmund Leach's structural analysis of animals in English folktales:[15] trustworthy up to a point, but forgivable in breach of that trust. Furthermore, as the rats in the foregoing quotes may have acted as metaphor for 'reds' in the red scares of the early 1920s, so also the dingo stands as a metaphor for thieves, criminals and the poor in Australia, as metaphor for aggressors against property, in fact, rather than as murderer.

Hence, the widespread 'sympathy for the dingo' movement is as much a refusal to accept the scapegoat as it is a protest against injustice. Even in Lindy Chamberlain's words, 'the dingo has *taken* my baby', the dingo is a thief rather than a murderer, and its representation as murderer is itself contradicted by such popular definitions as that of 'a dingo's breakfast'—'a drink of water and a good look around', as cited in the *National Times*, March 1981—a situation that applies to an increasing number of Australians living below the poverty line.

Inasmuch as the dingo maps in with images of other folklore characters such as the coyote (or Roadrunner, or Tom of *Tom and Jerry*), there is also a lot of sympathy for the dingo. In Roadrunner cartoons, for instance, the coyote's fate is usually to be torn to pieces, but then to turn up in one piece again. If indeed the dingo is a displacement for the unspeakable, but nevertheless much spoken of, rumoured sacrificial fate of Azaria, then the dingo's own fate (confirmed by the Adelaide Zoo experiments in the eyes of the TV audience) mirrors that of Azaria as narrated by her mother:

> I wanted someday to find a shred of her clothing to know what happened so the world would know . . . but not my beautiful Azaria torn to shreds by dingoes.

Or later:

> At that stage, Michael was full of hate for all dogs, especially dingoes and, minister of religion though he is, he could have torn them limb from limb. (*Woman's Day*, 1 October 1981)

In part also, the sacrificial displacement of baby into dingo was produced by the 'appearance' of Azaria as in fact whole and well in the large photograph of the child held up by both the Chamberlains at the end of the Barritt inquest 'to show what a beautiful baby she was' (*Daily Mirror*, 23 February 1981). The photo, perhaps a metre across, was certainly big enough for the TV cameras present, and presented, or rather re-presented, Azaria as 'a beautiful dream', the 'princess', 'such a little lady', or 'quite the most beautiful baby I have ever seen' that Lindy Chamberlain spoke of in her *Woman's Day* interview. The appearance of a 'whole' Azaria via this image and its visibility to the cameras might also have given impetus to rumours that another being, the dingo, was the dead underdog.

POPULAR CULTURE: A LAUGH AT LIFE

> The most bourgeois of all phenomena, gossip, comes only because people do not want to be misunderstood. The destructive character tolerates misunderstanding, but not gossip . . . The destructive character obliterates even the traces of destruction.
>
> Walter Benjamin, *The Destructive Character*[16]

> Ayers Rock and the Olgas comprise the visible ends of a huge sedimentary conglomerate of great geological and scenic importance.
>
> Denis Barritt, ABC TV 20 February 1981

In drawing attention to the function of gossip, jokes and speculation as an extension and partial subversion of dominant/dominating decoding practices in reading and viewing, and then discussing these in terms of something called 'popular culture', I have perhaps been perpetuating a notion of 'popular culture' that has recently come under scrutiny and criticism[17] (for instance, by Tony Bennett in his 'Popular Culture: A Teaching Object', *Screen Education* No 34, 1980). Specifically, one of the points taken up in such recent discussion concerns the dangers in taking up the idea of 'popular culture' only as an oppositional category—the study, say, of working people's or unemployed people's culture defined in terms of what it is set against (elite culture, hegemonic bourgeois culture). And in Australia, the idea of a confrontation between, as Bennett puts it, 'forms that are opposed from "above" and those that emerge from "below"' certainly co-incides with the Australian soft spot for the 'ocker knocker' as the local form of apolitical anti-authoritarianism. Gossip, rumour and jibes certainly may have been bourgeois forms in the world that Benjamin knew (see first quote above), but in Australia, they constitute the productive remains of working class oral virtuosities that have been increasingly converted to literate ones by schooling and the media. Denis Barritt's comments (second quote above) might almost be a metaphor for the relation between rich hegemonic signifiers such as Ayers Rock and the 'invisible' but still active 'conglomerate' from which it obtrudes.

However, an important aspect which a discussion of 'popular culture' in Australia might start with is this: the way in which oral practices such as joke and rumour articulate silences in 'official' discourses, such as those of the media, in such a way as to destroy their legit-imacy and the 'self-evidential'[18] regimes of sense that they perpetuate. In the dingo-baby jokes that proliferated in early 1981, the function of the rumoured sacrifice is taken over by the dumb animal (dingo), the silent continent, the silent race[19] (women, Aborigines), socially and sexually persecuted minorities, voicing the subject who is 'subjected', but not yet subjectified, socialised or sexualised. For example:

What did one dingo say to another outside the maternity hospital?
Shall we eat here or take away?

What could have changed the course of history?
A dingo at Bethlehem.

Baby jokes, and dingo–baby jokes, traverse the space of socially constructible meaning, articulating what has been evacuated from 'official' language and laughing at the vulnerability of that language. As popular culture, baby jokes in general deal usually with the torture, mutilation and death of humans before they have themselves become capable of language, when, as babies, they have yet to enter the Sym-bolic of language, when they are still 'speechless'. In this sense, baby jokes are not about babies so much as about being the oppressed of a situation in which one likewise 'has no voice'—eg, being poor. Baby jokes 'make sense' by laughing at 'made' sense.

In the gossip and speculation that surrounded the reportage of the Azaria case, then, media and magisterial discourses were elaborated and made to exceed themselves, making a non-sense of officially articulated closures of sense (the *Daily Mirror* headline 'Dingo did it' [20 February 1981], for example). The recent discussions on 'popular culture' that appeared in *Screen Education* have tended to reduce the anti-authoritarian and anti-hegemonic force of popular cultural practices by reducing a theory of resistant cultural forms to an algebra with dominant discourses and practices on one side of the equation and subdominant discourses and practices on the other. Rather than reducing the force of popular cultural practices in this way, in order to produce an account of how hegemony is attained and maintained (which is also necessary, but perhaps not at the expense of a 'popular' notion of 'popular culture') and to produce a reasonable 'teaching object' out of what is, after all, not only a set of cultural practices, but also the subject of a range of discourses on those practices by the people who engage in them, perhaps an 'engaged' study of popular cultural practices in Australia might consist in identifying, elaborating and perpetuating ruptures that dominant discourses and practices either exclude or incorporate or re-interpret or re-analyse or re-symbolise.

Gossip, rumour and joking are subdominant forms in which the 'play' of meaning is, anyway, produced, is acknowledged and exceeded. 'Making sense' of the various practices that constitute 'the social whole', as Francis Mulhern[20] has proposed for a study of culture ('the unity of those practices that produce sense'), may be only one part of such a study. But equally, 'making sense' also means doing so *at the expense of sense*, by indicating its limits, and in the 'making' of this 'sense', identifying whose 'sense' it is and how it has been constructed; and also, by carrying it to an extreme, showing how tenuous is its legitimacy and capacity to enact and perpetuate hegemony. The algebra of an 'above' and a 'below' must perhaps still be taken into an account, for it is not only an algebra with 'a' and 'b' terms, but also excess and whys.

April 1982

NOTES

1 EH Gombrich, *The Story of Art* (13th edition), London, 1977; M Foucault, *Madness and Civilization*, New York, 1973.
2 EH Gombrich, op. cit., p. 385.
3 M Foucault, op. cit., p. 280.
4 Ibid.
5 Ibid.
6 *Sydney Morning Herald*, 21 February 1981.

7   *Woman's Day*, 1 October 1980.
8   Ibid.
9   Cf J Lacan, *The Four Fundamental Concepts of Psychoanalysis*, passim, Penguin, Harmondsworth, 1977.
10 C Lévi-Strauss, *The Raw and the Cooked*, New York, 1970, pp. 153–4.
11 This distinction is a reference to one made by R Barthes (eg in *The Pleasure of the Text*, Jonathan Cape, New York, 1976) between a text, such as the realist novel, which produces in the reader a sense of pleasure and the fulfilment that comes with consumption, as against the text of 'jouissance'—bliss, orgasm, rupture, loss, unrest. This latter category is supposed to describe the effects of reading, say, avant-garde novels or seeing avant-garde films.
12 'Intertextuality' seems like a very useful term for indicating the way in which the way one reads a sign in one text is also supported by the way one has read the same sign (eg 'dingo' or 'Ayers Rock') in another text. The introduction by Leon S Roudiez to J Kristeva's *Desire in Language*, Blackwell, Oxford, 1980, p. 17, warns, however, that 'the term has . . . been much used and abused on both sides of the Atlantic'. So here's one for Australia.
13 *Sydney Morning Herald*, 10 May 1920, and quoted by H McQueen in his *Social Sketches of Australia*, Penguin, Harmondsworth, 1978.
14 DH Lawrence, *Kangaroo*, Penguin, Harmondsworth, 1978, p. 56.
15 E Leach, *Lévi-Strauss*, London, Fontana, 1974, p. 56.
16 W Benjamin, *One Way Street*, London, Verso, 1979.
17 See, for instance, Tony Bennett, 'Popular Culture: A Teaching Object', *Screen Education* 34, 1980.
18 Cf an interview with M Foucault, 'Questions of Method', *Ideology and Consciousness* No 8, Spring 1981, p. 6.
19 Cf J Kristeva, 'Signifying Practice and Mode of Production', *Edinburgh Magazine '76* No 1, p. 65 on women as 'the silent race, silent support of the symbolic function, permanent appeal to a forbidden incest, object of anguished male identification'.
20 F Mulhern 'Notes on Culture and Cultural Struggle', *Screen Education* 34, Spring 1980, p. 32.

PART III
The uses of popular culture

7

Homage to Catatonia: Culture, politics and Midnight Oil

McKENZIE WARK

Cultures are not manufactured, they grow of their own accord.

George Orwell, *1948*

I DON'T WANT TO BE THE ONE

It all began with a slight but suggestive sartorial detail. A little thing easy to miss amid the wash of bogus Australian Bicentennial pseudo-events and bogus Australian champagne. It was at the press conference to launch the first advisory report of the Constitutional Commission where to my eyes one little thing stood out from the usual run-of-the-mill meet-the-press bunfight. There, wedged in between the bespectacled, grey-suited dignitaries, with their tastefully conservative ties perched like floppy kippers between neatly pressed lapels, there sat Mr Peter Garrett in a faded black denim jacket and an open-necked shirt. As the report being launched tells us, Garrett is 'Lead singer for Midnight Oil; lawyer'.[1] Evidently he was dressed in the style of the former of these two capacities.

It seems to me that the 'lawyer' appellation was less important under these circumstances than the 'Lead singer'. This is what is most curious about the whole show. How is it that 'Lead singer for Midnight Oil' has become the sort of qualification one lists at the front of advisory committee reports? How is that the most striking thing about Mr Garrett's curriculum vitae is the discreet non-mention of his most remarkable achievement: the fact that this lead lawyer-singer came within a hair's breadth of winning a seat in national parliament?

---

* This essay originally appeared in *Meanjin* 47/2 (1988), pp. 298–309, as 'Homage to Catatonia: The Rise and Rise of Peter Garrett'.

Midnight Oil are a rock'n'roll band after all. A popular act, admittedly. Yet if that were the main criterion, why not Michael Hutchence of INXS, Jimmy Barnes or Neil Finn of Crowded House? Or even Australian of the Year, Mr John Farnham himself—surely still a household name in this land. After all, these are the entertainers which the industry itself considers its 'favourite sons' [sic].

Clearly, something else is going on here. The perennial presence of Peter Garrett in the public eye seems to me symptomatic of a whole range of things that can be pinpointed in the relationships between our popular culture, political culture and the 'culture industries' as they stand at the moment. This essay seeks in part to use Garrett as the thread for a rumination (summary as it is) on how these relationships might work.

The critic has to be careful in territory such as this. Take the opening trope of this essay. The critic as the one who has an eye for the telling detail. The suspicious mind which seizes on the metonymic part that will explain the whole business. But by what right? While the primary interest of what follows is in the 'micropolitics' of certain pop music, it is important also to lend an ear to the politics of the critic's relation to all that. A straightforward critical detachment may turn out to be not quite so straight after all—particularly if the critics have detached themselves too well. 'Critical distance', if you can bear the pun, can be taken too far. Hence this essay runs back and forth between the business of music and the business of criticism.

OILS AIN'T OILS

There is a marked lack of solid, critical writing about popular music in Australia. Perhaps this is partly due to the fact that there is a marked lack of popular music. A preliminary distinction may help explain this state of affairs.

On the one hand we have the music industry; on the other, popular music. I define *popular music* for present purposes as being that which enjoys the devoted, sincere, dedicated and even fanatical support and affection of a distinct and distinctive section of the general public. Which is to say, these people are prepared to buy this music off their own bat without being told to do so. In popular music, some relationship, some necessity, links the audience to the music. Demand precedes supply, but those supplying the music, the musicians, have to work damned hard to prove to their audience that they are indeed the genuine article, faithful and true, a suitor who will love, honour and obey.

Once they become firmly wedded to popular music, its audience is usually tenaciously faithful to it—often for decades. This courtship occurs through the dense network of channels and capillaries which forms the media landscape of our time: clubs, pubs, parties, jukeboxes, record stores, fanzines. Like any other small business, a rock'n'roll band starts small, investing a little capital, doing solid business, generating goodwill, word of mouth interest, building up a working stock of material, improving the product. Sooner or later, it will reach the stage where it needs a major injection of liquidity, capital or access to a big distribution network. Particularly if the band wants to break out of a small domestic market and get into big, international ones.[2] This is when the band, as it were, 'sells out'.

If it is lucky, the band will succeed in negotiating a deal with the big firms in the business which doesn't damage the goodwill the band has with its small family of loyal clients. In other words, a band will use the credibility it has garnered as purveyors of popular music as a bargaining chip to play against the majors in the business, so it can turn credibility into a base for financial success and exposure, and get a reasonable piece of the action as well.

Such is the story of Midnight Oil. The legion of Midnight Oil fans, from teenage tearaways and surfologists to middle-aged suburban public servants, are just such a loyal audience, and Midnight Oil have tried to keep the faith and keep their independence even though they now have a distribution deal with CBS, the most major of the major corporations in the music industry. 'The Oils', as they are affectionately known, have worked long and hard over the last ten years to achieve this.[3]

This is something of a contrast to how things work right at the heart of the music industry. The music industry is that branch of the 'culture industry' responsible for pumping out *prepackaged music*—be it popular in origin or not. Most prepackaged music fails in the marketplace. Some prepackaged music sells by the tonne, though not without the assistance of those branches of the industry whose job it is to promote the product, comb through it for the most bankable 'unit shifter', give it the stamp of approval of the leading style authorities—and flog it for all it's worth. Here the major company has to invest heavily in packaging, promotion and so on, and the band itself will be obliged to *sit still* for this, to allow itself to be marketed, to be cling-wrapped in cellophane, fondled and pawed by magazine and TV people. Particularly if the act is lacking in *credibility*. That is to say, hasn't spent years scraping and saving and gigging and accumulating capital, goodwill and so on out there in the capillaries or tendrils of the information landscape. If it lacks this kind of base, then the act has little bargaining power with the major recording and publishing companies, and will more or less have to do as it's told, more like hired hands than a subcontractor.

Prepackaged music may indeed sell, but without for all that becoming popular music. The distinction lies in the fact that the impulse to buy the package comes from above—from the marketeers and style leaders of the 'culture industries'. Supply precedes demand. The aim is to seduce the buyer into picking up what's on offer, giving it a fling or a spin. For the band, everything hinges on getting it right on the first date—it's all or nothing. Obviously the major and the band want the public to flirt with it on a regular basis, but for the major this is merely desirable, not essential. The majors know—as the public knows—there is always another act to be had down at the singles bar.

I don't want to give the impression that I'm making a value judgment about the 'lifestyles' of popular music as opposed to prepackaged music. One can't exist without its complement; the monopoly sector of industry can't exist without the competitive sector; monogamy and promiscuity mutually define each other; one meets demands the other can't. The central point, in terms of Midnight Oil and Peter Garrett's style of agit-pop politics, is that the impetus in prepackaged music comes from above, and in popular music it comes from below.

What I am trying to suggest is a model of 'culture industries' in Australia which does not reduce the circuit between music and audience to a crude theory of *manipulation* or *simulation*.[4] Neither could account for the tension and complementarity between popular music and the music industry. These two phenomena coexist in a dialectical relationship of adjustment, absorption and indifference—and daylight robbery. On the one hand, the slick music coming out of the industry may or may not enjoy success but can never accrue credibility without a spectacular, tragic and premature death. On the other hand, there is popular music, the music coming in out of the blue, supported by popular taste or burning conviction. Popular music can build up a steady stock of capital, but will rarely make 'the big time' without striking some kind of bargain with the monopoly sector of the business—Faustian or otherwise.

After money, credibility is the most precious commodity in circulation. As far as the majors are concerned, once you buy that the rest is easy. This is why the majors are prepared to deal with acts like Midnight Oil and cede a certain amount of business and artistic autonomy to them. Unlike money, credibility can only be earned the hard way. Credibility is inseparably wedded to the mythology of 'paying yer dues' and is also a system of peer assessment, competition and support. Midnight Oil (touted in their early days as the hardest-working band in the country) have earned it—and enjoyed not a little commercial success along the way. Oils ain't oils; there is a complicated politics of credibility and success which traverses the whole of the 'culture industry' and blurs its boundaries.

THE POWER AND THE PASSION

Within this framework, we can understand the double success of Midnight Oil and Peter Garrett. Midnight Oil are as well if not better known for their extra-musical activities as for their art. This is in no small measure due to the activities of Garrett, who is 'frontman' in more ways than one. He achieved national media exposure as the Nuclear Disarmament Party candidate in the 1984 election. Since then, his distinctive high-domed pate and bush hat have become familiar icons on television and in the press. The Garrett presence has mounted the soapbox for everything from the Uluru/Ayers Rock handover ceremonies, through the anti-ID card campaign and 'Surfers Against Nuclear Destruction' (SAND), to a symbolic visit to the US base at Pine Gap, loudhailer in hand. Not to mention being hypothesised about on the TV discussion program *Hypotheticals*. For an act which consistently refused to appear on ABC TV's pop music show *Countdown* both Garrett and the Oils have achieved remarkably wide media exposure.[5] One is almost tempted to suggest that Garrett's baldness has resulted from wearing too many hats.

Garrett has succeeded as a populist and progressive figure in the public domain precisely because Garrett and Midnight Oil have achieved credible success in producing popular music, supported from below, rather than turning out prepackaged music, promoted from above. Its authenticity is not really an issue. The Oils convey the *sign* of authenticity according to the conventions of their fans, and that's what counts. There is an organic link between the Oils and their patrons which precedes the machinations of the powers that be in the industry. Precisely for this reason, Garrett is able to appear in public, wear many hats, give voice to populist causes, vent his spleen in op-eds for the tabloids,[6] stand for office, sit on subcommittees, all without appearing ridiculous to the fans of Oils music. This is the precious stuff of credibility: the magic elixir of rock'n'roll power and passion— and politics.

As such Midnight Oil are a *practical* critique of a lot of what passes for critical practice. A critique from 'within' the so-called culture industries which is consequently far more credible than critiques which claim the alibi of coming from without. Let's face it, criticism itself is as much inside the beast as music, and the rules of the game, the network economy it is enmeshed in, are not so very different. The education industry is just as much a part of the 'culture industry' as the music industry. Yet by failing to include such obvious observations within their criticism, critics of the music business continue to misinterpret what they hear. Here are a few examples of criticism which consistently call the wrong tune.

Cochrane and Plews complain that there is a 'great need for radical cultural workers inside the machine'[7] but make no proper effort to analyse, let alone support, so central and obvious an example of what *can* and *can't* be done inside the machine as the Oils. One suspects they are happier prescribing what *should* and *shouldn't* be done. Since their prescriptions are aimed at rock musicians with acute cases of industrial deafness, they cannot be heard—and the critics remain pessimistic about the beast of pop culture which has stuffed all and sundry down its ravenous maw.

The more knowledgeable pessimism of Marcus Breen has it that regardless of how 'sound' the songs may be, when they 'suffer a transformation and become an extension of the marketing nexus of the dominant cultural and social values, their meaning is changed'.[8] Or, no matter how pure your intentions, 'they' will turn it into something evil. Criticism in the paranoid mode, in which ordinary people are assumed simply to consume meaning, rather than participate in its production. A difficult position to sustain without slipping into a patronising 'holier than thou' tone in order to explain exactly how the critic remains immune to 'dominant cultural and social values' which somehow get injected into the mainline consciousness of everyone else.

Michael Birch quite rightly stresses the 'ongoing relationship between the nature of cultural products and the technology of production and distribution'.[9] He also gives an account of the influence of the 'Birmingham school' on the study of popular culture, and the way that they look at it as 'a field of struggle, a battleground of ideology, a field in which dominated groups win space for themselves'. So far so good. He also ticks off 'scholarly work' which has 'taken a phenomenon through which millions have found expression, and has spilled quantities of academic ink to find a definition of popular culture'. Which is even better (though one wonders why it's in the past tense). Birch is admitting to the futility of attempting to define pop culture other than *nominally* and *relatively*.

Just when things are going so well, Birch succumbs to the most tedious error of all: *nostalgia*. He can't resist an invocation of 'the real sixties', as he experienced it, and expresses a desire to rescue the critic's own times from younger critics who evidently don't understand them at all.[10] This application of selective memory culminates in dark mutterings to the effect that 'the "political role" of popular music seems to have disappeared' and that for Australians 'the implications of recent developments are even worse'. Sadly, this is a position which could only be sustained by keeping one's ears as firmly closed as one's mind.

The bottom line with all of these critical approaches is pessimism about culture industries other than education and about cultural practices other than criticism. They all seem to derive from an excess of exceedingly general arguments of the sort where you take away the number you first thought of and the answer always adds up to an admission of hopelessness.

For example, Birch argues that successive cultural technologies tend to be more and more alienating, and estrange the performer more and more from her or his own work. The example given is video: 'the innocent days when a live band were just filmed making their music are gone forever'. Innocent days? This is really nothing more than the commonsense supposition that 'they don't make hotdogs like they used to'. Notice that the alienating technology of today is compared with . . . the day before. As if the culture technologies of the 1970s were not alienating to those who first experienced them, relative to what went before. Let's not forget that the Frankfurt school fell out over such 'alienating' technologies as photography, cinema and jazz music. There is nothing historical or dialectical about Birch's view of alienation here. No sense of the capacity of commodity production and the division of labour both to enslave and enliven; liberate and estrange.

Too often in Frankfurt-influenced culture studies alienation becomes the original sin which irrevocably adulterates every morsel of (non-academic) cultural sustenance. It becomes the intellectual's alibi for an orientation to a theological beyond—nostalgic past or utopian future.

Returning to Birch, on the subject of Garrett and the Oils we get this:

> The effect of a 'political' band like U2 on Irish politics will always be negligible. The example of Peter Garrett's failure to enter the senate, despite an enormous vote, is a perfect example of the treatment of performers in the world of popular music once they attempt to step outside it. Right wing bad actors can do it, but not people with bald heads. The business is now not just commercialized but industrialized.

Firstly, politics is collapsed into culture. U2's white flag raised against hundreds of years of bloody history, Garrett putting the wind up the Sussex St Labor hacks and debating Bill Hayden live on national TV are not considered for what they are—symbolic action, ethical parables—but lamented for what they are not: instrumental political acts. The second and third sentences are the pessimism of insatiable criticism: hard to please, never satisfied. It would be just as easy to be overjoyed at how rattled the ALP were by Garrett's showing. The last sentence takes off on a new tack, and sees the root of the problem in the evil *industrial structure*. Yet if we take this metaphor seriously, would we not have to argue that teachers and metal workers and soapie actors are all equally in hopeless political situations because they work in 'industries'? Perhaps that's why, like musicians, teachers and metal workers and actors sometimes form and join unions. The network economy of power, information and money is still there for all and sundry to struggle in, be they in 'industries' or not. Only when we measure such efforts by some imaginary, utopian standard do they pale, which is a good reason not to conduct criticism on such a basis lest we all get miserable and depressed. What politics is, criticism should be—the art of the *possible*.

Truly there is no shortage of pessimism when it comes to pop culture. 'The Frankfurt school is alive and well and living in Australia' indeed![11] Ironically enough, while these critics are busy 'pitting themselves against the working class' (as John Docker puts it), Garrett is busy trying to do the opposite. Whether he passes some critics' ideological soundness inquisitions on all counts is not really the issue. The point is that Garrett's is a practical critique of critical practice as practised in the academy. Perhaps the soapbox orator has a better understanding of the armchair critic than the armchair critic has of soap on the box.

BEST OF BOTH WORLDS

To return to the main point: I'm arguing that credibility sets popular music apart from prepackaged music, and that the Oils and Garrett are fine exponents of the former. This suggests two things. Firstly, that popular music of this sort is the heir to the tradition of folk music. Perhaps we could say that popular music is the folk music of monopoly capital. Any politics, any culture which is not merely utopian dreaming must take place within the social formation which prevails, and that is no cause for grief.

Secondly, within the particular beast that is our own social formation, the organic links between the Oils and their audience have been the springboard for Garrett to establish quite another kind of organic social relation and credential. To my mind, Garrett represents the figure of the organic intellectual in our time. Not quite the organic intellectual Gramsci spoke of: this is not quite the same conjuncture as fascist Italy in the 1920s. The traditional intellectuals, to whom Gramsci contrasted the organic intellectuals, are certainly no longer principally the clergy, although the structure of their moral beliefs today may be rather similar.[12]

Still, I think the analogy holds. Garrett uses his position in a particular set of social relations which are to do with the business of manufacturing music in order to give voice to his *constituency*. Garrett sees the constituency with whom and for whom he speaks as being more or less the same as the audience for whom he makes music as part of the collective entity that is Midnight Oil. While Garrett takes care to distinguish these roles in public life, the credibility of both is founded upon the same sort of rapport. It is a simple thing so hard to achieve. There is nothing formal or institutional about this relationship, but from this double position Garrett acts as a mouthpiece for certain conflicts and negotiations—which is the very stuff of our hegemonic culture.

David Rowe puts the up side of this very nicely:

> Rock and overt politics collide only intermittently, at particular moments when broad social movements meet performers with Brechtian aspirations. Garrett hopes to use his over-18 fans as a block vote and to link them to the heterogeneous clutch of organizations which is anti-nuclear. At the same time, he is playing Pied Piper to the nation's current and emergent youthful constituency. Garrett is . . . a spectral repudiation of Hawke's consensus, a metonym for the excluded and the dissident. It is encouraging to feel that . . . rock can still provoke dreams of a new synthesis in the slumber of fiscal austerity.[13]

As independent outsiders with their own base of support, both Garrett and the Oils can 'deal' with the business end and the press without being captive or captivated by either. This 'relative autonomy', besides bestowing an aura of credibility, has certain other advantages. It helps give Garrett access to the press and makes him a relatively recognisable 'talking head'. The Oils spent some ten years building up a name and a reputation, so they don't totally need either CBS or the media to put them into circulation. Garrett is quite well known without all that, which not only gives him some leverage *vis à vis* the publicity machinery of the music business, it also gives him a tiny, tiny bit of leverage with the non-music media. Editors want Garrett because he is already known and hence good copy.

Midnight Oil and their management try to use this to extract some degree of *control* over their image and message. Interviews are granted selectively, and they may retain the power of veto over a photo session. Needless to say there is very little room to manoeuvre when it comes to dealing with the mainline press, but 'The Office' which runs Midnight Oil's affairs have applied the lessons learned in the music media to the media in general. There is certainly a lot to be learned from their example about messages that 'suffer a transformation' (as Breen puts it) in the media process.

Thus, Garrett has two of the things political figures aspire to—constituency and media access—without a political party. His attempt to be part of one, the Nuclear Disarmament Party, was not in the end a success. Garrett's split with the NDP is a complicated affair,[14] but part of the problem may have been that Garrett's methods of work were so much at variance with those of a political party. Garrett worked up out of an organic relation to a grass roots musical culture, into the electronic media. Perhaps his style did not translate very well into the rorting and wrangling of a quite different kind of grass roots organisation—the mass social movement. *Individualism* is both the strength and weakness of Garrett's personal, populist style.

It is no surprise that Garrett is fond of quoting Orwell. Like Orwell, Garrett is popularly credited with a knowledge of politics without being tainted by *too* close a complicity with it. He retains (for some) the dignity of the committed artist who is both half in and half out of political life for the selfsame reason: the absolute necessity to retain moral integrity. This is what we might call the Orwellian dilemma, or the Catalonian tragedy . . .

Garrett is ideally placed to act as a populist figure: not totally dependent on the culture industry, not answerable to the 'politics industry' either. For a pop populist, the best of both worlds is to work with both but be identified with neither. Garrett uses this double position to advance a vision of a stripe which is uniquely his own. It combines appeals to 'Australian-ness' with elements from the agendas of the social movements of the 1970s. (Perhaps Garrett imbibed the spirit of these while studying for that law degree.)[15] Some of its elements are: environmentalism, anti-Americanism, Aboriginal land rights. At the same time, Garrett nods towards an older tradition of radical nationalism: republicanism, egalitarianism, participatory democracy, the rights and needs of the little people. A fair go for all. Garrett's most interesting contribution to our political culture is in demonstrating ways in which older values can be aligned with more recent and seemingly different ones, and may be made more palatable to younger generations—who may not even be aware of our progressive traditions.

Of particular interest in this respect is the visual iconography. That bald head is such an inspired symbol in this regard. Together with his catatonic dancing and open, outstretched hand, the bald head has always been an integral part of Garrett's stage presence, but off stage it has come to mean rather more. To return to matters of sartorial detail: if hairstyles signify anything in this day and age, it is age itself. A haircut, particularly a 'public' one, is always some sort of compromise between what befits one's years, what is fashionable, and how one wore it in one's youth. Garrett sidesteps the whole problem by abolishing it. The gleaming skull bridges the gap between the old left and the new left; the counterculture and post-punk marginalism; city and surf subcultures. Certainly, all the songwriting members of Midnight Oil (principally Jim Moginie, Rob Hirst and Garrett) are of an age which puts them somewhere in between the student radicalism of the late 1960s and the punk rebellion of the late 1970s, but the eclectic mix of attitude, iconography, ideology and musical styles which characterises the band's art tries to speak to like-minded souls from any and every period of cultural formation.[16] Hence the bold bald shine under the follow-spot at centre stage: a sign of open, honest neutrality, catatonically animated.

The Aussie bush hat is another key icon here. While the bald pate has gathered significance accidentally, the bush hat does have a slightly more calculated air about it. As far as I'm aware, its first public exposure was when Garrett launched the NDP campaign. It also appeared in the context of a public event connected with the Constitutional Commission: the re-enactment of the proclamation of Australia as a nation.[17]

The bush hat's connotations are obvious, and therein lies its appeal. More interesting are subsequent attempts to appropriate it. In a daring display of image scavenging, Ian 'Molly' Meldrum took to wearing one as host of *Countdown* to cover his receding hairline, and made a big show of symbolically giving Bob Hawke one when the latter appeared one night in the guest compere's seat. Thus Garrett, the wearer of many hats, has put one particular hat in circulation which has since been worn on many formerly hatless heads.

At the very last *Countdown* annual awards show, Molly removed the hat to reveal a clean shaven pate, à la Garrett—no doubt meant as a show-stopping joke to commemorate the antagonism there has always been between Meldrum and the Oils. The joke was on Meldrum. We all knew at the time that the avuncular Meldrum was going bald (and losing his grip on Australian teen consciousness), but not even Garrett himself knows if Garrett is going bald. The spokesperson for the aspirations of youth, now 33, is reserving the right to grow old, but not grey, gracefully. So far the press and the industry have let him, and that in itself seems to me to be a powerful tribute to the Garrett–Oils credibility. Something worth paying homage to—at least this once.

Of course, it would be possible to approach this whole business in a more critical vein. Neither Garrett nor Midnight Oil nor their management are beyond reproach, not all of their judgments along the road have been good ones, as they are themselves aware. Still, I think it is necessary to appreciate that stance for what it is before denouncing it from that more traditional seat of intellectual judgment—the armchair.

NOTES

1 Constitutional Commission, *Individual and Democratic Rights*, Report of the Advisory Committee to the Constitutional Commission, Canberra, 1987, preface.

2 The question of the relationship of the local to the international is a separate question from that of the relationship of popular music to the music industry, which is the focus of of this essay. These two sets of relations are logically distinct even though in practice they overlap. It is difficult to compare the Oils to overseas acts which may also have a political 'aura' because the structure of the industry differs from country to country, and one can really only compare industries, not individual acts.

3 On the history of Midnight Oil, cf Wendy Milson & Helen Thomas, *Pay to Play*, Penguin Australia, 1986; and Toby Creswell in Clinton Walker (ed), *The Next Thing*, Kangaroo Press, 1984. The archiving of pop newspapers and magazines leaves a lot to be desired, so interviews and articles from ephemeral publications are not easy to get hold of. Pop journalism is nevertheless the best source of detailed information. Here is a selection: Andrew McMillan, *RAM*, 9 September 1987; Toby Creswell, *Rolling Stone* (Australia), No 397 (April 1986) and No 411 (October 1987); Samantha Trenoweth, *Countdown Magazine* No 51 (October 1987); Bill Wolfe, *Spin* (USA) Vol 1 No. 4, 1985; Ken Wark, *Hero*, No 14, Summer, 1987 and *On The Street* No 333 (29 April 1987). A selection of earlier articles is reprinted in *Oil Rag* Vol 1, 1987, published by Midnight Oil's 'Office'. On the four types and three strategies of pop journalism cf 'Chat, Clatter & Pop', *Tension* 12, 1988.

4 Cf the popular culture forum papers printed in *On the Beach* 10, 1987. On popular culture I have been influenced by the work of Lawrence Grossberg, *It's a Sin: Postmodernism, Politics and Culture*, Power Foundation Publications, Sydney, 1988.

5 Not all publicity is good publicity. See *Centralian Advocate*, 16 July, 1986; *Age*, 15 July 1986; (Melbourne) *Sun*, 19 February 1987; (Melbourne) *Herald*, 16 July 1986.

6 Garrett wrote a number of 'Comment' columns for the (Melbourne) *Herald*. For example, 'Goose-stepping with the New Right', 11 September 1986 and 'Is Our Constitution in Crisis?', 9 October 1986. Also 'The Beat Goes On' *Rolling Stone* 409, (August 1987). Some of his political writings are collected in *Political Blues*, Hodder & Stoughton, 1987.

7 Peter Cochrane & Barry Plews in *Arena* 66, 1984.

8 Marcus Breen in *Arena* 74, 1986.

9 Michael Birch in *Meanjin* 43/4 and in Marcus Breen (ed), *Missing in Action*, Verbal Graphics, 1987. All quotes are from the latter, revised version.

10 Cf McKenzie Wark, 'Spirit Freed From Flesh', *Intervention* 21/22, 1988.

11 John Docker in *Arena* 65, 1983. The Docker article which launched the extensive debates in *Arena* on popular culture was in No 60 1982. This

was in some respects a return to much earlier debates in the pages of *Overland*, launched by Ian Turner. See also Tim Rowse, *Australian Liberalism and National Character*, Kibble Books, Melbourne, 1978, p. 239ff.

12 In the original context in which this essay appeared, my use of Gramsci's argument was intended to have an ironic register to it as well as an analytic one.

13 David Rowe in *Australian Journal of Cultural Studies*, 3, 2, 1985.

14 On 'The Rise and Fall (?) of the NDP', cf Marian Quigley, in *Current Affairs Bulletin* 62, 11.

15 There have been two sorts of movement out of educational institutions into pop: those which emanate from the universities (such as the Oils) and those which come from the art schools (Mental as Anything). Mid-1970s punk provided 'role models' for both, giving rise to 'agitpop' (Soritti Politti, Gang of Four) and the 'artful dodger' himself, Malcolm McLaren. (Cf Cathy Lumby & Ken Wark in *Tension* 10, 1986.) While the former may appeal to Fredric Jameson and the latter netted the biggest slice of the press coverage at the 1986 Sydney Biennale, the general influence of tertiary education and its values on pop is currently on the wane. One hopes this is not a reflection on what we are teaching . . . Cf Trevor Howard & Simon Frith, *Art into Pop*, Methuen, London, 1988.

16 Cf Megan Cronly's excellent analysis in *New Music Articles* 3, 1984, Melbourne.

17 Constitutional Commission *Bulletin* 2, September 1986.

8
Style, form and history in Australian mini-series
STUART CUNNINGHAM

I

In retrospect, the program that is generally regarded as the first Australian historical mini-series, *Against the Wind*, can be seen to have pioneered many of the protocols of production and reception that have characterised this distinctive television drama format. Produced in 1978 for the Seven Network at, for the time, the considerable cost of $76 000 per episode, the program consisted of thirteen one-hour episodes and dealt, with critical historiographical insight, with the first decades of colonisation in Australia. *Against the Wind*—with its large number of episodes and its discrete as well as continuous episodic structure—tended to resemble earlier Australian historical serials (such as the thirteen-episode *Luke's Kingdom*, 1974–75) more than the mini-series proper. However, its epic historical thematics and narrative coverage, its widely discussed revisionist account of the historical record on early convictism, its promotion and reception as history as well as drama, and its huge critical and ratings success all foreshadow the contours of the historical mini-series phenomenon of the 1980s.

And quite a phenomenon it has become. From 1980 to mid-1986, fifty mini-series were made in Australia, and the Bicentennial year has seen the release of another considerable group (*Captain James Cook, Melba, True Believers, Dirtwater Dynasty, The Alien Years, All the Way*) together with the recycling of several series. The mini-series boom is very much an outgrowth of the 10BA tax legislation: its inauguration

* This paper first appeared in its present form in *Southern Review* 22 (November 1989). An earlier, shorter version was published in *Filmviews* 136 (1988). Dates for mini-series discussed are dates of first broadcast in the major metropolitan areas; in some cases these differ from year of production.

in 1980, and the diminution of its benefits and effective replacement by 1988, neatly bound the 'high' period of mini-series production.[1] These close links indicate something of the complex of institutional preconditions and contexts for the prioritising of the mini-series at the high-budget end of film and television financing in the 1980s in Australia.[2] These favourable conditions have given us such memorable critical and ratings successes as *A Town Like Alice* (1981); *1915* (1982); *The Dismissal, Waterfront* and *Power Without Glory* (1983); *The Last Bastion, Bodyline* and *Eureka Stockade* (1984); *Anzacs, The Dunera Boys* and *Cowra Breakout* (1985); *A Fortunate Life* and *The Lancaster Miller Affair* (1986); and *Vietnam* (1987).

However, it is not my purpose here to analyse these preconditions and contexts, nor to survey in broad strokes this contemporary plethora of mini-series. Rather, I want to be both more abstract and more particular than either of these approaches would determine. I want to address the distinctiveness of the mini-series as a televisual format and to indicate some of the innovations and challenges that Australian historical mini-series present in both their representations of national history and in their expansion of the 'horizons of possibility' of televisual form. Such an approach attempts to construct a stylistic and generic map of the Australian mini-series, demonstrating continuities and variations within the format.

II A HYBRID FORM

The mini-series is a quite recent addition to the established array of television formats—news, current affairs, light entertainment, series and serial drama, documentary, sport and so on. It is a veritable hybrid, split between the series and serial drama formats, and between documentary and dramatic modes. It can be defined as a limited-run program of more than two and less than the thirteen-part season or half-season block associated with continuing serial or series programming, with episodes that are not narratively autonomous (as they are in the series format). Thus, strictly speaking, the term 'mini-series' is a misnomer. However, it is closer to the series format in so far as it moves to conclusive narrative resolution across a limited number of episodes—unlike the serial, with its indefinitely (and what seems at times, infinitely) deferred denouements. Its hybridisation of documentary and dramatic modes creates real definitional problems, perturbs many viewers and commentators because of the ethical, legal and political imponderables raised by its taste for 'impersonating' history, but excites just as much rapturous response for the risks and challenges it takes as it 'inscribes the document into experience'.[3]

The mini-series' hybrid status, as might be expected, poses further problems for general theories of televisual form. Commentators have thus sought family resemblances between cinematic forms and modes of promotion, and the mini-series. While there are intriguing connections, the dramaturgical structures deployed in mini-series defy

118

easy assimilation to a cinematic model. Finally, the approaches to issues and events taken up in the most interesting examples of the format move easily around traditional categories usually held to divide televisual material into entertainment and information/education. I want to look at these questions more closely now.

III QUALITY TELEVISION

Taking perhaps the most evident aspect first, the Australian historical mini-series is 'quality', 'event' television. Its status is analogous to that of the art cinema in relation to mainstream commercial cinema, albeit without the financial and promotional marginalisation typically experienced by art cinema. Historical mini-series are produced on regularly record-breaking budgets for television, are accompanied by major promotional campaigns, often as flag-carriers leading into new ratings periods, and in turn attract lavish spin-off campaigns and critical and ratings successes, all of which contributes to their status as 'exceptional' television.

The mini-series' placement as quality television registers at several interrelated levels. At an institutional level, it can be traced to the need for the major US commercial networks to inaugurate and market their own genre of up-market material in order to counteract the allegiances public television, cable and subscription services were soliciting from the demographically sensitive market sectors with high disposable incomes. It is evidenced by the diverse and high-profile circulation of the mini-series as event in contiguous formats—from glossy presentations on production history (Brian Carroll's *The Making of A Fortunate Life*), novelisations (Sue MacKinnon's *Waterfront*), reprints of journalistic accounts (Paul Kelly's *The Unmaking of Gough* reprinted as *The Dismissal* upon the release of the mini-series by the same name), coffee-table records of the series (Kristin Williamson's *The Last Bastion*), through to voluminous numbers of letters to the editor, historical reminiscence by actual protagonists, lavish and detailed critical reviews by more usually dyspeptic newspaper critics, and many educational packages produced for secondary students of history, media and social studies.

Further, it is on display in the textual forms and protocols of production of the mini-series. With their high production values—a fastidious attention to historical verisimilitude, epic shooting schedules, the use of film rather than videotape as shooting stock, the highly publicised use of theatrical workshopping techniques to prepare actors exhaustively for historical impersonation—mini-series bear direct comparison with other established zones of quality such as the BBC and ABC classic serials *(The Windsors, The Sullivans)* or the Australian period film of the mid- to late 1970s *(The Getting of Wisdom, The Irishman)*. The way this textual and production rhetoric of quality marks out a difference for the mini-series now requires further analysis

119

in terms of its modes of historical representation, its patterns of dramaturgical and narrative structure, and in terms of its inflection of the hybrid form of documentary-drama.

IV HISTORICAL REPRESENTATION

Consider the relation of historical mini-series like *The Last Bastion*, *The Dismissal*, *Cowra Breakout* or *Vietnam* to other forms of Australian historical drama, such as the period film—*The Getting of Wisdom*, *The Irishman*, *The Mango Tree*, and so on—and television series like *Rush*, *The Sullivans* and *Carson's Law*. These texts typically centre around fictional characters who achieve a form of 'everyman' status such that they can be considered representative of a nation and its experiences (in youth, in war, in depression). Thus *The Sullivans* presents a 'typical' wartime Australian family. Crucially, these texts operate to set predominantly fictional narratives and characters' lives against the backdrop of historical events: wars, depressions. Tom Ryan notes of period film protagonists, however, that they are people who do not influence the course of history to any extent: they are victims of, rather than participants in, historical events.[4] They achieve representative status precisely because of their historical anonymity.

In contrast, the historical mini-series often deals directly with actual historical events—the Eureka Stockade, the First and Second World Wars, the dismissal of the Whitlam government, the Kelly story, the Castle Hill rebellion—and offers accounts of those events. Moreover, it often deals with 'large' historical figures—Menzies, Curtin, Churchill, Roosevelt (*The Last Bastion*), Lalor (*Eureka Stockade*), Kelly (*The Last Outlaw*), Bradman, Jardine (*Bodyline*), still familiar politicians (*The Dismissal*), Melba (*Melba*), Kingsford Smith (*A Thousand Skies*). Rather than being victims of history, or in some cases actually attempting to evade historical change, these characters tend to be represented as the *makers* of history, determining and directly influencing the course of events. In centring such figures and constructing accounts of the events in which they participated, the historical mini-series attempts to accede to history in direct rather than mediated terms—ie, as merely the backdrop for a narrative. In doing so, it operates in different conceptual terms from the period film. For in so far as the protagonist of the period film achieves a sort of everyman status, the genre itself operates in a literary or mythical rather than a historical register. This point is underscored when one considers the reliance on literary adaptation in the period film—for example, *Picnic at Hanging Rock*, *The Getting of Wisdom*, *My Brilliant Career*, *We of the Never Never*—and the lack of it in the most pertinent instances of the historical mini-series. This, in turn, invites a rather different position for the viewer of the mini-series: as knowledgeable citizen, rather than distracted consumer.

The period film tends also to reconstruct the past in nostalgic terms. It presents the past as a lost, desirable time, as a golden age of lost ways and values. In contrast, the historical mini-series' representation of the past is not so much nostalgic as it is critical and interventionary. While the period film trades on this mythic representation of a national past, the historical mini-series frequently recreates Australia's past in less nostalgic terms. Thus it criticises the Austalian's naivety (rather than innocence) in *The Last Bastion* and *The Dismissal* and presents lazy, prejudiced Australian soldiers as prison guards in *Cowra Breakout*. *A Fortunate Life* is primarily an account of a young man's ability to survive a neglected childhood rather than an affectionate reminiscence of a difficult past.

Many mini-series, particularly those produced by the Kennedy–Miller organisation, also promote a more radical 'multiperspectivism', one that effectively displaces the unreflective chauvinism to which so much recent Australian media is prey. In doing so, these mini-series produce remarkably innovative *elliptical* approaches to major historical events in the nation's history. Thus almost half of *The Cowra Breakout* is spent on the Japanese side, encouraging empathy with their point of view. The Japanese scenes contain Japanese dialogue and English subtitles—an extremely unusual departure from the conditions of intelligibility of commercial television. Similarly, *Bodyline*—while more conventionally reverting to a 'little Aussie battler' mode in its latter stages—constructs much of its account with reference to the point of view of Jardine (captain of the MCC tourists in 1932–33 and a convenient Lucifer in Australian sports hagiographies), Edith (Jardine's English sweetheart), and Fender (friend of Jardine and gentleman cricketer). *The Dismissal* multiplies perspectives and points of narratorial authority with dizzying speed. *Vietnam*, like *Cowra Breakout*, insists on Vietnamese perspectives and shows them to be as fraught with division as Australian positions with regard to the war and the personal tensions it provoked.

Further, it is arguable that these mini-series take seriously the radical historiographical dictum that 'the past is only interesting politically because of something which touches us in the present'.[5] Thus, *The Last Bastion* mounts a case, *inter alia*, for a greater multilateralism in Australian foreign policy at a time (1984) when the ANZUS alliance was in crisis over New Zealand's refusal to allow US nuclear warships into its harbours and the US's consequent withdrawal from bilateral defence arrangements. This much is explicitly claimed for the series by one of its producers and scriptwriter, David Williamson, in an interview in the documentary *The Making of The Last Bastion*. Similarly, it is clear that both *Cowra Breakout* and *Vietnam* are major documents contributing to setting the emergent discourse of multiculturalism on the national agenda. *The Dismissal* was deemed by the Ten Network to be a sufficient potential intervention in early 1980s politics to delay its broadcast twice until after the March 1983 federal election. It was held to be a unique, and uniquely courageous, staging so close to the event of the most destabilising contravention of constitutional convention in Australian, and probably Westminster, political history.

121

V DRAMATURGY AND NARRATIVE

Second, the historical mini-series presents us with innovative narrative and dramaturgical models when compared with established television formats. All mini-series present themselves with a rhetoric of epic structuration, virtually all operate on the model of the nineteenth-century *Bildungsroman,* and several of the best engage with formative historical events in a documentary-drama mode. What are the salient implications to be drawn from these shared formal characteristics?

Epic structure means extreme etiolation of narrative trajectory. A good deal of the criticism that mini-series attract focuses on this point: skeletal narratives padded out to fit predetermined program durations. However, if we consider both the usual length of the mini-series—eight to ten hours of viewing time—together with the propensity for historical mini-series to rework events whose narrative consequences are already widely known, its dramaturgical cues for sustaining viewers' interest must lie outside narrative enigma. The commodious temporal format typically allows for a displacement of *event* by *causation* and *consequence*: the events inscribed in titles such as *The Dismissal, Bodyline* and *Cowra Breakout* occur well into the second half of the respective series; in the cases of *The Dismissal, The Last Bastion* and *Vietnam,* there is a pointed following-through of the political, social and public policy issues that are consequent on the events which are the series' *raison d'être.* In this sense, the historical mini-series offers an unparalleled upgrading of the terms within which historical information and argument are mediated through mainstream television. Consider, by comparison, that television's representations of history either trade on a comforting nostalgia or a superficial nominalism: on the one hand, history as a lost Eden of traditional values (*The Sullivans*) or as a pure spectacle of the 'otherness' of a national past (*This Fabulous Century*); on the other, history as merely an indefinitely prolonged series of discrete phenomena (news and current affairs).

The pull, then, of narrative enigma is displaced in the historical mini-series by the fact that its plot and resolution have gained social currency before the text is screened. The series' prologue might announce its resolution (the early narration of *The Dismissal*), the narrative may be familiar as social knowledge or as part of a canon of well-known literary texts (*Bodyline, The Dismissal, Eureka Stockade, The Challenge, A Town like Alice*). Regardless, the circulation of publicity around the screening of a mini-series guarantees such prior knowledge. As a consequence, a different viewing position is invited. The central place conventionally occupied by suspense in televisual drama is replaced by an emphasis on what John Caughie has called the 'documentary look': the terms in which the viewer is situated in relation to the text's careful reconstruction of the past. The ambience of this re-creation can become a central focus of the historical mini-series. This is not to suggest that there are never suspense structures. The known nature of the outcome of the plot, however, alters the function of suspense. One experiences a sense of pathos and tragedy in *The Dismissal because* of the knowledge that Whitlam will be sacked. Similarly, we attend to the *mode* of debate about Japanese honour in the Cowra internment camp *because* its consequences are foregiven.

Much of this 'foregiven' status of the mini-series text has been ascribed by less sanguine critics to an all-pervading 'recognition-effect' that secures a safely confirming viewing position.[7] This criticism, however, overlooks or elides crucial aspects of audience composition and response. Not all audiences recognise the historical material with the facility and smugness implied by such criticism. On the contrary, for younger audiences, the historical mini-series may be an unparalleled means by which the 'document is inscribed into experience', if the number of educational packages produced to accompany mini-series into the classroom is any guide. Second, far from being lulled, many viewers regard mini-series as significant—verifiable or falsifiable—historical arguments, if the amount and nature of public corre-spondence generated around them is taken into account. Third, such a criticism smacks of a governing aesthetics of suspicion: the pleasure taken in the recognition-effect need not necessarily be ideologically complicit in principle.

Perhaps the most crucial narratorial and dramaturgical modality of the historical mini-series, however, is its multiperspectivism. By this I mean the way in which the epic length and structure of the mini-series both necessitates and makes possible a multiplication of author-ising perspectives within a sprawling narrative field characterised by the *Bildungsroman* format. Albert Moran puts it this way:

> Structurally, such narratives tend to sprawl. Although the focus is on one or two individuals, nevertheless, as part of an epic sweep, there is often a variety of stories and the accumulation of much social material, the latter often characterised by a painstaking accuracy of detail. The historical cre-dentials of the form are often doubly secured; the elongated time scheme, as well as the extended social and even geographic dimensions and the narrative trajectory of the central figures, is frequently intermeshed with the narrative of more public events. Such narratives often require a 'slow-ing-down' of the main story. With the accumulation of parallel plots, tan-gential episodes, multiple themes and so on, the main narrative is frequently displaced. In the end such a narrative may accumulate so much diverse material that it is difficult to bring it to a close. Endings are often not so much a climax as a 'point of let-up' where certain resolutions are achieved and the story is over.[8]

In the most interesting examples, there is a foregrounded battle for enunciative authority where narrative order is put under considerable stress by contending claims on the historical record. The entrusting of narrative authority on the English side for most of the first half of *Bodyline* was certainly a controversial displacement of enshrined

Australian chauvinism. *The Dismissal*'s radically complex mode of narration disseminates narrative authority across time and political combatants. Commentators have variously equated the line the program takes with that of Fraser, Kerr or a Left-Labor position of 'maintaining the rage'. Whatever else such differing readings suggest, they attest to the innovative multiperspectivism that certain historical mini-series produce.

VI DOCUMENTARY-DRAMA: A STYLISTIC AND HISTORICAL CONTINUUM

A third general issue of the nature of the historical mini-series as a textual system concerns the vexed question of documentary-drama. The BBC's banning of Peter Watkins's *The War Game* and the diplomatic crisis between Britain and Saudi Arabia over *The Death of a Princess* are two of the more explosive events which attest to the legal and political as well as textual volatility of the form.[9] This volatility should caution against attempts to define the format; rather, it is more constructive to consider documentary-drama in the historical mini-series on a continuum between two sets of limiting markers. Towards the 'conservative' limit, one might situate mini-series like *1915*, which presents itself as a straight literary adaptation, is structured around fictional characters against a backdrop of historical events, and which attempts little, if any, textual work integrating archival material into the dramatic reconstruction. Towards the 'innovative' limit might be programs like *The Dismissal* and *Vietnam* which work from original screenplays and make complex use of mixtures of fictional and historical protagonists and archival and reconstructed diegetic material. Somewhere between the two are situated mini-series like *Power Without Glory*, derived from an innovative *roman à clef*; *Anzacs*, *The Last Outlaw* and *Against the Wind*, historical mini-series with original scripts written by experts on their respective subjects which attempt some measure of historical revisionism, but which are essentially 'straight' historical dramas; or *The Last Bastion* and *Bodyline*, with their original scripts, mainly historical protagonists and set piece mixtures of archive and drama.

Let us consider this question of a stylistic and representational continuum comprehending a broad range of approaches to televisual form and to history in Australian mini-series in some detail. There are, of course, many methods of constructing critical parameters for the sixty or so series—more than four hundred television hours!—under consideration. We could start with their consistent and undoubted importance as rating successes, and pursue the implications of this for the reinvention of indigenous, serious drama with commercial potential.[10] The industrial emergence and fortunes of the format might be the focus.[11] Alternatively, we might follow topic, period or source groupings in the mini-series, producing an account such as the following:

(1) literary adaptations: *1915, A Fortunate Life, Water Under the Bridge, For the Term of His Natural Life, A Town Like Alice, Robbery Under Arms, Lucinda Brayford.*

(2) non-historical: *Return to Eden.*

(3) contemporary history: *The Dismissal, The Challenge, Tracy, Vietnam, Sword of Honour, All the Way, Shout!*

(4) early history: *The Timeless Land, Captain James Cook, Against the Wind, The Last Outlaw, For the Term of His Natural Life, Eureka Stockade, Robbery Under Arms.*

(5) early twentieth-century history: *Anzacs, 1915, A Fortunate Life, Melba, The Alien Years.*

(6) mid-century: *The Weekly's War, Nancy Wake, The Lancaster-Miller Affair, The Petrov Affair, True Believers, The Last Bastion, Cowra Breakout, Bodyline, Dunera Boys, A Town Like Alice.*

(7) generational sweep: *Dirtwater Dynasty, Women of the Sun.*

Rather than pursue these kinds of groupings, however, a stylistic and representational continuum would attempt to establish qualitative criteria for discriminating amongst mini-series in terms of their use of the format and their approach to historical reconstruction. Employing the criteria introduced above, this would involve setting 'conservative' and 'innovative' markers on two axes, the stylistic and the historical.

A grid like this, gross as it is, can act as a heuristic device to suggest some fruitful means of categorisation, enabling us to specify the stylistic and representational parameters of Australian mini-series. Let us plot, then, some of the points on this grid.

VII THE LAST BASTION

The Last Bastion (1984) is significant for its uncompromising focus on the historical moment of Australia's greatest danger during the Second World War. It is one of the only mini-series (*The Dismissal* is the only other significant example) to suppress romance as a major dramaturgical motor and concentrate throughout on political-diplomatic-military vectors in order to structure the drama of the series. It is thus peopled entirely by large historical figures in what are at times complex narrative interactions, which are nevertheless rendered as classically dramatic. This mini-series marks the only contribution to the format by the pre-eminent scriptwriter David Williamson (who was also co-producer). In contrast, *The Petrov Affair* (1987) attempts a reconstruction of a similarly complex historical moment, but fails to develop a co-herent dramatic field. Like *Against the Wind* (1978) and *The Last Outlaw* (1981), *The Last Bastion*'s principals claim to have done ori-ginal research on their subject that will 'substantially rewrit[e] Aus-tralian history'.[12]

As we have seen, the series also makes a strong political argument against Australian diplomatic and military dependency, and by its resilient focus on the drama of diplomatic manoeuvres against the backdrop of a nationalist reading of Australia's marginal international status it takes a reasoned stand against the moralist doxa of both conservative populism and *gauchiste* purism that parliamentary poli-tics and allied diplomacy is a corrupt and corrupting game. Through-out *The Last Bastion*, the effect and affect of political rhetoric is centred and successfully dramatised, as it is in few other mini-series, *The Dismissal* and *Vietnam* excepted. This is a considerable achievement in and of itself.

One of the most intriguing issues a series like *The Last Bastion* raises is that it arrives at a classical Whitlamite position of greater diplo-matic and military independence for Australia by a route which runs counter to the way the same position is argued by contemporary Left historians; Michael Dunn, for instance, in the tradition of the anti-nationalist Left historiography of Humphrey McQueen, puts Curtin in the position of having merely shifted dependencies from Britain to America.[13] It suggests much about the commercial and dramaturgical imperatives of research and scripting for television mini-series that Curtin is produced as a Whitlamite *avant la lettre* in *The Last Bastion*. But it also suggests something of the import of such television work that it is ordering 'popular memories' to provide antecedents and traditions for what is still today (within political agenda-setting) considered aberrant and utopian.[14]

VIII THE PETROV AFFAIR AND THE DISMISSAL

Compare *The Petrov Affair*, on the one hand, and *The Dismissal* (1983), on the other, with *The Last Bastion*. The latter series, by the insistence of its achieved political and diplomatic focus, creates a kind of cor-relative formal interest when considered against dominant character structures of television drama. *Petrov*, by comparison, is an 'incoher-ent' text both at the level of political-historical argument and of dra-matic structure. Drew Cottle, in his discussion of this series, needn't have worried so much over the pernicious New Right ventriloquism of the series, because it has failed to find a line—dramatic as much as political—through the dense weave of issues surrounding the Petrov affair.[15] Nevertheless, *Petrov* is an interesting failure because it suggests something of the difficulties posed by the hybrid form of the mini-series. In this case, the genre recipe of the spy thriller and the complexities of political and popular address around an excessively localised moment in Australian history don't play off each other productively.

The Dismissal, by contrast, succeeds spectacularly in finding a dra-matic style appropriate to an equally complex and divisive political moment, the sacking of the Whitlam government. This is the mode of reconstructed Greek tragedy: an audacious hyperdramatisation that grasps the literal import of the cliché 'political theatre', attempting as it does to perform the psychic-social ritual of turning solipsistic left-wing melancholy into a more productive work of 'national mourn-ing'.[16] It is within this global purpose that the radical stylistic gestures of *The Dismissal*—the overwrought omniscience of narratorial voice, the dramaturgical and character architecture of classical Greek trag-edy, the quasi-Method actors' preparation and physiognomic and gestural impersonation—should be understood. *The Dismissal*, as its producer and scriptwriter Terry Hayes has noted, 'changed the land-scape of Australian television'.[17]

IX MELBA AND SHOUT!

Another obvious pairing of mini-series is that of *Melba* (1988) and *Shout! The Story of Johnny O'Keefe* (1986). What a strange text *Melba* is, ex-emplifying as it does so many of the stylistic imponderables of the mini-series format. It has all the hallmarks of the conservative spirit of reconstruction: period costume, chamber drama, and a straight biographic focus cutting against any claims to multiperspectivism. On the other hand, this only describes perhaps half the program time; after the first episode, the rest is given over to enormous chunks of Linda Cropper deftly mouthing a veritable *catalogue raisonné* of Melba's operatic career. Like *Cowra Breakout* and *Vietnam*'s expansive periods of subtitled Japanese and Vietnamese, the mere fact that commercial network television is taking to its bosom such 'marginal' interests—opera, multiculturalism—is cause to suggest stylistic departures of some moment.

Look also at the demands that the dramaturgy of *Melba* places on audiences: its ponderous pacing and movement (or rather, lack of it), its mostly unrelieved reliance on a talking heads/chamber drama

127

format, and the evaporation of narrative tension or enigma through excessive signposting. The success of *Melba* must point to the successful marketing of mini-series as addressing the heightened civic consciousness of audiences, as providing informative 'history lessons'. This form of address legitimises a divergent (reflective, conscientious?) mode of dramaturgy within the regimes of commercial television and therefore creates a space, however underdeveloped it is in many mini-series, for such strangenesses as, here, the oracularity of opera repeatedly suspending an already extremely leisurely narrative movement.

Interestingly, though, the address to a heightened national consciousness in *Melba* can be regarded as very much balanced against the more recent industrial imperatives to sell the high-budgeted mini-series in overseas markets. The series' investment prospectus claims *Melba* 'will be an international series which combines a major title, momentous events and international locations'.[18] As can be seen from this series, as well as such examples as *The Last Frontier* (1987), *Nancy Wake* (1987) and *The Dirtwater Dynasty* (1988), these industrial vectors have decided effects on choices of location, generic convention and cast.

The same could not be said for *Shout!* Arguably one of the most tightly narrativised mini-series (written by Robert Caswell), it also has a highly complex form of local address and a powerful approach to the relation of archive and drama. Historian Ray Evans's fine analysis of this series dwells on some of the problems posed by its compelling attempt to represent the dialectics of cultural dependency in an import culture such as Australia's.[19] The historian will still find much that falls short of the full amplitude of considered analytical research in even the most outstanding television drama, but that should not divert our attention from the achievements of such television drama, of which *Shout!* is indisputably an example. Let us look briefly at *Shout!*'s achievements in the areas of dramaturgical form, cultural politics and relations of archive and drama.

For a mini-series, *Shout!* has a frenetic, almost hysterical, narrative pacing and a central characterisation, Terry Serio as the The Wild One himself, who stands alone amongst principal characters in mini-series (Nicole Kidman's performance as Megan Goddard in *Vietnam* comes to mind as similar) as a whirlwind presence. The opening sequence sets this tone: the oneiric camera movement through an empty Sydney Stadium, *into* the past, into the big production theme number 'Shout', and then out again, in slow motion, to a surreal gesture of childhood psychodrama, with little Johnny O'Keefe screaming to get his own way with his mother, and teacher Brother Mazzerini ominously laying down The Law of the Father. The dense circumambient aurality, the oneirics, the performer as ritual sacrifice—it all recalls Martin Scorsese's *Raging Bull*, and not simply because it's set in a converted boxing ring.

The dream theme is doubly appropriate, because it is the dream of movement within the fixed rules of exchange in a culturally dependent nation that is the narrative crux of *Shout!* 1954: Johnny courts Maryanne at the flicks; they watch a Cinesound Review item that tells them that Australian car manufacturing can't at the moment be as good as overseas models—'in the meantime, we can always dream'. Lee Gordon, displaced American, has a dream of 'world-class entertainment for Australia'. 1956: Johnny and Maryanne kiss at a shopfront display of televisions as Shirley Strickand and Betty Cuthbert win gold at the Melbourne Olympics, giving Johnny the opportunity to demand recognition that Australians can be as good as anyone in the world.

But *Shout!* is minimally chauvinistic in its cultural politics. If anything, as Evans points out, it accords too great a role to the enabling status of Lee Gordon, and its strict bio-pic parameters move the focus away from developments parallel to that of O'Keefe in Australian rock. Nevertheless, it 'performs' the dialectics of exchange in an import culture brilliantly and, on the way, provides—as does *Melba*—an extraordinary repertoire of the aural and visual archive running, in *Shout!*, from the 1950s to the 'psychedelic' 1970s.

X SWORD OF HONOUR AND VIETNAM

Finally, consider another comparison between two mini-series with similar thematic foci, *Sword of Honour* (1986) and *Vietnam* (1987). Both deal with the effects of the Vietnam war on several members of a family; both cover similar time frames—the mid-1960s to 1972 (in the case of *Vietnam*) or 1975 (in the case of *Sword of Honour*). Both map generational difference and conflict on to national conflict; both deal with the intensified intra-generational conflict posed by war service on the one hand and the counter-cultural peace movement on the other; both have major reconciliatory finales. However, the manifest differences between the two can serve as a telling demonstration of the kinds of issues that I have considered central to an appreciation of style and representation in Australian mini-series.

These two series belong towards opposite ends of my stylistic and historical continuum. *Sword* is a straight character drama which does little with the capacious narrative potential of the mini-series format except fulfill its worst-case scenario: slackness of narrative movement unrelieved by anything else punctuating or layering the plot at the level of archival inscription, the insertion of large historical figures, or even a heartfelt chauvinistic nationalism. Gestures towards some of these bottom-line elements help to salvage bits of otherwise equally awful series such as *All the Way* (1988), *The Challenge* (1986) or *Captain James Cook* (1988). Even in its central theme—the fortunes of an extended family group over an extended time span—*Sword* manages little, because the characters undergo little fundamental reorientation, as *Vietnam*'s central quartet of characters do. Perhaps the only moment of layering or arresting intensity in the eight hours is in the third hour, when Tony is taken to Frank's private altar to military glory, mateship and death. *Sword* might have elegant symmetries of character construction, as Ina Bertrand's analysis of this and other treatments of Vietnam in recent film and television posits, but they never move off the analyst's page.[20]

Vietnam, by contrast, has all the hallmarks of an omega point in Australian mini-series production. It has invented a dramaturgy of the archive, going further than any other series not only in archival inscription, but in integrating that into a complex, multiperspectival dramatic structure. Each pivotal character—Douglas, Evelyn, Phil and Megan—has their own narrative trajectory, which interweaves with other pivotal trajectories as well as providing the focus for a series of relatively autonomous subsidiary narrative worlds. Historical movement—eight years from November 1964 to December 1972—also means the slow accretion or layering of perspectives such that when the family finally re-forms at the end, we have learned to think of them historically. To think of the central characters historically is to decentre them in purely characterological terms. They gradually assume the status of markers of sectoral divisions within a historically delineated population, itself undergoing irreversible sea-change. Their tentative reconciliation at the end is strongly overdetermined by its taking place on the night of Whitlam's 1972 electoral triumph. This propitiatory utopianism is probably the most breathtaking example of the mini-series best-case scenario—the successful mapping of the personal on to the public and vice versa. The narrative architectonics are constantly enlivened by a prodigiously pleasureful amount of archival quotation, aural as much as visual, which can be read both for its own sake—the texture and pathos of instant recognition and impossible difference—and in terms of its layering of narrative. *Vietnam* can lay claim to constitute a remarkable *Gesamtkunstwerk* of Australian television.[21]

XI

Consideration of the general characteristics of the Australian mini-series in this discussion has prevented extensive analysis of more than a few important examples, but it has suggested that such work is valuable: the mini-series offers a rich field for investigating the potential for innovation in contemporary television. The format, and the uses to which it has been put in certain series at the 'innovative' end of my continuum, might suggest a greater range of possibility for broadcast television than general accounts of it and of its differences from cinema have suggested.[22] Further, the mini-series has arguably given local and international audiences many memorable representations of major determinants of Australian history.

NOTES

1 The history of the 10BA tax legislation and issues surrounding it are presented in accessible form in Susan Dermody & Elizabeth Jacka, *The Screening of Australia* Vol 1: *Anatomy of a Film Industry*, Currency Press, Sydney, 1987, pp. 211–16. See also *Film Assistance: Future Options*, Allen & Unwin, Sydney, 1987, p. 2.

2 For more detailed accounts of the institutional history of the mini-series, see Paul Kerr, 'The Origins of the Mini-Series', *Broadcast*, 12 March 1979, pp. 16–17; and 'A Little Plot in Colorado', *Time Out*, 25–31 May 1979, pp. 20–1; Bart Mills, 'Washington Behind Closed Doors', *Stills* April–May 1984, pp. 26–8; Henry Castleman & Walter Podrazik, *Watching TV: Four Decades of American Television*, McGraw Hill, New York, 1982, pp. 262–76. For Australian background as well as international antecedents, see Ewan Burnett, 'Mini-Series', *Cinema Papers* 44/45 (1984), pp. 32–6; and Albert Moran, *Images and Industry: Television Drama Production in Australia*, Currency Press, Sydney, 1985.

3 John Caughie, 'Progressive Television and Documentary Drama' in *Popular Television and Film*, eds Tony Bennett et al, BFI, London, 1981, p. 346.

4 Tom Ryan, 'Historical Films' in *The New Australian Cinema*, ed Scott Murray, Nelson, Melbourne, 1980, pp. 122–5.

5 Colin MacCabe, 'Memory, Phantasy, Identity: *Days of Hope* and the Politics of the Past' in Bennett et al (eds), op. cit. (note 3).

6 Caughie, op. cit. (note 3), p. 342.

7 See, for example, Jodi Brooks, 'Dismissing', New South Wales Institute of Technology *Media Papers* 19, (1983).

8 Moran, op. cit. (note 2), p. 207.

9 See Andrew Goodwin et al (eds), *Documentary Drama*, BFI, London, 1983 for accounts of these and other significant controversies around documentary drama.

10 See Australian Broadcasting Tribunal, 'Ratings of Australian Drama, Mini-Series, Films and Telemovies', *Australian Content Inquiry Discussion Paper*, ABT, Sydney, March 1988.

11 Burnett, 'Mini-Series' (op. cit. note 2); Elizabeth Jacka, 'The Industry'; 'Films'; Stuart Cunningham, 'Kennedy–Miller: "House Style" in Australian Television' in *The Imaginary Industry: Australian Film in the Late '80s*, eds Susan Dermody & Elizabeth Jacka, AFTRS, North Ryde (Sydney), 1988.

12 Cited in Peter MacGregor, Australian Teachers Curriculum Package on *The Last Bastion*. On the two earlier mini-series, see the comments of their co-scriptwriter: Ian Jones, 'The Historical Mini-Series—Problems and Priorities' in *The First Australian History and Film Conference Papers* 1982, ed Anne Hutton, AFTS, North Ryde (Sydney), 1982, pp. 73–88.

13 Michael Dunn, *Australia and the Empire: From 1788 to the Present*, Fontana, Sydney, 1984, especially Chapter 6.

14 For a much fuller treatment of *The Last Bastion*, see the well-argued piece by Geoff Mayer, one of the very few that engages with questions of both style and representation. '*The Last Bastion*: History or Drama?', *Cinema Papers* 48 (1985), pp. 38–41, 87.

15 Drew Cottle, '*The Petrov Affair*: Constructing the Right Past?', paper to the Fourth History and Film Conference, University of Queensland, December 1987.

16 See Freud's distinction between 'mourning' and 'melancholia', which this point follows: 'Mourning and Melancholia' in *On Metapsychology*, Penguin,

Harmondsworth, 1984, pp. 245–68. Within a social psychology framework, the point is developed brilliantly by Alexander Mitscherlich & Margarete Mitscherlich, *The Inability to Mourn*, Grove, New York, 1975.

17 Terry Hayes, interview with Keryn Curtis, 6 February 1988. For more detail, see my chapter '*The Dismissal* and Australian Television' in Stuart Cunningham et al, *The Dismissal: Perspectives*, AFTS, North Ryde (Sydney), 1984, pp. 1–6; and Cunningham, op. cit. (note 9).

18 'Comments from the Producer' in *Melba* Investment Prospectus, 1985.

19 Raymond Evans, 'Heroes Often Fail: "Shout!", Johnny O'Keefe and Another Australian Legend', *Cinema Papers* 71 (1989), pp. 38–42.

20 Ina Bertrand, 'From Silence to Reconciliation', paper to the Fourth History and Film Conference, University of Queensland, December 1987.

21 For more detail, see Stuart Cunningham, 'Jewel in the Crown', *Filmnews* 17,4 (1987) pp. 8–9.

22 See, for example, John Ellis, *Visible Fictions*, Routledge & Kegan Paul, London, 1984.

9

In the name of
popular culture
ADRIAN MARTIN

[My mother] declared one day, that I would have to know what other boys of my age were reading, otherwise I soon wouldn't be able to understand my schoolmates. She got me a subscription to *Der Gute Kamerad* (a boy's weekly), and incomprehensible as it now seems to me, I read it not without enjoyment, at the same time as Dickens. There were exciting things in it, like 'The Gold of Sacramento', about the Swiss gold-hunter Sutter in California, and the most suspenseful thing of all was a story about Seianus, the minion of Emperor Tiberius.

—Elias Canetti[1]

I

Since its introduction in 1991, public reaction to the Victorian Certificate of Education (VCE), at least as filtered by the media, has been relentlessly hostile. A memorable Liberal Party billboard of early 1992 starkly captioned a particularly unflattering mugshot with only three little words: JOAN 'VCE' KIRNER. The introduction of the VCE marked an unexpected triumph for progressive ideals of education in the secondary education system—especially unexpected by those observers in the tertiary sector still struggling with the massive restructurings of a post-Dawkins era. It is hardly surprising, then, that the VCE aroused a number of familiar social worries: the fear that competiveness will be replaced by 'mothering', common denominator educational standards;[2] anxiety over the introduction *en masse* of trendy or 'soft option' subjects; a *Quadrant* or *News Weekly* mode of paranoia over the surreptitious (and strangely belated) coming-to-power of a generation of 1960s radicals.

---

* This is a shortened and revised version of an essay which appeared in *Metro* 89 (Autumn 1992), pp. 35–46.

But perhaps no aspect of the VCE has focused argument more intensely than the new English curriculum—and the role within it of a certain 'popular culture'.

Published negative reactions to the VCE English curriculum make for a puzzling spectacle. One revisits, as if in a time machine, the dark ages of this century when the spread of mass culture (first cinema and popular music, later comic books and TV) was seen in terms of an infectious, invasive disease, complete with germs that attacked the sober, discriminatory faculties of hitherto normal citizens. Suddenly, in the 1990s—when, to believe some voices, Pop Culture is All, and furthermore we All know it—one could again read hysterical denunciations of the insidious effects of 'non-print' media (usually boiled down to 'comic strips and videos') couched in the jargon of a flagrant ideological witch-hunt.

A sampling of the ongoing letters, reports and editorials in the (Melbourne) *Sunday Herald* during the hottest period of this debate in 1991 gives a good idea of the strategies and assumptions of those guardians of education who have recently come out of the closet on the offensive against popular culture. The dominant strategy is one of mutual exclusion, with great literature (pre-eminently Shakespeare) and popular culture (invariably, 'TV soapies') figured as the extreme points of a vast and unbridgeable cultural divide—as if (as so many have incredulously pointed out) soap (ie melodrama) doesn't saturate the fictions of Dickens, Shakespeare, and much more besides of the various great traditions of literature.

It seems that soap, to some, is not only the dead opposite to Shakespeare, but actually—and this is where hysteria sets in—poses a terrible threat to the proper dissemination of the Bard. A *Sunday Herald* editorial conjures the unthinkable horror whereby schoolchildren will be 'giving their attention to *Neighbours* and *A Country Practice* as an alternative, *or even in preference to*, Shakespeare, Milton and Dickens' (my emphasis).[3] Part of the fear is that children will be actively denied access to, and thus disenfranchised of, this particular heritage.

There is a paradoxical ideal of *cultural literacy* held high by the conservatives in this war. It is not what one might reasonably, innocently expect cultural literacy to be—the imparting of an ability to 'read' and understand all cultural texts, be they written, visual or aural, which is clearly one of the basic aims of the curriculum in dispute. It is, more restrictively, an education in those preselected, time-honoured classic (literary) works—a passing on of the right ways to love and uphold the established canon of artistic excellence.

It comes as a rather delightful surprise when, in the VCE debate, just about anyone working on behalf of popular culture is immediately labelled a rabid 'left winger', insidiously carrying out the program of a 'Socialist Left philosophy'—if not a downright ideologically correct member of the newly emergent thought police. I'm quite sure some of the teachers involved in formulating the VCE English curriculum would have been shocked to find themselves thus interpellated.

What a fantasy: the notion that innocent fans of *Terminator 2* or *Home and Away* could have taken hold of such enormous social power—or that, at the very least, such power is somehow *at stake* in the exercise of their cultural tastes.

Maybe there's a truth in that fantasy. One of the most suspect catchcries heard over and over in the VCE debate is the appeal to that endangered species, 'our cultural heritage'. Ours? Who is 'us' in this figure of speech? (After all 'Milton, Shakespeare and Dickens' sounds suspiciously like a straight, obsequious adoption of *Britain*'s cultural heritage.) The VCE debacle in this regard provides a local echo of the debate about political correctness that has raged for some time now in the US—the continuing, vicious attack on all those 'tenured radicals' who are reputedly undermining, through their courses, the fabric of US life. According to Sylvia Lawson,[4] at stake in this debate are the 'traditional norms of scholarship' that have for so long dominated US education: white, Western notions of objectivity, truth, reason, and the collective cultural good. There too, a particular constructed heritage is being invoked, and hysterically shored up.

Questioning and opposing this heritage is an array of other forces, among which Lawson includes 'the impact of new and not-so-new thinking on popular culture and the media' alongside the rise of feminism, multiculturalism and the critiques of institutions, power and authority. And it seems still true that any public sign of an embrace or even a non-judgmental consideration of popular culture can make a conservative ideologue see red immediately. Why, otherwise, would a *Quadrant* writer be moved to argue that pretending that *Dallas* and Dante are on a par contributes mightily to the spiritual decline of our age?[5] And why would the lordly statement appear, amidst the VCE debate, that 'education should include an understanding of such things as: the Westminster parliamentary tradition, the Judaeo-Christian ethic, the history of Western civilisation, and the type of learning associated with a liberal education'?[6]

II

Despite what might be imagined from reading the various missiles in the VCE debate, it's clear that some who support (even militate for) moves to give popular culture its due attention are hardly inspired or driven by a radical, anti-liberal vision. On the contrary, the invocation of popular culture is these days easily taken up and smothered within a certain soft, mushy, populist sentiment. Popular culture is 'us', our nation, our daily life—and little more that is in any way thoughtful (let alone critical) needs to be said.

There is an anxiety underlying this soft option: the anxiety of seeming too intellectual, too esoteric, too highbrow in one's public approach to a common, popularly accessible art. This is a very widespread anxiety amongst those who have been dubbed the pop culture intelligentsia, as if the very role of being an intellectual engaged in popular culture is an impossible, schizophrenic, absurd one. There is a valid point to this anxiety; Thomas Elsaesser has diagnosed it as 'the conflict of the intellectual when trying to articulate the value inherent in non-intellectual art, or indeed any art that grows from different cultural social preconditions: doomed to resort to his own language, he necessarily distorts his own intuition and transforms the object of his study into a metaphor'.[7]

My feeling, however, is that this particular rendering of the conflict of the intellectual can function as a cover for another kind of life-and-death conflict played out on a rather more social stage—the struggle between serious and unserious approaches to popular culture.

'There may well be reasons why some attention should be given by students of English to intellectually unchallenging samples of light entertainment',[8] wrote the editor of the *Sunday Herald*, obviously at a loss as to what these reasons could be. 'Intellectually unchallenging': these ominous words are echoed in many an everyday description of popular culture as providing, essentially, 'light entertainment'— diversion, simple amusement, escape, relief, and the like. Melbourne *Age* journalist Jim Schembri speaks what I take to be the sentiments of many when he muses about the Australian film *The Big Steal*. 'I tried getting deep about it while talking to a friend and my tongue came out in a rash. It was only when I got back to phrases such as "delightful family film" and "a lot of fun" that the spots began to clear up'.[9] Getting deep about popular culture is obviously, for some, an embarrassingly misplaced endeavour—save depth for arthouse movies and quality TV.

We live in an interesting time when popular culture has transformed itself into pop. What's the difference? Once upon a time, certified intellectuals like Robert Warshow,[10] working in the 1940s and 1950s, would pluck particular texts from the stream of mass-produced cultural artefacts and critically explore their specific, distinctive themes, styles, values, modes of functioning. Popular culture might be best understood as the idea that these critics were trying to identify. The study of this culture—in writing and teaching—pretty much went on its merry way for quite a time afterwards. It was naturally and fairly shamelessly intellectual in orientation, discussing issues of philosophy, aesthetics, metaphysics, ideology. It did not feel it had to be validated by that mythic mass of ordinary folk known as 'the people'. It did not experience any great anxiety about its lack of general accessibility (although neither was it, in many instances, strictly academic in its manner and social circulation). This perhaps golden age of innocence in the study of popular culture includes much of the auteur and genre work on cinema in the 1950s and 1960s: David Will, for example, unselfconsciously declaring that 'If [Douglas] Sirk discovered the universal relevance of *The Reader's Digest* and *True Confessions*, [Roger] Corman is the seer of *Astounding Stories*, *Marvel Comics* and He-Man magazines'.[11]

By the 1980s, no one could make (or hear) such a statement publicly without smiling, or at least surrounding it with an elaborately defensive justification. This has occurred because whereas popular culture was, in a sense, a minority idea, the newer idea of pop is vigorously marketed and policed in most corners of the public sphere. Pop, as I am defining it, is the acute self-consciousness of mass culture and its consumers. Nowadays (as McKenzie Wark has rightly put it) the official policy of a leisure-driven society is 'pop till ya drop'[12]—where even the pursuit of fun has a certain manic grimness about it. And this regime of pop enforces some remarkably strict and ungiving ideas about what popular culture texts are allowed to be, and do. As never before, consumers are moved to identify themselves as representatives of 'we the people', who demand only to be entertained by those objects labelled entertainment commodities.

In a pop climate, certain responses to popular culture rule over other responses that have been, or could be. Pop raises the camp attitude, itself once a minority idea, to a majority religion. Camp, kitsch, schlock, trash: these are the various synonyms for pop, and the mooted pleasures of pop, which is a deeply, forcibly unserious business. Pop is certainly a reversal of elite, high culture snobbery—it knows what low experiences it likes, positively revels in them, hungrily demands more and more of them. Yet it also displays a deeply defensive, shamed attitude which betrays a continuing, obedient deferment to superior cultural values. Pop's motto, endlessly reiterated in the film, TV and popular music columns of our daily newspapers, is: 'I know it's not great art, but it's good, relaxing fun'.

Pop works very hard to ensure that its films, TV shows and the like are taken as simply, as straightforwardly, as ephemerally as possible. It abhors any sign of intellectualism brought to bear on its goods and services. One effect of this is that, where the kitsch attitude reigns, serious fans of popular culture are likely to be credited with a sophisticated perversity every time they open their mouth in earnest praise of a lowly item. Yet the wilfully perverse response, like the camp attitude, conspires to keep the same old, most conservative coordinates of culture in place—not only high art snobbery, but also entertainment industry philistinism.

By the same token, strenuous efforts to intellectualise popular culture fall prey to another, equally socially defined, equally debilitating kind of anxiety: legitimation anxiety. The history of attempts to get popular culture taken seriously and accepted by (for instance) the Academy or the Museum often reveal a pained (and perhaps ultimately doomed) tendency to push this culture upwards on the scale of artistic respectability. William Routt suggests that one (mainly unconscious) drive underlying the heroic push of auteurism in cinema studies was to see 'only the virtues of elite art in the eminently popular films pouring out of Hollywood', grasping the presence of artists and Big Themes, but not any new aesthetic experience that 'might tumble some preconceptions'. Routt cites the embarrassment of critics who realised, fatally late in the day, that *Citizen Kane* was 'a magic show and not a Shakespearean drama, a Hollywood movie and not an art film'.[13]

Prevalent myth approaches to popular culture tend also to contribute to this legitimating sleight-of-hand. I am thinking of those commentaries that are only really at ease invoking and discussing a popular film when its characters or plot events fit one or other of the grand, universal archetypes bequeathed to us by storytellers at the dawn of time. Thus, Mad Max is the 'hero with a thousand faces' described by mythologist Joseph Campbell; *Fatal Attraction* dramatises the Jungian duality of the Two Faces of Woman; Hannibal the Cannibal in *The Silence of the Lambs* is merely the latest incarnation of the Dracula archetype buried deep in our collective unconscious. There's surely a pertinence to these observations; what they tend to overlook or erase in any specific popular culture case, however, is usually enormous.

To put it in the strongest possible terms, I think the legitimating approach—just as much as the embarrassed, let's-not-get-too-deep attitude—*betrays* popular culture, refuses to see its possibility, sells it off to the highest bidder. Is there something inherently special about popular culture that has never been directly confronted, never been taken on board in its own terms, in the variously pinched, too-careful sectors of public culture? Routt observes that, in many instances and places, popular art is denied 'what is conceded without saying to elite art: the ability to take one unawares, to question what one thought one knew, to confront one with one's self'.[14] So I think that 'we' (at least, those of us who care about popular culture in passionate and angry ways) should be open to the serious possibility that popular culture is offering us its own, unique aesthetic character, its own ways of thinking profoundly about some things, its own mysterious strangeness and 'otherness'.

III

But is it really productive to speak of popular culture as an identifiable force, a quasi-mystical entity, with characterising traits and dynamics, and its very own, full-blown aesthetic? It is against such idealism that other voices have spoken up, wanting to reinstate more rationally descriptive terms like 'mass culture' and 'the culture industries' with which to explore the media landscape of our contemporary world. The necessary value of such terms is that they sever something which is materially produced and transported along the consumption networks of society—a bunch of films, videos, books, records and the like—from any necessary tie to fanciful inventions like 'the people' and popular taste (not to mention the collective unconscious). Indeed, popular culture means no more, on one level, than *available* culture, the texts made available through one outlet or another.

One of the great problems that has stuck ferociously to many recent accounts of popular culture touched by idealism is the tendency to *reify* this culture—to turn it into a static object with values that will always and everywhere be the contestatory opposite of those values that belong to high culture and its works. Just as in the fantasies of those who oppose Shakespeare to soap, the popular culture critic can trap her/himself inside an imperishable dichotomy of high versus low. In this move much is repressed, especially the knowledge that much popular culture is very often precisely stage-managed, calculated ('the trade response to market responses', as Raymond Durgnat once put it),[15] and that, in the realm of celebratory cultural criticism, '99 per cent of anything we might talk about will be turned back on itself, ground up and dissolved' (Greil Marcus)[16]—in short recuperated, to use an unfashionable critical term.

John Fiske's work is increasingly influential over the way popular culture is studied in schools and universities under the recently emergent subject area Cultural Studies. In the essay 'Popular Discrimination' he reiterates his particular high vs low model of culture:

> Popular films, novels, and TV narratives such as soap opera are frequently dismissed by highbrow critics for three main sets of reasons: One set clusters around their conventionality, their conforming to generic patterns and their conditions of mass production. Another set centres on criteria such as superficiality, sensationalism, obviousness, and predictability, while the third is concerned with their easiness, their failure to offer any challenge. Yet these qualities, which in aesthetic or critical discrimination are negative, are, in the realm of the popular, precisely those which enable the text to be taken up and used in the culture of the people.[17]

It is one thing to argue that part of the aesthetic of popular art is its superficiality or spectacularity (although I think this deserves a more sophisticated and sensitive account than one usually gets); it is another thing altogether, and an extremely reductive move, to hold popular culture texts to (and in fact celebrate them for) a reputed 'failure to offer any challenge'. This is a crippling dichotomy; far from leaving us open to be 'taken unawares' by a work (low *or* high), it leads us always to expect and then see in it the dutiful fulfilment of the same, preordained cultural–textual function. 'There is no requirement, in the popular domain, for a text to be difficult, challenging, or complex. In fact, just the reverse is the case'. This is an astonishingly reified characterisation of 'the people', the 'culture of the people', the 'realm of the popular' and 'popular meanings'.

The theories of Mikhail Bakhtin, as they have been rediscovered and promoted in cultural studies, have also been extraordinarily influential. In his study of Rabelais and other popular texts and events, Bakhtin explored the folk notion of the *carnivalesque*—the cheeky, deliberately grotesque turning-upside-down of a society's respectable values. Bakhtin was sensitive to the complexity of the carnivalesque moment—its fleetingness and fragility in relation to the world which circumscribes and contains it. Many of the modern-day appropriators of Bakhtin, however, can be accused of no such sensitivity. John

139

Docker freezes the TV show *Hey Hey It's Saturday* into an instance of eternal carnivalesque revolt—a perpetual pageant of 'festive abuse' of authority, decentred anarchy and participatory popular humour—in order to propose that, 'With the help of communication technologies, popular culture remains outrageously omnipresent'.[18] An unchanging and monolithic good thing, popular culture again acquires in this account attributes which high culture can presumably never share—attributes of vulgarity, unselfconscious playfulness, anti-authoritarianism, a will to democratic levelling, and so on.

In one of the more interesting discussions of the useful relation of Bakhtin's work to modern film and TV comedy William Paul suggests, with due modesty and caution, that, 'If "high" and "low" could be stripped of their evaluative connotations, they might well offer fine descriptive terms for differing kinds of art'.[19] Low has a literal significance in a certain kind of art—as in Paul's example of Charlie Chaplin's films, which are (as he shows) obsessively focused on 'base', lower-body functions. Yet the 'evaluative connotations' of low and high have become more determining on critical practice than ever before—even if they have undergone a striking inversion since the mythical bad old days. For many popular culture critics, low is now definitively mightier and better than high: body, distraction and anarchy are better than head, contemplation and order.

Given this, it's hard for some of these new popular culture zealots to resist including intellectualism and seriousness on the bad, high culture side of the great divide. In an article on the teen movie *Ferris Bueller's Day Off*, RL Rutsky and Justin Wyatt argue, in a remarkably circular fashion, that entertainment movies cannot be discussed convincingly in any of the available weighty modes, since *fun* in popular culture has as one of its principal aims the mockery of pompous seriousness.[20] They claim that any textual analysis of a film like *Ferris Bueller* would inevitably read like a parody of those dour Marxist–feminist–psychoanalytic theoretical practices which cannot account for the viewing pleasures of savvy fans. By reducing all *conceivable* serious approaches to popular entertainment to this (highly caricatured) humourless reading, Rutsky and Wyatt dodge the possibility that there might be a supple, critical, validly intellectual approach that could be (or, in specific cases, has already been) evolved.

In this climate, the prospects for evolving a frankly serious discourse on popular culture are especially difficult; more difficult, I feel, than ever before. On the one hand, from the conservative side come charges that all popular culture critics are to be suspected and exposed: either because they are secretly and hypocritically aristocratic ('Instead of reading Henry Fielding, they look at *The Simpsons* and *Twin Peaks*. They are actually engaging with a small elite group'),[21] or because they are intellectually vacuous. John McDonald tries to create an impossible double bind for any aspiring worker in the field by suggesting that, considered in the light of the kind of 'kitsch criticism' which simply celebrates its pop subject matter, 'to treat with scholarly seriousness the mass-produced objects of mass culture is perhaps an even more pronounced form of kitsch criticism'.[22]

On another flank, within the merry halls of pop journalism (or kitsch criticism) itself, we find contortions that are no less disabling. In a brief but revealing commentary on the TV show *LA Law*, playwright-screenwriter-essayist Joanna Murray-Smith begins by chiding the program—implicitly from high culture premises—for its fakeness, unreality, absurd glossiness, and its too-clean resolutions, ie, not being serious, authentic, dramatic enough. Then she does a twist and takes the pop perspective of 'hey, don't get me wrong, I *like* inane trash'— by which criterion *LA Law* is now judged as *too serious*, too earnest, too heavy (better by far if it were chintzy, good-looking and superficial).[23] Neither serious popular culture critics nor serious popular culture texts stand much chance of thriving in these booby-trapped discursive fields.

At present, many commentators have lost the ease (which I think belonged to some popular culture analysts of previous generations) of passing between high and low texts, and noting the kinds of exchanges that go on between them. Such crisscrossing (the ideological motives and phantasms of which are often highly devious) is evident everywhere in culture—and not only since postmodernism reputedly inaugurated the 'mixing' of high and low. There have always been high works with calculatedly low elements (*Proof* is a good example, with its drive-in hi-jinx punctuating a Losey-like chamber drama), and low works with painfully high aspirations (such as the TV ads with Molly Meldrum flogging classical greats). *Pretty Woman* offers a fascinating model of the diverse, schizophrenic cultural tendencies that can cross any one text: it's both celebrated and damned as the purest of pop entertainments; within the story itself, the upward cultural move of Julia Roberts from prostitution and Prince to Shakespeare, chess and opera is clearly offered as an ideal trajectory for viewer identification; there's a big opera scene in the movie, but on the soundtrack album only rock and pop songs.

If popular culture is reified, then this kind of traffic becomes less and less evident and significant to the analyst's eye. One reason that this reification has been so complete and successful is that critics including Fiske and Docker have been too keen to conflate and collapse levels: they confuse what is *made* of texts (what is claimed of them and for them, the gestures and appropriations performed in their name) with what is supposedly *in* them. In his article on disco music, Philip Brophy provides a different model for understanding the relation between gestures and texts in culture: 'One could call [disco] shallow, cheap and crass, but of course, to call one music style these things, one must be able to justify supposedly contrary styles as deep, subtle and of high quality.'[24]

For Brophy, neither high nor low works in themselves possess depth and meaning; what can differentiate them (not once and for all, but in specific, changing situations) is a 'history of meaning', of meanings attributed, read in, taught and passed on. This insight can be taken further because now, in the age of pop, we have behind us not only histories of meaning (generally a feature of high culture) but also histories of non-meaning: claims that the virtue of this or that text is that it is purely meaningless, playful, kinetic, spectacular, camp, and so on. So just as it is entirely possible and necessary to argue these days that some low texts are profound, it is equally possible to turn the tables on high culture's self-definition and demonstrate that its own (even canonical) works can be seen as superficial, mad, formulaic, market-driven, glamorous . . .

The values that get ascribed to texts, and the readings we make of them, are not the same as the texts themselves. This is not only because all texts are to some extent naturally more-or-less polysemic (complex and multifactorial); it is also because different cultural contexts and frames of understanding cause us to see (and invent) these texts in radically different ways. In a way, criticism (in all its forms) happens in the ever-malleable space *between* texts and values.

Inevitably, our frames and contexts of understanding are political (although in no simple way). It has been a queer and disturbing feature of much recent work on popular culture that the drive to defend, uphold and celebrate this culture at all costs has led, not only to a theoretical reification, but further to a queasiness about being (or seeming) politically engaged in its unfolding dynamics. Issues of gender provide one obvious barometer: Rutsky and Wyatt grant the seriousness of the claim that *Ferris Bueller* has some sexist elements, but have no way of pursuing them critically within their fun-centred framework; Docker's account of *Hey Hey It's Saturday* works to pre-empt any killjoy suggestion that the show's running sexual politics are, frankly, disgusting. It is one thing to suggest that gender relations in low culture texts can get pretty tricky and complex; but it is simply an artful evasion then to wipe off questions of sexism and patriarchy without even trying to come to new terms with the way they function today.

This point about gender issues can be extended to everything that used to go under the rubric of *ideology* in politically motivated media and cultural studies. In their overwillingness to err on the side of popular culture as a fundamental good thing, many critics of late have thrown out the baby of ideology with what they perceived to be the tepid bathwater of 'Freudo-Marxist' determinist readings of that ideology. But, although it has certainly been fashionable for some time to conjure popular culture as the best of possible worlds while casting out the memory of those left pessimist spoilsports of the Frankfurt School, it's hard not to credit Theodor W Adorno with some residual intelligence when he suggested that, while 'numerous so-called utopian dreams have been fulfilled—for example, television', one can feel that

> insofar as these dreams have been realized they all operate as though the best thing about them had been forgotten—one is not happy about them.

As they have been realized, the dreams themselves have assumed a character of sobriety, of the spirit of positivism, and beyond that, of boredom (...) one sees oneself almost always deceived: the fulfilment of the wishes takes something away from the substance of the wishes (...) one could perhaps say in general that the fulfilment of utopia consists largely only in a repetition of the continually same 'today'.[25]

To claim that anyone writes, speaks or teaches in the name of popular culture implies that, in an important sense, this culture is not in fact a real, material, objective thing or field that can be defined and delimited. Rather, popular culture is more like a phantom site around which things happen, an idea or dream that is variously pursued. In the name of popular culture, people are driven to gestures of love or hate, defense or aggression. These gestures are, inescapably, as social, cultural and political as they are personal. And the disputes over this site will naturally be marked by 'tension, conflict and violence... abrasion and aggravation' (Brophy).[26] For—except in a certain highly elaborated and theorised fantasy—no one simply loves popular culture. Meaghan Morris has referred to the tendency of Cultural Studies to erase 'the moment of everyday discontent—of anger, frustration, sorrow, irritation, hatred, boredom, fatigue'.[27] We might do well to think of everyday cultural experience in terms of sadomasochism—as potentially and actually full of tiresome, ritual repetitions and impossible, painful binds as of liberating and imaginative pleasures.

If popular culture is not a place but a name, such a (purely fanciful but deadly serious) distinction makes me recall the intoxicated words of Gilles Deleuze:

To say something in one's own name is very strange, for it is not at all when we consider ourselves as selves, persons or subjects that we speak in our own names. On the contrary, an individual acquires a true proper name as a result of the most severe operations of depersonalization, when he opens himself to multiplicities which pervade him and to intensities which run right through his whole being.[28]

In trying to return to the task of describing and bearing fair witness to that which is possibly unique (and even sublime) about popular culture, one path that offers itself is an imaginary journey or two through such 'severe operations of depersonalization'. For an individual, the act of becoming cultured—whether in high or low modes—has always necessitated some pretty rigorous, socially prescribed lessons about how to tell good objects from bad ones, how to identify texts, and one's own proper response to those texts. Tellingly, for McDonald (following Harold Rosenberg) the clear original sin of popular culture criticism is that it 'ducks the question of the quality of the object it is examining' and 'avoids making valuations'.[29]

This is perhaps the true sense in which the idea of popular culture can lay claim to an anti-authoritarianism: it is the name for that precious moment, that utopian space in which 'no one knows for certain which popular artworks are "good" and which "bad"'(Routt).[30]

Popular art is, by its mass-produced, often anonymous nature, a fugitive beast: more of it is lost than is ever reclaimed, and, without a canon to call its own, it perhaps comes most alive in the fleeting stories that are told about it, the critically engaged gestures that can light up this or that text as a site of sudden, furious importance.

Philip Brophy ends one of his articles on horror cinema with the statement that his writing is 'impelled by the belief that some of the films mentioned here—for good or for bad—will in the hopeful future be more widely recognized as illustrative of a sublime cinematic invention'.[31] Everything about this statement—the impulsion, the dream (against all likely odds) that culture at large will one day pick up on any of this, the invocation of sublimity, and especially the suspension of good and bad—indicates the sort of feverish, unearthly, liminal state from which perhaps the best and most vital popular culture criticism proceeds. Let the final judgment over good and bad fall tomorrow; let the officers of public culture come along for the ride or not as they please. Today, we speak in name of a phantom popular culture; we'll have to stick around to see whether, at the next turn, the best things about it have already been forgotten.

> The fable is profound, and without ostentation.
> Michel Serres on *The Adventures of Tintin: The Castafiore Emerald*[32]

NOTES

1 Elias Canetti, *The Tongue Set Free*, Picador, London, 1988, pp. 156–7.
2 In a letter to the *Sunday Herald* ('VCE's cultural cringe a perverse protectiveness', 10 March 1991), Dr Fredrick Toben proposed that the VCE curriculum is driven by a 'misplaced and perverse motherhood instinct', aiming to overprotect the disadvantaged from the hard slog of an 'academically demanding curriculum'.
3 *Sunday Herald*, 'Education: We Knew It Well' (Editorial), 3 March 1991.
4 Sylvia Lawson, 'Sorry, We Have Other Plans', *Australian Society*, January–February 1992, pp. 39–41.
5 Harry Oldmeadow, 'The Past Disowned: The Political and Postmodernist Assault on the Humanities', *Quadrant*, March 1992, pp. 60–5.
6 Kevin Donnelly, 'Students Lose Out on Cultural Heritage' (letter), *Sunday Herald*, 17 March 1991.
7 Thomas Elsaesser, 'Two Decades in Another Country: Hollywood and the Cinephiles', in *Superculture: American Popular Culture and Europe*, ed Bigsby, Bowling Green University Popular Press, 1975, p. 213.
8 *Sunday Herald*, 'Education: We Knew It Well'.
9 Jim Schembri, 'The Big Steal', *Cinema Papers* 81, December 1990, p. 53.
10 Robert Warshow, *The Immediate Experience: Movies, Comics, Theatre and Other Aspects of Popular Culture*, Athenium, New York, 1970.
11 David Will, '3 Gangster Films: An Introduction', in *Roger Corman: The Millenic Vision*, eds Will & Willemen, Edinburgh Film Festival, 1970, pp. 69, 71.

12 McKenzie Wark, 'Towards a Post-Pop Language', *Tension* 20, March 1990, p. 25.
13 William D Routt, 'The Hollywood Screenwriter', *Australian Journal of Screen Theory* 4, 1978, p. 15.
14 Routt, 'The Progress of Romance', *Arena* 83, Winter 1988, p. 171.
15 Raymond Durgnat, 'Nostalgia: Code and Anti-Code', *Wide Angle* Vol 4 No 4, 1981, p. 76.
16 Chris McAuliffe, 'Heresay & Heresy: An Interview with Greil Marcus', *Tension* 22, August–September 1990, p. 20.
17 John Fiske, 'Popular Discrimination', in *Modernity and Mass Culture*, eds Naremore & Brantlinger, Indiana University Press, Bloomington, 1991, p. 108.
18 John Docker, 'In Defence of Popular TV', *Continuum* Vol 1 No 2, 1988, p. 98.
19 William Paul, 'Charles Chaplin and the Annals of Anality', in *Comedy/Cinema/Theory*, ed Horton, University of California Press, 1991, p. 111.
20 RL Rutsky & Justin Wyatt, 'Serious Pleasures: Cinematic Pleasure and the Notion of Fun', *Cinema Journal* Vol 30 No 1, Fall 1990, pp. 3–19.
21 Cassandra Pybus quoted in Helen Trinca, 'A New Age for the Humanities?', *Weekend Australian*, 'Focus', 1–2 February 1992, p. 27.
22 John McDonald, 'Implosive Pops', *Age Monthly Review*, June 1985, p. 11.
23 Joanna Murray-Smith, article on *LA Law*, (Melbourne) *Age* 'Green Guide', 11 July 1991.
24 Philip Brophy, 'What Is This Thing Called "Disco"?', *Art & Text* 3, Spring 1981, p. 63.
25 TW Adorno, 'Something's Missing: A Discussion between Ernst Bloch and Theodor W. Adorno on the Contradictions of Utopian Longing', in Ernst Bloch, *The Utopian Function of Art and Literature: Selected Essays*, The MIT Press, Cambridge, Massachusetts, 1988, pp. 1–2.
26 P Brophy, *Trash & Junk Culture* (catalogue), Australian Centre for Contemporary Art, 1989, p. 10.
27 Meaghan Morris, 'Things To Do With Shopping Centres', in *Grafts*, ed S Sheridan, Verso, London, 1988, p. 197.
28 Gilles Deleuze, '"I Have Nothing to Admit"', *Semiotext(e)* II, 3, 1977, p. 113.
29 John McDonald, 'Implosive Pops', p. 11. The first phrase quoted is Rosenberg's.
30 William D Routt, 'Todorov Among the Gangsters', *Art & Text* 34, Spring 1989, p. 111.
31 P Brophy, 'The Body Horrible: Some Notions, Some Points, Some Examples', *Flesh: Intervention* 21/22, 1988, p. 67.
32 Michel Serres, 'Laughs: The Misappropriated Jewels, or a Close Shave for the Prima Donna', *Art & Text* 9, Autumn 1983, p. 14.

PART IV
The politics of publics

10
What's 'ethnographic' about ethnographic audience research?
VIRGINIA NIGHTINGALE

Cultural studies, in its current state of development, offers two overlapping methodological strategies that need to be combined, and the differences between them submerged, if we are to understand this cultural struggle. One derives from ethnography and requires us to study the meanings that the fans [of Madonna] actually do (or appear to) make [of her]. This involves listening to them, reading the letters they write to fan magazines, or observing their behavior at home or in public. The fans' words or behavior are not, of course, empirical facts that speak for themselves; they are, rather, texts that need 'reading' theoretically in just the same way as the 'texts of Madonna' do.

The other strategy derives from semiotic and structuralist textual analysis. This strategy involves a close reading of the signifiers of the text—that is, its physical presence—but recognizes that the signifieds exist not in the text itself, but extratextually, in the myths, countermyths, and ideology of their culture. It recognizes that the distribution of power in society is paralleled by the distribution of meanings in texts, and that struggles for social power are paralleled by semiotic struggles for meanings. Every text and every reading has a social and therefore political dimension, which is to be found partly in the structure of the text itself and partly in the relation of the reading subject to the text.

John Fiske, *Television Culture*[1]

I must confess to a perverse fascination with this quotation from Fiske's (1987) book, *Television Culture*. My fascination centres around both the understanding of 'cultural studies' presented and the terminology used to describe it. The *perversity* of my fascination, on the other hand, emanates from a sense of the impossibility of the task so glibly outlined, from a sense of horror at the breadth of the theoretical and

* This essay was first published in the *Australian Journal of Communication* 16 (December 1989).

methodological abyss such a project presents for the serious researcher, and from my own obstinate inability to ignore the contradictions inherent in the statement. The disquiet and bewilderment is intensified by the actual research Fiske calls on to corroborate his summary of the cultural studies project and in the gap between what is desired of the research and what is realised. This paper, then, grows out of a commitment to such a cultural studies project and to popular cultural research which recognises the importance of audience–text interactions. Nevertheless, the commitment to cultural studies is matched by an equal commitment, an obstinate commitment, to the necessity to consider the theoretical and methodological difficulties and implications of such research.

The developments in cultural studies to which Fiske refers above derive from two theoretical projects formulated in the 1970s by Stuart Hall: the research project encompassed by the encoding/decoding model and the marrying of the 'two paradigms of cultural studies', British Culturalism and the European structuralisms.[2] The research initiatives inspired by these projects reference other Cultural Studies projects, that is, the subcultures and deviance research of the late 1960s and early 1970s, as much as they reflect contemporary theoretical debates about texts, discourse, knowledge and power.

Four central characteristics of such cultural studies research are worth noting. Firstly, the research characteristically focuses on *texts*, and specifically on high-rating television programs or the more popular music videos as its objects of research, followed by a variety of attempts to 'read' the audience. Secondly, this body of research characteristically focuses on, and legitimates, the study of *popular culture*. In particular, it legitimates the study of the texts created, produced and distributed by multinational media companies as well as particular approaches to the study of the people who enjoy such commodities. Thirdly, the research usually recognises the importance of *discourse* as the form in which cultural meanings circulate, even though cultural studies researchers appear increasingly reluctant to pursue an *analysis* of such discourse.[3] And last, the research either claims, or has attributed to it, the quality *ethnographic*. It is with this last characteristic that I will deal in this paper, even though separating the *ethnographic* from issues of *text* and *discourse* may appear to minimise the complexity of each and the importance of the interaction of all four characteristics (issues which I have pursued elsewhere).[4]

The apparently simple formula (suggested by Fiske in the quotation above) of using semiotics to study texts and ethnography to study audiences depends for its coherence on a refusal to acknowledge the theoretical and methodological inadequacies inherent in the enterprise. Such inadequacies include:

• the possibility/impossibility of 'reading' the audience using ethnography.
• the lack of specificity as to the appropriate hermeneutic principles

required to analyse letters, transcripts of interviews, personal docu-ments and so on, compared to the sophistication of semiotic ap-proaches to the analysis of texts produced as cultural forms within institutionalised structures.

• the lack of any justification for treating letters (for example) differ-ently from television programs as texts.

• the lack of justification for 'reading' the accounts people give of their television-related practices at face value, with a crudity remi-niscent of the grossest content analysis, rather than with the sophisti-cation of semiotics, psychoanalysis, discourse analysis and the other 'cultural' research methods—methods which constitute the finest achievements of cultural studies over the last twenty years.

• the apparently absolute refusal to apply principles of 'readership', particularly those which stress the recognition that meaning is as much in the reader as in the text, to the reading of research 'texts' (as read by the researcher) such as interviews, letters, diaries and so on.

These inadequacies reflect a lack of resolution of two fundamental contradictions inherent in such research—contradictions about where the meaning of a text is likely to be found and contradictions about the nature of 'ethnography' and what the researchers expect of it.

The first contradiction stems from a lack of resolution of the problem of textual meaning—the supposition that the text can stand alone, separate from its 'readers', in order to be 'read' semiotically, while at the same time being dependent on readers for its meaning. This is the fundamental contradiction which surfaced in Morley's 1980 study of *Nationwide*'s audience[5]—the problem of matching two sets of in-commensurable readings: the disciplined reading of the researchers[6] with the 'unschooled' reading of the casual viewer. In this case the meaning of the text, *Nationwide*, is considered commensurate with the reading produced by the researchers, an assumption which is in itself tenuous. Preferring to interview fans rather than casual viewers (a solution to this problem chosen by several of the studies mentioned below) fails to solve this dilemma, for what is needed is some analysis of how the program schools/teaches its 'fan' viewers to read sym-pathetically—fans, by definition, *always* read sympathetically and actively—as well as some criteria to distinguish between the readings of fans and casual viewers. While Buckingham[7] has made a start on this problem in his application of Iser's reader-response theory to the analysis of the textual invitations offered by *EastEnders*, the task is far from complete.

The second contradiction, the one on which I will focus for the rest of this paper, involves the audience, and specifically the suggestion that it is possible to 'read' an audience *ethnographically*. The contra-diction for 'ethnographic' audience research seems here to be based in a confusion between 'ethnography' and 'interpretive anthropology', a confusion of the descriptive and classificatory work of ethnography with the interpretive work possible once cultures are seen as metaphors for texts.[8] Within cultural studies for example, this contradiction can be seen in the failure to distinguish between the 'ethnography' of Paul Willis[9] which applies 'ethnography to projects of broader purpose and theoretical significance'[10] and the 'interpretive anthropology' of Dick Hebdige[11] which draws more directly on the structuralist theories and methods of Lévi-Strauss. The audience 'ethnographies' produced in encoding/decoding research follow Willis in the use of naturalist research methods[12] but refrain from sharing his focus on broad social process, and stop short of the interpretive work needed to 'read' the audience. In this sense the studies are unfortunately compromised, drawing on interpretive procedures to understand the texts around which the audience clusters and on descriptive measures only to account for the audience. Such an account must be a non-account.

What, then, is 'ethnographic' about ethnographic audience research? Is 'ethnographic' an appropriate description for research of this type? In attempting to answer this question, I will refer to research carried out about five popular television programs: *Nationwide* (Brunsdon and Morley 1978; and Morley 1980);[13] *Crossroads* (Hobson 1982);[14] *Dallas* (Ang 1985);[15] *A Country Practice* (Tulloch and Moran 1986);[16] and *EastEnders* (Buckingham 1987).[17] Morley, Ang and Hobson are all cited by Fiske[18] as examples of the use of ethnography to carry out audience research. These studies use, among them, a combination of research methods which include participant observation (Hobson; Tulloch and Moran), group interviews (Morley; Tulloch and Moran; Buckingham), letters solicited by the researcher (Ang) or written (unsolicited) to newspapers or television channels (Hobson; Tulloch and Moran), as well as informal discussions with students (Tulloch and Moran). In each case the audience component of the research complements an extensive commitment to description/explanation of the television program. In the work of both Hobson and Tulloch and Moran the work on the television program is based in participant observation, and is every bit as 'ethnographic' in character as the audience research, but for some reason seldom actually described as such.

The description of such work as 'ethnographic' describes its research techniques rather than its research strategy. The use of participant observation, observation, interviews, group interviews, personal documents are all included among the naturalistic techniques of ethnography. While the research techniques are ethnographic, the research strategy is not. Marcus and Fischer have defined ethnography as:

> A research process in which the anthropologist closely observes, records, and engages in the daily life of another culture—an experience labelled as the fieldwork method—and then writes accounts of this culture, emphasising descriptive detail. These accounts are the primary form in which fieldwork procedures, the other culture, and the ethnographer's personal and theoretical reflections are accessible to professionals and other readerships.[19]

Clearly there are differences between this definition and the 'ethnography' of the above studies. Firstly, they do not set out to provide an account of an 'other' culture; secondly, in many of them the only contact with the 'other culture' is an interview or the reading of a letter. Indeed the senses in which the mass audience, or parts of it, can be seen as an 'other culture' are also tenuous. At their most 'other', the participants in the above research may be described as 'working class', but in several instances (such as Morley and Ang) even this distinction does not hold. The relationship between the researcher and researched is foregrounded as problematic once the term 'ethnography' is used to describe it. In this sense, the very use of the term acts as a reminder of the differences (of class, education, religion, gender, age etc) between them, differences which are often unacknowledged, especially when the researcher is of equal or lower status than the researched, as where television executives or production personnel are concerned. Similarly, a singular lack of commitment to 'recording' or to the provision of 'descriptive detail' is evident. Transcripts of interview, accounts of interaction, are substituted for descriptive detail—in the case of group interviews or household interviews, little time is spent describing where the interview is held, whether the interviewees are interested in the discussion or not, or what interactions (verbal or non-verbal) take place within the group in deciding who will speak for the group or how the group responds to what is said on its behalf.

What occurs, then, in the absence of rigorous ethnographic observation and description, when the techniques of ethnography are divorced from ethnographic process, is a co-opting of the interviewee's experience of the text by the researcher, and its use as authority for the researcher's point of view. This can best be described as a disproportionate reliance on the authenticating quality of ethnographic data, a reliance which can be argued to constitute what Rosaldo has described as 'the false ethnographic authority of polyphony',[20] in which the researchers' voices and the voices of their interviewees are equally heard, and yet which demonstrates no sensitivity to the power relations or to the cultural differences which operate when the data is obtained. In both the *Crossroads* and *EastEnders* studies, for example, there is an openly stated denial of the possibility that such factors could influence the research. The quality of the relationship between researcher and interviewee is sometimes even claimed to overcome such methodological problems.[21] The problem then is to account for the determination with which writers such as Fiske (above) describe this body of research as 'ethnographic'.

THE ETHNOGRAPHIC CONVENTION

Since description of the studies as 'ethnographic' cannot be justified by the nature of the research actually undertaken, other reasons for the use of the term must exist. One possibility is that the application of the descriptor 'ethnographic' to these studies has acquired conventional status within cultural studies as the way of referring to the empirical audience research undertaken within the field. Accordingly, the term is used not to classify the research as belonging to, or even as having any links with, ethnography, but to signify the allegiance of the research to the academic heritage, cultural studies. The term 'ethnographic' possesses connotations which include *cultural, community-based, empirical,* and *phenomenal,* all of which can legitimately be applied to the encoding/decoding studies. The term 'ethnographic' can then be a way of talking about research which possesses *these* characteristics, but which is also defined by its difference from 'cultural' research which possesses *other* characteristics, such as textual studies and perhaps even psychoanalytic studies. The encoding/decoding studies can be seen as an attempt by cultural studies to colonise a new realm, the realm of audience research. In this respect the term 'ethnographic' acts to legitimate the research, to denote its cultural, phenomenal and empirical methods, and even to signify its emphasis on 'community'.

The problem is that the term 'ethnography' has other lives. It has a life within the discipline of anthropology and a life within the research traditions of symbolic interactionism, both of which affect the ways in which the encoding/decoding research is enacted and evaluated. These other lives of the term 'ethnographic' provide both historical and theoretical links with the past of cultural studies, with its past triumphs as well as its failures. The other lives of 'ethnographic' also suggest possibilities for an 'ethnographic' future for cultural studies, especially since the discipline of anthropology, particularly interpretive anthropology, is currently appropriating many of the theoretical insights from literary studies which 'met' in cultural studies in the 1970s.[22]

USING 'ETHNOGRAPHIC' TO EVOKE THE 'CULTURAL STUDIES' PAST

A second reason for using the term 'ethnographic' may therefore be motivated by a desire to retain something, be something, achieve something it does not (at least not yet). The case for the use of the term as an attempt to 'retain' something from the past of cultural studies is obvious. During the 1970s cultural studies was characterised by intense interest in subcultures and deviance, and drew on the 'ethnographic' research methods popularised by symbolic interactionism to pursue its ends. The term 'ethnography' was used to refer to symbolic interactionist methods,[23] as it is still by symbolic interactionists.[24] The use of these 'naturalistic' methods, derived from ethnography and applied to modern society, suited the reformist agenda of the deviance research and its critique of capitalist processes of exploitation and domination, as demonstrated in Willis's *Learning to Labour.*[25] It is in Willis's work that this 'ethnographic' heritage comes close to producing the sort of 'social realist' research advocated by Williams.[26]

To this British culturalist research heritage identified by Williams and evident in Willis's work, other researchers such as Hebdige[27] added structuralist, interpretive techniques. The combination of these heritages has shaken the symbolic interactionist underpinnings of cultural studies (as cultural studies researchers such as Willis had always argued it must)[28] and led to the ascendance of literary and structuralist approaches—the interpretive paradigm—instead. The meeting of these two research heritages has not been achieved without struggle. Yet it is worth noting that the struggle between the two, characterised as a struggle between culturalism and structuralism by Hall,[29] has now been played out in many of the social sciences. The most recent example is anthropology, where exploration of the implications for ethnographic practice of 'textual criticism, cultural history, semiotics, hermeneutic philosophy, and psychoanalysis'[30] is under way. A similar process has affected the practice of archaeology.[31] In each case what began as a critique of practice has ended in a more rigorous concentration on texts, a revaluation of hermeneutic as opposed to positivist social science practices, and a greater tolerance of relativism.

In cultural studies during the mid- and late 1970s, the interpretive revolution resulted in an almost exclusive concentration on media texts. The study of media audiences, however, 'belonged' to positivist social science. The 'ethnographic' tradition of cultural studies had for the most part focused on how the media exploited subcultural groups or appropriated and neutralised their resistance to the dominant culture. This approach was constructed in diametrical opposition to positivist and mainstream audience research which presupposed an 'administrative' perspective,[32] and presumed the purpose of audience research to be the management of audiences. It was the hiatus between the phenomenological orientation of subcultural research and the administrative orientation of mainstream audience research which promised to be remedied by an encoding/decoding attempt to understand audiences. Using the term 'ethnographic' to describe this research initiative asserts a continuity between the encoding/decoding studies and the earlier subcultural research, even though the encoding/decoding studies are text-centred not subculture-centred. That desired continuity, which the encoding/decoding studies have so far failed to demonstrate, is for a quality of research which allows the particular cultural experiences of broadcast television viewers to be understood in the context of communication in capitalist society.

The work of Paul Willis[33] is still widely regarded as the model for the cultural studies ethnographic method, and it is currently being cited as the direction for cultural studies reception research,[34] for symbolic interactionist 'cultural' research[35] and as challenging the anthropological tradition of ethnography to undertake broader and more critical research appropriate to the conditions of the modern world order.[36] What Willis's work offers, as Marcus points out, is a demonstration that the cultural (in Willis's case, capitalist society) defines the particular (school non-conformity and labour conformity). Willis achieves this not by a positivist attempt to prove Marxist theory by his observations, but by invoking Marxist theory as given. As Marcus again points out, Willis's purpose is achieved by the exploration of 'the cultural meanings of the production of labour and commodity fetishism' which 'provides textual means for bringing the larger order into the space of ethnography'.[37] Willis's adherence to the notion of cultural totality, to the structuralist project of reading the culture *in* its forms—the legacy of Raymond Williams—is seen by Marcus as a positive achievement for anthropology emerging from Willis's work. As Marcus puts it:

> Nonetheless, Willis does pose the challenge for the anthropological tradition of ethnography, underlain perhaps by an unattainable ideal of holism not to be taken literally, to apply ethnography to projects of broader purpose and theoretical significance, like his own. This entails the writing of mixed genre texts, similar to those envisioned by Raymond Williams for social realism, in which ethnographic representation and authority would be a variably salient component.[38]

TECHNIQUE VERSUS STRATEGY

Nevertheless, if a continuity is *assumed* between the 'ethnographic' practice of Willis and the 'mixed-genre texts' of Morley, Hobson, Ang, Tulloch and Moran, and Buckingham, crucial differences *between* them may be overlooked; for while encoding/decoding audience research uses the same research techniques as Willis, its practitioners' research strategies are quite different. Willis's aim was to demonstrate the working of social process, to explain cultural reproduction through the interlocking of education and the labour process. This type of broad social aim, with its singularity of focus, is missing from the encoding/decoding studies, which concentrate on several, and more limited, aims such as explaining the popularity of the text,[39] teaching about British cultural studies,[40] or demonstrating the operations by which pleasure is encoded in the text.[41] The encoding/decoding studies use their 'ethnographic' data to achieve textually defined aims rather than to explain social process. Their strategy, characteristically, involves a multi-focus approach. They use whatever observations, participant observation, interviews (individual and group), personal, commercial and/or public documents are available, all of which address some aspects of the broad range of issues which litter the field of popular culture research. The choice of research foci is usually eclectic, drawing on the personal interests of the researcher.

For example, Hobson's strategy involves interviews with and observation of selected personnel involved in the production of *Crossroads*, participant observation (viewing the program with women viewers), examination of letters written to the local press when changes to the program were proposed, interviews with representatives of the profession and the Independent Broadcasting Authority, and the use of television criticism from the daily press.[42] Tulloch and Moran use a broad array of interviews and observations as they follow the sequence of 'performances' of the program which culminate in its final performance by the audience.[43] The notion of 'text as performance' operates as a uniting theme, but is weak as a critique of popular culture. Ang tries to infer ideological approaches to reading popular cultural texts from a small number of letters about *Dallas*, taking up themes such as textual pleasure, feminism and popular culture, and the concepts of 'tragic structure of feelings' and 'melodramatic imagination' directly from textually oriented theory.[44] Buckingham uses interviews with the producers of *EastEnders*, programming executives, BBC audience research findings, interviews with groups of children about the program, a textual analysis based on Wolfgang Iser's theory of textual invitations, newspaper coverage and observation of public sector interest groups.[45] A recurrent trope in all of the research is the disparagement of the audience and the contempt for the text which is alleged to characterise television criticism, even after ten years of academic work to legitimate the study of popular cultural texts. Even though the research uses the techniques of 'ethnographic' research advocated by Willis, it is vastly different in its strategies, which so far fail to offer a satisfying critique of popular culture.

The problem is compounded in that the ethnographic strategy outlined by Willis does not address the problem of reading complex cultural forms like popular television programs in their particularity. Reading the significance of the signs of a subculture (dress, argot, behaviour, rituals) and its relation to the cultural totality is qualitatively different from reading television and from reading people's readings of television. The direct communal authorship of the signs of a subculture is qualitatively different from the highly institutionalised, conventionalised and commercially motivated production of television. The relationship of the community to the televisual cultural form is one of appropriation rather than authorship; an appropriation of ideas authored by agents of discursive formations, as Turner has noted, an appropriation in which the operation of 'bricolage' is much more complexly articulated than in the appropriation of other objects.[46] The professionalisation of television production and the complexity of the text as appropriated object (appropriated by the audience, that is) place constraints on the reading of such appropriation which demand more sophisticated techniques of analysis than those offered by ethnography. The things people say about television cry out, I suggest, for innovative approaches to discourse analysis combined with the now familiar 'ethnographic' techniques.

MIXED-GENRE RESEARCH

Even though the presence of the ethnographic convention in cultural studies research seems more nostalgic than progressive, other aspects of this embryonic research tradition constitute an innovation in cultural research practice. If the encoding/decoding studies are seen as first attempts at mixed-genre research, research which integrates the study of audience discourse and data obtained from audience observation with qualitatively different observations and materials about television texts, production, distribution and industries, the value of the work is better appreciated.

As mixed-genre research, the work establishes an elaboration of the 'triangulation' strategy. The use of triangulation strategies is advocated when 'the nature of the problem under investigation demands a multi-method approach'. It is a characteristic of community studies, as I have argued this research to be.[47] As Gorden puts it:

> Community studies must triangulate information from public records, personal documents, newspapers, direct interviews with the focal persons, participant-observation, and pure observation merely to obtain the many types of information needed to cover the complex phenomenon we call a community. Experimental studies, naturalistic communities studies, and statistical surveys can be fruitfully combined in many instances.[48]

The encoding/decoding model suggested discourse as the uniting focus of such triangulation, but the focus on the 'discursive form of the message', and even any notion of message, has been progressively discarded and the focus of the research, its critical edge, thus lost. The central focus, for example, in the *Nationwide* studies was on the ideology of the program and its reflection in the verbal discourse of the audience. This centrality of focus gave way in the subsequent studies to more disjointed research strategies, leading to a lack of coherence in the research, as Craik has noted.[49] The value of the attempts at triangulation in the studies was thus dissipated and, as is perhaps most obvious in the *EastEnders* research, the research focus fluctuates from explaining the popularity of the program to justifying the interpretive 'work' of the audience and providing background information for teaching about the program in school. In the *Dallas* research, by contrast, the focus is more firmly held on the 'pleasure' of *Dallas*, yet in this case the empirical research is slight (consisting of only forty-two letters, which are not analysed as texts) and coupled with attempts to combine the letters and the program through theoretical exegesis and description of current trends in feminism. Once again the sense in which the study coheres is tenuous, and the focus fluctuates between explaining the processes by which *Dallas* is experienced as 'pleasure', and justifying feminine and feminist interest in the programs, as well as teaching about the program.

The multiple foci of these studies, then, are used to justify the study of popular culture, to teach (often both students and the general public) about the mass media, to validate the mass television audience (or sections of it) and its interest in such programs, rather than to engage in cultural critique or analysis. In all the studies (except Morley),[50] the ethnographic initiative is not the central research strategy but is used only to validate the production and textual research initiatives. While the research does pioneer writing for multiple audiences, it falls short of offering any critique of cultural practice, either of production or of reception. In this sense it contrasts with the strong attraction of similar research in anthropology. Marcus and Fischer correctly identify such writing within anthropology as experimentation which is likely to re-vitalise academic practice. As they put it:

> Writing single texts with multiple voices exposed within them, as well as with multiple readerships explicitly in mind, is perhaps the sharpest spur to the contemporary experimental impulse in anthropological writing, both as ethnography and as cultural critique.[51]

Needless to say, this position is proposed within the context of discussion of structured research strategies such as 'cross-cultural juxtapositioning'. In this regard, it seems the encoding/decoding studies have new lessons to learn from anthropology.

While the central concern of the encoding/decoding studies remains the account of the text, and while the diversity of the research focus is centred around a particular television program, rather than around a critique of audience–text bonding, we will continue to produce writing about such programs which situates the research more as apologia than as critique. It is time to look again at anthropology and at ethnographic research techniques, to re-evaluate their use in cultural studies audience research both as a heritage and as a future direction. It is time to learn our lessons from the pioneering work which has been done and to develop strategies for cultural critique which provoke critical appraisal while retaining respect for and appreciation of the popular texts which accompany and orchestrate our lives.

NOTES

1 J Fiske, *Television Culture*, Methuen, London and New York, 1987, p. 272.
2 S Hall, 'Encoding/Decoding' in *Culture, Media, Language*, eds S Hall et al, Hutchinson, London, 1980; 'Cultural Studies: Two Paradigms', *Media, Culture and Society* 1980, 2, pp. 57–72.
3 See especially J Tulloch and A Moran, *A Country Practice: Quality Soap*, Currency Press, Sydney, 1986; and D Buckingham, *Public Secrets: Eastenders and Its Audience*, BFI, London, 1987.
4 V Nightingale, 'Researching People as Audiences: The Cultural Studies Experiment', PhD thesis, Macquarie University.
5 D Morley, *The 'Nationwide' Audience: Structure and Decoding*, BFI, London, 1980.
6 See C Brunsdon & D Morley, *Everyday Television: 'Nationwide'*, BFI, London, 1978.
7 Op. cit. (note 3).
8 See GE Marcus & MMJ Fischer, *Anthropology as Cultural Critique: An Experimental Moment in the Human Sciences*, University of Chicago Press, Chicago, 1986, pp. 17–44.

9 Paul Willis, *Learning to Labour: How Working Class Kids Get Working Class Jobs*, Gower Publishing, Aldershot, 1977.

10 GE Marcus, 'Contemporary Problems of Ethnography in the Modern World System' in *Writing Culture: The Poetics and Politics of Ethnography*, eds J Clifford & GE Marcus, University of California Press, Berkeley, 1986, p. 188.

11 D Hebdige, *Subculture: The Meaning of Style*, Methuen, London and New York, 1979.

12 See B Roberts, 'Naturalistic Research into Subcultures and Deviance' in *Resistance through Rituals*, eds S Hall & T Jefferson, Hutchinson and CCCS, University of Birmingham, London and Birmingham, 1975.

13 Brunsdon & Morley, op. cit. (note 6); Morley op. cit. (note 5).

14 D Hobson, *Crossroads: The Drama of a Soap Opera*, Methuen, London, 1982.

15 I Ang, *Watching Dallas: Soap Opera and the Melodramatic Imagination*, Methuen, London and New York, 1985.

16 Tulloch & Moran, op. cit. (note 3).

17 Buckingham, op. cit. (note 3).

18 Fiske, op. cit. (note 1).

19 Marcus & Fischer, op. cit. (note 8), p. 18.

20 R Rosaldo, 'From the Door of His Tent: The Fieldworker and the Inquisitor' in *Writing Culture: The Poetics and Politics of Ethnography*, eds J Clifford & GE Marcus, University of California Press, Berkeley, 1986 p. 82.

21 Hobson, op. cit. (note 14), p. 107; Buckingham op. cit. (note 3), pp. 158–9.

22 See J Clifford & GE Marcus (eds), *Writing Culture: The Poetics and Politics of Ethnography*, University of California Press, Berkeley, 1986.

23 See G Pearson & J Twohig, 'Ethnography through the Looking Glass: The Case of Howard Becker' in *Resistance through Rituals*, eds S Hall & T Jefferson, Hutchinson and CCCS, University of Birmingham, London and Birmingham, 1975; B Roberts, op. cit. (note 12); P Willis, 'Notes on Method' in *Culture, Media, Language*, eds S Hall et al, Hutchinson, London, 1980/1976; R Grimshaw et al, 'Introduction to Ethnography at the Centre', in *Culture, Media, Language*, 1980.

24 See E Wartella, 'Commentary on Qualitative Research and Children's Mediated Communication' in *Natural Audiences: Qualitative Research of Media Uses and Effects*, ed TR Lindlof, Ablex, Norwood NJ, 1987.

25 Willis, op. cit. (note 9).

26 Marcus & Fischer, op. cit. (note 8), pp. 77, 78.

27 Hebdige, op. cit. (note 11).

28 Willis, op. cit. (note 23); Grimshaw et al, op. cit. (note 23).

29 Hall, 'Cultural Studies', op. cit. (note 2).

30 J Clifford, 'Introduction: Partial Truths' in Clifford & Marcus, op. cit. (note 22), p. 4.

31 I Hodder, *Reading the Past: Current Approaches to Interpretation in Archaeology*, Cambridge University Press, Cambridge, 1986.

32 T Gitlin, 'Media Sociology: The Dominant Paradigm', *Theory and Society* 6, 1978, pp. 205–53.

33 See, especially, op. cit. (note 9).

34 D Morley & R Silverstone, 'Domestic Communication—Technologies and Meanings', Paper presented to the International Television Studies Conference, London, July 1988.

35 P Traudt & C Lont, 'Media-Logic-in-Use: The Family as Locus of Study' in *Natural Audiences: Qualitative Research of Media Uses and Effects*, ed TR Lindlof, Ablex, Norwood NJ, 1987, pp. 144, 159.

36 Marcus, op. cit. (note 10).
37 Ibid, p. 173.
38 Ibid, p. 188.
39 Hobson, op. cit. (note 14); Tulloch & Moran, op. cit. (note 3).
40 Ang, op. cit. (note 15).
41 Ang, op. cit. (note 15); Buckingham op. cit. (note 3).
42 Hobson, op. cit. (note 14).
43 Tulloch & Moran, op. cit. (note 3).
44 Ang, op. cit. (note 15).
45 Buckingham, op. cit. (note 3).
46 V Turner, 'Frame, Flow and Reflection: Ritual and Drama as Public Liminality' in *Performance in Postmodern Culture*, eds M Benamou & C Caramello, Coda Press, Madison Wisconsin, 1977.
47 Nightingale, op. cit. (note 4).
48 RL Gorden, *Interviewing: Strategy, Techniques and Tactics* (4th edn), Dorsey Press, Chicago, 1987, p. 12.
49 J Craik, 'Soft Soap', *Australian Left Review* 102 (Nov/Dec 1987), pp. 34–7.
50 Morley, op. cit. (note 5).
51 Marcus & Fischer, op. cit. (note 8), p. 163.

11
Invisible fictions
JOHN HARTLEY

Although television as an institution is dependent upon audiences, it is by no means certain what a television audience is.

However, it seems that this is not the only uncertainty facing those working in the field of television studies. Ann Kaplan, for instance, in her introduction to *Regarding Television*, remarks:

> The structure, form, content and context for British television are so radically different from those of its American counterpart that everything has to be rethought by critics in this country [the US]. Television scholarship is simply not exportable in the easy manner of film criticism.[1]

The idea that international television criticism is a contradiction in terms is not confined to the US side of the Atlantic. In fact it has been taken even further by British writer John Ellis, who suggests not only that television scholarship is unexportable but also that one nation's television is 'incomprehensible' to observers from other nations. In the preliminaries to his *Visible Fictions* Ellis confesses that at the time of writing he had never visited the United States, and continues:

> This really demonstrates an insuperable problem with all writing about broadcast TV: unlike cinema, which in its commercial sectors has a highly integrated international aspect, broadcast TV is an essentially national ac-

* This article also appears as Chapter 6 of John Hartley's 1992 collection, *Tele-ology: Studies in Television*, Routledge, London and New York. It was first published as 'Invisible Fictions: Television Audiences, Paedocracy, Pleasure', *Textual Practice*, 1, 2 (Spring 1987), pp. 121–38; published in the US in *Television Studies: Textual Analysis*, eds Robert J Thompson & Gary Burns, Praeger, New York, 1989.

tivity for the vast majority of its audience. Broadcast TV is the private life
of the nation-state . . . incomprehensible for anyone who is outside its scope.[2]

Neither Kaplan nor Ellis qualifies these remarks with customary
scholarly caution. Both write in absolute terms: television is incomprehensible for those outside its scope; television criticism is simply
not exportable; everything has to be rethought; the problem is
insuperable; it applies to all writing about broadcast television; television is essentially national. Furthermore, their remarks are not
isolated. Quite a lot of media criticism in recent years has been conducted around a perceived gulf, as wide as the Atlantic Ocean, between
North American and Anglo-European perspectives.[3] This gulf, once
invoked, is made to explain such divisions as those between empirical
and theoretical approaches; so-called transmission and ritual models
of communication; liberal-pluralist and Marxist theories; even the disciplinary location of media studies—in North America it's a social
science, in Britain it's in the humanities.

If these divisions really constitute an insuperable problem, then of
course international television scholarship does become impossible.
Or, more accurately, the kind of criticism that constructs as its object
an *essential* form, on the model of 'cinema' or 'literature', becomes
impossible. What the uncertainties noted above do imply is that there
is no such thing as 'television'—an abstract, general form with in-
variable features. Neither does television have any *essential* mode of
production, distribution and consumption, despite the very obvious
fact that many television shows, series and formats display exactly
that 'highly integrated international aspect' claimed by Ellis for cinema.

As for television studies, a certain uneasiness with the erection of
essential, national boundaries around television scholarship has been
voiced by Willard Rowland and Bruce Watkins in their introduction
to *Interpreting Television*. They discuss 'this old and contentious issue',
largely with reference to a myth of US 'dependence' on European
thought, and show that, although that dependence is mythical, the
consequences of reiterating the myth have been real enough. They
argue that, although it is tempting, it is inadequate to categorise current
research by means of a 'bipolar, European/critical versus American/
liberal dichotomy'. They conclude that 'it is becoming increasingly
difficult to speak about any pure national or even regional tradition
of thought, especially in communication and cultural studies'.[4] If it
is indeed difficult to speak of pure national traditions of thought in
this context, it may be easier, certainly more productive, to speak of
impurity. It may even be possible to see in impurities not a problem
but a fundamental criterion for cultural studies.

The productivity of impurity, of transgressing national boundaries
unawares, has been amply illustrated, paradoxically enough, by John
Ellis. Having erected pure—insuperable—boundaries between British
and US television, and between British and US writing on television,
he then subverts this line of thinking completely:

Sudden exposure to the often bizarre practices of broadcast TV in another country can stimulate fresh thinking about the whole phenomenon of TV. This is the case with Raymond Williams's concept of 'flow' which resulted from his culture shock on seeing US TV. Seeing another country's broadcast TV has the effect of 'making strange' something we normally take for granted: TV, normally habitual and bound into the life of the nation, suddenly becomes an alien and inexplicable series of events.[5]

Thus, transgressing the frontiers of the familiar, the national, produces culture shock, the bizarre, the alien, the inexplicable—which turns out to be the very condition for understanding, stimulating fresh thinking by breaking habitual bonds. Even so, it has to be noted that some bonds remain taken for granted: Ellis is still presuming that there is such a thing as 'the whole phenomenon' of television, in the teeth of his own evidence to the contrary.

TELEVISION: ANOTHER COUNTRY?

Since the concept of the nation seems to play such an important role in specifying both television and TV scholarship, it would seem to be a good idea to look at what the concept of the nation might mean. However, it wouldn't be such a good idea to substitute for the essentialism of 'television' another kind of essentialism, for instance, the notion of an essential 'America', or 'Britain', or 'Australia', or even 'the nation'. Nations cannot be understood 'purely'—that is, from their own supposed intrinsic or essential features. Neither television nor nations can be understood at all, in fact, except in relational terms. They have no pure, intrinsic properties but only differences from other, related domains. Benedict Anderson has argued that they are by definition limited or impure, because each nation is defined by *other* nations:

> Even the largest of them, encompassing perhaps a billion living human beings, has finite, if elastic boundaries, beyond which lie other nations. No nation imagines itself coterminous with mankind [sic]. The most messianic nationalists do not dream of the day when all the members of the human race will join their nation in the way that it was possible, in certain epochs, for, say, Christians to dream of a wholly Christian planet.[6]

It follows that nations can only be defined by what they are not; their individual identity consists in the recognition and establishment of finite boundaries that are simultaneously elastic. This formula generates a well-known definition not only of nations but also of signs; like signs, nations are constructs. But, like signs, nations are constructs not of any external, referential world but of *discourses*: Anderson calls nations 'imagined communities'. They are communities because everyone has confidence in the existence of others within their nation; they are imagined because there is absolutely no external warrant for this confidence:

An American will never meet, or even know the names of more than a handful of his 240 000 000-odd fellow Americans. He has no idea of what they are up to at any one time. But he has complete confidence in their steady, anonymous, simultaneous activity.[7]

Where does this confidence come from? Among other sources, Anderson mentions the newspaper as a mechanism for providing imaginary links between members of a nation. Newspapers are at one and the same time the ultimate fiction, since they construct the imagined community, and the basis of a mass ritual or ceremony that millions engage in every day: 'What more vivid figure for the secular, historically clocked, imagined community can be envisioned?' asks Anderson.[8] Of course, a more vivid metaphorical figure for the imagined communities of nations can indeed be envisioned. It's called television. Like newspapers, television may be more than merely a metaphor for imagined communities; it is one of the prime sites upon which a given nation is constructed for its members. And, as we have seen, the nation is, concomitantly, one of the sites upon which television has been constructed as a concept.

Like nations, television as an institution is limited, impure, with no essence but only difference from other television, other forms, other institutions. Nevertheless, television does frequently transgress national boundaries—the idea of its essential national-ity is as imagined, or fictional, as the idea of the nation itself. Certain program types, especially sporting championships, Olympic Games, news pictures, beauty and other contests, award ceremonies within the general showbiz domain, together with the more recent genre of 'aid' shows, may be seen more or less simultaneously by hundreds of millions of people, sometimes making it possible for producers to dream, as it were, of a wholly tuned-in planet. As well, television transgresses national frontiers in more routine ways, notably at the level of transnational ownership and control of both production and distribution, and at the level of international sales of individual shows and series. It follows that if television can be imagined as an 'essentially national activity', as Ellis puts it, it can only be so imagined on behalf of the experience of audiences: the audience is constructed as comprising those for whom television is indeed the 'private life of the nation-state'. In short, one unwarranted, invisible fiction—the imagined community of the nation—is used to invent and explain another: the television audience.

INVISIBLE FICTIONS

Television is, like nations, a construct of specific institutions; what it 'means' turns on how those institutional discourses construct it for their own specific purposes. Among the institutions that construct television discursively, three stand out: the television industry (network, stations, producers, etc); political/legal institutions (usually formalised as regulatory bodies, and intermittently as government-sponsored inquiries and reports); and critical institutions (academic, journalistic and—surprisingly rarely—self-constituted audience organisations or pressure groups). Each of these institutions is, of course, marked by internal contradictions, hierarchies and historical shifts, and by manifold differences from each of the others. However, despite the fact that they don't speak with one voice, all three tend to legitimate their actions and interventions in the name of the same imagined community. All claim to speak, albeit with quite different voices, on behalf of the audience.

It follows that audiences are not just constructs; they are the invisible fictions that are produced institutionally in order for various institutions to take charge of the mechanisms of their own survival. Audiences may be imagined empirically, theoretically or politically, but in all cases the product is a fiction that serves the need of the imagining institution. In no case is the audience 'real', or external to its discursive construction. There is no 'actual' audience that lies beyond its production as a category, which is merely to say that audiences are only ever encountered *per se* as *representations*. Furthermore, they are so rarely *self*-represented that they are almost always absent, making TV audiences perhaps the largest 'community' in the world that is subject to what Edward Said has dubbed the discourse of 'orientalism',[9] whereby disorganised communities which have never developed or won adequate means of self-representation, and which exist almost wholly within the imagination or rhetoric of those who speak on their behalf, become the 'other' of powerful, imperial discourses.[10]

What kind of fiction is the orientalised audience imagined to be? In the critical domain, two influential recent developments in the theoretical conceptualisation of audiences are noteworthy. The first, elaborated in relation to cinema and associated largely with the journal *Screen* in the seventies, is applied by John Ellis to television. Here the audience is imagined as 'the subject', positioned or constructed as a textual/institutional effect of television. However, Ellis's 'viewer' is far from being an effect of television; Ellis's viewer is an effect of Ellis's stated project, which is to produce an argument about the general aesthetics of broadcast television in comparison with those of cinema. Ellis is preoccupied with the idea that television has, or might have, a 'specific signifying practice', and that such a thing is what unifies television. Hence the argument is driven, ineluctably it seems, to imagining a unified viewer to go with this unified signifying practice:

> The viewer is constituted as a normal citizen. This is the position constructed for the TV viewer by the processes of broadcast TV; many viewers occupy the very position which TV addresses, even if they would never consider themselves to be such a strange being as a normal citizen.[11]

A strange being indeed, and one produced by that totally unwarranted confidence in the existence of the nation noted above. Indeed, Ellis's viewer is imagined as coterminous with the ideal bearer of the concept of the nation: the 'normal citizen'. Not content with imagining the 'normal citizen' as a fictional construct or textual position produced by television's signifying practice, however, Ellis then asserts (on their behalf, without consultation) that 'many viewers occupy [this] very position'. Thus Ellis's viewer is an invisible fiction, a construct that is a figment of the argument's imagination.

The second influential recent approach to audiences is that of David Morley in and following his study *The 'Nationwide' Audience*. Morley's work was ground-breaking when it appeared, offering the hope of integrating theoretical approaches such as those of *Screen* and the Centre for Contemporary Cultural Studies in Birmingham, in their different ways, with the more traditional concerns of empirical audience research. Thus, although Morley is astute and convincing in his account of theoretical issues, his work retains a commitment to an 'actual' audience that—the research paradigm *requires* it—is an independent entity. Empirical research is based on the presumption that audiences are not merely the product of research into them but exist prior to, apart from and beyond the activities of both television and television research. Unlike Ellis, but like traditional audience researchers, Morley sets off in search of the audience. Unlike traditional researchers, however, he tramps the country seeking not preferences, attitudes, opinions and tastes but the relation between television and class. Thus he seeks his audience among already-constituted groups which he feels able to identify in class terms—groups of students taking courses in various kinds of educational establishment. The shop stewards, trade union officials, bank managers, apprentices and students of various other kinds are described in terms of their class 'background', though no warrant is ever offered for the very precise labels Morley uses. He never explains how he distinguishes between, for instance, 'skilled working class', 'skilled upper working class', 'upper working class', and 'working class'.[12] The fact that some of his chosen groups were unfamiliar with the chosen show (*Nationwide*), because he showed them a different regional version or because they habitually watched the commercial channel, is not deemed significant. And the fact that the show was screened to them in a setting that is itself discursively productive in ways that necessarily affect what the 'social subjects' said about it was, says Morley, merely 'situational'.[13]

Clearly then, for Morley, an audience is an audience, whether it is 'responding' in an educational/work setting or 'decoding' in a family/home context. For Morley, the 'cultural and linguistic codes a person has available to them' is a matter not affected by the 'situation' in which those persons are watching a program dealing with financial and union issues during courses in banking or trade union studies. And an audience's cultural competence to 'decode' is not significantly affected by the fact that they've never seen the show before. An audience is an audience at home or at work, despite the fact that Morley's groups are carefully chosen and sorted into class 'background' rather than being interviewed at home. Clearly, Morley's audience too is an invisible fiction, produced by his project, which was itself a product of academic/critical institutional discourses. His audience is no more real than Ellis's, and no more independent of the research than any other experimental subject. It's Morley's *method* that is empirical, not the audience he constructs for his research.

In Morley's more recent *Family Television* the method is more sensitive to audience situation and the project more interested in gender than in class. But I would still be cautious about accepting the families Morley interviews as 'the TV audience', not only because twenty or so families in the south-east of England aren't readily generalisable, but also because the whole point of the project is to test *Morley's* imaginings (against 'real' or 'natural' audiences), which means the audience as we know it in the book is called into being by the project, and is not self-constituted in ways it would recognise, let alone choose for itself. For instance, the preoccupation with gender is Morley's, not that of the families, and it derives from Morley's institutional/theoretical situation. Of course families are engaged in gender politics, but the choice to foreground them was Morley's, not theirs, as can be demonstrated by his relative neglect of gender, in favour of class, in The 'Nationwide' Audience. In short, *Family Television* makes sense in relation to Morley's intellectual commitments, not in relation to those of the audience.[14]

A PAEDOCRATIC REGIME

Not even innovatory and critical work such as Ellis's and Morley's, whether theoretical or empirical in mode, is exempt from a tendency to essentialise the audience. Ellis makes it the 'normal citizen'. Morley's 'social subject' is more complex, being inflected by class differences in particular, but even so his project assumes that audiences have intrinsic (observable) properties, and his very title implies that they are to be found with the same properties 'nationwide'. If audiences can be understood in this way in critical, academic discourses, then the tendency to imagine them as independently existing, essential entities that are also nations is abundantly amplified in the practical discourses of the TV industry and of its regulatory bodies. This is no doubt partly because both the industry and its regulatory bodies are obliged not only to speak *about* an audience but—crucially, for them—to talk *to* one as well: they need not only to *represent* audiences but to enter into *relations* with them.

The way in which corporate executives and professional producers imagine audiences is particularly important, since it determines to some extent what goes on air, and it may help to explain why the industry acts as it does. Conversely, the way in which regulatory bodies imagine the audience may help to account for some of the things that don't get on the air. Turning, first, to the industry, it is clear that as far as private opinions of producers are concerned there may be as many views of the audience as there are personnel, and certainly such views will display contradictory aspects. However, in so far as audiences can be understood as imagined communities that are also nations, then it is relevant to ask what system or manner of rule or government—what regime—characterises such communities. In other words, it isn't the personal opinions of individuals which are at issue here but an institutional system—a construction of the audience that organises the industry's practices and serves its institutional needs and purposes. The institutional needs and purposes of the television industry are survival and profitability, to be achieved (hopefully) by audience maximisation and by minimising risks and uncertainties.

Audiences are *paedocratised* to serve these needs. For the industry, television is a *paedocratic regime*. The audience is imagined as having childlike qualities and attributes. Television discourse addresses its viewers as children. This regime does not govern all television everywhere all the time, of course. But there may be a 'law' which states: the bigger the target audience, the more it will be paedocratised. Thus American network television is the most paedocratic regime of all. However, smaller networks and stations are by no means exempt from the tendency to paedocratise audiences, if only because they buy network product and operate according to models of popular television generated by network. Indeed, it isn't the absolute size of a target audience that determines whether or not it will be paedocratised but rather the proportion of the population (local, state or national) that might conceivably be attracted: the higher the proportion, the more paedocratic the regime.

What do those who work at the centre of US network television imagine about the audience? How do they fill out their invisible fictions with plausible attributes? Often the fiction is invested with those attributes that best explain or justify the professionals' own practices. Many examples can be found in Todd Gitlin's *Inside Prime Time*. In fact, Gitlin saves one of these comments for the last paragraph of the book, where it refers not just to audiences but to the whole television industry, and it serves as an epigraph not only for the industry's view of its practices but for Gitlin's too. Gitlin cites Michael Kozoll, co-creator of *Hill Street Blues*:

> Which truth to conclude with...? Let the last word go to Michael Kozoll...Halfway through the second season [of *Hill Street Blues*], Kozoll said he had finally found the metaphor for television he had long been seeking. Doing episodic television, he said, is like raising a retarded child. By which he meant that there are only so many things it will ever learn to do, no matter how much you love the child, no matter how much effort and care and intelligence you lavish upon it. It will never shine. One could add: Its little accomplishments are also miraculous.[15]

So says Todd Gitlin, whose pessimism about television seems matched only by his pessimistic and very conservative view of 'retarded' children. Elsewhere, however, Gitlin cites Marvin J Chomsky, director of *Attica*, *Holocaust* and *Inside the Third Reich*, who justifies network paedocracy by reference to its need to win ratings:

Our audience is the guy who's used to walking around and getting a beer. We've got to reach him. He's a guy who hasn't made much of a commitment to give his rapt attention to what we're offering, right? We're going for the eighty million who will watch something. An infant in a cradle likes to watch things that move. So there you are. We go in for close-ups and we try to find the conflicts.[16]

This 'conventional wisdom'[17] is perhaps best exemplified in the work of Aaron Spelling ('in a class by himself', for network successes, says Gitlin), producer of *The Rookies, SWAT, Starsky and Hutch, Charlie's Angels, The Love Boat, Fantasy Island, Vega $, Hart to Hart, TJ Hooker* and *Dynasty*, among other top-rated shows. Spelling has called his products 'mind candy' and 'fast-food entertainment'. His shows have 'tennis-match dialogue' and 'show and tell' plots—'on a Spelling show any plot point important enough to be signalled once is signalled twice'.[18] Gitlin cites a lengthy insider's anecdote which is designed to show that even the smallest details of scripting, representation and semiosis are determined by the concept of a childlike audience. In particular, narrative suspense is constructed according to the conventions of children's theatre. The insider explains Spelling's methods:

The villain walks out onstage and says 'Heh-heh-heh! I have the secret matchbook, and I am going to hide it. I am going to put it behind this basket, and the heroine will never find it. Heh-heh-heh!' And he walks off. Now the heroine comes on and says, 'Where oh where is the secret matchbook?' And all the kids in the audience say, 'It's behind the basket! It's behind the basket!' That's what Aaron does. He believes that's what the American audience is you see.[19]

And Gitlin comments: 'by any Network standard, it all works'. Indeed, according to Gitlin, 'Spelling embraced the form's simplifications so fervently he left his personal impress on the medium', in the shape of 'two-generation pairings' of a father-like 'sage and authoritative elder' overseeing a team of youthful, sibling-like peers who in turn oversee the rest of the diegetic world, 'patrolling the street nasties and keeping recalcitrant, childish reality under control'.[20] In short, the mechanisms of representation, together with the diegetic world that they produce, are paedocratically organised to communicate with an audience which is itself believed to relate to television paedocratically.

CHILD'S PLAY

Why do industry professionals invent the audience in the image of a retarded child, or of an infant in the cradle—with or without a beer— who is just about sharp enough to spot the movement of moustache-twirling villainy? One reason is that audiences are, literally, unknowable. Gitlin quotes Scott Siegler, the then CBS vice-president for drama development: 'Because it's a mass audience—it's an unimaginably large audience—the audience tastes are so diffused and so general that you've got to be guessing'.[21] But guess they must, since communication depends on what Valentin Vološinov has identified as dialogic orientation towards an addressee. For Vološinov, this fundamental characteristic of communication applies to books (and we may add, allowing for technological developments, to television and the electronic media) just as much as it does to interpersonal speech. He calls such public performances 'ideological colloquy of large scale',[22] and producers can't escape it: not only must their programs talk about something, they must also talk to someone. Since that someone is unimaginable, with attributes that are diffused and general, it is perhaps not surprising to find the image of a child, or an infant, being used to humanise the unknown interlocutor with eighty million or more heads.

There are, in fact, other options open to broadcasters, but for historical and political reasons these options have narrowed. In the past, and in other discursive regimes, audiences have been hailed variously as 'Workers!', 'Citizens!', 'The People!' etc, but such appellations have been abandoned for most purposes in Western mainstream media, probably because of the leftist rhetorical connotations that such terms have been invested with since at least the Second World War. Similarly, there are unacceptable rightist connotations in some mobilisations of national identity, so care has to be exercised in this area; patriotism and commitment to what even Superman calls the American way may be understood as an automatic, natural reflex—but the knee-jerk must not be mistaken for the goose-step.

Thus broadcasters have to maintain an uneasy equilibrium; without being too populist or too nationalistic, they must strive to be popular, and speak to, for and about the nation. In addition, their popularity is organised not around citizenship or jingoism, but primarily around pleasure; the chosen path to survival and profitability is entertainment, understood as universally intelligible narrative fiction and spectacle. What this means in practice is that broadcasters tend not to insist on allegiances and identities that might be constructed on other sites but, on the contrary, to persuade audiences to abandon any such allegiances and identities, especially those of class (rendered as 'demographics' in television, of course), ethnicity and gender. Other 'variables', like region, age, education, family structure, even nation itself, may be significant, but the whole point of popular television is to cut across such divisions and to reconstitute the people involved into one unified constituency: the audience. The mechanism broadcasters have hit upon to do this impossible job is that of paedocracy. This isn't to say that television is merely infantile, childish, or dedicated to the lowest common denominator—those would be certain mechanisms for losing the audience. On the contrary, broadcasters paedocratise audiences in the name of pleasure. They appeal to the playful, imaginative, fantasy, irresponsible aspects of adult behaviour. They seek the common personal ground that unites diverse and often directly antagonistic groupings among a given population. What better, then, than a fictional version of everyone's supposed childlike tendencies which might be understood as predating such social groupings? In short, a fictional image of the positive attributes of childlike pleasures is invented. The desired audience is encouraged to look up, expectant, open, willing to be guided and gratified, whenever television as an institution exclaims: 'Hi, kids!'

FAMILY-CIRCULAR ARGUMENTS

The paedocratic regime is not confined to the imagination of broad-casters, nor to the North American networks. Broadcasters are encouraged in this view of audiences and the television medium itself by regulatory bodies that lay down broadcasting policy and program standards. Such bodies tend to express little uncertainty about the audience and its attributes; indeed, so strong and obvious is this knowledge that it is used to account for the 'nature' of television, presumably on the principle that you grow like the people you live with. Here, for instance, is the Annan Committee, a Royal Commission whose report on the *Future of Broadcasting* was the biggest ever government-sponsored inquiry into television in Britain. The report is prefaced with this definition of television:

> We ourselves agree that it is in [television's] nature to communicate personalities more successfully than ideas, emotional reflexes better than intellectual analysis, specific detail better than universal principles, simplicity better than complexity, change, movement and disorder better than permanence, tranquillity and order, consequences better than causes. The broadcast audience does not require education or even literacy to understand and enjoy programmes.[23]

This is another version of the 'retarded child' model of television, and once again it is fictional imagining. Television doesn't have an essential 'nature', so—like 'the nation'—it is explained anthropomorphically (paedomorphically) by investing it with the very attributes that the Annan Committee imagines belong to preliterate children: personality, emotional reflexes, specific detail, simplicity, change, movement, disorder, consequences, non-literacy, lack of education.

Reserving to itself the opposing (parental) attributes—ideas, intellectual analysis, universal principles, complexity, permanence, tranquillity, order, causes, literacy, education—the Annan Committee goes on to speak on behalf of the audience which, like a preliterate child, may not need education but does require protection:

> The audience for a programme may total millions: but people watch and listen in the family circle, in their homes, so that violations of the taboos of language and behaviour, which exist in every society, are witnessed by the whole family—parents, children and grandparents—in each other's presence. These violations are more deeply embarrassing and upsetting than if they had occurred in the privacy of a book, or in a club, cinema or theatre.[24]

172

The television family is not just orientalised; it is tribalised. The image of a three-generation family sitting in a circle round a television set under the spell of taboos is a complete fiction. Three-generation families are statistically quite rare; where they exist, there's no evidence that they watch television together (quite the reverse, in many cases); television cannot be watched in a 'circle'; there are no universal 'taboos'. Even so, this strange, tribal family is imagined as paedocratic: all its members are defined in terms of their relationship with children; they are not people, or even adults, but 'parents', 'grandparents'.

The child-orientated sensibilities of this family circle are not its own private affair; on the contrary, for Annan they are matters of the highest public policy. This is because 'whatever is published is presumed to be in some way approved, or at least condoned, by the society which permits its publication'.[25] The Annan Committee doesn't say exactly who does the presuming, approving, condoning or—more importantly—the permitting, nor does it extend its notion of privacy ('the privacy of a book') to watching television in the privacy of the home. It simply equates television with 'the society', and then closes the circle by equating 'society' with the 'whole family', which, as we've seen, is governed by children.

Along the way, a potentially useful model of the relationship between television and TV audiences is invoked and then ignored in favour of protective paedocracy. This is the model of broadcasting as *publication*. But the model of book and magazine publishing is not followed through. Instead, the 'privacy of a book' is imagined as essentially a solitary affair, while television, as a social phenomenon, is understood to require a 'permit' from 'society'. Of course, publishing is just as social as broadcasting, but printed publications can cater for a much wider range of political, personal, sexual, aesthetic, generic and other tastes—with or without 'violations' of taboos—than broadcasting ever has, without each item ('whatever is published') being seen as approved of by the whole 'society'. Publishing has had its own long history of regulation and censorship, but never in modern times has *everything* been subject to permit. If broadcasting is a form of publication, the question arises: why is it treated so differently? But the question does not occur to the Annan Committee, so strong is the image of the 'embarrassment' that would ensue if children were to be seen by their parents and grandparents witnessing 'violations' of language and behaviour (another interesting question they do not address is exactly who is imagined to be 'upset'—the parents or the children). Such is the power of paedocracy.

Turning from policy recommendations to the regulations that enforce them, and turning from Britain to Australia, it is clear that the 'publication' of television is governed by children down to the most surprising details. The Australian Broadcasting Tribunal issues a manual to commercial broadcasters ('licensees'). Having equated the 'Australian community' and the 'general public' with 'adults and children', the writers of the *Manual* go on to warn licensees of their 'overriding obligation' to 'avoid televising program material which can give offence to sections of the public or can be harmful to the young people who make up a large part of the audience at certain times of the day'.[26] Once again, it turns out that 'the Australian community' as a whole is governed by that 'large part' of the audience comprising 'young people'—the tail wags the dog. This is especially evident in the standards laid down for 'family programs', whose 'special provisions' are:

(a) The selection of subject matter and treatment of themes should be wholesome and fresh in outlook. The more sordid aspects of life must not be emphasised.

(b) The following in particular should be avoided—
   (i)   torture or suggestion of torture;
   (ii)   horror or undue suspense;
   (iii) the use of the supernatural or superstition so as to arouse anxiety or fear;
   (iv)   any matter likely to lead to hysteria, nightmares or other undesirable emotional disturbances in children;
   (v)   excessive violence.

(c) Morbid sound effects intended to anticipate or simulate death or injury should not be used.

(d) Particular attention should be paid to the treatment of child or animal characters, as a child's imagination can be readily overstimulated by suggestions of ill-treatment of such characters.

(e) Particular attention should be paid to the use of correct speech and pronunciation; slang and incorrect English should be avoided, except when necessary for characterisation.[27]

Like their British counterparts, the writers of the ABT *Manual* are confident they speak on behalf of 'a child's imagination', and they are equally certain that they know what goes on in that imaginary, tribal 'family circle'. Here is one of the regulations covering advertising (now under review):

> Because some products (especially those of a personal nature) are considered unsuitable as topics for conversation in the family circle, licensees should exercise discretion in accepting advertisements for them; if such advertisements are accepted, great care should be taken in selecting times appropriate for their transmission. Products of a particularly intimate nature which are not freely mentioned or discussed in mixed company should not be advertised through television. Illustrated advertisements for brassieres, girdles, briefs or similar items of underwear making use of live models should not be televised between 6.00 a.m. and 8.30 a.m. or between 4.00 p.m. and 7.30 p.m. on weekdays or at any time before 7.30 p.m. on Saturday, Sunday or weekdays which are not schooldays.[28]

REGIMES OF PLEASURE

Broadcasters are required to conform to a fictional image of the family circle and to an extraordinarily outdated notion of 'mixed company' on pain of losing their licence to broadcast. However, a more constant threat for television networks is losing not their licence but their market share. Does it follow, then, that audiences do in fact exert a powerful influence on broadcasters in the form of demand? Television as an industry is subject to certain market forces, but the institutional organisation of the industry seems designed not to enter into active relations with audiences as already constituted trading partners, but on the contrary to *produce* audiences—to invent them in its own image for its own purposes. Certainly the relationship of the television industry to its audience is not the classic market relation of supply and demand. This is because television, as one of the culture or consciousness industries, is not like the traditional producer of goods or services which are then sold to a market. Television shows are not commodities in the usual sense—they are 'non-material' commodities—and audiences don't buy them. The exchange is not goods for money, but symbols for time. If, as Nicholas Garnham has put it, culture is 'above all the sphere for the expansion of difference',[29] then it follows that the use value of cultural commodities like television shows is very hard to pin down or to predict. Television executives do their best. Todd Gitlin cites a list of 'mysteries' that executives offered to him as explanations for a show's success: 'whether a concept was "special", "different", "unique", even (wonder of wonders) "very unique"; whether a show had "chemistry"; whether it "clicked", whether "it all came together"'.[30] But clearly the demand for novelty or difference, for the 'very unique', is so unspecific that it barely counts as demand at all. The only discipline such demand imposes on the industry is that of variety: television, like other culture industries, cannot standardise its product but must offer a repertoire. Further, such demand cannot be stabilised. Despite the tendency to minimise uncertainty and risk by the use of repeats, long-running series (in both drama and news), recombinations of successful formulae, and spin-offs, uncertainty remains: out of around 3000 new ideas put up to each of the three US networks each year about a hundred will be commissioned to the script stage; of these, twenty-five will go to pilot stage; after testing the pilots, perhaps five or ten new series will go on the air; of these, perhaps only one will go to a second season.[31] In the face of such uncertainties, television networks are driven to ever higher production costs per item in order to maintain novelty and difference, which in turn means that they are driven to seek ever larger audiences to justify the unit costs.

But for their part, audiences treat television shows not as scarce commodities but as public utilities for which they are not prepared to pay. Like other cultural goods, such as radio shows, advertising and free newspapers, television shows are not purchased. Furthermore, they are not consumed; they are not used up in the act of reading or viewing. This means both that the products of the past are available for reconsumption, and that audiences are apt to use television when and how they like, and (despite piracy laws) to save what they like for consumption later on—an increasing tendency since the introduction of video recorders. This means it is hard for the industry to maintain scarcity (and thus price), especially given the need for audience maximisation.

In this context—where the industry's product cannot be standardised, where demand cannot be predicted or stabilised, where the commodity is 'non-material' and neither purchased nor consumed, and where vast capital investment is required to manufacture goods that are then virtually as free as the airwaves that carry them—in this context audiences are not television's real market. There is one sense, of course, in which audiences are literally the product of the television industry: in the commercial sector, networks sell access to their audiences to advertisers; in the public sector, the corporations must convince their funding agencies that an agreed proportion of the public is tuned in often enough to justify the enterprise. Thus audiences—or, more accurately, *ratings*—are the key to profitability and survival in the television industry, and access to them is the key to power. It follows, as Garnham has argued, that in line with other cultural industries, but unlike traditional manufacturing industries, distributors (networks) are more powerful and profitable than producers (authors). However, it does not follow that audiences have power over networks: they are created, organised and maintained *by* networks, and not vice versa. Indeed, the real relations of broadcasters are not with audiences as such but with other professionals in the industry: with advertisers, funding agencies, suppliers and—it's about as close as they get—with audience research organisations. In this context, the 'power' of the audience is contained within the networks themselves, taking the fictionalised form of ratings and of those imaginary, paedocratised representations of the audience that the networks promote throughout the industry. Networks minimise their risks by stabilising not demand but supply, but neither networks nor producers know what will 'sell'; they don't know who they're talking to and they don't 'give the public what it wants' because they don't know what the public is. This structural uncertainty at the heart of the television industry means that networks and producers alike are afraid of the audience: afraid of offending it, of inciting it, of inflaming it—above all, of losing it.

At the level of programming, in the 'ideological colloquy of large scale', this structural uncertainty is reproduced as a constant effort to reconcile an irreconcilable contradiction. On the one hand, audiences must be appealed to and won; they must voluntarily forgo other activities and choose not only to watch television but to watch this channel, during this time slot, today. On the other hand, audiences must be disciplined and controlled; they must learn to recognise that what's on offer is, despite its requisite novelty or difference, just that kind of pleasure for the enjoyment of which they have both forgone other activities and invested scarce time resources. A further contradiction facing broadcasters is that between the audience as an unimaginably large mass and the audience as an individual viewer. Without having the slightest notion of each or any viewer's identity, the ideological colloquy has to address each in order to amass all.

In practice, such contradictions produce what can be called television's regimes of pleasure. Like other publishing forms, television channels provide a montage or repertoire of different kinds of elements in order to convert as wide a spectrum of the public as possible into the audience. Far from seeking to fix just one 'subject position', least of all that of Ellis's 'normal citizen', television, as Ien Ang has argued, has developed its cultural form as a heterogeneity of modes of address, points of view, program genres, styles of presentation, codes of recognition.[32] Television is characterised, in effect, by excess, providing audiences with an excess of options which can nevertheless be easily recognised, and offering an excess of pleasures (one of which is to choose between those on offer) which can nevertheless be disciplined into familiar, predictable forms. Thus in order to produce an audience, television must first produce excess. But, like the audience whose demand it is supposed to represent, pleasure is a diffuse and irrecoverable concept; it must be regimented in various ways in order for the television industry to be able to supply it, and so to survive, profitably. Thus television is a pleasurable institution, but one offering a complex of channelled, disciplined pleasures which are driven towards corporately achievable forms; television operates *regimes* of pleasure.

ILLEGAL IMMIGRANTS?

But all the time the efforts of television networks and producers to regiment the audience are subverted by the audience's own excess—its tendency always to exceed the discipline, control and channelling of television's regimes, and its tendency always to exceed the imagination of television's corporate executives. Thus the interests of the audiences and of television are in principle opposed. Television as an industry needs regimented, docile, eager audiences, willing to recognise what they like in what they get; and audiences need a relationship with television in order to exist at all as audiences, but that relationship is not organised, nor even represented very directly, in the institution. Their interests are discernible only as random: childish, unfocused desires for excess, transgression, novelty, difference; for play, escape from categorisation, and occasionally for that characteristic childish demand—'Do it again!'

The politics of television, then, consist in a very unequal struggle between different interests within a wholly fictional (that is, discursively/rhetorically/textually imagined) community. Since audiences don't exist prior to or outside television, they need constant hailing and guidance in how-to-be-an-audience—hailing and guidance that are unstintingly given within, and especially between shows, and in

THE POLITICS OF PUBLICS

the metadiscourses that surround television, the most prominent among which, of course, are those publications aptly called television guides. Thus television is not just a regime, or complex of regimes, of pleasure; it is a pedagogic regime too. What this means, in effect, is that television producers haven't got the courage of their convictions. For, if television audiences are subject to a *pedagogic* regime of pleasure, then it follows that they do not live, while acting as audiences, in a democracy. But neither do they live in a paedocracy, since a pedagogic regime cannot be governed *by* childlike qualities but on the contrary constitutes government *over* them. In fact, the paedocratic regime of television discourse is itself, in the end, an invisible fiction, because audiences have no voice of their own to speak within the institution. Like the discourse of orientalism, paedocracy too often functions within the industry not to explain audiences but to explain them away, to contain their potential threat, to render obvious their need for protection, regulation, rule. The paedocratised image of television audiences that circulates within the industry and around its academic and regulatory observers as an obvious truth is not necessarily devoid of force for those who actually watch television—but its primary function as a discourse is to serve the purposes of the professionals engaged in professional survival. For them, any irruption of actual audiences would spoil their routine assumption of the power to speak on behalf of a disorganised community which hitherto has existed almost wholly within their own imagination and rhetoric. Thus it is true that television networks act, as Todd Gitlin has put it, *in loco parentis* for the audience, but it is not the childishness of the audience that produces this situation; nor is it, as Gitlin is tempted to conclude, 'a projection of their [the networks'] own childishness'.[33] On the contrary, it is a system for imagining the unimaginable; for controlling the uncontrollable.

NOTES

1 E Ann Kaplan (ed), *Regarding Television: Critical Approaches—An Anthology*, American Film Institute/University Publications of America, New York, 1983, p. xi.
2 John Ellis, *Visible Fictions: Cinema, Television, Video*, Routledge and Kegan Paul, London, 1982, p. 5.
3 See, for instance, Raymond Williams, *Television: Technology and Cultural Form*, Fontana, London, 1984; James Carey, 'Mass Communication Research and Cultural Studies: An American View', Chapter 16 in *Mass Communication and Society*, eds James Curran et al, Open University/Edward Arnold, London, 1977; Stuart Hall, 'The Rediscovery of "Ideology": Return of the Repressed in Media Studies' in *Culture, Society and the Media*, eds Michael Gurevitch et al, Methuen, London, 1982; 'Ferment in the Field', *Journal of Communication* 33, 3 (1983).
4 Willard Rowland and Bruce Watkins (eds), *Interpreting Television: Current Research Perspectives*, Sage, Beverley Hills CA, pp. 25, 33.

5   Ellis, op. cit. (note 2), p. 5.
6   Benedict Anderson, *Imagined Communities*, Verso, London, 1983, p. 16.
7   Ibid, p. 31.
8   Ibid, p. 39.
9   Edward Said, *Orientalism*, Routledge and Kegan Paul, London, 1978.
10 Edward Said, '*Orientalism* Reconsidered', *Race and Class* 27, p. 7.
11 Ellis, op. cit. (note 2), p. 169.
12 David Morley, *The 'Nationwide' Audience*, British Film Institute, London, 1980, pp. 40, 42, 46, 48.
13 Ibid, p. 27.
14 David Morley, *Family Television: Cultural Power and Domestic Leisure*, Comedia, London, 1986.
15 Todd Gitlin, *Inside Prime Time*, Pantheon, New York, 1983, p. 324.
16 Quoted in ibid, p. 188.
17 Ibid.
18 Ibid, pp. 136, 137.
19 Quoted in ibid, p. 138.
20 Ibid, p. 139.
21 Quoted in ibid, p. 22.
22 Valentin Vološinov, *Marxism and the Philosophy of Language*, Seminar Press, New York, 1973, p. 95.
23 Annan Committee, *Report of the Committee on the Future of Broadcasting*, HMSO, London, 1977, p. 25.
24 Ibid, p. 246.
25 Ibid.
26 Australian Broadcasting Tribunal, *Manual*, Australian Government Publishing Service, Canberra, 1984, p. 11.
27 Ibid, p. 15.
28 Ibid, p. 27.
29 Nicholas Garnham, 'Concepts of Culture: Public Policy and the Cultural Industries', *Cultural Studies* 1, 1 (January 1987), p. 31. The phrase '*expansion* of difference' does not in fact appear in the more accessible published version of Garnham's paper referenced above. It is corrected to the much less interesting phrase '*expression* of difference'. I have retained 'expansion' from the first published version, which was issued as a house-printed pamphlet (giving no author or date) by the Greater London Council in 1983.
30 Gitlin, op. cit. (note 15), p. 26.
31 Ibid, p. 21.
32 Cf Ien Ang, 'The Battle between Television and Its Audiences: The Politics of Watching Television' in *Television in Transition*, eds Philip Drummond & Richard Paterson, British Film Institute, London, 1986.
33 Gitlin, op. cit. (note 15), p. 300.

12
Semiotic victories:
Media constructions of the
Maralinga Royal Commission
GRAEME TURNER

Between 1952 and 1957 Britain conducted twelve full-scale nuclear weapons tests on Australian soil. The first, in the Monte Bello islands in 1952, was followed by two at Emu Field in South Australia in 1953. A further two devices were exploded at Monte Bello in 1956 before testing was transferred to the permanent site at Maralinga where it continued until 1958. As well as test explosions of atomic bombs, there was also a series of 'minor trials' in which the effects of nuclear accidents on military installations and equipment were inspected. These minor trials, we now know, spread plutonium over a vast area, making a more insidious contribution to the irradiation of the land than the bombs themselves. All of this occurred with the acquiescence if not the full knowledge of the Australian government of the time.

I have two interests in this history. One is a continuing analytic interest in the function of discourses of nationalism in the decade of the Bicentennial in Australia—roughly, the decade of the 1980s.[1] The history of the 1980s in Australia emphasises, not these discourses' monolithic predictability, but their canny flexibility, their readiness for continual appropriation and redeployment as they participate in the construction of a national culture. The discourses of nationalism dealt with in this essay are those of a 'modularised' nationalism: that is, a nationalism thought of as a relatively established set of discursive formations which can be moved into place on a variety of terrains in the service of a range of interests. As we shall see, it is not always easy to tell which, or whose, interests are being served in any one instance. My second concern is more substantive and emerges directly from the histories dealt with in my discussion of the Maralinga Royal Commission, which ran from 1984–85. I want to suggest how the work of this commission was given its dominant meaning: that of a process through which the Empire struck back to expose the devastating material effects of colonial domination. This account demands challenge and criticism, not only because of its singularity but also because of the effects its dominance has produced.

It is hard to tell what meanings the 'Australian public' attributed to the tests at the time they occurred. If one is to deduce public opinion from press reports of the tests, it would seem to have been whole-heartedly in favour of the exercise. However, although these reports are our major category of primary evidence, to see them as a direct or 'accurate' reflection of popular opinion is extremely risky—in theory and in practice. Researchers have found traces of greater opposition than is acknowledged in the contemporary news media. We know, for instance, that 'Ban the bomb' demonstrations did occur, that the Labor Party pressed energetically but unsuccessfully for an enquiry into the safety precautions for the second Monte Bello bomb, that the letters pages in the newspapers were dominated by protests, and that a Gallup poll at the time showed 60 per cent of Australians opposed the tests.[2] Little of this surfaces in press reports at the time. In Adelaide, *The Advertiser* rarely mentioned the likelihood of any safety problems resulting from the exercise despite its taking place so close to home. Indeed, as the tests were repeatedly postponed because of unfavour-able weather conditions, *The Advertiser*'s reporters began to represent the safety precautions as excessively bureaucratic, even silly. Inevitably, Chapman Pincher was covering the event for the paper and he likened the wait for the momentous event to the experience of an expectant father waiting for a baby that never arrived. Quick to take the hint, Oliphant produced a cartoon which depicted a chain-smoking father pacing outside the Maralinga Maternity Ward. The day after the test did occur, there was the sequel: the father shouting joyfully, 'It's a bomb'.[3]

Tame and Robotham describe the Australian press response to the tests in the following way:

> ... the Melbourne *Argus* of 27 September 1956 captured the mood best with its coverage of the Maralinga test of the same date. 'Bombs Away!' trumpeted the paper's front-page headline, followed by the immortal first paragraph: 'Maralinga Thursday: the atom bomb's gone up at last'. Worse was to follow. 'Minutes after the explosion, Government members cheered and Labor MPs shouted "Thank goodness" and "At last, at last" as Mr Beale, Supply Minister, announced in the House of Representatives the test had been successful.' Still later in the story the euphoria and hysteria increased: 'As the cloud [radioactive] faded, convoys of trucks and jeeps brought back the servicemen who'd faced the blast at close range. AND EVERY FACE WORE A SMILE [sic] . . . They could have been coming back from a picnic.[4]

If it is hard to tell who might be speaking through the discourses used to construct such reports, the Minister of Supply, Howard Beale's, description of the tests might help; to him, they were 'a striking example of inter-Commonwealth cooperation on the grand scale—England has the bomb and the know-how, we have the open spaces and the willingness to help the motherland. Between us, we shall help to build the defences of the free world.'[5]

Noel Sanders describes a similarly contradictory brew of discourses—of nationalism and Empire, of destiny and modernity—in his discussion of the exploration for and marketing of Australian uranium in the 1950s.[6] The Australian government seized on uranium and the atom bomb as signs of a transformed modernity, a chance to leap from an agricultural past to a technologised future in the new role of supplier to the major powers. Sanders notes the *Sun-Herald's* inevitable claim that the 1953 test had, like so many other events before and since, 'put Australia on the map', as well as the opinion of WC Wentworth MP who saw it as the most important material event in history, second only to that more spiritual event—the birth of Christ.[7] The *frisson* of playing a part in the geopolitics of the Cold War, of assisting Britain's attempt to remain a world power (by finessing what amounted to a technical breach of their non-proliferation agreements with the US and Canada), is discernible in government rhetorics of the time. In government pronouncements, a scenario emerged: from a position in the front row of the imperial chorus, Australia would stand on the world stage not quite in partnership with, but certainly in some re-lation to, the major atomic powers—in any case, a long way from riding on the sheep's back. A sea change in Australia's sense of itself was at hand. Within such a climate, Sir Ernest Titterton's extraordi-nary remarks seem entirely appropriate: he saw it as 'axiomatic' that, as a consequence of our implication in nuclear politics, 'one or more of our capital cities will be destroyed in the next 50 to 100 years'.[8] Such a probability merely underlined the national aggrandisement sure to follow.

Plausibly constructed though it was, this euphoria could not last long. Even the Menzies government soon realised how little care had been taken in the testing and how it had encouraged the British to act like unruly house guests; once it became clear the host would give them the run of the house, they started to put their feet on the furniture and drop ash on the rug. The first scientific reports to question British claims about the limits of the fallout were completed and suppressed in 1957; they detected fallout as far from Maralinga as Townsville and constructed an entirely pessimistic map of its disper-sal.[9] I need not elaborate the details here but over the next 25 years there was a steady stream of claims, accusations, scientific research and attempts to contain the damage. Britain was called back for a limited clean-up in 1967 (Operation Brumby) but this merely involved ploughing the scattered plutonium and bomb debris into the ground. A further operation in 1979 removed some of the contaminated soil but still left the majority of the site untouched.[10]

As the years went by, and as information about the dangers of radiation were more generally understood, survivors of the tests started to question the extent to which they had been informed of the dan-gers. Pilots had been instructed to fly through the nuclear cloud to collect dust particles; ships had been instructed to sail into the drop zone off the Monte Bello islands; soldiers had been sent into 'ground zero' within minutes to commence cleaning up—mostly without any kind of protective clothing ('just a slouch hat and shorts', as one survivor put it on *Hinch* in 1991.)[11] As white Australia began to acknowledge the importance of the land within Aboriginal culture, the forced evacuation and irradiation of the Maralinga people's country assumed the dimensions of an outrage. The inadequacy of the attempts to evacuate all Aboriginals from the area also came under scrutiny; warning signs in English and the patrols of a solitary officer were the sum total of these attempts. Finally, as the environmental dangers of nuclear energy and the dumping of toxic waste became of general concern, the enormity of what had occurred at Maralinga began to sink in.

By the late 1970s, the trickle of reports had become a flood of accusations about the inadequacy of the clean-up methods, the plight of the surviving servicemen and women, the callous incompetence of those in charge of safety during the tests, the silencing of scientists who had evidence of widespread nuclear contamination, the dispossession of the Aborigines from their land, and the long-term effects on the site area itself. With the change in government in 1983 and the gathering of more evidence about the condition of the test site, and with the Labor government needing to restore some of its environmental credentials after overturning Labor Party policy on uranium mining, the royal commission was set up in 1984. The primary issues to be dealt with are usefully laid out in a series of articles in the *Canberra Times* published the month before the commission commenced.[12] It highlighted the relationship between Britain and Australia in the administration of the tests; what it called 'the modern-day massacre' and de-tribalisation of Aborigines in the test area; the management of safety by the British and in particular the role of the Australian nominee, Sir Ernest Titterton, on the safety committee which was meant to safeguard Australians' interests; and the question of whether or not we were told the truth about the size of the bombs exploded or the hazards they presented to Australians.

On Anzac Day, 1992, Paul Keating delivered a speech at a memorial on the Kokoda Trail in Papua New Guinea which established him for the first time as a nationalist. The speech revised some of the standard components of Australian mythology in order to write Kokoda in and Gallipoli out, and it renewed the licence for some other components— the British used us in World War I and lied to us in World War II which helped stitch this new mythology back into the old one. Keating's reading of World War II history—'Churchill sold us out'— raised something of a storm here and in Britain; whatever its virtues as history, its political acumen lay in its successful exploitation of many Australians' apparent (Oedipal) readiness to view the British– Australia relation as a treacherous one. The Australian news media's treatment of the Maralinga Royal Commission was similarly exploitative. While the commission was still in Australia, reporting was often factual, issues-oriented and low-key. The full range of issues raised in the *Canberra Times* articles did seem likely to be addressed. This changed when the hearings moved to London. Once there, the range of issues raised and meanings generated contracted as the story slotted itself into a popular history of British–Australian colonial relations that has us as the resistant victims of British hegemony. The story took on a higher profile and became, consequently, more sensationalised: the coverage was increasingly personalised and opinionated as it acquired bigger headlines and moved closer to the front page.

The president of the commission, 'Diamond Jim McClelland', has admitted deliberately provoking Her Majesty's Government with some strategic pommy-bashing on the opening day of the London hearings.[13] In order to speed up the British provision of files and witnesses, and to puncture any illusions that the commission could be fobbed off by a bunch of Sir Humphreys, McClelland issued a statement attacking the lack of cooperation and preparedness he had encountered. It had the desired result, both in the increased media attention and in the fact that the commission received more rapid and thorough cooperation from the British, in the end, than from the Australian Public Service.[14] Within the British press, it must be said, McClelland's outspokenness won him a great deal of support; he was applauded for cutting the red tape that was, after all, also restricting British servicemen and women from gaining access to information that would assist their own claims against their government.[15] It should also be noted that the commission took place within a slightly different context for the British press; it became part of a series of 1980s investigations into Britain's political management of its official secrets—a later episode of which was played out in Australia during the *Spycatcher* trials.

Within the Australian press, evidence of the British support for the commission's work was buried. From the first day, the hearings were constructed as a juicy opportunity for an avenging Australian nationalism to punish a complacent and undifferentiated British Establishment. In a piece headlined, 'Her Majesty's Govt gets a taste of the colonial birch', Evan Whitton gushed like a fashion reporter: McClelland, he found, was as 'handsome as ever', an 'impeccable dresser' presenting 'a delightful study in pink and grey'. For the British counsel Robert Auld, Whitton could only manage 'a plump man with thinning hair'. Nevertheless, throwing disinterest to the winds, Whitton did muse that 'it must have been quite a treat for Mr Auld to hear a colonial judge giving his client, Her Majesty's Govt, such a thorough birching but it has to be said that his client has made a quite remarkable ass of itself'.[16]

Robert Milliken, in his book *No Conceivable Injury*, has suggested that the real entity on trial in these hearings was science itself; if so, it was a particularly Anglo formation of science. Even Milliken ends up describing the hearings as 'total war' between the British and Australian counsel.[17] And although McClelland's initial outburst may have fanned the flames, the situation does seem to have been ripe for a colonial battle before he said a word:

The first hearing was marked by chaos, confusion, threats of violence and strident Australian nationalism, as Fleet Street reporters jostled for space in the overcrowded conference room with Australian television crews. One Australian cameraman demanded to know if a stenographer was English or Australian and, on learning she was English, set about haranguing the hapless woman for walking in front of his camera—'deliberately' . . . and preventing Australian audiences from getting the full picture.[18]

From such a start, it is no surprise that within two weeks the London sittings had become, in the *National Times'* words, 'one of the most bitter wrangles between Australia and Britain for many years'.[19] Of course, it wasn't any kind of wrangle between 'Australia' and 'Britain' at all; at best, it was a wrangle between a group of Australian lawyers with unprecedented access to the British and Australian media, their British counterparts, and some sections of Whitehall.[20]

Once given the 'McGuffin', however, the media continued to develop the narrative. Much was made of Australian attempts to extract information from the British—both during the hearings and in the 1950s. Menzies emerged from the hearings as a hopeless Anglophile, but even he had been reduced to sending a frantic telegram to Britain after fallout from the second Monte Bello (Mosaic) test in 1956 was detected drifting over the mainland. 'What the bloody hell is going on!' his telegram read; the phrase was widely taken up in headlines as a metonym for the whole set of colonial relations. The effect was to construct, inferentially, an homology between Menzies' predicament, that of the royal commission itself, and ultimately that of the Australian people.[21] As secret after secret was uncovered, the headlines were less and less restrained in their accusations about British 'lies'.[22] One of the tests in 1956 turned out to be twice the magnitude the Australians had originally been informed it was—a bomb, the headlines told us, five times the destructive power of the one which wiped out Hiroshima. It seemed entirely plausible that commentators should conclude the revelations would 'further strain Australia–UK relations already fragile since hearings in Australia indicated 27 years of British duplicity over the tests'.

For most Australians reading these reports, such fragility bothered us not a jot. Even though my interest here is in challenging the media representations, it would be hypocritical to deny how exciting it was to read the daily revelations from a position of absolute moral superiority. The spectacle of an instrument of the Australian government bullying the British establishment into hurt submission was a deeply satisfying one. Coupled, as it was, to a genuine attempt to defend the rights of citizens against a callous and incompetent bureaucracy (leaving aside the question of *whose* bureaucracy), it was a heady mixture. The effectiveness of nationalist discourses lies in the fact that their seductiveness is assured in advance; in this case, as in so many others, they offered us pleasures that were irresistible.

McClelland himself became something of a national hero; he began with the impeccable nationalist credentials of an Irish-Australian background and service in the Whitlam government. His abrasiveness in London and his 'fuck you' attitude to British officialdom[23] endeared him to the British and the Australian public for much the same reasons: he was the perfect stereotype of the Australian in Britain and he was on the side of the angels. According to the position one can construct from the press reports, particularly those in the *Sydney Morning Herald*, his Anglophobia was far from being a disqualification; rather it was a perfectly appropriate attribute which could only bring him credit since his commission produced the objective correlatives for his condition daily. His outspokenness was legitimated by his nationalist principles; interviewed on *Sixty Minutes* when he returned from London (but before the commission had completed its hearings), McClelland accused Menzies of being a 'lickspittle to the British' and defended his actions in London as the only way 'a colonial' was going to get any results.

The nationalism which provides the major discursive frame for the reporting of the Maralinga Royal Commission dramatically narrowed the meanings of the enquiry. Progressively displaced from the foreground were the effects upon Aboriginal people, their land, and their communities; the extent of the contamination of Australian land is still unknown and was not vigorously pursued by the commission at all; even the plight of the British and Australian veterans depending upon the findings of the commission as support for their own claims for compensation gradually gave way to this narrative of postcolonial politics, this melodrama of duplicity and betrayal—of British lies, British stooges, British bastardry. The story settled into the genre of the political thriller rather than the historical mini-series, the climax occuring with the naming of the guilty, the uncovering of the plot. Issues such as who would pay, who *should* pay, what needed to be done and who would do it, were all left to the report itself and thus would always risk being ignored.

The discourses of nationalism served at least two further functions in this case. Firstly, as I have suggested, they unequivocally defined the royal commission's activities as in the national interest, effectively conflating the interests of the government which set the commission up with those fractions of its people who were its subjects—the Maralinga Aboriginals, ex-servicemen and women. This, despite (for instance) the Australian government's long and uninterrupted history of obstructing veterans' claims for compensation on the basis of sickness produced by their exposure to radiation at Maralinga. One could see how the government's interests might be served by this representation, however implausible, of its role as champion of its citizens' rights. Better still, once established, the nationalist narrative made it clear the British were to blame.

It should go without saying that this was a gross misrepresentation of, at least, the Australian government's degree of culpability. On the issue of the evacuation of the Aborigines, for example, while McClelland took some delight in pointing out British ignorance of Aboriginal culture, the Australians involved were certainly not much better. Among the reasons why the evacuation was so difficult is that Aborigines were not even included in the Australian census during the 1950s. Australians were responsible for the traumatic treatment of two Aboriginal families found in the drop zones after tests began; one family was sent off to a destination 650 km away on foot—three of its members are said to have died on the journey. Insensitivity to the effect of the dispossession and evacuation on the Aboriginal communities is not solely attributable to British ignorance. As Kingsley Palmer puts it, 'it suited the British and Australian governments in the 1950s to believe that the land was of no importance to desert Aborigines, and that the area, which was the ideal place to perform the tests, was more or less empty'.[24] The expertise of Australian anthropologist AP Elkin was sought in order to see that the Aborigines' 'well-being was not interfered with in any way'. However, Elkin's advice was entirely consonant with the objectives of the British and Australian governments, complicit in the eventual dispossession of the very people whose 'well-being' he was supposed to protect:

> [T]he potential effect of the bomb tests on the sacred sites and on the socio-religious life of Aborigines was ignored [by Elkin] because it was considered irrelevant. According to Elkin, in time Aborigines would leave their traditional ways and lifestyle behind, and all of its associations, and would develop into 'modern' men and women . . .[25]

In relation to this issue, as with many others, evidence of Australian culpability was submerged under the weight of another story.

The second function served by the discourses of nationalism in this case was, however, even more destructive. The clarity of the position McClelland took against the British allowed the report, when tabled, to be seen as irredeemably tainted by McClelland's Anglophobia. Alexander Downer—currently shadow Defence Minister—launched one of several attacks on the report in *Quadrant* as politically biased ('antagonistic to the tests'), and on McClelland himself—'that embittered, gaudy relic of the Whitlam government'. Itself a vigorous political document, Downer's article reversed all of McClelland's orthodoxies, defending Menzies, Titterton, the lot.[26] Some editorial writers had also taken this line. *The Age* confined itself to ticking off the commission for its lack of diplomacy, while accepting the arguments it presented.[27] The *Sydney Morning Herald*, though (whose reports had been among the most rabidly nationalist), attacked the 'standing of the commission' itself. Its credibility was damaged by the 'Pom-bashing antics of its chairman', and thus in need of renovation if its recommendations were to have any hope of implementation.[28] With the pomposity of a newspaper intent on slaying the monster it had largely been responsible for creating, the *Sydney Morning Herald* agreed the commission's case was proven but saw it as unlikely to be of any use to a government stuck with the 'embarrassing dilemma' of asking the British to shell out. For the rest of the press, the story was a dead duck almost as soon as the report came out; the government, whatever it might have pretended at the time, must have felt the same.

As I say, this is not surprising, given the meanings attributed to the event. For many Australians, the report of the Maralinga Royal Commission consigned its subject to the past; it represented the completion of a ritual of separation which had to be performed if Australia was finally to be its own place. *The Age* editorial on the report said as much, smugly suggesting that 'what happened in Australia in the 1950s would not happen today'. Historian Stephen Alomes, writing in 1987, also felt confident that the royal commission had 'put the last nail in the coffin of Australia's colonial relations with Britain':

> An Australian commission exposed British deceptions and Menzies' colonial servitude through hearings held in part on British soil. Furthermore, Jim McClelland savaged contemporary English inefficiency. The colony was no longer deferential and obedient.[29]

Here the press's chosen narrative is delivered unalloyed, raw mythology offered as history. But neither *The Age* nor Alomes should go uncontested.

For a start, it *could* happen again. In 1987, Kim Beazley approached the Maralinga community to allow NASA to use the Woomera range for rocket tests. Beazley's letter sought community agreement but it did contain the threat that the government 'reserves the right to make use of the Prohibited Area [the irradiated area of the test sites, which borders on inhabited Aboriginal land] for rocket launchings if that becomes necessary or expedient in the interests of the Commonwealth'. By May 1989, Beazley had expanded the plan to that of a 'military mega-range', testing 'rockets, missiles and other war material' over Aboriginal land. He faxed the Maralinga community asking for permission to use their land for this weapons research on a more or less permanent basis.[30] The request presumably depended on the assumption that since, once again, the Aborigines were not making use of this land they would not mind if it was used by the government. There is a Defence Department plan to turn the area into an international 'war games park', although its current status is not known.[31] There have been reports suggesting the area has been offered to the US as a replacement for their Philippine bases, and there is also evidence of French interest.[32] It could happen again.

From a second angle of attack, the media narrative of British guilt and Australian innocence has started to break down into its constitutive fictions. Between 1989–91, the British journalist Robert Cockburn published a series of reports—largely in the London *Times*[33]—of further scientific evidence from Maralinga being covered up by the Australian government. Cockburn produced two television documentaries—one for SBS' *Dateline* (screened on 17 August 1991) and one for the BBC's *Nature* series (screened in the UK, 28 October 1991). Both drew on a report by the Australian Radiation Laboratory which had been hushed up by the Department of Primary Industries and Energy, and which revealed that contamination of the test sites and surrounding areas was even more extensive than previously thought. Some of the areas thus surveyed included those to which Aborigines had been allowed to return under the misapprehension the land was safe. The *Dateline* story was about an Australian cover-up in British interests, accusing the Australian government of having no intention of pursuing the British to implement the royal commission recommendations but rather aiding and abetting them in their attempts to avoid public scrutiny. Indeed, the story presented the interests of the Australian and British governments as largely identical, and thus antithetical to those of the Aborigines.

A chilling moment occurred in the *Dateline* program, when Jim McClelland was taken into the studio and shown the footage the viewers had themselves just seen. He was devastated: 'It's news to me', he said, lamely, painfully aware of how futile this made his own best (and hitherto apparently successful) efforts appear. The 'British bastardry' thesis got more complicated as we watched: 'the colonial cringe is alive and well', he finally admitted as the complicity of a succession of Australian governments (including the Hawke government) in a series of cover-ups stood revealed.

The *Dateline* story produced a burst of media interest which threatened to undermine conclusively the royal commission mythology. *Hinch* presented a story on the survivors, the soldiers who participated in the tests and were now dying of cancer. The Australian government's obstruction and callousness were the key themes of the story. The Aboriginal delegations' visits to London also caught the attention of newscasts, although none that I saw drew the inference that this direct approach indicated a loss of faith in the good will and intentions of their own government. There has been no sustained revision of the narrative I have presented, however; since mid-1991, Cockburn has found it very difficult to get his articles published in Australia and has largely given up trying. There are still many further questions to be asked, and there has been no class (as distinct from individual) compensation to any of the groups claiming it.

My initial interest in the Maralinga Royal Commission was related to my interest in the apparently programmatic way the media's use of the discourses of nationalism accelerated for the Bicentennial. In the first half of the 1980s, even business was constructed as a nationalist, sporty activity; the Australian version of high risk business practices was valorised as the expression of the national character—larrikin capitalism. Here, it was suggested, in the most unlikely of domains, Australians were once again challenging the traditionalists and breaking the rules. A sense of a growing national independence or maturity is customarily seen to mark the 1980s—to excess, in most accounts. Within such a formulation, the reporting of the Maralinga Royal Commission would seem to be homologous with such a cultural movement and explicable in its terms (as in Alomes' account, for instance). And yet, my research suggests it is also explicable as the product of, for example, strategies adopted by the Australian press to make the commission into a story, of the government's defence of its own interests in deflecting blame and discouraging closer scrutiny of its own files, or of the royal commissioner's own weakness for self-promotion.

Whatever we might agree on as the appropriate constellation of contributing sources for these discourses, I want to close by saying what were in my view their consequences. The effect of the dominance of these discourses in this case was to make it seem as if a victory had been won; disclosure was complete even before the report was written. As we have seen, however, the victory was only at the level of semiosis; material compensation never eventuated. Instead, veterans have continued to die before their claims come to court, the life expectancy among those Maralinga people displaced from their lands has dropped to thirty years, and a section of Australia the size of the UK in one estimate, five times its size in another, has been rendered uninhabitable for 240 000 years. That our government should, first of all, oversee such a series of events, and then attempt to ameliorate its effects, achieve nothing, and still appear to be serving the national interest is due, at least in part, to the power of those discursive strategies during the reporting of the commission which told the Australian public it was all fixed when Jim McClelland was rude to Whitehall and Evan Whitton called Her Majesty's Government a remarkable ass.

NOTES

1 I would like to gratefully acknowledge the research assistance of Jo Robertson in gathering material for this project, and for this paper.
2 Lindy Woodward, 'Buffalo Bill and the Maralingerers', *New Journalist*, 43, April 1984, p. 18.
3 ibid. p. 22.
4 A Tame and FPJ Robotham, *Maralinga: British A-Bomb, Australian Legacy*, Melbourne, Fontana/Collins, p. 10.
5 Janine Perrett, 'Diamond Jim Shuts Up the London Shop', *The Australian*, 20 March 1985, p. 9.
6 'The Hot Rock in the Cold War: Uranium in the 1950s', in Ann Curthoys and John Merritt eds, *Better Dead than Red*, Allen & Unwin, Sydney, 1986, pp. 155–69.
7 ibid. pp. 155–7.
8 Sanders, ibid. p. 162.
9 Deborah Smith & Deborah Snow, 'Our Atomic Cover-Up', *The National Times*, 4–10 May 1980, p. 3.
10 Brian Toohey, 'Plutonium on the Wind: The Terrible Legacy of Maralinga', *The National Times*, 4–10 May 1984, p. 3.
11 There are a number of accounts of the history of the tests and their implications. See Robert Milliken, *No Conceivable Injury*, Melbourne, Penguin, 1986, and Denys Blakeway and Sue Lloyd-Roberts, *Fields of Thunder: Testing Britain's Bomb*, George Allen & Unwin, London, 1985.

12   These were written by Paul Malone and Howard Conkey and ran daily
     from 28 September to 1 October 1984. The titles: 'Inquiry into nuclear
     tests has great deal to consider' (p. 2, 28 September 1984); 'Impact on
     Aborigines: the loud bang and black cloud linger' (p. 15, 29 September
     1984); 'Confusion on contamination' (p. 12, 30 September 1984); and
     'Mosaic tests: were they H-bombs?' (p. 12, 1 October 1984).
13   See Jim McClelland, *Stirring the Possum: A Political Autobiography*, Viking/
     Penguin, Melbourne, 1988, p. 210.
14   See Milliken, *No Conceivable Injury*, pp. 334–5.
15   Milliken, for instance, quotes this comment from *The Guardian*, which had
     been particularly positive about the 'refreshingly informal' but 'persist-
     ently inquisitive Australians': 'The whole story amounts to another
     swingeing indictment of British official secretiveness, and it is to our
     shame that it was left to the Australians to expose it' (p. 319).
16   *Sydney Morning Herald*, 5 January 1985, p. 4.
17   See Milliken, pp. 330–8 for an account of the deterioration of relations
     between the British and Australian counsel.
18   Robert Milliken, 'The Nuclear Fallout in St James's Square', *The National
     Times*, 11–17 January 1985, p. 4.
19   ibid. p. 3.
20   The Australian government was careful to maintain a low profile to avoid
     being cast as a defendant, while the British put off appointing a counsel
     until it was clear there was nothing they could do to avoid being cast as
     a defendant.
21   Papers which ran lead stories using this headline include *The Australian*
     (5 January 1985), the *Sydney Morning Herald* (5 January 1985) and the *Sun-
     Herald* (6 January 1985).
22   For example, Sue Morgan's front page story in the *Sydney Morning Herald*
     on 10 January 1985, headlined 'Atomic Tests: How UK Lied'.
23   See Milliken, *No Conceivable Injury*, pp. 316–17.
24   'Dealing with the Legacy of the Past: Aborigines and Atomic Testing in
     South Australia', *Aboriginal History*, 14:1–2, 1990, p. 205.
25   ibid. p. 200.
26   'McClelland's Royal Commission: An Exercise in Practical Politics',
     Quadrant, 30:3, March 1986, pp. 33–8.
27   6 December 1985, p. 13.
28   6 December 1985, p. 16.
29   *A Nation at Last? The Changing Character of Australian Nationalism 1880–
     1988*, Angus & Robertson, Sydney, 1988, p. 230.
30   Robert Cockburn, 'Maralinga tribal lands for war games park', *The Bul-
     letin*, 25 July 1989, pp. 35–6.
31   See also Max Hawkins, 'Defence Update', *Australian Aviation*, September,
     1989, pp. 82–4. The office of the Minister of Defence responded to my
     enquiries as to future plans of this kind in a letter on 12 December 1991.
     It largely endorsed the outline given in Hawkins' article but denied any
     use of ordinance was intended. At that date the Maralinga people had not
     responded, nor was there any 'planned development' of the war games
     park on a commercial basis.
32   David Lague, 'US may shift bomb ranges to Australia', *Financial Review*, (7
     November 1991), p. 6. The French connection is made in the *Dateline* story.
33   See, for example, 'Australia keeps wraps on UK bomb fall-out report', *The
     Times*, 5 July 1989 and 'Maralinga Aborigines want Britain to pay for
     clean-up', *The Times*, 9, 2–3, 1991.

13
(Mis)taking policy: Notes on the cultural policy debate

TOM O'REGAN

Much of the literature associated with cultural studies can be inter-preted as policy analysis. This is because, historically, cultural studies has been concerned centrally with the exploration and criticism of various strategies and programs of action and obligation, organised both discursively and institutionally. The forms of power exercised by state and private institutions, the forms of conduct they proscribe and the accommodations and resistances they meet are part and parcel of cultural studies' orientation. In this context policy tends to be under-stood in terms of its consequences and outcomes, and in terms of the actions of those affected by it as they attempt to exert some measure of influence upon the process. Cultural studies has adopted a deter-minedly 'bottom-up' policy towards all this, so as to emphasise the process of and need for negotiations on the part of those affected vis-à-vis the institutions and structures which formulate and design any-thing from texts to the built environment to administrative programs. Policy programs *per se* were not of so much concern as was their negotiation by intended subjects; whether the 'wild' viewers in media analysis,[1] the recalcitrant students destined, in the pedagogic analysis of *Learning to Labour*, for careers as labourers,[2] or the particular sub-cultural, ethnic and gender identities formed in response to social plan-ning, media logics, or prescriptive forms of moral and social conduct.[3]

In accordance with this largely bottom-up program, the policy of cultural studies involved foregrounding the recipient, the victim and the marginal in the exercise of social and cultural power. Sometimes this entailed a strategy of providing them with a voice they would not otherwise have;[4] sometimes it simply served as a kind of news func-tion;[5] at its best it encouraged forms of community-authorised speech

---

* This paper was first published in *Cultural Studies* 6/3 (1992).

or strategic intervention.[6] Cultural studies' polemical practice was one which often championed the restoration of community and ritual in the face of what James Carey calls a 'transmission' view of culture and communication (manipulation, control at a distance on the part of government and private agencies from broadcasters to the education system).[7] Cultural studies distanced itself, on the one hand, from political economy and cultural industry approaches by insisting on the degree of noise, negotiation, failure and contradiction attendant upon all social interactions in their passage from donor to recipient, TV institution to audience member, newspaper to reader, entertainer to entertained. On the other hand, it distanced itself from textual analysis approaches by situating the reading and consumption of symbolic goods in a multiplicity of audience settings—sociocultural, ethnic, subcultural and gendered. At its best cultural studies promoted a multilayered account of social practice in which the meaning of, say, a film or TV program would be traced not in one analytical exercise but in a series of texts where textual analysis, political economy and ethnography would all play a part.[8]

Coupled with this multidisciplinary approach, cultural studies was characterised by a particular ethical agenda, perhaps best expressed in the work of Eric Michaels.[9] His research was driven by a set of ethical concerns for the politics and conduct of research, of media practice, and of the consumption of media and artistic programming. In the process he transformed the visual anthropology of Sol Worth.[10] For instance, Michaels:

• took the enterprise of ethnographic filmmaking, already historically fraught with problems, one stage further. In the process he articulated a new and emerging role for the European in Aboriginal Australia as facilitator rather than creative collaborator.
• overturned some traditional 'policy' expectations about so-called disadvantaged or non-literate audiences, concentrating instead on the way in which video and TV technologies were incorporated in a dynamic way into their culture.[11]
• attacked the priority given by government to 'educating the white audience', directing Aboriginal media priorities towards inter- and intra-Aboriginal communication.[12]
• demonstrated the ethical issues of subjects' rights, typically overlooked by documentarists (filmmakers and social scientists alike), concerned as they were purely with the description of social problems.[13]
• eschewed the easy and simple divisions between audience studies, producer studies, and institutional studies; seeking instead to locate TV as part of wider social technologies, in an approach he sometimes called an anthropology of TV.[14]
• actively sought community authorisation of the research work which he conducted for and on behalf of a particular Aboriginal community.[15]

On such grounds as these, cultural studies engaged with the policy development of the state from the point of view of disadvantaged recipients or those who are excluded from such policies altogether, and it sought to defend or restore community. For instance, Tim Rowse in *Arguing the Arts*[16] rewrote Bourdieu[17] in the Australian context of arts policy, supporting forms of community arts as the basis of social equity and community involvement.

Cultural *criticism* in this universe entailed both cultural critique and policy engagement; some writers moved between the two poles. Sometimes cultural critique acted as a substitute for policy, at other times it was a priority in itself—it depended on where you were, and on the environment in which decisions were being made (whether decision-making was responsive to engagement or not). Things varied from sector to sector; in Australia, for instance, museum, art, film, and educational policy provided scope for policy engagement, whilst broadcasting policy presented more difficult (though not impossible) prospects. Things also varied from country to country; the Reagan and Bush years have not been highly conducive to even marginally left involvement in cultural policy in the US. In Britain meanwhile, the Thatcher period saw the disruption of connections between cultural initiatives and cultural criticism; radical criticism was excluded from the policy club altogether, as screen and arts policy were increasingly determined from the top. But in Australia, the same period saw the years of Labor ascendancy; in such a climate, progressive cultural criticism could and did 'count' rather more than in countries where conservatives were in office. Yet in Australia too it was a period when 'policy' seemed to come into its own, either in the form of a proactive consultancy role or in a reactive defensive political role, lobbying for the maintenance of existing programs. Either way the 1980s increasingly saw the ascendancy of a differently constituted 'policy' arena —and policy increasingly became known through governmental nomenclature, such as film policy, broadcasting policy, arts policy, equal opportunity policy and the like. It has become a more central political and public issue at a time when government resources for culture have been diminishing, when the management of the public sector has been overhauled, and when programs for educational relevance have gained favour in the political arena.

Enter the 'policy debate' in cultural studies in Australia.[18] Most of the intellectual running on behalf of the pro-policy position has been made by writers associated with or close to Griffith University in Brisbane—Tony Bennett, Stuart Cunningham, Ian Hunter, Colin Mercer, Jennifer Craik, Toby Miller (and, in a previous incarnation, myself)—especially since the founding of its Institute for Cultural Policy Studies (IPCS). The Communication Law Centre at the University of New South Wales and the Centre for International Research in Communication and Information Technologies (CIRCIT) in Melbourne are also active in 'policy' work. For these players, there is something wrong at the heart of the whole cultural studies enterprise. They call for the double reconstitution of policy: both as an object of study in its own right and as a political site of activity and analysis. They argue that the policy process as understood by governmental and private agencies should also be the centrepiece of cultural studies itself. However, since cultural studies was already concerned with policy, the current debate is over its orientation, and about what can count as policy; hence, they argue, cultural studies should reorient its concerns so as to coincide with top-down programs and public procedures, becoming bureaucratically and administratively minded in the process.[19] What is meant by 'policy' would also be narrowed in focus, towards those things which are called policy in political and bureaucratic terms—and these things, together with their agents and agencies, would constitute strategic targets for cultural policy studies. Such an orientation is therefore interested in creating a focused object with a definite inside and outside, assigning limited purposes to it, and in modifying the role of critical theorising and polemical analysis with regard to it. The policy-maker emerges in this scenario as an intellectual agent in his or her own right, making and intervening, not simply translating or putting into effect the ideas and plans of 'pure' intellectual cadres.

For policy proponents, adjustments in cultural criticism itself flow directly from policy activity; existing cultural criticism is criticised with reference to policy and policy analysis. Policy becomes the motor that drives cultural criticism, making it congruent with policy through impressing upon it 'appropriate adjustments of a theoretical and practical nature'.[20] As Tony Bennett concludes in the essay 'Useful Culture':

> In short we must recognise that cutting off the King's head in cultural theory means giving up the stance of the cultural critic and embracing instead that of the cultural technician. Not in a behaviourist sense but from a recognition of the complexity of the relations between culture, government and power which means taking account of the specific natures of different cultural institutions and technologies, the textual regimes that they give rise to and the specific forms of politics that they generate.[21]

Bennett calls for a change of mind-set on the part of cultural studies practitioners to adapt to this policy object. Those espousing a policy orientation on the part of cultural studies see their task as shifting it away from its present moorings and the prevailing 'rhetorics of resistance, progressiveness, anti-commercialism on the one hand, and populism on the other', as Cunningham puts it, moving instead 'toward those of access, equity, empowerment and the divination of opportunities to exercise appropriate cultural leadership'.[22] Specifically rejected in Bennett's words is 'the grand-standing of the cultural critic as an acceptable mode of intellectual work'[23] in favour of the cultural technician. In such a policy orientation 'cultural studies' becomes 'cultural policy studies'.

From this vantage point the existing project of cultural studies

195

appears to be hopelessly anarcho-romantic. Its commitment to community becomes identified as an act of faith; one which can be compromised (as in Raymond Williams's patriarchal Welsh working class, according to Bennett).[24] The goal is no longer to celebrate and help restore the community which survives and resists manipulative social and cultural programs; it is rather to accept the necessary lot of intervention and to recognise that such communities are themselves the by-product of policy.

Such a positioning of policy sees the humanities in general, and cultural studies in particular, as dependent upon *policy horizons*. This in turn has implications for the tertiary curriculum—especially since cultural studies is identified as actively disabling student participation in cultural industries.[25] Cultural policy studies analysts no longer identify, or maintain solidarity, with a broad political front operating on behalf of a loosely organised group of agencies and individuals. Instead, they accept a role as nodal points operating in the context of a set of polycentric institutional forces—that is, they constitute themselves as participants in a policy process.

The proponents of policy of this kind have conducted their arguments in deliberately provocative and binary terms, setting up divisions such as: policy versus post-modernism; cultural policy versus cultural criticism; reformist versus oppositional political practice; contextualist versus textualist emphases; Foucault the theorist of 'governmentality' versus Foucault the libertarian. Promoted as choices, these binaries entail quite different forms of conduct and self-recognition, directing engagement towards very different ends.

For those promoting this debate the central concern is with the utility, effectiveness and adequacy of cultural criticism on the one hand (seen as deficient on all counts), and the kinds of emergent practices and writing and reading protocols stemming from a policy orientation on the other. At the very least the debate signposts the possibility of self-consciously extending humanities work to include policy writing, advice and involvement. It also reminds us to take account of the quotidian histories, techniques and strategies of cultural governance which underlie the international agenda of cultural studies itself. It suggests an alternative career—that of cultural technician as opposed to cultural critic. Being a 'cultural technician'—in the sense of securing policy resources, consultancies and engagements—becomes in this moment as critical to the CV as do articles in refereed journals and books. The policy debate emerged as a bid to make the humanities—its programs, its knowledges, and its self-projections—count in policy development and the policy process by means of 'attached' intellectual work rather than just through the 'unattached'[26] involvement of cultural and social commentary.

The debate was about the direction of cultural studies as an academic or theoretical enterprise because those making the bid made it so. That they were taken so seriously resulted from shared perceptions of a 'crisis in the humanities', in terms of its relation to government and its curriculum.[27] The controversy assigns cultural studies a centrality in discussions over the future of the humanities that is at first glance surprising, given the tenuous hold of cultural studies as a disciplinary project in Australia and elsewhere. But in such Australian cultural journals as *Meanjin*, the term 'cultural studies' has become almost synonymous with the humanities in general, legitimating the humanities' effectivity in relation both to aesthetics and to everyday life. In the process cultural studies has become synonymous with the humanities' most 'relevant' aspects—be they the study of media, criticism of contemporary texts, historical studies, the study of social practices, or whatever. Cultural studies in this context comes to mean the broad mix of cultural criticism involving history and anthropology, literature and fine arts, communication and media studies. In such circumstances cultural studies becomes both a pedagogic ambition in its own right and a label for departmental and research organisation—there are, increasingly, schools of communication and culture, and centres for research in culture and communication, in Australian universities.

Why this peculiar assignment of centrality to a vaguely defined cultural studies? It is a reaction to perceptions of the diminishing role and importance of cultural criticism generally in contemporary educational, political and social processes in Australia, which has contributed to a palpable sense of crisis of identity and practice in cultural criticism. It is also a response to the demand for cultural planning and external advice-taking in government and interest group politics, in areas as diverse as communications, broadcasting, museum, heritage, arts, and educational policy. Under the looser kinds of policy development of the immediate past, various humanities researchers and graduates were able to find important places in policy, but with the ascendance of ('rationalist') economics and more centralist policy development these kinds of opportunities and competences have lost ground. The governmental 'main game' in policy has been transformed in social and cultural sectors, from styles of advice-taking that accommodate consensus formation and diverse inputs, towards a more profoundly centralist, less publicly accountable, and therefore limited style of advice-taking, marked by the ascendance of economic knowledges in public policy.[28] This 'game' has threatened to remove other knowledges from administrative horizons altogether, particularly those concerned with culture, forcing them at best into an accommodation with economic orthodoxy. Recognition of this governmental logic may account for the slightly desperate tone of some of the pro-policy contributions to the policy debate; the fear is that cultural studies is fiddling while Rome burns.

The policy bid can be seen, then, as a kind of reclamation exercise in circumstances where the injunction to be socially relevant has been given a significant, alternative and much more specific 'policy' definition. Bennett, for instance, advocates the production of 'positive knowledges that can be effectively used within actually existing spheres of cultural policy formation'.[29] Here work is to be regarded as relevant insofar as it participates in and extends administrative processes. The formerly loose and all-inclusive generality of what might *count* as social relevance is radically limited, narrowed to policy practice: that which can be made governmentally or corporately actionable, can be publicly endorsed, and can be institutionally sanctioned and found useful by government, tribunals, policy-makers and interest group lobbyists *directly* involved in forming policies. Of course these competing terms of 'relevance' are not new, but what is different here is that the pro-policy position has been lent extra weight and has gained powerful allies by virtue of the contemporary policy movement and adjacent changes in tertiary education.

For some, like Bennett and Hunter, the turn to narrowly defined policy is also a consequence of a re-theorisation of the humanities in the light of Foucault's later writings. In this re-theorisation the humanities as such become a cultural policy instrument, whose workings can be disclosed by a Foucauldian attention to administrative programs and their attendant 'technologies of the self'.[30] In this respect the 'administrative' side of the controversy has been lent extra weight by Ian Hunter's *Culture and Government*,[31] a thoroughgoing, sophisticated and ideological reading of the formation of the humanities as a technique of governance and social power. This analysis has wrong-footed certain routine justifications of non-intervention in the humanities (academic freedom, tenure etc), and made it difficult to assert that those promoting policy are reliant upon some untheorised pragmatic politics of the existent.

Even so, it must be said that Hunter's is a limited reading of Foucault, using his notions of governance to foreground the production of 'well-tempered subjects', to the exclusion of his focus upon 'unruly subjects' (to use Toby Miller's happy phrases).[32] Foucault's insistence upon regulation and governmentality as critical to the modern era is reconstructed by Hunter as an injunction to participate in that regulation as if that were the only socially forceful position to take. It is worth considering Foucault's position here. He argued that his work should be regarded not so much as providing answers but as providing resources that certain sorts of activists—such as prisoners' rights groups—might find useful in their own practice.[33] It was up to such groups to make Foucault's work 'useful'; he would not legislate how that use should occur. By contrast, the current policy polemic proposes a reading of Foucault which supports not relay and mediation, and therefore a gap between policy analysis and practice, but a means of acting in the social directly on behalf of and for governmental agencies. There is no gap here between cultural criticism and concrete intervention—only applicability; intervention is thus closely defined in terms of the occupation, consideration and development of policy.

These theoretical and practical developments mirror changes in the 'external' economic, structural and political environment, where far-reaching reforms in Australia, the US and Britain have brought social, industry, communications and arts policy issues to the top of the public agenda. They have also encouraged its proponents to argue for the advantages that a policy orientation can confer on cultural studies and on the humanities in general. But debate about these issues has been divisive. I have been part of this debate and associated with the cultural policy push. For I do have a certain regard for the practice of cultural policy: it is too important to remain under-examined in cultural studies. Like others who have discovered policy participation and the complexity of policy processes, I found cultural studies' current emphases and ethical imperatives to be a barrier rather than a vehicle for analysis. Unlike those who berated cultural studies in its more utopian and gestural manifestations, I simply set up shop somewhere else, and have variously gone by the label of cultural historian, film critic, sociologist, and political scientist. My criticisms of cultural studies were every bit as unflattering as Bennett's or Cunningham's; they were merely made in private (and on the questionnaire circulated by Stuart Cunningham as part of his research for *Framing Culture*), and remained at that personal level through which one's own institutional and writing trajectory is negotiated. No wonder then that my own reluctance to endorse the cultural policy push wholeheartedly, and to take a calculated distance from it, was surprising to those who expected my support. I could not give this support and was critical of the form and direction of this debate. But this was a criticism within cultural policy studies about its direction and orientation, rather than a thoroughgoing defence of cultural studies.

With this preamble in mind I will now propose an alternative view of policy to that proposed by Bennett. Foucauldian policy analysis can take two alternative directions: the one pursued by Bennett and Hunter which is reliant upon propositional contents and a reading of Foucauldian 'rationalities' as 'technologies'; and the other, my preferred direction, in which policy is approached as a technique of information handling in much the same way as Bruno Latour approaches science—as 'policy in action', as a cultural technology.[34] Such an approach has no argument with many of Bennett's fundamental tenets. Policy is interlocked with adjacent fields of cultural criticism, intellectual debate, administration, and lobbying. But I don't think policy, seen as particular intellectual programs for machining the social, is the structural engine room which powers everything else. Policy is a particular kind of informational practice with its own limitations, potentialities and linkages to other kinds of public discourse, including cultural criticism and journalism, over which it holds no necessary pre-eminence.

Bennett attends to the 'rationalities' or 'intellectual technologies' of government—ie the specification of the policy process itself as a knowledge-producing program designed to render the social field intelligible, calculable, and productive of certain desired effects. But a policy focus could equally concentrate on the 'rhetorical', 'information-handling' practices of governmental and other lobbying groups;

their particular techniques of verbal assemblage and the attendant reading protocols, the procedures through which other groups and individuals are enlisted, the machinery for the organisation of advice taking. Each brings into relief different aspects of the policy process. The Bennett–Hunter position foregrounds the propositional contents of policy as so many 'rationalities'; the Latourian position foregrounds the 'rhetorical' or persuasive aspects of the policy process—its network of actors, disposition of institutions, enunciative dimension. I don't think that a cultural studies account of policy can do without each focus.

This 'rhetorical' understanding of policy informs my analysis of the policy debate itself. I consider policy-making and cultural criticism as taking place in different sites and mobilising differently organised actors. I see the two sites as routinely exchanging personnel, ideas, words and phrases; in addition, policy actors will typically use cultural criticism sites to secure advantages in the policy-making process, just as cultural critics will use cultural policy involvements to gain advantages for themselves and their constituents. But the focus on the information handling practices of policy allows attention to turn to the uses made of inscriptions—the reading and writing practices undertaken, the disposition of ideas and their subsequent 'careers' in texts, and the networks of actors engaged in policy. Such a focus assumes that cultural policy and cultural criticism are both part of the larger political process (along with journalism). This suggests that policy and cultural criticism should not be counterposed as either mutually antagonistic forms of life, or as forms of life possessing any intrinsic conceptual, political or ethical advantage over each other. Rather a set of historically determined relations organise their differences and similarities over time, rendering the form of the relation between the two unavailable to general prescription.

In the Australian policy debate, however, the specificity of cultural policy as opposed to cultural criticism has been sought in terms of the character of their respective propositional contents—the words and phrases that they use. It is argued that cultural criticism could become cultural policy if it used different and more appropriate phrases and words—if it acquired a policy language and a reformist orientation.[35] I see this as a fundamental category mistake. The difference between cultural policy-making and cultural criticism consists as much in the kinds of reading, writing and manipulation that is practised upon 'proposition contents' as those contents themselves. Policy and cultural criticism are contiguous styles of reasoning involving shared discursive resources and reasoning procedures, but they deploy such shared resources in different ways. (The same distinction holds for the ways in which politicians, journalists and interested others argue, criticise, add to, and consider policy.)

So a choice cannot be made between policy and cultural criticism: we simply do one or the other depending upon the circumstance, and sometimes we do both at the same time. This is not to have it a bob each way. It is simply to point out that our contemporary society has a number of different information-handling practices and ways of acting and intervening in the world. Such diversity cannot and will not be 'remedied' by fiat, by turning cultural critics into bureaucrats, or by taking no account of the *varieties* of textual, critical and analytical techniques that are associated with the humanities and cultural studies.

Policy thus needs to be understood alongside a range of other activities and sites, including cultural criticism, journalism, cultural production, capital-P Politics. Sometimes it may act in a command position with regard to these sites, but mostly it does not, remaining instead another minor player, alongside the much maligned 'cultural critic', whose social power therefore also needs to be understood. This power may be difficult to mobilise concretely and resembles in important ways 'star' or 'personality' power. Yet such figures may shape the public agenda in ways that permit policy actors to act, providing them with valuable resources and arguments. For instance, I have shown elsewhere that there simply would not have been the kind of publicly funded support for feature film production if it were not for the cultural criticism of the late 1950s and 1960s.[36]

As far as intervention and self-conduct are concerned, the very issue of choosing between policy and cultural criticism—which to write for, which to inhabit—must turn out to be a question admitting no general answer. There are no *a priori* principles for choosing policy over cultural criticism. Nor can any presumption be made about social utility and effectiveness as necessarily belonging to one or the other. Cultural policy and cultural criticism are not hermetically sealed but are porous systems; open enough to permit transformation, incorporation and translation, fluid enough to permit a great range of practices and priorities. To put this crudely: terms like 'social class' and 'oppression' (and their attendant rhetorics) may not enter the vocabulary of government policy, but without their social presence in credible explanatory systems, any policy directed towards securing equality and equal opportunity would be diminished in scope and power. The recognition of oppression informs the policy goal of access, the persistence of social class underwrites the goal of social equality. Cultural policy and criticism are different forms of life, but they often need each other, they use each other's discourses, borrowing them shamelessly and redisposing them. Under some conditions they may clash, but normally they go happily along their more or less parallel, more or less divergent paths.

It seems to me that a critical regard for policy may end up serving four different purposes:

- state purposes—efficiency, equity, excellence, etc
- reformist purposes—which involve working 'within' administrative knowledges but with the aim of effecting changes
- antagonistic purposes—which involve critique and opposition, both general and policy-specific

THE POLITICS OF PUBLICS

• diagnostic purposes—in which policy emerges as a politics of discourse in a descriptive enterprise.

These are also the purposes for policy analysis and cultural studies. In Foucault, Latour and Michaels, policy can serve each of these purposes and the writer adopts one or the other depending upon the circumstance.

By contrast, for those involved in the 'policy debate', it appears to be a priority to expel *antagonistic* and *oppositional* purposes on an *a priori* basis, at least those identified as tendencies in cultural studies itself. This hostile orientation to cultural studies can, I believe, be explained by reference to the purpose of the 'policy debate' for those making it. Its purposes may be listed as follows:

• The debate serves to legitimate a focus on policy and governmental process as the object of attention on the part of a broad left constituency.
• It provides a way of promoting 'policy' in the theoretical and historical self-understandings of cultural studies.
• It promotes the adjustment of the tertiary curriculum, to take account of policy.
• It orientates academic and general intellectual attention towards policy uptake, and away from less direct, eccentric, and antagonistic cultural engagements.
• It makes a bid for the humanities to count on policy horizons, and serves to connect the humanities to the social sciences in ways cultural studies has neglected.
• It seeks to ensconce policy participation in career, reputation and reward structures.
• It promotes an edifying purpose for policy—intellectual, moral and social, rather than simply pragmatic, instrumental or opportunistic reasoning.

Meanwhile policy involvement has become a live issue for its participants as it has proceeded apace, become a routine practical ethical issue, and has started to impose its own logics on those who participate in it. It has led to a number of different orientations to policy involvement, which are coming to regard it:

• as a professional service being provided by specialists;
• as a holding operation, justified on the grounds of the special needs of a particular sector (this has led a number of left-leaning intellectuals, previously distanced from the film policy process and critical of it, to become central to the projects of the things they once criticised);[37]
• as a means of holding out for different techniques of policy engagement—more bottom-up rather than top-down policy development, more tribunal and public commission and less consultancy;
• as a means of going on the offensive; 'if you can't beat them join

them, and then you might be able to develop counter-programs and institutions' (policy becomes a way of meeting a more sharply defined 'relevance' agenda, setting 'new horizons' and sometimes working on the principle of getting in before the political right does, occupying the policy domain to pre-empt a more complete overhaul).

These pro-policy responses have in turn engendered a backlash because of their institutional threat to critical reasoning, which is justified by reference to 'academic freedom', 'freedom to think', as a non-instrumental reasoning historically aligned with oppositional, oppressed and marginal groups. The policy push is criticised as a kind of 'asset-stripping' operation, which denies the specificity of the techniques, orientations and practices that cultural studies may be good at. It appears to those engaged in cultural studies that the policy push would leave cultural studies as a mere social science policy project, stripped of both humanities and critical social science knowledges. Questions have also been raised about the very narrow view of policy as simply policy development, government process, consultancy and the like, as opposed to a wider view which includes other participants and knowledges, beyond commissioned policy documents, published procedures and so on. There is a related questioning of the way consultancies are conducted, and the ethics of arranging fields of knowledge and assuming a relative importance through that arrangement. Finally there is the criticism that those promoting the debate have ensconced a 'pragmatic' politics as the horizon of the thinkable— thereby assuming a solidity rather than fragility to those politics and political processes. That is to say, this program tends to assume a rightness of current politics and agenda setting. It relies less on principle than upon identification of political needs to be met.

These tendencies can lead either to a consideration of the ethics of policy involvement and the limits of pragmatism or to the creating of scapegoats in cultural studies and intellectuals for helping to bring about the present environment. Such scapegoating can be quite poignant as it involves identifying as culprit one's own past history or what Bennett has called his 'erstwhile theoretical self'[38] yet this is no substitute for addressing the site-specific politics and ethics of contemporary policy involvement.

In cultural studies we often make a topic of other people's contestive conduct, but there are few ethnographies of intellectual communities in conflict—we rarely consider our own handling of controversy as an information handling priority. The policy debate certainly says much about styles of engaged performance in an area which has defined its boundaries in terms of definite moral and ethical imperatives. Such imperatives license the *engagé(e)*, help organise the performance of a passionate engagement with methodology, procedure and orientation. They authorise forms of public recanting which don't function to shift the recusant *off* the stage but to push him or her further into the limelight. And they authorise an either/or, for-or-against logic, in which colleagues are deemed to hold up, inhibit and prevent the realisation of the critical and interventionist program proposed, because of their articles of faith, research priorities and political emphases. Consequently there is a turning inward rather than outward; a few heads are kicked, rather than a different story being told or a different intervention in the social field being organised.

The controversies that result from the exercise of these logics are tailor-made for another sort of intervention. This is one which seeks to hold the diverse projects together, to diminish the scale of the controversy, to dissolve it by pointing to fundamental continuities between positions. I've tended to occupy that position. For me the policy debate raises questions rather than providing any answers. The varying meanings of policy for cultural studies and cultural policy studies admit no general answer. The debate does however put policy at the very heart of the critical enterprise, which in turn informs and speaks through even those like Bennett who in their explicit policy orientation seek to make it an object and topic of analysis.

NOTES

I would like to thank John Hartley and Ien Ang for their comments on this and earlier drafts. This article has particularly benefited from John Hartley's editorial eye.

1 See Ien Ang, 'Stalking the Wild Viewer', *Continuum* 4, 2 (1991), pp. 19–35.
2 Paul Willis, *Learning to Labour: How Working Class Kids Get Working Class Jobs*, Saxon House, London, 1977.
3 Marie Gillespie, 'Technology and Tradition: Audiovisual Culture among South Asian Families in West London', *Cultural Studies* 3, 2 (1989), pp. 226–39; Dick Hebdige, *Subculture: The Meaning of Style*, Methuen, London, 1979; Gillian Dyer and Helen Baehr (eds), *Boxed In: Women and Television*, Pandora, London, 1987.
4 Anne Krisman, 'Radiator Girls: The Opinions and Experiences of Working-Class Girls in an East London Comprehensive', *Cultural Studies* 1, 2 (1987), pp. 219–29.
5 Annette Hamilton, 'Beer and Being: The Australian Tourist in Bali', *Social Analysis* 27 (April 1990), pp. 17–29.
6 D Crimp (ed), *AIDS: Cultural Analysis, Cultural Activism*, MIT Press, Cambridge, MA, 1988.
7 James Carey, *Communication as Culture*, Unwin-Hyman, Boston, 1989, passim.
8 Eric Michaels, 'A Model of Teleported Texts (With Reference to Aboriginal Television)', *Continuum* 3, 2 (1990), pp. 8–31.
9 For a bibliography of Eric Michaels's work see 'Eric Michaels: A Partial Guide to his Written Work', *Continuum* 3, 2 (1990), pp. 226–28. This issue is devoted to an appraisal of Eric Michaels's intellectual and political projects.
10 Sol Worth, *Studying Visual Communication: The Essays of Sol Worth*, Larry Gross (ed), University of Philadelphia Press, Philadelphia, 1981.

11 This is a central concern of *For a Cultural Future: Francis Jupurrurla Makes TV at Yuendumu*, Artspace, Art and Criticism Series v 3, Sydney, 1987.
12 Eric Michaels, *For a Cultural Future*, p. 72.
13 Eric Michaels, 'Hundreds Shot in Aboriginal Community: ABC Makes TV Documentary at Yuendumu', *Media Information Australia* 45, 1987, pp. 7–17.
14 See Michaels, 'A Model of Teleported Texts', pp. 8–31.
15 Eric Michaels 'Ask a Foolish Question: On the Methodologies of Cross-Cultural Media Research', *Australian Journal of Cultural Studies* 3, 2 (1985), pp. 45–59.
16 Tim Rowse, *Arguing the Arts*, Penguin, Ringwood, 1985.
17 Pierre Bourdieu, 'The Aristocracy of Culture', *Media Culture and Society* 2 (1980), pp. 225–54.
18 The debate is registered most forcefully in the following essays and publications: Tony Bennett, 'Useful Culture', *Cultural Studies* 6/3 (1992); and 'Culture: Theory and Policy', *Culture & Policy* 1, 1 (1989), pp. 5–8; Toby Miller, 'Film and Media Citizenship', *Filmnews* Feb. 1990, p. 5; Stuart Cunningham, 'Cultural Critique and Cultural Policy: Handmaiden or No Relation', *Media Information Australia* 54 (1989), pp. 7–12; 'Cultural Studies from the Viewpoint of Cultural Policy', *Meanjin* 50, 2/3 (1991), pp. 423–34; *Framing Culture*, Allen & Unwin, Sydney, 1992; Helen Grace, 'Eating the Curate's Egg: Cultural Studies for the Nineties', *West* 3, 1 (1991), pp. 46–9; Graeme Turner, 'Well-kept Secrets: The Public Role of Media Studies', *Atom News* 5, 4 (1990), pp. 7–17.
19 See Bennett, 'Culture: Theory and Policy', pp. 5–8.
20 Tony Bennett, 'Useful Culture', *Cultural Studies*, 6/3 (1992).
21 Bennett, 'Useful Culture', *Cultural Studies*, 6/3 (1992).
22 Cunningham, 'Cultural Studies from the Viewpoint of Cultural Policy', p. 434. This quotation was cited approvingly in Bennett's Dismantle paper.
23 Bennett, 'Culture: Theory and Policy', p. 7. The cultural critic is rejected in Bennett's mind because of his/her orientation to: 'a purely rhetorical politics, highly prone to denunciatory stances, in which positions are deduced from general principles and applied across different policy fields with scant regard for their different histories, organisation, characteristic mechanism, institutional arrangements, and so on' (p. 7).
24 Bennett, 'Useful Culture', *Cultural Studies*, 6/3 (1992).
25 This is a point that Stuart Cunningham and Ian Connell and Geoff Hurd make. See Geoff Hurd and Ian Connell, 'Cultural Education: A Revised Programme', *Media Information Australia* 53 (August 1989), pp. 23–30; and Cunningham, 'Cultural Studies from the Viewpoint of Cultural Policy', p. 432.
26 Terminology adopted from Robert K Merton, *Social Theory and Social Structure*, Free Press, New York, 1968, p. 266. 'Unattached intellectuals' refers here to those 'intellectuals who do not perform a staff function in helping to formulate and implement policies of a bureaucracy'. For Merton academics are unattached intellectuals despite their connection with 'academic bureaucracy' in that 'they typically are not expected to utilize their specialized knowledge for shaping the policies of the bureaucracy' (p. 266).
27 Dieter Freundlieb, 'Calculating the Incalculable: Governmental Reasoning and the Humanities', *Meanjin*, 49, 2 (1990), pp. 368–447; Stephen Knight, 'Searching for Research or The Selling of the Australian Mind', *Meanjin* 48, 3 (1989), pp. 456–62; Ann Curthoys, 'Unlocking the Academies: Responses and Strategies', *Meanjin* 50, 2/3 (1991), pp. 386–93.

28 See Michael Pusey, *Economic Rationalism in Canberra: A Nation Building State Changes Its Mind*, Cambridge University Press, Cambridge, 1991.
29 Bennett cited in Ann Curthoys, 'Unlocking the Academies: Responses and Strategies', *Meanjin* 50, 2/3 (1991), p. 387.
30 Ian Hunter, 'Personality as Vocation: The Political Rationality of the Humanities', *Economy & Society* 19, 4 (1990), pp. 391–430.
31 Ian Hunter, *Culture and Government: The Emergence of Literary Education*, Macmillan, Basingstoke, 1988.
32 Toby Miller, 'The Well-Tempered Self: Formations of the Cultural Subject', PhD Thesis, School of Humanities, Murdoch University, 1991.
33 Michel Foucault, *Power/Knowledge: Selected Interviews and Other Writings, 1972–1977*, edited by Colin Gordon, Pantheon Books, New York, p. 62.
34 Bruno Latour, *Science in Action*, Harvard University Press, Cambridge, Mass., 1987.
35 Stuart Cunningham, 'Cultural Studies from the Viewpoint of Cultural Policy', p. 434.
36 Tom O'Regan, 'Australian Film-making: its Public Circulation', *Framework* 22/23 (1983), pp. 31–6.
37 In the area of Australian screen studies Elizabeth Jacka and Stuart Cunningham are the most significant in this respect, providing supportive comment to the Australian production industry in their published articles, letters to the editor, consultancies, and books. But this has become a more general condition. I too have found myself regularly dealing with the Australian Film Commission and the Screen Producers Association of Australia.
38 Bennett was responding to a demand 'to name names' at the Dismantle conference.

PART V
The practice of place

14

Camera natura: Landscape in Australian feature films

ROSS GIBSON

> But the spirits have to be recognized to become real. They are not outside us, nor even entirely within, but flow back and forth between us and the objects we have made, the landscape we have shaped and move in. We have dreamed all these things in our deepest lives and they are ourselves. It is our self we are making out there...
>
> David Malouf

Mad Max fights for hegemony over it. Picnickers are subsumed into it, never never to return. The man from Snowy River spurs his small and weedy beast in a race to master it. It maps out the sorrow of the stoic shearer's wife who sees cause to lament that on Sunday Jack Thompson is too far away.

The common denominator in all these situations, the leitmotif and ubiquitous central character, is the Australian landscape. Its foregrounding (plus midgrounding and backgrounding) is such that the country becomes something much more significant than the environmental setting for indigenous narratives. In so many ways these films are *about* the Australian landscape. Cinematographers— Boyd, McAlpine, Hansen—become *auteurs*, as infinite space and light and colour are combined to elicit audience-gasps at sublimity. It's *our* inexpressibly bloody beautiful country! (This point about cinematographers is especially relevant in the light of the sham(e)-elegiac tone that advertisers adopted to promote *We of the Never Never* as the *chef d'oeuvre* of the late Gary Hansen. Implicitly, this is a film from the soul, about the Australian ethos. The film-maker apotheothised speaks for the nation.) Human beings wander through the frame—minuscule strangers in a strange landscape with figures. The five films already invoked don't furnish the only examples. Think also of *My Brilliant*

---

* This essay first appeared in *On the Beach* No 1, Autumn 1983.

209

New South Wales Lands Department aerial survey map of the Boggabri district.

Career, Chant of Jimmy Blacksmith, Journey Among Women, Plains of Heaven, or the early stages of *Gallipoli.*

I don't intend to pass judgment on films, to say this one gets it right, that one is lost in a wasteland. Rather I want to understand why mainstream film-makers, audiences and critics in Australia are currently under the spell of some spirit of the land. Why this (money-spinning) obsession with the natural environment? (It's too easy to say, 'Because it's there'.) What can the preoccupation tell us about Australian culture, cinematic and general?

A trek toward some answers might start in the territory of Australian art history. A cliché can be a point of reference and departure: non-Aboriginal Australia is still a ludicrously young society. The country is sparsely populated and meagerly historicised. Every plot of earth, every spike of spinifex hasn't accrued a story, hasn't yet become a sign in the arbitrary system of meaning which is history. To white sensibility

210

most of Australia is empty space, devoid of inhabitants, architecture, artefacts. It hasn't been incorporated into the symbolic order, except as a signifier of emptiness, a cultural *tabula rasa*, a sublime structuring void louring over all Australian culture. Compare Terra Australis with England's green and pleasant(!) land. Every Old World hectare has been ridden over, written over, inscribed into an elaborate, all-engrossing national culture. Virtually every region is a signifier in the chain of English history. East Anglia isn't just arable land; it is Constable country, habitable symbol of the pastoral dream. Cornwall refers to Celtic pre-history. Even the few regions like Dartmoor which do signify a certain obstinacy of nature can actually be quoted, in the context of English history, to emphasise the extent of cultural inscription over the land; Dartmoor stands as an exception that proves a rule. Hampshire evokes maritime myth and history. The Midlands are 'about' industrialisation and transport. And so on in a semiosis which is limited only littorally. English people inhabit a culture that covers their countryside. Australians, by contrast, are neither here nor there. Extensive tracts of the continent remain practically unsurveyed, even as considerable expanses (Botany Bay, the Never Never, Kelly Country, the Overflow, Van Diemen's Land) bear up under mythic connotations. Analysis of Australian landscape moves from questions of habitat to terms of hermeneutics, from referent to reference.

Australia is still being historicised, but we can't presume that, with the decades, the landscape will become systematised or artificed to the same degree as either the English countryside or an American urban environment such as New York, which nowadays is a semantic country unto itself—a symbol first and a city second. Factors of Australian nature and history impede the traditional processes of national acculturation. (It must be said, however, that Sydney is becoming a mythic city, on the way to being a symbol.) For a landscape to be regarded as the material of artistic discourse, the people utilising it need to identify with it, need to feel that they have control of that material, unless they want it to signify nothing but awesome indomitability. The geography must have been domesticated (or at least regarded as such), rendered safe for human manipulation and consumption. Such is the state of mythic England, where almost a millennium of concerted agriculture has wrought the earth to human design. In Australia, however, a different attitude is currently installed. The idea of the intractability of Australian nature is essential to the national ethos. It is a notion that was instigated by commentators like William Dampier long before European settlement; a notion promoted by the First Fleet journalists who detailed the anguish of a harrowed and perverse society struggling to understand and survive in a bizarre habitat; later certified by explorers whose diaries detail activities in an other-worldly wasteland at the centre of the continent; and ultimately perpetuated by the sundry legends of the Bush, the mythic region of isolation, desolation and a terrible beauty of 'nature learning how to write'.[1] Not exclusively the field of indigenous natural forces, nor the domain

211

Transcontinental railway. JT Furner at the border, 1901. (Courtesy of the National Library of Australia)

of artificial social constructs, the barely populated continent is formulated as a nether-world with an unplummetable vortex—half-tamed yet ultimately untameable, conceding social subsistence but never allowing human dominance. The mythic centre draws Australian arts onward, around and inward in quest of selfhood just at it lured so many early explorers.

Australian culture is propelled in an environmental dialectic in the region of drought and flood, dearth and plenty, nothingness and enormity, attrition and creation, while culture waveringly keeps its traditional adversary, nature, in check. The landscape becomes the projective screen for a persistent national neurosis deriving from the fear and fascination of a preternatural continent. (Hardly any of us ever see the never never, but we all know it's there, behind our backs.) Because Australians habitually regard the land as an awesome opponent rather than as a placid locale for the arbitrary organisation of life, and since the culture has not yet managed to subdue the nature (or at least to convince people that it has), Australian art is often 'anachronistically' concerned with 'primitive' themes. Generally speaking, Australian art is barely classifiable in terms of modernism (let alone postmodernism), where culture self-referentially creates more culture from existent culture rather than from nature. Of course, individual painters, sculptors, composers and writers have imbibed the modern European sensibility, but a great many Australian artists, and film-makers especially, are still processing Australian nature.

The culture has developed a short-circuit, traceable to the supra-social outback, which impedes the arts from switching on with the gaudy pyrotechnics of European modernism and postmodernism. Different region, different history. Is this such a bad thing? And is Australia presently 'third world' even as it is post-industrial? Eisenstein once wrote with regard to early twentieth-century Europe: 'At the intersection of Nature and Industry stands Art.'[2] Of Europe in the 1980s it might be said: 'Art is the industry of constructing new artefacts out of old signs that have already blotted out Nature'. And of Australia in the 1980s one could say: 'After incessant collisions between Nature and Industry, Art is scattered across the landscape, marking but never covering the continent'. At this stage of history, the Australian landscape shimmers in the collective consciousness as a mirage-like environment phasing in and out as sign.

In discussion of Australian cinema specifically, this notion appears enigmatic and convincing enough to shelter a seductive implication which marshalls so much lyrical panoramic cinematography to persuade us that, because human beings haven't cluttered the ground with their artefacts and connotations, the continent still stretches out as the text of some divine and immanent (as opposed to social and arbitrary) system of native, *Australian* meaning. If you want the real Australia, look at the earth, not the people. The landscape extends unsullied, the handiwork solely of nature, inscribed and subscribed with innate messages. Quintessential Australia hasn't yet been papered over by an alien Anglo-Saxon culture. So the story goes.

All this reverence (obscuring the unspecified fear) of the landscape is clearly the *result* of an alienated society's experience around the ridges of a vast, unpopulated and speciously indomitable country. But what of the *effects*? The legends of the awesome land imply the negligibility of social action. The society can't be seen to be directing the environment in its own interests (despite the multinationals' iniquitous ads about their quiet achievements in the ecosystem). It can't stretch out to cover all the unsubdued continent. In response to this implicit futility, the more heroic myths of individual-versus-the-environment fill the screen (*Mad Max, Sunday Too Far Away, The Irishman*). The society *en masse* can't make a mark on the land, so individuals set about carving niches for themselves, communing with the spirit of the land, reading its messages, jotting down hints for survival. In the inhuman landscape humanism flourishes. It is an aesthetic that André Bazin would have applauded. His remarks about the geography of Rosselini's *Viaggio in Italia* are startlingly apposite when applied to the environments presented in, say, *Mad Max* or *Sunday Too Far Away*: we are given 'a mental landscape at once as objective as a straight photograph and as subjective as pure personal consciousness'.[3] As Australian feature films survey this country of the mind, they enlist the connotations of verisimilitude which are still popularly

213

Transcontinental railway. Survey party at the border, 1901. (Courtesy of the National Library of Australia)

ascribed to photography at the same time as they present a Romantic image of geography. The implication is: 'This extra-human beauty, so sublime, is essentially Australian. Undeniably. There it is up on the screen. The camera doesn't lie'. Now maybe it *is* true that, the apocalypse notwithstanding (after Armageddon there'll be nothing left to talk about), there is a vast and incommunicable beauty which is untouched and untouchable by humanity. But the point is that once such geography is visualised and emphasised within a diegesis, it stands as something other than simple description; it has been transmuted into an element of myth, into a sign of supra-social Australian-ness. The *land* is installed as the country. The people don't get a look-in.

   This argument could be thrown out immediately if we could say, 'we all know the camera can and does lie', but unfortunately we don't all acknowledge such cinematic mendacity. In popular mythology, the filmic image (whether static or moving) still connotes denotation. The attitude espoused by Bazin in 'The Ontology of the Photographic Image' has never been fully discredited. Indeed it has received reiteration and seeming verification by no less an oracle than Roland Barthes:

> The (photographic) image is not the reality but at least it is the perfect analogon and it is exactly this analogical perfection which, to common sense, defines the photograph. Thus can be seen the special status of the photographic image: it is a message without a code.[4]

To be fair to Barthes, he writes of still photography here, but this 'common sense' view is often applied to motion pictures as well. It

214

Transcontinental railway. Terminal peg and cairn at border, 1901. (Courtesy of the National Library of Australia)

is problematic because it disregards a couple of crucial points about the image in motion-photography. Firstly, once a cinematic image is screened it must be read as an element of the systems of culture. It is not the re-presentation of some unmediated reality; it is a presentation, a newly created portion of reality. Secondly, given the linear progression of film, every image in a narrative is elaborately coded through its location in culture generally and through its insertion in a specific diegetic flow which must give rise to some meaning (even if the narrative is only 'about' incoherence).

Delusive 'common sense' prevails especially when a moving picture of a static, seemingly unartified landscape is presented. It is tempting to say, 'Well, there it is, untouched, panoramically extensive, simply photographed, objectively true'. But this would be to ignore the many selected and manipulated variables in a photographic image of the landscape: time of day; camera into sun; camera away from sun; stature, visibility and actions of human beings within the environment; choice of lens; static shot; tracking shot; duration without edit; soundtrack; location of landscape shot within the narrative progression. The list could go on. Evidently the fact that the landscape can't 'act' on cue doesn't render its filmic presentation any less manipulable. The shots of sublime geography which are so prevalent and connotative in Australian feature films are deliberately constructed to give off their seemingly objective messages. The presented *image* of a landscape is necessarily a sign. And in the Australian setting, it is a sign of nature as opposed to a sign of a sign; Australian film culture remains 'innocent' or 'primitive', declining to graduate to the (post-)modernist

215

worlds of second and/or third degree (re-)presentations of pre-existent social constructs.

The impression so far may be that human beings in their Australian habitat and culture are entirely powerless, struck expressionless by that huge uninscribable outback. That is only the impression. We can make a mark simply by persisting in subsisting. As Hegel put it, national culture entails a continuous process of shaping the environment to the society's needs even as the society adapts to the environment:

> Man [sic] realizes himself through *practical* activity, since he has the impulse to express himself, and so again to recognize himself, in things that are at first simply represented to himself as externally existent. He attains this by altering external things and impressing on them the stamp of his own inner nature, so that he rediscovers his own character in them. Man does this in order that he may profit by his freedom to break down the stubborn indifference of the external world to himself, and may enjoy in the countenance of nature only an outward embodiment of himself.[5]

Hegel's thesis seems especially pertinent to Australian culture. It allows us to think of our environment as a developing social creation while never denying that the society is also to some extent a 'natural' outgrowth of the habitat. In cinematic terms it means that a movie screen which shows images of a landscape can be regarded both as a window on the existent world and as a canvas on which a created world can be presented. And it is through the rendition of Australian landscape as sublime and supra-social that film-makers are attempting to create Australian culture even as, paradoxically, they are promoting the view that a society can't really make much of an impression on such a habitat. Or to approach it from another direction, they are attempting to read some innate Australian-ness in the landscape even as they are aiming to stamp their own inner natures on the external nature of the continent. Borrowing another notion from the rhetoric of Italian neo-realism, we 'note that the place where we were born and where we have lived has contributed to making us different from one another'.[6] It is not by chance, I think, that a crop of extensively publicised and acclaimed films highlighting a unique Australian landscape have come to light during this decade of resurgent nationalism. The landscape cinema asserts an Australian difference. The films say, 'Here is a key to our identity'. (Certainly this is how they are being marketed both at home and abroad.) Just when it seemed that the cultural cringe and strut were obsolescent, a burgeoning film industry comes along to display and participate in Australia's historical adolescence. This assertion is not in itself a cringe; it is simply an observation based on the tally of white Australia's age—fewer than two hundred years. Australian landscape films grow out of, and point to, the fact that Australian art is still propelled by a primitive dialectic of nature and culture. Nor is *this* a cringe. Indeed, at the risk of strutting, this very primitivism is what the jaded nomads from pluralist

216

Transcontinental railway. Officers of the South Australia Survey Party, 1901.
(Courtesy of the National Library of Australia)

Europe and New York find so refreshing, indeed inspiring, in Australian cinema. While raw-boned Australian aesthetes crave the energy
of the crisis, observers living on ground-zero in the northern hemi-
sphere yearn to put down roots in the wide open spaces. As the
societies of signs are primed to burn, the sophisticates are nostalgic for
solid earth. And certainly, Australian producers are canny enough not
to let anything interfere with that nostalgia. One reason for the list
(long as a country mile) of Australian costume-dramas set in colonial
outposts derives from the fact that the time-setting allows the film-
makers to focus without obfuscation of the theme of individuals, or
isolated groups of 'primitives', in confrontation with nature (*Jimmy
Blacksmith, Never Never, Picnic, Brilliant Career, Snowy River, Irishman*...). There is really no need to hark back so far: *Mad Max, The
Last Wave* and *Plains of Heaven* have demonstrated that the 1900 themes
can be contemporarily transposed. The landscape still seems to hold
the key to Australian mythologies. However, as accountants and many
reviewers would agree, there's no point in complicating things: put

217

Production still from Canberra Natura, *16mm film produced by John Cruthers and directed by Ross Gibson.*

those 'eternal' themes in a setting that shows them off with 100 per cent clarity.

Inevitably there is a hidden irony complicating all this. Or maybe it's another short-circuit. The camera, the instrument through which all this clamour for difference is being mediated, is actually constructed so that some innate Australian-ness (regardless of whether it exists or not) cannot be presented. The movie camera, as so many commentators have shown, is a quintessentially Western-industrial artefact designed to produce other artefacts that are suffused with the incumbent ideology of naturalistic representation.[7] Designed during the insurgence of the European bourgeoisie ca 1840–60, the camera still produces the type of image which, like painting of that time, served to locate the viewer in a situation where s/he could feel scopic control over an entire scene rendered completely comprehensible and consumable for the individual who, in bourgeois ideology, was necessarily the centre of the universe. The camera is a tool for constructing a viewing-individual centred in a spectacle which is posed as complete and colonisable. The camera is not a machine designed for expressing sublimity—either of the Romantic pantheistic kind or of the post-modernist, supra-systemic kind before which the cohesive, centralised self begins to disintegrate. The camera does not express inexpressibility. Quite the opposite. It is designed not to warp the perspectival codes which were installed in art practice during the

218

Renaissance (after the waning of the medieval world-view which had devalued the secular personality) and which have served to persuade generation upon generation that the secular status quo is immutably 'natural'.

To change the way you think, you've got to change the way you see, and vice versa. And Australian film culture, despite its pursuit of its own difference, is plugged into the vicious circuit. Under Australian skies we are looking with Western eyes. The contradiction is manifest in the films. Because the Australian film industry subscribes increasingly to the Hollywood 'ethic' of investment entertainment, the Hollywood narrative format is endemic. As a rule it features a naturalistically related, unilinear story which purports to concentrate on the fortunes of intimately known individuals acting and reacting in a 'real' universe which exists for human action. It sounds like an uncomplicated formula for success. But in Australia the not-quite-different filmic landscape is always there, claiming priority of place as the point of fascination, as the central character. Australian nature resists colonisation by dominant film discourses. Yet, even as the film-makers are rejoicing in this, even as they are saying, 'This is where we are different; look at that landscape; it's our bloody unique country', their Western culture is refusing to allow a distinctive nature to imprint itself on Australian film form. For the film-makers are obeying all those rules of dimension and ocular clarity which inscribe the images of the continent with traditional European attitudes about landscape art, attitudes which have grown out of and bolstered a specifically European view of nature and culture. A continent which has spent eons in its own geographical and cultural locales is promptly framed within European parameters. And even when it is shown to be a different land from, say, Claude's Lorraine or Gainsborough's greensward, it is different definitively with reference to traditional European models. (See the Manet-like tableaux in *Picnic*.) In yet another way the Antipodes become a reflection of Europe.

Thankfully this system of cultural colonisation isn't hermetic. Some films get through to uncharted centres of meaning, thereby blazing a trail for later explorers. The most recent and instructive example is *Two Laws*, made by the Booroloola people in conjunction with Carolyn Strachan and Alessandro Cavadini. A cognition of new ways of seeing the land and its history underlies much of the vociferous praise and discussion surrounding the film. Two cinematic laws clash as a deliberately rationalised Aboriginal world-view is codified both through the use of unedited (which is not to say unselected) shots with a wide-angle lens and through the avoidance of a foregrounding or hier-archising of individuals within the spiritual and social ecosystem of the Aboriginal environment. *Two Laws* takes a deliberate stand outside dominant film culture, eschewing formal 'normalcy' and refusing to partake of a humanist personality cult which focuses on the actor. This is not to say that the film is free of rhetorical tropes; nor is it to say that the film has finally captured 'true Australia', as if there were some Platonic Austral ideal immured in a Booroloola cave. Any film is an artefact after all. *Two Laws* is just as much an arbitrary presentation of a world-view as, say, Nicholas Roeg's *Walkabout*, which (brilliantly) exploits the Australian setting as the background for a characteristically passionate, percussively edited 'European' drama of culture shock and primal desire. But *Two Laws* does present an unfamiliar impedance to dominant film culture in Australia. A cynic could argue that the project of the film is an inadvertently reactionary one of oppositional reference to mainstream cinema; but the degree of difference which is intentionally set up refracts the light which is thrown by white culture and which purports to illuminate a way toward 'civilised' control of the land. The film is saying, 'There are other, perhaps indigenous, ways of seeing the country'.

The search for Australian specificity is one of the motivating chimeras of Australian cinema, drawing thoughts and gazes centripetally into the unsubjected outback. Of course, white Australians will never arrive at anything other than a predominantly white Australian ethos, but in a necessary process of self-definition they habitually seek more 'native' vision, waiting for the land of Dreamtime to stamp itself on the culture. The gaze of the camera turns toward the oneiric uncivilisable centre. The unknowable heartland, representing a crucial lack, becomes a 'gravitational' pole which attracts obsessions and stands as the essentially unattainable zone of meaning where all outstanding enigmas might be explicated (not unlike the 'unplummetable centre' of Freudian dream analysis).

In 1849 Charles Sturt wrote:

> A veil hung over Central Australia that could neither be pierced nor raised. Girt around by deserts, it almost appeared as if Nature had intentionally closed it upon civilized man, that she might have one domain on earth's wide field over which the savage might roam in freedom.[8]

Terra Australis in camera. Thirteen decades later this seventh Salomaic veil still eroticises the landscape, causing Australians to project their definitive desires on to it. Even as white culture attempts to ravage the land, the land seems perversely to seduce the culture. Must it always be so violent? And futile?

> The country grows
> into the image of the people,
> and the people grow
> into the likeness of the country
> till the soul's geographer
> each becomes the symbol of the other
>
> Max Dunn, 'Portrait of a Country'

NOTES

1   Marcus Clarke, 'Preface' to *The Poems of the Late Adam Lindsay Gordon*, Samuel Mullen, London, 1887, pp. v–vi.

2 SM Eisenstein (ed & trans Jay Leyda), *Film Form: Essays in Film Theory*, Harvest, New York, 1946, p. 46.
3 André Bazin (ed & trans Hugh Gray), *What is Cinema?* Vol II, University of California Press, Berkeley, 1971, p. 98.
4 Roland Barthes, 'The Photographic Message' in his *Image–Music–Text* (ed & trans Stephen Heath), Fontana, London, 1977, p. 17.
5 FW Hegel in EF Carritt (ed), *Philosophies of Beauty*, Clarendon, Oxford, 1931, pp. 161–2.
6 Giuseppe de Santis, 'Towards an Italian Landscape', in *Springtime in Italy: A Reader on Neo-Realism*, ed David Overby, Talisman, London, 1978, p. 125.
7 See Brian Henderson's 'Towards a Non-Bourgeois Camera Style' in *Film Theory and Criticism*, eds Gerald Mast and Marshall Cohen, Oxford University Press, Oxford, 1979.
8 Charles Sturt, *Narrative of an Expedition into Central Australia* (2 vols), T & W Boone, London, 1849, Vol 2, p. 2.

15
History on the Rocks
TONY BENNETT

The more spick and span the work is, the greater the happiness of all the army engaged in the work of restoration. It is like the satisfaction of the tradesman in the new brass plate displayed in front of his shop window . . . with all its letters sharply cut. Whereas to us every item which is spick and span and new . . . is something which requires an apology.[1]

It was thus that Sidney Colvin disparaged the cult of 'restoration' at the inaugural meeting of the Society for the Protection of Ancient Buildings in 1878. Opposition to the practice of restoration—that is, to the fabrication of idealised pasts by stripping ancient buildings of their subsequent accretions so as to restore to them the architectural purity they were once thought to have had or, more pliably, to be essentially and spiritually theirs no matter what the historical record might say—had developed considerable momentum over the previous two decades. It had first been voiced by Ruskin who, in 1856, had argued that it was not a matter 'of expediency or feeling whether we shall preserve the buildings of past times or not. *We have no right whatever to touch them.* They are not ours. They belong, partly to those who built them, and partly to all the generations of mankind who are to follow us'.[2] The part of the 'preservationists' against the 'restorers' was also taken up by the Society of Antiquaries in 1855 when it recommended that 'no restoration should ever be attempted otherwise than . . . in the sense of preservation from further injuries'.[3] However, the clarion call that resulted in the establishment of the Society for the Protection of Ancient Buildings was made by William Morris who, on learning that Tewkesbury Abbey was to be 'restored,'

* First published in Don Barry and Stephen Muecke (eds), *The Apprehension of Time*, Local Consumption Publications, Sydney, 1988.

wrote to the *Atheneum* calling for an association 'to keep watch on old monuments, to protect against all "restoration" that means more than keeping out wind and weather, and by all means, literary or other, to awaken a feeling that our ancient buildings are not merely ecclesiastical toys, but sacred monuments of the nation's growth and hope'.[4]

The distinction between restoration and preservation is, of course, hardly unproblematic and, as it turned out, Morris's ideas of preservation—as those of the Society for the Protection of Ancient Buildings and, subsequently, the National Trust—could hardly be described as having been committed to the project of preserving the past as it had really been. The shift from restoration to preservation in late nineteenth-century English culture was a shift of emphasis rather than a qualitative rupture; what was exchanged in the transition was less the aesthetics of Romanticism for the sober realities of history than one idealised version of the past for another.[5] Nonetheless, and even though the dust has long settled on these disputes, the distinction is worth recalling. And nothing recalls it quite so much as a visit to The Rocks, where the past does indeed have that spick and span, highly polished appearance to which Colvin took such exception. At The Rocks the past is, so to speak, brand new. It is a site where the passage of time has been halted and thrown into reverse, its marks effaced so that, in the renovated façades of the shops on George Street or those of the terraced cottages on Argyle Terrace and Sergeant Major's Row, the past shines forth once again in the gleaming newness it once had, or is thought to have had.

Move away from these high-spots of the tourist's itinerary, however, and the past wears a different, more dilapidated face in the ruined houses, only too visibly marked by the passage of time, which line the sides of Harrington Street and Essex Street. 'All that is old does not glitter': so we are told in the official guide to The Rocks published by the Sydney Cove Redevelopment Authority. And, if it doesn't glitter or cannot be made to do so again, the text goes on to inform us of its likely fate:

> It cannot be denied that there are many buildings still standing in The Rocks which are a sad reflection on any city.
> These buildings of a slum standard are neither chalk nor cheese. They have no historical or architectural significance. It is planned to remove them just as the Authority is retaining all worthwhile [sic].
> It has to be accepted in today's society that future generations cannot be expected to continue living in such circumstances. The Sydney Cove Redevelopment Authority emphatically rejects the belief that people on low incomes should have to live in substandard conditions.[6]

It would be otiose to comment on the real estate calculations which lie behind such formulations. The cynical manoeuverings of the Sydney Cove Redevelopment Authority and its disregard for the expressed wishes of the communities which had traditionally inhabited the area have been well documented.[7] Important though such matters are, the

Argyle Terrace, before and after renovation.

question of the interests of the local community versus those of developers and planners has not been the only issue at stake in recent struggles at and over The Rocks. For rather more has been, and is being, developed there than property values. The Rocks, in its transformation into a site of historical tourism, now furnishes the locale for the development of a sanitised and mythical past which, in its

All that is old does not glitter.

commitment to eradicating all the marks and signs of the area's set-tlement that cannot be harmonised with the glittering facade which (in its officially instituted form) the past is obliged to wear, functions as an institutionalised mode of forgetting. In brief, The Rocks supplies the site for an encounter with an idealised and fabricated past which has been substituted for, and made possible by, the erasure of those marks which bear a testimony to the real and contradictory com-plexity of the area's history.

Of course, plenty of lip sevice is paid to the rhetoric of preservation, both at The Rocks itself and in the literature relating to the area. In his foreword to the official guide to the area, Eric Bedford, the NSW Minister for Planning and Environment at the time, thus writes:

> The Rocks is not yet 200 years old. What is important for all of us to remember is that our responsibility to the preservation of our heritage does not end in 10 years time or even in 100 years. Our actions will be judged by future generations and we must all ensure that the plans and actions of today will retain the heritage of our past for the future.[8]

If that sounds like Ruskin or Morris, the practice of the Sydney Cove Redevelopment Authority has been more like that of the 'restorers' whose activities Ruskin and Morris opposed, clearing The Rocks of history in order to make space for the shining new past the Authority is committed to developing. Of course, the tendency to refurbish and renovate the past so as to put it to new purposes is not limited to The Rocks. Jim Allen has commented on the ambiguities inherent in the recent transformation of Port Arthur into a museum via the reconstruction and restoration of the main buildings relating to the period of its use as a penal settlement. The very project of restoration, he suggests, entails the loss of one of the more important historical lessons that might have been learned from the site had it simply been preserved, retaining the ravages of time and disuse intact rather than removing them in an attempt to return the buildings to their original condition. 'The system (of penal settlement)', he thus argues, 'should be *seen* to have failed and the ruined buildings are the most poignant testimony of its failure. This chapter of history was grim and bitter and should not be deflected by the creation of moods of "relaxation and quiet tranquility"'.[9] At Port Arthur, moreover, the project of restoration is simultaneously and explicitly one of *improvement* also in the sense that the structural deficiencies of the original buildings are to be corrected in order to increase their future life-span. Allen comments as follows on the kind of institutionalised forgetting this entails:

> That foundations were insufficient, that damp courses were not used, that bricks were poorly made are the products of real events. Just as the monumental nature of the buildings reflects the virtually limitless supply of time and labour to be had under the transportation system, so do these technical shortcomings underline the inadequacies of the system—a lack of skills, a lack of understanding of the environment, and the imposition of an alien culture by force. To replace original building standards with modern ones of greater durability cannot be historical restoration but merely renovation—the creation of a grotesque silhouette which does violence to the past and defrauds the future.[10]

The restoration of The Rocks has subjected history to a similar process of ideological revision, and one in which it has been violently shaken rather than merely gently stirred, as, in terms of the predominant discourses which organise the visitor's experience, the site has been returned—as is the case with Port Arthur—to the moment of its origins.

A CENTRE OF ORIGINS

> Throughout its fascinating, lively, though sometimes turbulent and distressing history, The Rocks has ever remained the place where Australian society began. The Rocks with its rich variety of buildings, its winding streets, its umbilical links with the nearby harbour, its parks and public houses, is part of the heritage, not only of the people of Sydney but of all Australians.[11]

This passage, the opening of Eric Bedford's foreword to the official guide, aptly summarises the discourse of origins which predominates in the tourist literature relating to The Rocks in its representation as 'the birthplace of the nation'.[12] It also provides an important key to the criteria of historical value which have governed the restoration policies of the Sydney Cove Redevelopment Authority. As we have seen, the remnants of those aspects of the area's history which might be regarded as 'turbulent and distressing' either have been, or are destined to be, effaced. The evidence of social distress and discord suggested by the housing stock bearing the marks of many generations of working-class settlement is thus to be removed, either through demolition or, if they occupy key sites—as at Argyle Terrace—through their restoration to sentimentalised workers' cottages which resonate with the prevailing quietism of the area. Such evidence, in effect, is destined to survive merely as a footnote to the Authority's good intentions ('It has to be accepted in today's society that future generations cannot be expected to continue living in such circumstances') which, viewed as part of a broader process, serve merely to mask the fact that the restoration project is committed less to the eradication than to the relocation of substandard housing conditions—there has been a notable shortage of proposals to 'restore' Sydney's western suburbs— as The Rocks is cleared so that it might function as both a tourist showpiece and a gentrified residential zone for the middle classes.

Against this, of the various buildings and sites which have been or are to be preserved and restored, pride of place is given to those which, in one way or another, can be regarded as having come first. 'See the sites of many Australian firsts: the first hospital, the first cemetery, the oldest surviving house and the places where many famous colonial figures lived'.[13] Of course, this is not particularly surprising. Nor, in itself, would it amount to much. What matters rather more is the way in which such firsts have been transformed into origins and, correspondingly, The Rocks itself into a centre of origins in the sense of being not merely the first area of settlement but one which contains the seeds of future and broader developments. In this respect, The Rocks is governed by what, in another context, Eugenio Donato has called 'an archaeological epistemology' according to which 'each archaeological artifact has to be an original artifact, and these original artifacts must in turn explain the "meaning" of a subsequent larger history'.[14] For this to be possible, it is necessary that origins be cast in the mould of the larger history whose meaning they are then called on to explain.

In The Rocks this is achieved by organising the visitor's experience within the terms of a rhetoric of consensus nationalism which, in overlayering the various objects and buildings encountered, enables them to function as origins of the subsequent unfolding of the nation's history told as the gradual rise of a free, democratic, multicultural citizenry. The *modus operandi* of this archaeological epistemology is centrally dependent on the mechanisms it uses to exorcise conflict from the origins it constructs as well as from the subsequent history which flows from those origins. The means by which the second of these effects is produced have already been commented on. With regard to the actual moment of origin itself, this is cleared of conflict by two means. First, as is true of all bourgeois myths of origin, the site is represented as a *tabula rasa* prior to European settlement; it functions as an origin by means of the neglect of any prior history which might disturb its status as origin or mark that origin as a conflictual one.[15] In brief, apart from an Aboriginal craft shop in the Argyle Centre, Aborigines are represented as absent from the moment of settlement, which is thus established as an encounter between man and nature rather than one between two cultures and civilisations. The Rocks, in this respect, is like Robinson Crusoe's island but without the anti-mythical presence of a Man Friday.

Second, and perhaps more distinctively, conflict is exiled from the moment of origin by being represented only as deriving from elsewhere—rather than as being endemic to the nation's foundations—and in forms that were soon removed and retrospectively eradicated once the true trajectory of the nation's development had been established. This cleansing of origins is particularly in evidence at the two key symbolic markers of The Rocks as 'the birthplace of the nation'— Cadman's Cottage, the first of all firsts at The Rocks, and, in The Rocks Square, the First Impressions sculpture commemorating 'the isolation, hardship and bondage common to all early pioneers'.[16]

At Cadman's Cottage the story of Sydney and, thereby, of Australia is recounted via a pictorial display. The text accompanying the first picture, which depicts the First Fleet at anchor and the signs of early settlement on the shore, invites us to imagine the convicts and marines working together in close harmony. However, we are told that if we look more closely the marines will be seen to be standing guard over the convicts, labouring in chain gangs under the stern and watchful eye of British authority represented by the encampment of the Governor, Judge and Provost. Here, then, is conflict—but a conflict derived from the contradictions of British society, an alien blight on these new shores and one which is overcome as soon as 'Australian history proper' gets going: the next panel in the display tells the story of Macquarie's support for the emancipists, enabling them to take their place alongside free settlers in laying the real foundations of the nation.

The First Impressions sculpture suggests a similarly sanitised version of the nation's origins. This consists of three figures—one of a convict, one of a marine and one of a family of settlers—depicted in bas-relief on sandstone quarried from the area. These figures are backed onto one another and joined at the centre, thereby creating the impression that these three foundations of the nation, knitted together through their backbones, form a non-antagonistic unity. This impression is reinforced by the plaques which accompany the figures. The plaque relating to the marines recounts how many of these received land

Cadman's Cottage

grants to make them the colony's first free settlers, whereas the one relating to the convicts portrays them as the victims of the conditions prevailing in Britain at the time. Finally, the plaque relating to the settlers—who form the *telos* of the composition—constructs unity out of difference in remarking how the land grants made to both marines and emancipated convicts enabled them to join the free settlers, placing particular stress on the Gold Rush as the period which laid the foundations for the many nationalities which make up contemporary Australia. Once again, imported contradictions have been eradicated and no new ones admitted in their place.

In his *Thoughts Out of Season*, Nietzsche argued that what he called 'monumental history'—the attitude to the past evident in the deeds which come to be monumentalised in a nation's statuary—constructs the past as a chain of examples for action in the present that is orientated to the future, a spur to deeds that will push the life of the nation to new peaks. 'The great moments in the individual battle', he wrote, 'form a chain, a high road for humanity through the ages, and the highest points of those vanished moments are yet great and living for men; and this is the fundamental idea of the belief in humanity, that finds a voice in the demand for monumental history'.[17] The past that is produced by monumental history, Nietzsche goes on, consists of ' "effects in themselves"—in other words, effects without sufficient cause' in that they function without regard to 'the real nexus of cause and effect, which, rightly understood, would only prove that nothing quite similar could ever be cast again from the dice-boxes of fate and the future'.[18]

It is certainly true that, at The Rocks, the past is figured forth as a series of 'effects without sufficient cause'. However, if the foundational figures of the marines, convicts and settlers are cast in the mould of monumental history, their deeds, while leading to the present, do not act as a spur to action beyond it. Michael Bommes and Patrick Wright have argued that, in order for the past to be rendered as an object of the tourist's gaze, history must be portrayed as 'completed and fully accomplished'.[19] And so it is at The Rocks where the symbolic markers of the nation's foundations serve as the origins of a history that has nowhere to go because it has realised its goal. We, the citizenry whom that history addresses, are its point of arrival, and are called on to do no more than to contemplate the process of our own making. It enjoins us to do nothing because what might need to be done has already been done in that the tendency toward unity enshrined in the nation's origins has been brought to a fulfilment in our own consensual and multicultural selves. The most we might do, perhaps, is to complement and individualise the site's archaeological epistemology by conducting a personal odyssey into our origins via a visit to the State Archives.

A place to live.

DEPOPULATING HISTORY, PEOPLING THE PAST

There is, however, another face to history at The Rocks, an attitude to the past which, in somewhat scathing terms, Nietzsche characterised as that of the antiquarian:

> All that is small and limited, mouldy and obsolete, gains a worth and inviolability of its own from the conservative and reverent soul of the antiquary migrating into it, and building a secret nest there. The history of his town becomes the history of himself; he looks on the walls, the turreted gate, the town council, the fair, as an illustrated diary of his youth, and sees himself in it all—his strength, industry, faults and follies. 'Here one could live', he says, 'as one can live here now—and will go on living; for we are tough folk, and will not be uprooted in the night'.[20]

And so The Rocks, we are told in the official guide, is not merely a place to visit; it's a place to live and work, too, and where, in doing so, one might daily rub shoulders with the past:

> Working in The Rocks is different. There is an inherent and all-pervading sense of history. The people working there may not know the Argyle Centre was originally a vegetable garden for Sydney's first hospital, or that Francis Greenway the architect lived opposite, but the feeling of the past is there.[21]

A matter, then, not of knowledge but of feeling the past insinuate its presence into the rhythms of daily life, marking it off from the present—the hurly-burly of city life—as a zone of tranquillity. Those who work there can 'take a leisurely stroll at lunchtime in the historic streets' or 'sit and dream on the harbour front' while, for those who live there, The Rocks offers the peace and stillness 'of a village atmosphere'.[22] Simply to live there, moreover, is to acquire something of the resilience of the people, to become a part of that 'tough folk' who 'will not be uprooted in the night'. If, as we are told, 'the attitudes and independence of the inhabitants of the area played a part in the moulding of the Australian character',[23] these qualities are to be transferred to newcomers via a process of historical osmosis:

> Those who were born in The Rocks have always claimed it with a fierce pride. As the scheme emerges, the pioneers, those who came later and those yet to come will be living in one of Sydney's most desirable neighbourhoods.[24]

In the meantime, of course, those of the area's residents who did display qualities of fierce pride and independence in their struggles to preserve their homes and way of life *have* been moved in the night, and by no means solely in order to realise real estate values. Their removal, like the demolition of the slums, was an ideological necessity, a matter of depopulating history—clearing the area of those whose lives testified to the real complexity of its history—in order that 'the conservative and reverent soul of the antiquary' who migrates there,

231

whether to live, work or visit, might find it peopled by an idealised folk appropriate to the tranquillised past, the ideal city of the mind, which The Rocks now embodies.

But for whom has this past been tranquillised? For whom is The Rocks an ideal city of the mind? Consideration of an analogous case throws some light on these questions. In the 1970s, the cotton mills of Manchester, New Hampshire, were largely swept away under a government-sponsored program of urban renewal. In the midst of this program, Tamara Hareven and Randolph Langenbach conducted an oral history survey of local community reactions to the clearance of the past which this program entailed. They summarise their findings as follows:

> It is the mistaken impression of middle-class civic leaders (many of whom are from regions other than the city in question) that since conditions were worse then than they are now, people must wish to forget the past and would prefer to see its manifestations erased.
>
> The assumptions of social reformers and planners that the working-class past in these industrial settings must be eradicated because it symbolised poverty, grimness and exploitation, misses what the workers themselves feel about their world. Most of the former industrial workers whom we interviewed for the Amoskeag oral history project remembered the good and the bad as inseparable parts of their life's experience . . . Both were part of their entire life story and were deeply enmeshed with their sense of place. Memories of struggle with poverty, daily two-mile walks to the factory, unemployment and strikes, illness and death were all part of that story, and were intimately linked to the buildings. Beyond their individual experiences, buildings were so significant to people's memories because of their associations with other people, such as family members, friends, neighbours, and fellow workers with whom they had shared these experiences . . .
>
> Those whom we found to hold negative attitudes had advanced into the middle-class, and felt that association with these buildings conflicted with their efforts to escape from their parents' working-class background. As is often the case, however, the grandchildren of those who had worked in the mills have sometimes turned to appreciate and value the world of their grandparents, while the intervening generation rejects them.[25]

Clearly, at least some part of what has happened to history at The Rocks might be accounted for in terms of similar mobility anxieties on the part of middle-class planners and reformers. The full picture, though, is more complex, and mainly because The Rocks is marked by a double relation to history: the institutionalised mode of forgetting, which is the product of practices of erasure; and a fabricated mode of remembrance constructed by practices of restoration and development. Between them, these do not merely remove the vestiges of a past marked by any signs of working-classness, thus facilitating the passage of the mobile middle classes; they also construct a past for those classes to return to—an amalgam of a conflict-free past of origins and an urban idyll, a past which weighs on the brains of the living like a petit-bourgeois daydream in which that class finds itself always-already there.

However, this is not merely the result of the past that has been removed through the program of slum clearance or of the one that has been installed in its place by means of the rose-tinting practices of restoration. It is equally an effect of the kind of economic re-vitalisation policies pursued by the Sydney Cove Redevelopment Authority in installing a set of socioeconomic relations at The Rocks which itself functions ideologically. Rather than seeking to renew the area's traditional industries and sources of working-class employment, the Authority has eradicated any signs of the economic and social relations of contemporary capitalism. In their place, it has instated the social relations of petty commodity production and distribution, attracting a rush of small businesses to the area—mainly craft pro-ducers, tourist shops and restaurateurs. These businesses, in catering to the tourist trade, also blend in with the mythic past of The Rocks so that they function as a part and parcel of its message in materialising an idealised set of social relations which seems to flow from the past to the present in an unbroken continuity. In being steeped in the past, these social relations come, in turn, to saturate that present so that the two, past and present, merge as the relations of petty com-modity production seem to arise naturally out of their own back-projections. For there is no intervening history (it has been erased), except for that of a momentary absence, which might interrupt their continuity.

> The area always attracted an assortment of business. The blacksmith in Harrington Street, the barber shop—the source of local gossip—the pawn-broker in Argyle Street who did a roaring trade before pay day, the iceman and the 'fisho' who delivered daily.
> As the population dwindled, these shopkeepers and merchants were forced to close their doors. In the return of business to The Rocks the former names have been retained where possible, as in Unwins Store.[26]

In his discussion of the Ironbridge Gorge Museum complex in Britain, Bob West notes that practices of historical preservation/restoration, when implemented within active communities, often severely disrupt the local economy in promoting the non-essential sector of that economy (ie, that geared to the needs of tourists) at the expense of services essential to sustaining the local community. In brief, through the tourist infrastructure which they bring in their tow, such practices often destroy the basis for a functioning local community which, as at The Rocks, they then reinstate in an idealised and nostalgic form. West also notes that it is sometimes the fate of those whose lives have been transformed under the impact of those practices to be turned into parts of the idealised historical displays they organise. He thus remarks how his local pub which faces the Blists Hill Open Air Mu-seum—a part of the Iron Gorge Museum complex—has become a haunt where the tourist can rub shoulders with the past by mingling

with the museum workers who drink there attired, as their employment requires, in the period-costume of a sentimentalised working-
class of yesteryear:

> Here at lunchtime at the bar one finds young men in sub-Victorian garb;
> heavy hobnail boots, plain serge trousers or mock Halifax corduroy gath-
> ered at the waist with binder-twine, hauled up with wide braces, pulled to
> at the ankle with gaiters. Old jackets, dull, nondescript but suggestively
> 'old', open to reveal grubby collarless workingmen's shirts, or the occa-
> sional plain waistcoat perhaps with the stylish flourish of a watch fob and
> chain. Needless to say, these phantoms of the past-present quaff real ale,
> 'brewed traditionally', itself a sort of liquid history bearing silent witness
> against the present.[27]

Workers in disguise, the current class position of these museum
employees is masked as they bear testimony to an allowable working
class, allowable because it belongs safely to the past. The Rocks has its
similar points of rendezvous with the living past—the Hero of Water-
loo Hotel, for example, where drinking is transformed into a historical
ritual and where the locals, just by being there, lend authenticity
to the display. So, too, do the remaining residents—many of them
elderly—who are encountered on the tourist's itinerary, particularly in
the outlying areas of The Rocks such as Cumberland Street and Lower
Fort Street. Lending an aura of age and authenticity to the buildings,
these remnants of earlier days perform unpaid bit-parts in the ideological economy of The Rocks, peopling the past as, in ways that they
are powerless to avoid, they are transformed into historical curios,
moving props in a tourist peep-show.

IS THE PAST TOO MUCH WITH US?

In his useful survey of the development of national traditions in the
late nineteenth century, Eric Hobsbawm accords particular importance
to those practices through which, in Europe and elsewhere, national
pasts came to be organised and officially instituted as such.[28] The
development of museums of national history; the erection of statues
to national heroes; the preservationist activities of national heritage
lobbies: these and related practices all served to give the discourses
which organised the terms in which national pasts were constructed
a concretely materialised and officially sanctioned public presence. Of
course, the relations of such pasts to the verifiable historical record
were frequently tenuous. Although the pasts that resulted from these
practices were usually represented as being anchored in the structures
of deep time (by back-projecting the continuity of the nation into the
structures of classical antiquity or embedding it in the subterranean
continuities of a folk), they were, in spite of the venerable age which
seemed thus to attach to them, *new pasts* whose currency was established, as Hobsbawm puts it, by a 'quasi-obligatory repetition'.[29]

There is no reason to suppose, however, that this in any way diminished the effectiveness of such pasts. In a useful neologism, Michael Bommes and Patrick Wright have suggested that the institutions engaged in the business of producing and circulating such national pasts are best regarded as comprising a 'public historical sphere' to be investigated less with regard to its accuracy in relation to the historiographic record than as 'a publicly instituted structuring of consciousness'.[30] This is not to imply that such public historical spheres should be viewed as superstructural phenomena and, therefore, as consequential only in reflecting or reinforcing the economic or political imperatives which supply the 'real' basis for nation-state formations. The unity of a nation, Poulantzas argued, requires the mapping onto one another of the *'historicity of a territory and territorialisation of a history'*, a process which is organised, institutionalised and materialised, Poulantzas further suggests, by the state.[31] The production of national pasts in the late nineteenth century through the activities of museums, heritage movements and the like was thus not an incidental accompaniment to the formation of nations. Rather, in simultaneously *historicising the territorial space of the nation and nationalising the past*, these processes played an essential role in organising the time–space coordinates of nation-states. They were, and are, *constitutive* of nations and not their *reflections*. Nor is there any doubt that the state accorded considerable priority to this area of its activity. Bazin, for example, argues that, by the late nineteenth century, the museum had become 'one of the fundamental institutions of the modern state'.[32] If that seems an exaggeration, it is worth noting that, in the 1870s, the British Museum had 344 staff and an annual vote of £110 000 compared with the Colonial Office's staff of 65 civil servants and annual vote of £36 210.[33]

It was writing in this context that Nietzsche regarded his essay *The Use and Abuse of History* as being 'out of season'. It was so, he argued, 'because I am trying to represent something of which the age is rightly proud—its historical culture—as a fault and defect in our time, believing as I do that we are all suffering from a malignant historical fever and should at least recognise the fact'.[34] Historical culture, Nietzsche proceeded to argue, 'is really a kind of inherited grayness, and those who have borne its mark from childhood must believe instinctively in *the old age of mankind*'.[35] In maintaining this, Nietzsche had in mind the effects of those histories which represent the present as the outcome and fulfilment of the pasts they construct and which, in so far as they project a future, do so only by envisioning it as a perpetuation of the present. Such pasts, while they may trace their foundations to a generation of 'first-comers', address their recipients as 'late-comers'—as the ripe fruits of history conceived as a process that is over and finished, except that the present it has produced might be augmented according to the formula 'more of the same', rather than as active participants within a process that might be carried forward by breaking with and disrupting the continuities of the past. Poulantzas had something similar in mind in arguing that the state 'constitutes the people-nation in the further sense of representing its historical orientation; and assigns a goal to it, marking out what becomes a path'.[36] It is a path, however, that is merely the completion of the state's own becoming in that in 'this oriented historicity without a fixed limit, the State represents an eternity that it produces by self-generation'.[37]

Nietzsche did, however, speak of a third orientation to the past, one which would bring it 'to the bar of judgement, interrogate it remorselessly, and finally condemn it'.[38] The suggestion is just as much 'out of season' now as then, but all the more timely for that and nowhere more so than in Australia which is currently in the midst, and has been so since the 1960s, of what will undoubtedly count as *the* main moment in the organisation and production of its national past. The initiatives directed toward the public institution and materialisation of a national past that have been sponsored, directly or indirectly, by the various branches of the Australian state over the past two decades are comparable, in range and scope, to those evident in Europe in the late nineteenth century when, for the greater part, an Australian past was regarded as an absent or impossible object, as something that had yet to be made rather than as something to be preserved or restored.[39]

The reasons for this need not concern us here. Suffice it to say that, in a comparative perspective, there was a relatively underdeveloped public historical sphere in late nineteenth-century Australia and that, to the extent that such a sphere did exist, its associations were largely colonial.[40] The past, understood as a publicly instituted structuring of consciousness, was relatively thin on the ground and was scarcely, if at all, nationalised. Moreover this has remained so for the greater part of the twentieth century. There are, of course, exceptions—most notably the Australian War Memorial—but very few of them, and mostly ones which confirm the rule.[41] If the Australian War Memorial constituted the first concerted attempt to institute and lend official sanction to an Australian past, fashioned in the image of the digger, that past did not stand entirely on its own but, in a variety of ways, was referred to and anchored in the deeper times of European history and the militarised modes of national commemoration derived from the British state.[42]

The period since the 1960s, by contrast, has witnessed not merely a marked extension in the scope of the public historical sphere but also a refashioning of that sphere as, increasingly, it supplies the site for the representation of a clearly autonomised Australian past. The legislative landmarks of this period are soon summarised: the establishment of the Australian Council of National Trusts in 1967; the establishment of a Committee of Inquiry into the National Estate in 1973 leading, in 1975, to the appointment of an Interim Committee of the National Estate and, in 1976, to the enactment of the Australian Heritage Bill; and, finally, the establishment in 1974 of the Committee of Inquiry on Museums and National Collections leading to, as its single most important legislative outcome, the *Museum of Australia Act* of 1980. However, these are merely the most visible manifestations of what has undoubtedly been, at the State and local levels as well as that of the federal government, one of the most significant areas of cultural policy formation in Australia in recent years—and one which has both fed off and received a good deal of popular support. The 'quickening of interest in Australian history', as the Committee of Inquiry on Museums and National Collections put it, 'has been . . . one of the most unexpected and vigorous cultural movements in Australia in this century'.[43]

The fate of history at The Rocks needs to be considered in the light of these broader developments just as it, in turn, supplies a perspective from which the latter might be critically interrogated. This is not to query the desirability of organising an autonomised Australian past. Equally, though, it is clear that this process of autonomisation may bring a more questionable set of values in its tow, depending on the discourses which govern its implementation. This is not to suggest that the currently ongoing 'nationing' of the Australian public historical sphere is uniformly and consistently regulated by a discourse of origins similar to that in operation at The Rocks. To the contrary, the discursive strategies in evidence vary considerably from one historic site to another. There is even considerable variation as to how the time–space coordinates of the nation are organised. Eric Hobsbawm has suggested that the public historical spheres of different countries can sometimes usefully be distinguished in terms of the gradients of development exhibited by the national pasts they establish.[44] If the more usual case is that of a long, slow gradient as the nation emerges out of an immemorial time into which all its essential properties have been back-projected, some pasts, Hobsbawm argues, establish their own cut-off points—1789 for France, for example—from which they rise in a steep and rapid ascent.

Thus if, at The Rocks, the national past is figured forth in a similarly rapid ascent from the cut-off point of 1788, the discursive strategies in evidence at other sites display the contrary orientation. While it is too early to tell precisely how the national past will be organised and represented at the Museum of Australia—if it is ever completed—it seems likely, from the evidence of recent planning documents, that the pre-settlement history of Aborigines will be annexed to the history of the nation in order that that history might, in turn, be stretched back beyond 1788, flattening out its ruptural possibilities to ensure a smooth passage from an immemorial past to a multicultural present:

> As the nation approaches the bicentenary of European settlement it has become a complex multicultural society. The continuing story of the transformation of Australia from a country of hunter-gatherers to an industrial nation is one of tragedy, triumph, persistence and innovation.[45]

There are other respects, too, in which the coordinates of the national past have not been settled. But a stone's throw away from The Rocks the past wears a different, and more contradictory face, at Hyde Park Barracks where, although unevenly, a very real attempt has been made to halt and question the triumphalist and celebratory terms in which museums more usually represent the national pasts they organise. The representation of popular celebrations in the exhibition Sydney Celebrates, for example, works hard to undercut the discourses of national unity and consensus which those celebrations themselves fostered. Equally, and more generally, there is no doubt that the Australian past as it is currently being re-fashioned is a more open, demotic and inclusive past than was previously the case and, in good measure, is so because of the active part played by labour, social, feminist and Aboriginal historians—either as lobbyists or as museum workers—in contributing to the development of this area of cultural policy. The Museum of Australia, quite conscious of the newness of the past it will institute and anxious to dissociate it from the detritus of old pasts—

> Nor will the Museum be tied by existing buildings or traditions which could hamper its development. In effect, the Museum starts as a clean canvas on which the history of Australia and the Australian nation can be sketched and gradually filled in[46]

—thus stresses its commitment to a broad, open and generously inclusive representation of the life of the nation:

> The Museum will seek to highlight aspects of Australia which other museums in Australia may not have emphasised: for example, the everyday life—work and leisure—of people in both city and country.[47]

The signs are, though, that here as elsewhere—and the discourse of the National Estate is a prime example[48]—the rhetoric of consensus nationalism will predominate, as it is the notion of *difference* rather than that of conflict which gains admission to this expansive national past, a notion of difference, moreover, which serves mainly to support a story of the nation as one of an already completed process whereby unity has been developed out of diversity. Should this be so, the fate of history at The Rocks may indeed prove to be emblematic of a new Australian past that will turn us all into latecomers. To call this past to the bar of judgment, and condemn it, is unlikely to impede its development. But it may mute and qualify its effects.

NOTES

1 Cited in Martin J Wiener, *English Culture and the Decline of the Industrial Spirit 1850–1980*, Penguin, Harmondsworth, 1985, p. 70.
2 Cited in Wiener, op., cit. p. 68.
3 Cited in Hugh Prince, 'Revival, Restoration, Preservation: Changing Views about Antique Landscape Features' in *Our Past Before Us: Why Do We Save it?* eds David Lowenthal & Marcus Binney, Temple Smith, London, 1981, p. 45.
4 Cited in Prince, op. cit., p. 46.
5 The concepts of 'history' and 'the past' are susceptible to variable

definitions, with the consequence that the relations between them may also be subject to different interpretations. Here, and solely for reasons of rhetorical convenience, 'the past' is used to refer to those representations of past periods and events which are socially produced and circulated within the public arena via the practices of such institutions as museums, national heritage organisations, etc. 'History,' by contrast, refers to the (contradictory) archive of statements referring to past periods and events produced by the practices of historians rather than to any empiricist conception of the past 'as it really was'.

6   Sydney Cove Redevelopment Authority, *The Rocks: A Unique Revitalisation Project for the Birthplace of Sydney*, John R Pola and Associates, Sydney, nd, p. 22.
7   See Zula Nittim, 'The Coalition of Resident Action Groups' in *Twentieth Century Sydney: Studies in Urban and Social History*, ed Jill Roe, Hale and Ironmonger in association with The Sydney History Group, Sydney, 1980, and Jack Mundey, *Green Bans and Beyond*, Angus and Robertson, Sydney, 1981.
8   Sydney Cove Redevelopment Authority, op. cit., p. 2.
9   Jim Allen, 'Port Arthur Site Museum, Australia: Its Preservation and Historical Perspectives', *Museum*, 28, No 2 (1976), pp. 104–105.
10 Ibid, p. 105.
11 Sydney Cove Redevelopment Authority, op. cit., p. 2.
12 See the official tourist map of The Rocks.
13 Sydney Cove Redevelopment Authority, op. cit., p. 19.
14 Eugenio Donato, 'The Museum's Furnace: Notes Toward a Contextual Reading of *Bouvard and Pécuchet*' in *Textual Strategies: Perspectives in Post-Structuralist Criticism*, ed Josué Harari, Cornell University Press, Ithaca, 1979, p. 220.
15 For a discussion of the organisation of bourgeois myths of origin in the writings of Daniel Defoe and Jules Verne, see P Macherey, *A Theory of Literary Production*, Routledge and Kegan Paul, London, 1978.
16 As described in the official tourist map of The Rocks.
17 Friedrich Nietzsche, *Thoughts Out of Season* Part 2, Gordon Press, New York, 1974, p. 17.
18 Ibid, p. 20.
19 Michael Bommes & Patrick Wright ' "Charms of residence": the public and the past' in Centre for Contemporary Cultural Studies, *Making Histories: Studies in History-Writing and Politics*, Hutchinson, London, 1982, p. 291.
20 Nietzsche, op. cit., p. 24.
21 Sydney Cove Redevelopment Authority, op. cit., p. 20.
22 Ibid, pp. 16 and 20.
23 Ibid, p. 22.
24 Ibid, p. 16.
25 Tamara Hareven & Randolph Langenbach, 'Living Places, Work Places and Historical Identity' in Lowenthal and Binney, op. cit., pp. 116–17.
26 Sydney Cove Redevelopment Authority, op. cit., p. 20.
27 Bob West, 'Danger! History at Work: A Critical Consumer's Guide to the Ironbridge Gorge Museum', Centre for Contemporary Cultural Studies, History Series Occasional Paper: SP No 83, p. 1.
28 Eric Hobsbawm, 'Mass-Producing Traditions, Europe, 1870–1914' in *The Invention of Tradition*, eds E Hobsbawm & T Ranger, Cambridge University Press, Cambridge, 1983.

29 Eric Hobsbawm, 'Inventing Traditions' in Hobsbawm & Ranger, op. cit., p. 2.
30 Bommes and Wright, op. cit., p. 266.
31 Nicos Poulantzas, *State, Power, Socialism*, Verso, London, 1980, p. 114.
32 G Bazin, *The Museum Age*, New York, 1967, p. 169.
33 Edward Miller, *That Noble Cabinet: A History of the British Museum*, Ohio University Press, Athens, Ohio, 1974.
34 Nietzsche, op. cit., p. 4.
35 Ibid, p. 66.
36 Poulantzas, op. cit., p. 113.
37 Ibid, p. 113.
38 Nietzsche, op. cit., p. 28.
39 For details, see the final chapter of KS Inglis, *The Australian Colonists: An Exploration of Social History 1788–1870*, Melbourne University Press, Carlton, 1974.
40 Sally Kohlstedt notes the total absence of materials relating to the post-settlement period in late nineteenth-century Australian museums. See SG Kohlstedt, 'Australian Museums of Natural History: Public Practices and Scientific Initiative in the 19th Century', *Historical Records of Australian Science* 5 (1983).
41 A report commissioned by the Carnegie Corporation noted that, apart from the Australian War Memorial, only two other institutions were given over exclusively to the display of materials relating to post-settlement history. See SF Markham and HC Richards, *A Report on the Museums and Art Galleries of Australia to the Carnegie Corporation of New York*, Museums Association, London, 1933.
42 See KS Inglis, 'A Sacred Place: The Making of the Australian War Memorial', *War and Society* 3, 2 (1985).
43 *Museums in Australia*, report of the Committee of Inquiry on Museums and National Collections, Australian Government Publishing Service, Canberra, 1975, para. 5.8.
44 Eric Hobsbawm, 'Inventing Traditions' loc. cit., pp. 1–2.
45 Museum of Australia, *Plan for the Development of the Museum of Australia (Report of the Interim Council)*, Commonwealth of Australia, Canberra, 1982.
46 Ibid.
47 Ibid.
48 See, for example, Clem Lloyd, *The National Estate: Australia's Heritage*, Savaas Publications, Adelaide, 1983.

16
At Henry Parkes Motel
MEAGHAN MORRIS

A motel is a motel anywhere.
                    Robert Venturi

I
BRICK WALL

On the 24th October 1889 Sir
Henry Parkes Colonial Secretary
and Past Member for Tenterfield
made his Historic Federation Speech.
As a result of this Speech the
Commonwealth of Australia was
formed.

The Sydney Mail referred to Sir
Henry Parkes as Australia's Most
Farsighted Statesman. This Motor
Inn is located 180 metres from the
Place where that Famous Speech
was delivered. It is called 'The
Henry Parkes' in Honour of this
Great Statesman.

There is a Legend inscribed on the street-front wall of the Henry
Parkes Motor Inn, Tenterfield.

It tells a story about one of the representative Great Men of colonial
New South Wales—an immigrant, self-made man, traveller, poet, journalist, and an indefatigable patriarch in his family and political life—
founding the modern nation with a speech act.[1]

It is also the story of a journey famous only for being interrupted
in a small rural town. Parkes was returning to Sydney from Brisbane
after talks with Queensland leaders, and stopped in Tenterfield to
issue a press release (an after-dinner oration). The story of his speech
is repeated now to attract the attention of travellers passing through
that town today.

---

* This essay first appeared in *Cultural Studies* 2, 1 (1988).

I should like to be able to say that a reading of this Legend *in situ* could be a useful starting-point for a feminist essay in cultural studies.

It raises familiar questions about the past represented in the present (myths of nationality, origin, engendering). But it does so in a context formed by everyday cultural activities—driving, stopping at a motel, tourism, small-town life—in which the Legend is used to engender effects of *place*. It attempts to persuade passing tourists to stop, and to define the town to its residents. To thematise relations between past and present, mobility and placement, is the minimal semiotic (promotional) program of any memorial-motel. The Henry Parkes in this respect is usefully self-reflexive.

A feminist reading might question, for example, whether the myths of national and local history produced in the practices of tourism may also imply, and intersect with, a gendering of the spatio-temporal operations (movement/placement) on which those practices depend.

This is a question about representation: figures (moving) in a landscape. But a feminist reading would also want to invest any motel context with effective political significance. Motels are often used today as privileged sites of a road-runner *Angst* (the *Paris, Texas* model). In that guise, they usually signify a transcendental homelessness. But, with its peculiar function as a place of escape yet a home-away-from-home, the motel can be rewritten as a transit-place for women able to use it. On the one hand, motels have had liberating effects in the history of women's mobility. They can offer increased safety to that figure whom Trollope once described as the Unprotected Female Tourist, and promise decreased bother to women on 'holiday' with their families. On the other hand, they fix new sites of placement for domestic, affective, and sexual labour, paid as well as unpaid.

So the motel can be used to frame and displace, without effacing, the association of men with travel and women with home that organises so many Australian 'legends'—in academic as well as popular and recycled touristic forms. A memorial–motel is a complex site of production, and one in which conflictual social relations cannot sensibly be ignored.

■

But, if the text of a motel Legend seems to represent a likely point of departure, a tour of recent cultural studies can make it surprisingly hard to get there.

For each direction of research I've mentioned, there is a different kind of objection.

First, there's a problem about what counts as the proper use of *time* in analysis of popular culture. Iain Chambers, for example, declares in *Popular Culture* that, since 'in the end, it is not individual signs, demanding isolated attention, but the resulting connections or "bricolage"—the style, the fashion, the image—that count', we should, in response to popular culture, refrain from resubjecting it to 'the contemplative stare' of 'official culture'. To linger too long at a motel wall, or to 'read' its inscription too closely, requires a tempo inappropriate to my object: such reading 'demands moments of attention that are separated from the run of daily life'.[2] The past-in-the-present is now a look, not a text.

Then there is a problem about *placement*. For Georges Van den Abbeele in 'Sightseers: The Tourist as Theorist', studious reading does not contradict the daily pursuits of tourism. He sees them as fellow travellers: tourism is already a mode of cultural studies, and a contemplative mode at that. It can involve research, interpretation, and prolonged moments of intense attention. Yet, for him too, there is a trap involved in lingering at an inscription. The Legend of Henry Parkes is what he calls, following Dean MacCannell,[3] a *marker*—a sign constructing a 'sight'. In studying it, both tourist and theorist can be caught up in a metaphysical quest. Each is motivated by desire 'to make present to himself a conceptual schema which would give him immediate access to a certain authenticity (the "real nature" of his object of study)'.[4]

So if I insist to the first objection that the Legend of Parkes is a tourist tale of politics made on the run, and to the second that it marks for critical inspection a (phallo)logocentric myth, from either side this motel wall represents, as an object of reading, a desire to limit movement by constructing a singular place. Here comes a third kind of difficulty. For numerous theorists of travel (Fussell, Baudrillard, Virilio . . .) there is no such 'place' to start with. The trouble with a *motel* as a site of analysis is not the familiar gap between a text (a particular motel-in-place) and reading practices (the multiplicity of its uses). Nor is it the pertinence of talking in this way about a bit of the built environment, or a segment of everyday life. The trouble is that, whatever they may say, motels in fact *demolish* sense-regimes of place, locale, and 'history'. They memorialise only movement, speed, and perpetual circulation.

∎

So the project of reading should retreat, perhaps, and recommence, with a view on the run from the road. This is to follow the line of least resistance, a 'populist' approach—though to depart, in order to arrive, is a time-consuming, place-fixating activity. One reason for pursuing it, though, is that it's the kind of popular practice that motels work to foster. Another is that it lets me discard, *en route*, some encumbrances.

The glimpse

You can see from the highway it's a tempting motel, an obvious place to stop. If you come into town from the south, one surge brings you over the mountain and down a slope to the Motor Inn at the bottom. A radiant promise of SPA POOL SAUNA GYM (and, in these cold climes, CENTRAL HEATING) flares out, day and night, at the delicate moment dividing a long, hard haul from Sydney from an easy cruise into Brisbane. This is the last town before the Queensland border. As a scenic view on the northbound road, the Henry Parkes is perfectly timed.

From the north, the approach is less dramatic. Tenterfield is only the first real town in New South Wales, and you already would have driven through most of it. It's pretty, with willows and old stone buildings, but after some three blocks of deserted main street there's not a great deal to stop for. But there's a long, level view of the Henry Parkes on the other side of the highway. Its design is imposing enough to demand serious attention: verandahs curving grandly around a garden courtyard, white-sashed Georgian windows, and on the front wall of the nearest wing a large commemorative scroll. Clearly a motel, it might also be a gracious residence, a country resort, a health centre, a historic public building. From this direction, the Henry Parkes suggests serious leisure instead of a night's salvation.

Scan

Personified models of action (the weary itinerant coming to rest, the reflective tourist sampling the country . . .) are commonly produced by travel narratives set in and around motels. Any well-designed motel can cite and mobilise a number of these without 'imposing' any one too explicitly. Indeed, the motel form (or 'chronotope', in Bakhtin's terms) has become so richly mythic in our culture that any one motel anywhere must constrain the possibilities. An amorphous, general motelness can be commercially unconvincing at any price except to connoisseurs of the basic.

It isn't simply a matter of suggesting, for 'high speed comprehension' across vast space,[5] a competitive definition of style (cost, ambience, clientele). Motels are transit-spaces, charged with narrative potential. A motel should promise a scenario, and exactly the one you want: a good night's sleep, a stint of poignant alienation, a clandestine adventure, time off housework, a monastic retreat—promises which need have nothing to do with what anyone subsequently does. Veering off the road and into the drive of any motel setting, we seek shelter, rest, and safety, but we also assess a script (even, or even especially, at the lone motel, in the middle of nowhere, no commercial rivals for miles).

The Henry Parkes is distinguished from its close competition by the sense of a 'complex' it generates. The major rival is straight across the road—the Jumbuck, a Homestead Inn. The familiar 'H' sign for the chain *aficionado* is in thick nailed board, and its woodiness is the single concession, apart from the name, to a code of bush nostalgia. The Jumbuck is aggressively *serial* in theme ('You're Home', wherever you are): the asphalt yard is for parking, no nonsense with stately courtyards; a few routine flowers, no pretentiously landscaped shrubs; and, unusually for a New England motel, no effort at Georgian sashing.

244

The sliding windows are uncompromisingly functional, with mean proportions outlined by the plain aluminium of a hardline, no-frills modernism. The Jumbuck makes minimal use of allusiveness to other building forms. It could be, at best, a raw new home in a brand-name housing settlement. Anywhere else, the same design might merely be motel-basic. But opposite the florid expanse of the Henry Parkes it claims austerity and rigour. The Jumbuck is a real motel, for travellers on serious business.

So the reflective tourist arrives at a scholastic dilemma where Miles Street meets Rouse Street, Tenterfield. On one side of the road, a myth of the Modern Universal: seriality, chain self-reference, territorialisation by repetition-and-difference; *a Homestead is a Homestead everywhere*. On the other, Postmodern Particularity: *bricolage* individuality-effect, pluralist pastiche coding, localisation by simulated aura: *this motel is The Motel in Tenterfield*.

In each case, the major signifiers of these myths are equally myths of Australianness (the motel signs: Jumbuck, Henry Parkes) and of Home (the suburban referent of their design). But these function quite differently on either side of the road. The Jumbuck is a national-*identity* synecdoche, as internationalising in form as a Tudor Inn or a Ten-Gallon Hat; its model of 'home' is a standardised housing. The Henry Parkes, in contrast, advertises *personality*: a locale appropriates a 'historic' name, to claim special regional significance; and the 'home' it offers is a middle-class splendour, customised to connote 'unique-ness'. The Jumbuck is a motel to use, the Henry Parkes a place to visit.

Quandary

On the road, the choice can be quickly reduced to price, availability, mood. So, for some reflective tourists, there could be no choice in-volved. A motel, by definition, can never be a true *place*: the locality-effect of the Henry Parkes is an optical illusion.

Following an influential distinction derived from Daniel Boorstin, for example, any motel is necessarily one of the 'pseudo-places' defin-ing the tourist world.[6] For Paul Fussell, the characteristic sign of the pseudo-place (from Disneyland to the airport, Switzerland to the shop-ping centre) is a calculated readability.[7] True places are opaque to the passing observer and 'require' active response (ideally, the rich in-terpretation that was 'literature' in the lost era of 'travel'). Pseudo-places achieve an artificial transparency, inducing the passivity typical of 'tourism'. It follows that motels juxtaposed in space can only be rival pseudo-places. In Tenterfield (part place, part pseudo-place) the most that could be said is that, while the Jumbuck celebrates its pseudo-place status, the Henry Parkes tries to hide it. The difference is mere variation apprehended in a high-speed, empiricist *flash*. Indeed, the rapidity with which I can 'recognise' the difference is the sign of its pseudo-status.

With its dependence on cultural élitism and on a realist epistemology, the idea of the 'pseudo' has shown a surprising tenacity in recent cultural studies. Jean Baudrillard's concept of hyperreality owes a good deal to Boorstin's work, and can be written back into its terms. In the world of third-order simulacra, the encroaching pseudo-places finally merge to eliminate places entirely. This merger is a founding event: once it has taken place, the true (like the real) begins to be reproduced in the image of the pseudo, which begins to become the true.[8]

In this optic, my two motels can only be 'recognised' as generators of a hyperreal country town. Adjacent features—old houses, paddocks, sheep—become, like 'rural' faces in the street, indifferently either vestiges of the old order of the Real, or simulacra of the old (more true than the true, more rural than the rural) for the new order of hyperreality.

For both Fussell and Baudrillard, the irreality of motels is of an objective order. Both write allegories of subjects in movement halting here and there in an obdurately recognisable landscape: Fussell's tourist requires the known; Baudrillard's theorist always finds it.

Acceleration

A slightly different rejection of the Henry Parkes can be produced by simply not stopping—writing the subject as a zooming observer, tourism as a history of *speed*.

For Paolo Prato and Gianluca Trivero (scanning Fussell's use of Boorstin via the work of Paul Virilio), 'Speed undoes places; events [*faits*] become non-events [*défaits*] (Paul Virilio), and a succession of pseudo-places reduces the complexity of the environment to hotel chains, motorway restaurants, service stations, airports, shopping centres, underpasses, etc.'[9] And indeed, for Virilio, speed consumes time, narrative, and subjectivity as well as space: speed is itself a 'non-place', and the users of transit-spaces, transit-towns (like airports), are spectral—'tenants . . . for a few hours instead of years, their fleeting presence is in proportion to their unreality and to that of the speed of their voyage'.[10]

In the 'accelerated impressionism'[11] of an aesthetics of disappearance, 'the' landscape becomes a blur, a streak, and no sense of place can survive.

But, if there is a spectre haunting transit-space in these racy formulations, it is perhaps the figure of the peasant rather than that of the short-term tenant. Duration, stability, accumulated experience, reality itself are products of relative immobility in a permanent and singular place: which is to say, they are rhetorically immobilised *categories*. They don't really move in history, or transform in response to transit(ion). The founding myth here is not geographic (the progressive encroachment of the pseudo-sphere) but historical: the trauma of humanity's first train ride, the thrill of first contact with cinema.[12] Unlike Baudrillard's hyperrealist, however, the subject of zoom analysis is eternally fixed in her originary moment. Hurtling on in the accelerating placelessness of speed, she's a figure in chronic stasis.

U-turn

However, Paul Virilio's notion of the 'lodgment' as a '*strategic instal-lation*' (establishing 'fixed address' as a monetary and social value in the history of mobilisation)[13] allows for slowing the pace. A motel is a type of installation that mediates (in spatial, social, and monetary terms) between a fixed address, or domicile, and, in the legal sense, 'vagrancy'. It performs this function precisely as a transit-place, a fixed address for temporary lodgment.

Furthermore, the installation of any one motel can easily be seen as strategic. There is not only rhetorical competition with neighbours ('address' projected in space) but a conative effort at stopping the traffic over days as well as moments, to slow transients into tourists and divert energy to places (the motel and its vicinity). The aim of a specialist motel like the Henry Parkes is an elaboration on this—an attempt from a small-town highway spot to alter urban maps of sig-nificance. The ploy assumes the transience and plasticity, not the fixity, of meanings constructed in space. So to stop to examine such an effort is also to construct a strategic installation: rather than halt-ing for confirmation (collecting theoretical brochures) at exemplary places or performing their disappearance (hypostatising motion), it places reading transitionally *at* a site, in a process of place invention.

Tour

Highway clichés aside, the Henry Parkes foyer is in fact a place where the 'fixed' and the 'mobile' meet. Adorned with all the conventional signs of tourism and moteldom, it is both a front office to one wing of the motel and a work-space extension to the family home a few steps away on the left—with activity spilling between them.

To a new arrival looking around, the relationship between parts of the complex are hard to stabilise.

Behind the family home (designed to blend with the motel) is a public sports centre with a large and well-equipped gym; and the passage to it from the motel negotiates a garden-with-pool landscaped in suburban 'backyard' styling. Like many motels with a sporting motif, the Henry Parkes can double as an informal community centre: the therapeutic motel function extends into the local leisure economy. So at any moment, and in most of the spaces defining the complex, there is constant intermingling of the 'host' family's domestic life, the social activities of town residents, and the passing diversions of tour-ists. The motel's solidity as *place* is founded by its flexibility as *frame* for varying practices of space, time—and speed.

This art of motel extension projects rhetorical identity in space in a manner quite different from that analysed by Venturi, Scott Brown, and Izenour for façades on the Las Vegas strip. In those highway-inflected structures, they see a functional distinction between 'front' and 'back' reflected in formal design: 'Regardless of the front, the back of the building is styleless, because the whole is turned towards the front and no one sees the back'.[14] A front/back regionalisation model[15] is thus rewritten as a distinction between a surface (persuasive) rhetoric, which varies, and a deep (enabling) grammar, which does not— 'the neutral, systems-motel structures behind . . . survive a succession of facelifts and a series of themes up front'.

The Henry Parkes abandons these distinctions and the fundamentalism they foster. The façade theme is developed, not restricted or deflated, by the intricate regions behind. The country-resort experience begins on the street and runs all the way back to the fence. As a strategic installation, this motel works *against* the codes of highway inflection—and, in fact, against the pull of the highway. It intrudes into the traffic flow to inflect it towards the town.

It is as a small-business 'front', then, that the Henry Parkes effects a rural solution to the problem defined by Venturi. Its production of itself as a 'place' (and of Tenterfield as a tourist setting) isn't simply a logical progression from the dynamics of highway competition but an effort to reverse and exploit the highway's displacing effect on small towns. It is a common device of theme motels in locations of fragile importance, and one that still allows for variation along the lines described by Venturi. Other sports-theme motels, for example, may function primarily as wrenching body-conversion centres, or as exotic health-and-beauty farms. In this case, however, place is produced as a strongly built form of *'residency'*.

Inside the complex, the resident family, visiting locals, and motel guests all share in a pervasive production of 'home'. The Henry Parkes offers locals not only a little work (house and garden) and an inspiring architectural model of the 'beautiful residence', but the raw material ('strangers') for further home-town promotion. The coherence of the Henry Parkes complex is an embracing and durable familialism. The touristic, the neighbourly, and the proprietorial are related not by opposition (mobile/fixed, touristic/everyday, itinerant/domestic) but along a spectrum divided by degrees of duration, intensities of 'staying' (temporary/intermittent/permanent).

Being there

To change the hospitable rhetoric of the Henry Parkes could be a costly and senseless venture. The most removable, renovatable, and ignorable facet of the place is in fact the Legend of its patron personality inscribed on the scroll at the front.

Bannered across a brick wall, curved elegantly around a plaque and bust, is a Legend of a famous Visitor. This is the motel's 'foundation-stone', its anchorage in History—national (the Federation of Australia), regional (the Tenterfield Oration), and personal (the motel's baptism).

For a cursory glance, the ornate script of the Legend and the bronze effect of the bust need do little more than signify period nostalgia. For many tourists, no doubt, there it stops.

Another kind of cursory glance could read, yet again, the disappearance of history in myth. On this wall, the bitter class struggles of the late nineteenth century, the machinations of a fading patriarch still grasping at political influence, the displacement of the Aboriginal people, and so the very history of this town, this *site*, in battles for land, wealth, power, and the right to determine 'Progress'[16]—all, indifferently, are obliterated by a cloying and sentimentalised sign of the past as timeless colonial *style*.

An experienced history-tourist could even defy the anecdotal status of the Legend, and make it an accessory to the motel's familial myth. It was Parkes, after all (reformer and titular founder of housing, health, prison, transport, communications, and education programs), who married, in 1890, the dream of a white Australia to a nostalgia for Britain as 'home'—casting, in a memorable and much-commemorated form, the Imperial Family legend: '*The crimson thread of kinship*', his descendants would repeat, '*runs through us all*'.

Yet there's an imbalance between this all-embracing interpretation of the motel myth and the scroll's quite casual position. On the one hand, the Legend ascribes great powers to the Word (Parkes spoke, and as a result Australia federated) and to the authority of media citation (the *Sydney Mail* creates Parkes's status). On the other hand—who reads it? What powers does a scroll exercise? The cypress trees in front of it grow taller . . . the locals can ignore it, most tourists may not see it, and who has heard now, anyway, of Henry Parkes? It has the power, at best, to send some trade down the road to see the Place of the Oration. Few travellers, one must imagine, can be expected to take their pleasure in knowingly sleeping and eating 180 metres away from a site of enunciation.

Who can say? Who knows about 'the others'? This is one problem that the scroll can raise, with its story of an exemplary figure's fiat. What actions are performed by positing ideal models of a theoretical practice (and speaking position) appropriate to popular culture? The motel gives pause to think about the question. To give pause is the primary function of the motel as motel anywhere. Back in the rooms of this one, there is, in the midst of a comfortable mix of mod-cons and period-effects, strategically installed, under a window beside the TV, that contemplative place—a desk.

II
DOMESTIC PURSUITS

Political philosophy

Under which thimble—quick! if you please—
Under which thimble now are the peas?

Juggle on juggle, all the day long,—
Sir, you are right!—ah no!—you are wrong!
Then it was R, and now it is C,[17]—
None of your eyes could follow the pea;
How it was smuggled nobody shows,
How it was juggled nobody knows.

Juggle on juggle, day after day,
Life is a struggle, do what we may;
Wait for our next, and then you shall see
Which is the thimble holding the pea.

Juggle on juggle, all the day long,
None are quite right, and none are all wrong;
Life is a struggle ever up hill,
Life is a juggle, say what you will!
Henry Parkes, *Studies in Rhyme*, 1870

(Of all Parkes's features as a self-made man, few caused more hilarity to critics during and after his lifetime than his untutored efforts at poetry—except perhaps the 'wandering aspirates' that gave his class origins away. He published five volumes of verse, including many poems about the joys of travel, and others about domestic bliss enjoyed at home with his wife.)

■

In 'Sightseers: The Tourist as Theorist', Georges Van den Abbeele makes this comment on the kind of itinerary I've just produced:

> The ritualizing and/or institutionalizing of the voyage can also be an attempt to achieve a certain immediacy (of knowledge, of presence) through the realization of a priorly conceived project. One attempts to circumvent the delay in cognition by being there so to speak before one has begun, by preparing an 'ambush' so that when the experience takes place it can be grasped as fully present.[18]

His article is an intricate commentary on Dean MacCannell's book, *The Tourist: A New Theory of the Leisure Class*. MacCannell argues that tourism emerges in a society no longer dependent on alienated labour but on 'alienated leisure', in which 'reality and authenticity are thought to be elsewhere'.[19] Tourism is a quest to find them. But this quest is made impossible by the very structure of modern tourism. It is defined by a 'semiotics of attraction', in which something (the marker) represents a 'sight' to someone (the tourist). Claiming to indicate the sight, the markers delimit and produce it (since without the proliferation of information and itineraries the tourist would not be able to distinguish the 'sight' from its 'surroundings'). Thinking that he is grasping the reality of a different world, the tourist is in fact always reading the signs of tourism—that is, signs of difference.

In Van den Abbeele's gloss on this argument, a tourist does research for his trip, not merely to avoid discomfort in strange places, but to prepare himself, like an assiduous art student (or a pursuant of truth in politics), for *grasping* the eventual authentic 'sight'. So the tourist as autodidact is perpetually involved in producing and reproducing a metaphysics of presence. He hopes to 'ambush' the sight, but he is always already ambushed by the marker–sight relation.

The trap is unavoidable; and, in one sense, it is the inevitability of 'ambush' that is (like the pious moral of Parkes's cynical philosophy, the 'desk' in my writing on the wall) always already present to Van den Abbeele's argument.

Rather than retrace the path towards it, I want to sidestep to consider the political inflections of the moves by which Tourism and Theory are read as exemplary, parallel instances of a teleological *drive*.[20] It is difficult to do justice in summary to Van den Abbeele's text, not only because of its complexity but because of its shifting relations to the text of *The Tourist*. To simplify, I shall disarm my own ambush by exposing it at the beginning. Van den Abbeele will argue that the totalising projects of both Tourism and Theory could be displaced by a theoretico-practical Nomadism. I shall read his argument as developing from three major oppositions that he works to deconstruct: *voyage/home, Man/difference, theory/tourism*. They do not function as equivalents of each other, but I shall read each of them as marked by an implicit valorisation of the first term as 'masculine' (that is, unmarked human)—a valorisation which survives the deconstructive move, *and* in doing so enables an elimination of politics from Van den Abbeele's trajectory.

Voyage/Home

In his reading of MacCannell, Van den Abbeele accepts that a search for 'destination' is endemic to tourism. Doing so allows him to develop a strong analogy between 'tourism' and 'theory' using the classic epistemological metaphor of the voyage. He *also* limits that metaphor's deployment by reading it as a model of narrative structure. The key figures connecting these operations are *home*, or the *domus*, and *domestication*:

> The tourist theorizes because he is already en route and caught up in a chaotic, fragmented universe that needs to be domesticated. The very concept of 'the voyage' is this domestication in that it demarcates one's traveling like the Aristotelian plot into a beginning, a middle and an end. In the case of the tourist, the beginning and the end are the same place, 'home'. It is in relation to this home or domus then that everything which falls into the middle can be 'domesticated'. (p. 9)

The project of domestication fails, not only because of the gap between marker and sight, but because the tourist's interpretation always 'lags' behind the activity of voyaging. Domestication is an effort to catch up cognitively with the ever-fleeing experience, or the 'motion', of being *en route*. It is thus an attempt to contain and deny the precedence, as well as the excess, of process over structure. The tourist's problem with 'lag' here becomes, I think, a model of a more fundamental dilemma said to define the speaking being.

In this account of the 'circular structure of referentiality', the *domus* really functions as the ultimate ambush awaiting the tourist. As the fixed point to which the tourist's theorising attempts to refer, the *domus* is not only always receding as the voyage begins (the designation 'home' is an 'eminently retrospective gesture') but will never be the same when the tourist attempts to 'return'. Home has moved on while the tourist moved away, and the tourist returns transformed by the process of 'domesticating' experience elsewhere.

Van den Abbeele's tourist is trapped, of course, not only by his own myth of Presence and by the aporia of his empiricism, but by a literary variant of both—Tristram Shandy's dilemma. His tourist, chasing 'himself' in time, is a doomed but indomitable realist—forever pursuing a pea.

One problem with this account is the place it accords to 'activity', 'effort', and 'labour'. These terms are made operative only for the voyage, not for 'home' (the elusive ideal that motivates the journey). The *domus* is not reciprocally constructed as a site of work, theoretical or otherwise. Van den Abbeele is quite attentive to the significance of practical activities in tourism (boarding planes, checking in baggage, taking taxis, getting out of bed . . .), but it is strictly, as the ordering of this list suggests, in relation to the rituals of arrival and departure that extend the 'voyage' into the domestic space and make its beginning impossible to fix. That is say, 'home' is at once a space which is *blank* (so, impossible) and a site of recessiveness: the voyage intrudes into the home, not vice versa (except as a dream of nostalgia). The *domus*, therefore, is figuratively constructed not only as a womb, but as unproductive—a womb prior to labour.

Furthermore, if the work of tourism (research, reading the markers, theorising the voyage) is a 'domestication', it is because the domestic is understood in the romantic sense of a 'taming' and a 'naturalisation'. There is no necessary logical connection between the concepts of coherence and unity (which the tourist tries to impose on a 'chaotic and fragmented universe') and those of home and womb (between which, again, there is no necessary connection). But, of course, there is a very powerful cultural link—one particularly dear to a masculinist tradition inscribing 'home' as the site both of frustrating containment (home as dull) and of truth to be rediscovered (home as real). The stifling home is the place from which the voyage begins and to which, in the end, it returns.

An extreme version may be read in Sam Shepard's *Motel Chronicles*. On the left-hand page, a poem: the world-weary drifter declares, in a moment of 'domesticating' his experiences while not-at-home, 'I've about seen/all the nose jobs capped teeth and silly-cone tits I can handle/I'm heading back to my natural woman'.[21] On the right, a photograph of a woman in a house or motel laundry —her body balanced beautifully between the ironing board and the washing machine. Shepard, in this instance, is the more rigorous theorist of the *domus*. Labour is inscribed on both sides:

Man on voyage (writing poem) positions Woman in *domus* (with washing). In Van den Abbeele's text, the restriction of work to the voyage prevents this sort of crudity from emerging in his schema. It also blocks reflection on the schema's cultural history; it defines, for him, a purely epistemological problem ('the metaphorics of the voyage'). A feminist reading might ask, therefore, what happens to that problem (and the voyage/*domus* opposition) if 'home', rather than the voyage, is rewritten as chaos and fragmentation, labour, transience, 'lag'—or in quite different terms, since these remain a bit too parasitic on the voyage.

But in Van den Abbeele's text the possibility of rewriting 'home' cannot emerge any more than a feminist desire to do so does. The tourist leaving and returning to the blank space of the *domus* is, and will remain, a sexually in-different 'him'.

Man/Difference

One reason for this blankness is that Van den Abbeele follows Dean MacCannell at least some way towards displacing the 'working class' with the 'new leisure class' (of tourists) as a privileged site for analysing modernity. MacCannell considers 'work' used as a tourist spectacle (work displays) to be the very definition of 'alienated leisure' (we work to tour other people working). In Van den Abbeele's text, non-theoretical work drops from sight: the elision of work from the *domus* simply follows from accepting that the tourist's social 'home' is a society of alienated leisure.[22]

Another reason for it is that he goes further than MacCannell in theorising tourism (and thus 'modernity') as a production of differences, and spectacles of difference. This requires a digression to look at *The Tourist* in more detail.

MacCannell argues that, rather than being organised by simple dualities (such as capital/labour, men/women), modernisation is an institutionalised process of 'social structural differentiation'. This means 'the totality of differences between social classes, life-styles, racial and ethnic groups, age grades . . . political and professional groups and the mythic representation of the past to the present' (p. 11). In his version of this by now familiar diagnosis of the post-industrial condition, MacCannell sees differentiation as the 'primary ground' of the feeling of freedom, and also of contradiction, conflict, and alienation, in modern society. Tourism rests on this ground, as a 'collective striving' to transcend differentiation and discontinuous experience by grasping the Big Picture. The tourist as alienated but active cultural 'producer' is thus, for MacCannell, a model of *modern*-man-in-general (p. 1).

This also why the tourist, for MacCannell, always remains an ambivalent figure. On the one hand, '*sightseeing is a ritual performed to the differentiations of society*' (p. 13). Seeking signs of authentic difference elsewhere, the tourist carries modernisation further afield (imperialism).

His quest is foiled not only because tourist attractions have the same structure as the differentiations of modern society, but by the effects of his own action in spreading the 'totalizing idea' of modernity. Tourism correspondingly helps to secure a 'strong society' at home; therefore, it may be fundamentally conservative, as well as destructive in the field of modernity's Others.

On the other hand, the quest at least implies a discontent with 'home' (modernity). The issue is complicated by the fact that, while defining the quest as doomed, MacCannell also wants to reject denigration of tourist activity as *in*authentic. It's a matter not just of sympathy for popular culture, but of arguing that the 'rhetoric of moral superiority' to tourism is (especially in the form of touristic anti-tourism) in perfect conformity with the logic of differentiation that motivates tourism. Anti-tourism (contempt for 'the others') is not an analytical reflection on tourism but 'part of the problem' (pp. 10–11).

So the rehabilitation of the tourist is also achieved by suggesting that the tourist may, through his interpretative labour, have an experience of something *like* 'authenticity'. Unlike Paul Fussell, the tourist doesn't find his motels and sights and souvenir shops to be 'pseudo' but enjoys them and keeps on going. He helps to sustain 'a collective agreement that reality and truth exist somewhere in society, and that we ought to be trying to find them and refine them' (p. 155). He is, in his way, a social theorist.

It is only at the last step that Van den Abbeele parts company with MacCannell. He places much greater stress on differentiation as 'the marking process' in tourism—which he radicalises, in a formalist move, as the '*actual production*' of social differences, rather than the ritual performance of them (p. 10). He also points out that MacCannell's concept of 'social structural differentiation' does nothing to modify the totalising impulse of theory (or tourism), since 'nothing is so totalizing as a concept of differentiation—nor so apt to be undermined by the very play of differences it attempts to name and delimit' (p. 13).

The tourist never attains an approximation, or even an intimation, of authenticity, but produces social reality as a kind of 'figural displacement'. It follows that a 'radical politics' of tourism will mean actively affirming the 'supplemental play' of the 'inauthentic' marker, rather than trying to grasp the Sight (or insist on difference). That is to say, the radical tourist will not struggle for transcendence and the refinement of social realities, but will deconstruct his theoretical practice as tourist.

At first sight, it seems that Van den Abbeele's move should lead to a deconstructing of the figure of modern-man-in-general (Man). In fact, something different happens. MacCannell's Man acts out the logic of social-structural differentiation to which, and of which, he is Subject. That is, 'he' is always already socially differentiated (by sex, age, lifestyle, etc.) as a cultural producer, and may be uncomfortable

254

about it. His Manhood, then, is both a grammatical fiction and an unachievable ideal. Van den Abbeele's tourist is an indifferent producer of social reality *as* differentiation: his discomforts emerge not from his own social positioning in difference but from his philosophical mistakes (seeking authenticity, difference). His Manhood, then, is not an object of struggle—something to be achieved—but a presupposition. It still remains the *a priori* of the voyage.

Theory/Tourism

If the tourist, for MacCannell, is a social theorist, he is a 'primitive' one—he is 'mystified' about his role in constructing modernity, and his work historically precedes that of the social theorist: 'Our first apprehension of modern civilization ... emerges in the mind of the tourist' (p. 1). But he has a responsive potential, because of his own discontent. So, for MacCannell, some resolution of the problems posed by tourism may be achieved if social theorists rethink and develop it as a mode of 'community planning'.

Van den Abbeele recoils from both the prospect of 'planning' and MacCannell's claim that his theory of tourism can serve as a theory of social totality. Quite reasonably, he points out that it is really a theory of travel (of modernity seen as 'a perpetual narrative of adventure' (p. 11)), and turns instead to question the politics of producing such an 'all-encompassing' theory. For Van den Abbeele, what is finally at stake is 'less the ideology of tourism than the ideological function of theory' (p. 11).

He takes issue with what he sees as MacCannell's eventual reassertion of the 'superiority' of the social theorist over the tourist. By giving up his radical 'sympathy' for tourism, MacCannell not only reasserts the power of his own position as theorist but repeats the very *gestures* of mystified tourism. Both tourist and theorist attempt to ambush Presence. But the theorist has the greater pretension. He wants to be not just a sightseer but a *seer*—a prophet, in possession of knowledge superior to that of 'the others'. The circle closes: for Van den Abbeele, the theorist, even more than the tourist, is 'part of the problem'.

But whose problem? MacCannell's critique of anti-tourism is based not only on sympathy for the tourist (rejection of élitism) but on a concern for the social consequences of modernity's 'adventure' for the places and people *toured*. It is because of this concern that MacCannell returns in the end to the question of planning. His final position is not simply one of theorist differentiated *from* tourist but of theorist potentially working *with* particular communities planning to be toured. His position as 'seer', then, is more limited in its pretensions than Van den Abbeele can allow.

The 'toured' in fact disappear from Van den Abbeele's account as soon as he introduces his critique of the concept of *totality*. Oddly enough, this happens just as he points out that 'not everyone has either the political right or the economic means to travel' (p. 11), and that MacCannell's theory therefore only deals strictly with the 'leisure class' rather than society as a whole. Van den Abbeele then suggests that, if travel is 'relatively restricted, it must be because of some danger it poses to society's integrity'. This is consistent with his own desire to argue that the excess of the voyage can constitute a threat to the *domus*. But, surely, one might draw the opposite conclusion: if for some societies travel is relatively *unrestricted* for large numbers of people, it is because for the 'home' society it does *not* pose much of a danger to its integrity.[23] This is, of course, exactly why MacCannell sees the 'international middle class' as a problem in the first place.

For Van den Abbeele, however, sympathy for the tourist combined with a critique of totality implies a general transformation of theoretical practice. He proposes a politics of theory in which the excess of the theoretical voyage would not be restrained—and in which the process of theorising would not attempt to refer back to a *fixed*, 'theorist's', place in a *fixed* society. It is the very presupposition of a fixed position—or *domus*—that must be questioned.

This familiar, indeed 'domestic', conclusion to a deconstructive analysis of the politics of theory then provides a figure to supplant both the Tourist as realist/empiricist/metaphysician of Presence and the Theorist as totalising Seer. It is the Nomad—who 'renders impertinent' any opposition between rest and motion, between home and travel (p. 13). Invoking Deleuze to insist that the nomad isn't necessarily in motion but can travel '*sur place*', Van den Abbeele speculates that nomadic theory would 'travel from inauthentic marker to inauthentic marker without feeling the need to possess the authentic sight by totalizing the markers into a universal and unmediated vision' (p. 14).

It's a satisfying conclusion, from which it's hard to dissent. The trouble is that, where MacCannell's totalising concept of modernity does allow for a critique of 'present' social differentiation and for a disarticulation of modern-man-in-general itself by modernity's various Others at home and abroad (precisely because difference is so 'apt to be undermined' by the play it attempts to de-limit), Van den Abbeele's philosophically more sensitive trajectory has the opposite result. It erases social, political, and perhaps theoretical struggle altogether.

In 'Feminist Politics: What's Home Got to Do With It?' Biddy Martin and Chandra Talpade Mohanty argue that there can be political limitations to 'vigilante attacks on humanist beliefs in "man" and Absolute Knowledge wherever they appear', if these deny the critic's own situatedness in the social, and in an institutional 'home'.[24] Something like this has happened in 'Sightseers: The Tourist as Theorist' when, at the end of the road, we are ambushed by a figure who, erasing both the *domus* and difference (therefore becoming, in a sense, autogenetic), and marking a positive denial of situatedness in the social, might well be effectively a model for (post)modern-Man-in-general.

'Tis misconception all

A PHILOSOPHER *said, 'All the world is mad, I am the only sane man in it'.*

> *''Tis misconception all. The world is mad,*
> *And I alone am sane'. Such the words*
> *Of England's living sage, he rightly proud*
> *Of wisdom in the courts of wisdom.*
>
> *An unit in that full and flowing crowd*
> *Of miserable maniacs, I, like them,*
> *Was too intent to win the happiness*
> *And worth of life, to value high the search*
> *For possibilities, convertible,*
> *It might be, to the probable. Too full,*
> *Within the limits of a biassed mind,*
> *Of the sweet claims of many clinging friends,*
> *And the dear wisdom of kind deeds,*
> *The daily earnestness of common life,*
> *To yield, unquestioned, that high-voiced demand*
> *Of all-engrossing sanity. Wise, thought I,*
> *Mothers who bend o'er the helpless babes;*
> *And wise the husbandman, who brings*
> *From God's right hand our daily bread;*
> *And wise the toiler 'midst the clang*
> *Of mighty engines for the world's behoof;*
> *And wise, most humbly wise, the innocent,*
> *If ignorant, who bend the knee*
> *And bow the heart to learn of God.*
> *Thus, tho' yet in love with wisdom, I*
> *Shrank back with thoughts akin to hate or scorn,*
> *And called the wise man—egotist.*

Menie Parkes, Poems, 1866

(It's a bit hard to like Menie Parkes, although she is the brilliant daughter effaced by the father's Legend. She had a sad life, and found ferocious consolations in religion. She was Parkes's companion and counsellor, made money writing romances, and married a clergyman who soon died in a fall from a horse. Her own book of poetry was printed privately, as a Christmas gift to her father.)[25]

In 'Maps for the metropolis: a possible guide to the present',[26] Iain Chambers discusses travelling in terms quite different from those of Georges Van den Abbeele. But Chambers also suggests a figure of the modern intellectual, though one with more limited scope for movement and of more focused pursuits than the Nomad—the 'humble detective'.

But if the detective himself is humble, he works a grandiose territory. He cruises through everyday life in a place subsuming both the voyage and the *domus*—the city or, more accurately, the Metropolis (for Chambers, 'the modern world'). Not surprisingly, then, he travels a lot: 'A critical intelligence adequate to the fluid complexity of the present is forced to fly regularly' (p. 5). But eventually 'we also go home'.

The privileged metaphor for Chambers's argument is not the voyage but the *map*. Critical movement is defined not in relation to the temporal 'lag' that fascinates Van den Abbeele, but in relation to spatial shifts between 'perspectives'. There are two major and apparently conflicting ways of mapping the modern world: the *overview* (the theoretical view from the aeroplane—rarefied atmosphere, vast generalisation, flat earth as disappearing referent, possible implosion under pressure); and the *close-up* (the view on the ground—'down-to-earth' observation, local detail, stubborn and violent materiality of terrain, an overwhelming mass of complexities). A working mediation of these two perspectives is possible, however, on the 'giant screen' of the contemporary city. The streaming images of everyday life provide a fluid space of 'immediacy' between the extraterrestrial perspectives of postmodernism and the terrestrial prospects of lived popular culture—while maintaining a tension between the two in 'the semiotic blur' of the Present.

So, where Van den Abbeele's deconstruction of the temporal paradoxes of the travel story finally restructures his map of space (no more tour, no more *domus*), Chambers's mapping of perspectives for remapping space eventually generates a 'guide' to *time*—the empire of the Now, the Contemporary, the Present.

These two projects diverge in a number of ways, which make it difficult for a detective to compare them. One is about tourism, the other about everyday life (though, with their discussions of travel and flight, they overlap). One is situated institutionally by literary theory, the other by cultural studies: while one uses the Aristotelian plot as a trope to define its object, the other refers to punk. One situates itself historically by invoking a 'global' European tradition (the 'metaphorics of the voyage'), the other situates itself in a history of postwar British subcultures. One is an academic reading of a reading, relentlessly contemplative—and so emerges from what Chambers would call 'official culture'. The other scans a mixture of materials with the casual attention characteristic, for Chambers, of 'popular epistemology'.[27] (And there is another difference: Van den Abbeele's text does not make this kind of upstairs/downstairs class distinction, and so provides no counter-accusation to situate Chambers's project.)

In the casually contemplative spirit fostered by a room in a quiet motel, it's also fair to say that, while one is very hard-going, the other is an irresistibly amusing read. Both texts are serious, but one is arduous, like homework, the other fun, like a magazine. It's not just a matter of marking different desires for audience. Van den Abbeele does not, and of course cannot, attempt the 'theorizing without theory' he dreams of for the Nomad. He is searching for the possible, convertible—*it might be*—to the probable. Chambers's detective has no time for postponing the conversion: he writes of the daily earnestness and pleasure of common life, in the now codified pop-theory style that has become a contemporary, informal equivalent of traditional socialist realism.

So it seems in overview. But in close-up there are some interesting points of convergence in the trajectories of the Nomad and the Detective.

Both Van den Abbeele and Chambers establish their topics *territorially*, by a move of metonymic expansion. For the former, the ordinary tourist as social practitioner becomes the Tourist/Theorist as exemplary interpreter, before being transfigured and redeemed as the Nomad. In Chambers's text, expansion operates at the level of a field of action, rather than that of the actor's competence: postwar British (sub)culture becomes 'popular culture' which occupies the Metropolis which becomes co-extensive with 'the modern world', and with the Present. It's not a bad achievement for two moves towards affirming a logic of the local, the limited, the partial, the heterogeneous.

At the same time, both texts insist that the point of departure for such expansion *anticipates*, as well as preceding in practice, its conclusion. Van den Abbeele reclaims MacCannell's thesis of 'the tourist's anteriority to the social theorist' (p. 12) in order to make the Tourist prefigure the Nomad—by providing the structure of the dilemma which the latter must displace. Chambers overtly claims that the metropolitan cultures of the last twenty years have 'fundamentally anticipated' the 'intellectualizing' of postmodernism (pp. 5–7). So, in each case, it is the terrain of everyday life (lived tourist 'theorizing', for Van den Abbeele; cultural 'mixing', for Chambers) that anticipates a general theoretical program and its actantial 'hero' (Nomad, Detective).

That is to say, the social in each case is inscribed as prophetic of the theoretical conclusion to which each of these texts will come. And in each case that conclusion will assert the displacement of the intellectual as 'prophet'. As the Nomad displaces the seer, so for Chambers the Detective replaces the intellectual 'as a dispenser of the Law and Authority, the Romantic poet-priest-prophet' (p. 20).

At this point, it may appear that a point of departure is emerging, not from the messy complexity of metropolitan culture or the prophetic space of lived theorising *en voyage*, but from a bibliography of critical writings from the past twenty years—a point of departure retrieved as the ambush of conclusion, recycled, for ritual revisiting, as a *destination* that is inevitable, like the Eiffel Tower, on a tour of present possibilities (or politico-theoretical *markers*). Like Anne Zahalka's photographer in her series of images 'The Tourist as Theorist 1: (theory takes a holiday)'[28] we begin our planning from brochures and conclude with a review of our personalised images of the sights we set out to see.

When 'Theory takes a holiday', however, the interesting thing is not the reiterations of narrative structure but the re-emergence of a form of personification allegory to articulate that structure. For both Chambers and Van den Abbeele (unlike Zahalka), 'Theory' not only becomes the subject of the story of flight and transformation but divides, *in the end*, into two figures. The story is remotivated (for future development) by the splitting (and doubling) of Theory into good and bad characters—the Nomad versus the Seer, the Detective versus the Poet-Priest-Prophet.

In his classic study *Allegory: The Theory of a Symbolic Mode*, Angus Fletcher argued that the hero of personification allegory is above all a 'generator of other secondary personalities, which are partial aspects of himself'.[29] The traveller is a 'natural' conceptual hero for such allegory because he is 'plausibly led into numerous fresh situations, where it seems likely that new aspects of himself may be turned up' (pp. 36–7). Following this, the *tourist* would be a likely hero today precisely because he is plausibly led into *familiar* situations, where old aspects of himself may turn up for renewed recycling. Either way, the point for Fletcher is that the splitting-off of 'chips of composite character' is part of a progressive process of reduction that he calls 'daemonic constriction in thematic actions' (p. 38). The daemons of ancient myth share with allegorical agents, says Fletcher, the characteristic of *compartmentalising function* (p. 40).

Thus, as the Theorist splits into the Nomad and the Seer, the Intellectual into the Detective and the Poet-Priest-Prophet, two diverging daemonic programs emerge for further adventures by Theory. As the field of action of the hero expands (the nomad universe, the 'modern world'), so, correspondingly, his semantic function is reduced, condensed, and sealed off from that of his necessary Alter Ego.

If this is an odd outcome from what starts out in each case as an affirmation of the priority of complex social experience over totalising theoretical activity, it is particularly odd as an outcome for Iain Chambers, for whom '*the metaphysical adventure is over*' (p. 20; my italics). This is the claim that enables his displacement of the metaphorics of the voyage with that of the map. If the detective is certainly still an adventurer, he is, as ten thousand screen stories in the naked city have taught us, nothing if not pragmatic about the process of getting results, and the places where he goes to get them. The real mystery in this case is why, if the metaphysical adventure *is* over, the streetwise intellectual should begin his practice so strictly positioned in a constitutive opposition to 'the Other'—particularly since Chambers, like MacCannell, sees a weak sense of detailed differences (the 'others') replacing singular opposition.

But a binary value-system is probably as indispensable to the rhetoric of populism as the construction of emblematic tableaux of personae performing the functions that define them is to its social portraiture. Menie Parkes's scenes of mother with child, husbandman with bread, or toiler with engine can easily be read as prefigurations of Chambers's post-Rasta black Britons with Italian tracksuits and male gender-benders with falsettos—with the difference that Parkes's tableau assumes an eternal congruence of person and persona, while populism today predicates its pedagogy on their radical dissociation. In this sense, and in spite of its anti-academic or anti-'official' stance, populism may well be one political trajectory for which the metaphysical adventure can *never* be over.

One could conclude that if the rhetoric of touristic anti-tourism defines 'part of the problem' rather than a critical perspective, then in a comparable way an academic anti-academicism defines not a transformed politics of theory, but 'part of the problem'. But this formulation is misleading, in that (like the allegory it analyses) it assumes that anywhere and everywhere the problem of 'Theory' is the same. Not the least of the little imperialisms performed by these exercises is to place 'the modern world' as having-been or still-being under the sway of an intellectual Prophet-Despot who sounds for all the world like an elderly humanities professor in a venerable but declining European university.

'The problem' for me is the function performed by the figure of the Prophet ('the Other'), not in the history of the world, but in Iain Chambers's argument. Its main role seems to be to eliminate the difficulties raised fleetingly by Chambers as 'the relationship between...the machinery of capital, commerce and industry and ART or CULTURE' (p. 17).

Chambers reasonably points out that these distinctions are highly artificial and promote complacent myths of critical exteriority to culture, and that the 'struggle for sense' occurs inside the powers of the field mutually constructed by 'commerce' and (in his example) music. He argues for situating struggle in the complex 'immediate mishmash of the everyday', rather than in relation to a singular *or* 'free-floating' first cause.

However, in a move which has become increasingly common in recent cultural studies, Chambers immediately retreats from extending the principle of complexity to the problem of relations between the (global) 'machinery of capital' and (local) cultural machinations. Instead of entering the 'field' supposedly constructed 'mutually' by industry and culture, the former simply drops out of play. Put baldly, the result is that 'the immediate mishmash of the everyday' in this account still does not include rapidly changing experiences of the workplace, the home, family life, or mechanisms of state—because it does not include these at all. It certainly does not extend to any flickers of experience of the complexity of relations between high-tech culture and the international, and increasingly internationalised, division of labour that Richard Gordon has called the 'homework economy'.[30]

Instead, as an account primarily (and avowedly) based on the emblematic street experience of un- or under-employed males in European or US cities (or what then becomes its echoes elsewhere), it *restricts* the scope of enquiry to what may well be, in a grim sense, one of the 'growth' areas of that economy—but which does not necessarily thereby serve as a useful synecdoche from which general principles of 'culture' in 'the modern world' may be composed. Perhaps this is one reason why women, in post-subcultural accounts, still appear in apologetic parentheses or as 'catching up' on the streets when they're not left looking out of the window.[31] The ways in which economic and technological changes in 'the 1980s' (in Chambers's phrase) have been transforming women's lives simply cannot be considered—leaving them not so much neglected in cultural studies as anachronistically mis-placed.

Left as a restricted account of local developments, Chambers's 'possible guide' would have a different (more 'modest') force. It's the allegorical expansion that gives the lie, like the myth of the Metropolis, to the rhetoric of the local in Chambers's text, and to many accounts of popular culture which read the collapse of old dichotomies (production/consumption, industry/culture) as an occasion for simply effacing the first term and expanding the second (and most of its traditional content—pleasure, leisure, play, resistance). Yet it's a difficult reading to argue against, precisely because the imaginary figure of the Enlightenment Intellectual—prophet of Truth, poet of Totality, priest of a General Theory, and so on—is still so powerful in debate about culture that the Oedipal effort against him automatically resumes in response to suggestions that relations of production and reproduction, too, are now transformed and transforming in the mishmash of the everyday.

This is precisely how, and why, the figure of the Prophet appears in 'Maps for the Metropolis'. After raising the question of relations between industry and culture, and stressing the ambiguities and multiplicities of the 'mix', Chambers immediately rephrases the issue, in straight and simple terms, as one of intellectual 'hostility' to popular culture. Like Van den Abbeele reducing the problem of tourism to sympathy for or against, Chambers shrinks (and moralises) any critique of capitalism to 'talk of commerce and *corruption*' (p. 20; my italics)—and discovers that behind intellectual 'distaste' for popular culture there is 'a deeper drama. A certain intellectual formation is discovering that it is losing its grip on the world'.

This seems to me to be a nostalgic retreat—not least from the possibility of imagining that the 'deep' drama of anybody's anxieties today may have more generous and urgent resonances than a fear of loss of 'grip' (the intellectual as egotist). It's a retreat from the difficulties that follow once criticism of popular culture is already based on complex experiences of *taste* rather than distaste, of involvement rather than distance, so that a strategic 'siding' for or against the 'popular' becomes a quite pointless manoeuvre. Above all, it's a retreat from asking whether the humanist formation exemplified by the Romantic Prophet has not long ago lost out anyway to that quite different formation which Donna Haraway calls 'the informatics of domination',[32] of which the privileged figure might be (to maintain the allegorical imperative) that exemplary localist, the Stress-Management Consultant—from whose 'daemonic' program it is not always so easy to differentiate one's own as Other.

■

Installed in the assiduously stress-free environment of a family-theme motel, the Unprotected Female Tourist tidies her papers, stares at other people's children tumbling past the window on their way to the pool, and wonders whether the woman changing the bedclothes was a girl she went to school with. A feminist, she thinks uncomfortably, should really begin her 'voyage' from these familiar homely markers on the map of everyday life—rather than by chasing, like some raddled detective, the traces of their effacement from the itineraries of 'the others'.

But that's the trouble with travel stories written as Voyages and Maps. They relentlessly generate models of the proper use of place and time—where to begin, where to go, what to become in between. Among the most prescriptive of genres in the canon of modern realism (including 'speculative fiction'), the travel story seems strongly resistant to precisely the effort of transformation that 'Sightseers: The Tourist as Theorist' and 'Maps for the Metropolis' desire to see accomplished.

In Frank Moorhouse's *Room Service* (a useful counter-text to Shepard's *Motel Chronicles*), a story called 'The Anti-Art of Travel' demonstrates the difficulty of overcoming generic models of teleological drive. François Blase—a journalist and tourist who likes to 'rove the world in an inconclusive state'—is confronted in the bar of the Albuquerque Holiday Inn by one of his literary 'others', the Systematic Traveller. In the course of a chat, Blase is harassed by the ST for an account of his theory of travel. Blase resists, but cannot avoid altogether the ambush of reaching a conclusion:

> 'But how do you get a picture of the places you've been to?' the ST said, harriedly.
> 'I don't', I said glumly, 'I just don't. I can't generalize, that's my problem. I can't wrap up my observations in a dazzling conclusive verbal sachet. After all, travel is a damned expensive way to arrive at inconclusiveness . . .'[33]

He hurries on past, however—eventually to end in mid-sentence, muttering inconclusive comments about Boswell and street crime, to a politely bored bar.

III
BILLBOARDS

It was some 180 metres from the site of
this Motor Inn on the 24th October 1889
that Sir Henry Parkes whilst Colonial Secretary
and Past Member for Tenterfield
made his famous and historic federation speech
resulting in the formation of the Commonwealth of Australia.

The Sydney Mail of the time
quoted Sir Henry Parkes as
Australia's most far sighted statesman.

This Motor Inn is therefore named
The Henry Parkes
In Honour of this great statesman
A man to whom all Australians
should be proudly thankful
For the birth of a nation
In its own right.
A COLONY FOR A NATION AND A NATION FOR A COLONY.

restaurant plaque, Henry Parkes Motor Inn

■

There was a legend still circulating in town when I was a child that the Tenterfield Oration was a myth. The Clerk of Petty Sessions, a man then old enough to have witnessed the event as a boy, would swear that Henry Parkes had merely ridden down the main street of Tenterfield, hopped off his horse, relieved himself around the back of the pub, then headed straight out for Sydney.

When locals laughed at the efforts of booster families to mark their patch as a Place of far-reaching significance, they made a joke with antecedents. In 1882 Parkes, returning from an exhausting voyage to America, Britain, and Europe to face turmoil over land reforms, lost the poll in East Sydney. The candidate for Tenterfield, a Mr Edward Reeves Whereat, JP, immediately stood aside and offered Parkes his seat. Elected unopposed, Parkes was baptised by his opponents 'The Member for *Whereat*'.

But the joke wasn't really on the Tenterfield boosters. Making an equation between progress for the town and rhetorical contiguity to a prominent figure, the *Tenterfield Star* celebrated Parkes's election by noting that it would assure its future as a transit-town: 'With regard to the Clarence and New England Railway, the return of Henry Parkes must necessarily make him a firm adherent to the Tenterfield route'.[34]

For far-flung communities dependent on transport for economic survival and growth, to be traversed and attract traversals was obviously a means to, and not an end of, the process of settling 'place'. The railway here didn't blur the landscape but made it visible, legible, and liveable to whites—cutting 'culture' into the bush. This dependence, though, is one reason why country towns never really acquired organic 'roots' or sentimental 'main street' connotations in Australian popular culture. The pomposities of civic pride remain defensive against the more powerful mythic pull of the routes for comings and goings.

Whether or not Parkes's 'adherence' to the route contributed to Tenterfield's success in becoming a transit-town, his name was firmly established as a patron saint of *passage*. In the circular production of 'prominence' that organised regional politics long before the arrival of media and regimes of simulation, the Tenterfield landowners, dignitaries, and small business families dined out on his story for decades. Modern tourism finds in their storytelling its basic semiotic strategy.

■

In *The Practice of Everyday Life*, Michel de Certeau makes an interesting distinction between 'place' and 'space'. A *place* delimits a field; it is ruled by the law of the 'proper', by an orderly contiguity of elements in the location it defines, and as an instantaneous configuration of positions it implies an 'indication of stability'.[35]

A *space* is not the substance of a place but the product of its transformation. It exists only in relation to vectors of direction, velocities, and time variables. Space 'occurs'; composed of intersections of mobile elements, it is *actuated* by the ensemble of movements deployed within it. With none of the univocity or stability of the 'proper', it is produced by the operations that make it function in 'a polyvalent unity of conflictual programs or contractual proximities'.

'In short', says de Certeau, 'space is a *practised place*'. The street defined by urban planning is transformed into a space by walkers; and, in the same way, an act of reading is a space produced by a practice of a written text (a 'place constituted by a system of signs').

One useful consequence of this definition is that no distinction can be made between authentic and 'inauthentic' places. At the same time, it avoids any move to predetermine the kind—and the tempo—of spatial (reading, walking) practices deemed 'appropriate' to particular places. A written text on a motel wall or restaurant plaque may be spatially practised in ways, in directions, and at velocities as various as any street, or literary text. By definition, no one spatial practice can correspond to a 'proper' use of place, and there are no exemplary users.

Nor is there a simple disjunction between the place and its use as space. For de Certeau, stories act as a means of transportation (*metaphorai*) in the shuttling that 'constantly transforms places into spaces or spaces into places'.

There are two sorts of determinations in stories. One works to found the law of place by the *'being-there* of something dead'—a pebble, a cadaver (or perhaps the record of a speech). The other works to specify spaces by the *actions* of historical subjects—stones, trees, human beings (or a political rogue in a hurry). There are passages back and forth between them—for example, in a story of the putting to death (or putting into a landscape) of heroes who have transgressed the law of the place, and make restoration with their tombs (or their epitaphs on motels).

That is, both determinations can be at work in any one legend or story. So the memorialising of events occurring at a site cannot simply be divided into, say, bad petty-bourgeois fabrication (myths of place, sacralisation) and good popular contestation (semiotics of displacement, debunking). As an activity, memorialising is itself a complex spatial-story practice. Struggles (conflictual programs) occur in the shuttling between stories, and between competing determinations *in* stories. Thus the rival versions of the Tenterfield Oration ('Call to the Nation' versus 'Call of Nature') both commemorate a local event and invest a site with meaning, but the second *enlivens* the first—as well as marking its enshrinement of a something-dead as a socially placed aspiration (rather than a 'national' event).

This distinction can be useful in dismantling those lingering equations between the place and the *domus*, displacement and the voyage, which in recent years have made the projects of feminist history so fraught, despite the rhetoric of the local, with general-theoretical anxiety[36]—particularly since de Certeau's concept of story operates at the level of minute phrases and tiny events as well as larger narrative structures. His insistence that 'every story is a travel story—a spatial practice' (p. 115) refers to sentences, footsteps, or scraps of TV news rather than vast developmental schemas for ordering human life.

Thus he differentiates between 'tours' and 'maps', not in terms of teleological narrative drives in the one case and fixations of the Present in the other, but as competing modalities in a process of narrative description. In 'oral descriptions of places, narrations concerning the home, stories about the streets',[37] for example, indicators of the 'map' type ('There is a historic site 180 metres down the road') present tableaux (*seeing* as 'the knowledge of an order of places'), while those of the 'tour' type ('You go down to the School of Arts') organise movements (*going* as 'spatialising actions'). In narration, one form may be dominant but punctuated by the other: tours postulate maps, while maps condition and presuppose tours. It is their combination in a narrative chain of spatialising operations that defines for de Certeau the structure of the travel story: 'stories of journeys and actions are marked out by the "citation" of the places that result from them or authorize them' (p. 120).

The travel story, therefore, does not consist of process contained and directed by origin and destination, nor does it oscillate between 'perspectives' on reality. It is itself a movement organised (like any spatial story) between both prospective and retrospective mappings of place *and* the practices that transform them.

■

Various foundation stories wander around the Henry Parkes (on brochures, cards, and a menu in all the rooms) as well as up and down the streets. The front-wall legend, with its war-memorial layout and assertive historical statement, transmutes on a restaurant plaque into the visual form of a poem.

In this text, events are elegiacally distanced by a *tournure* of romance. It begins from place, not time ('It was some 180 metres . . .' versus 'On the 24th October . . .'); and an archaising syntax ('history-effect') combines with a proprietorial enunciative trace in a discourse of obligation ('all Australians should be proudly thankful'). This produces an aura of special importance, like saying grace before the meal. But it also makes the restaurant plaque a declaration of personal commitment rather than a simple touristic seduction.[38]

The plaque has another touch, however, which marks it off from the other stories and yet defines the type of movement that regulates them all.

It ends with a kind of slogan: 'A COLONY FOR A NATION AND A NATION FOR A COLONY'. It's a resonant, and memorable, phrase. But, when you stop to think, it doesn't make sense—or, rather, it maps an imaginary place. It works for a world in which New South Wales alone became 'Australia', or in which the whole of the Australian continent was occupied by one vast colony. Either way, the whole process of federating six distinct and mutually suspicious colonies into one nation would have been (like the Tenterfield Oration) quite unnecessary.

It could be called a misquotation. The original slogan, attributed to Edmund Barton (later to be first Prime Minister), was 'For the first time in history, we have *a nation for a continent and a continent for a nation'*. But this production of congruence between natural and political places occurred in a public speech. It begins its course of citation and recitation in Australian historiography not as a text certified by its author but as a reported 'memorable impromptu' made at a meeting. In his memoirs, Robert Randolph Garran claimed to have been its first inscriber: it 'would have been unrecorded if I had not happened to write it down'.[39]

What matters in this story is not a myth of the primacy of the spoken word but the movement (in this case, of hearsay) that runs between citings of the text—and that movement in one place of its migration, a plaque on a dining-room wall, transforms it from place-founding slogan to the 'score' of a lilting rhythm: a trill, a whistle, a jingle, a musical spatial story.

■

If you follow the story down the street and go on a tour of the town, several maps of the present and stories of the past begin to intersect. There's discord about it, not just a codified diversity-and-difference.

The School of Arts enshrines the site of Parkes's speech. It's disconcerting to enter with any sense of anticipation, for the inside turns out to be an everyday lending library. As Dean MacCannell points out, the most difficult sights to sacralise are places where something once happened (battles, speech events) but where there's nothing left to see. All that's left here is a lovely but still walked-on original wooden floor.

Down one end, however, there is a roped-off tiny museum of Henry Parkes memorabilia. Apart from a 1915 bust, and a portrait of Parkes in his favourite pose as a late Victorian Moses, most of the objects (wheelbarrow, dog collar, watch) seem to have been collected on the basis of their having been *touched* by Parkes or by persons in his vicinity. They are those objects most confusing and emotionally opaque to a media sensibility—genuine relics. But even this image of sanctum is jarred by pieces which seem to have nothing personal to do with Parkes: a modern book on *Georgian Architecture*, local histories of distant places, bits of twentieth-century pottery with a nationalistic theme.

267

It's a museum dedicated not to the remains of a person but to an old school of history—an inventory of unrelated, age-encrusted, national *faits divers*.

A few blocks away, a rival foundation-place offers something more familiar. It's a showbiz monument—an old shop restored as the home of the 'Tenterfield Saddler'. Built in the 1860s, it was created a few years ago from a song by US-based entertainer, Peter Allen (commemorating a family connection). It's an impeccable third-order simulacrum: even though the building is now 'in its original condition', it reproduces an image of a reality with no previous claim to existence. People treat it respectfully as a forebear of Tenterfield's modernity.

The Centenary Cottage museum tries for something completely different. It has long been in transition between an old house crammed with junk and a 'restored pioneer home'. An incipient program is readable: the highway-oriented, universalising pedagogy of simulation hovers as a possibility. But, even in the rooms already most organised towards this ideal, the period-effect is overwhelmed by local genealogies. In a clear case of what MacCannell calls 'obliteration by the markers', each item is clustered by the history of its donation: a bed is presented by A, handmade by B from a silky oak cut on property C located at D in 1881, and restored by Mr and Mrs E. This museum is unreadable to outsiders. It refuses to effect the gestures of labour, ownership, and gift in the manner essential to catching transient interests—not because it has a deep-rooted sense of 'reality', but because it has no idea of its own obscurity. This is a *dynastic* museum—a 'who's who *here*' display—and despite its touristic ambitions it primarily lectures the town.

Nothing much here means anything to me. But in the more disorganised parts of the Cottage two objects immediately provoke what is usually called 'nostalgia'.

One is in the yard, past an old weighing machine stranded in the grass and some singed-looking ferns by a drain. It's an old laundry copper, 'historic', but intimately stifling: hot, heavy, stubborn loads of washing to be stirred, stick circling round boiling water, in a misery of blazing heat every endless Saturday morning.

The other is in the chaos of junk inside. Next to a 1921 income-tax receipt are the 'Last Reservation Tickets for the Lyric Theatre'. My own first cinema memory rushes up from the 1950s. But it has nothing to do with hurtling through space, zooming through time, or an aesthetics of disappearance.

It's about *placement*, a memory of anxiety in the theatre about where to sit, just the same as in the schoolroom. A tension map of proximities to avoid: town Aborigines (all right, sort of); white West End louts (worse); and worst, in a row tacitly off-limits to everyone else, the Aboriginal and white-trash families from just out of town on The Common.

■

If within a few blocks it's possible to tour an archaic mode of pedagogy, a parochial display of current class and caste distinctions, and
a piece of postmodern aesthetics, then it is partly because tourism
here is as yet barely organised. Apart from National Parks and National Trust (historic buildings) activity, tourism operates as a local
response to economic distress.[40] It's also relatively innocuous—though
there's something devastating about the blatancy of a leaflet available
around town called *The Bluff Rock Massacre*. 'We punished them
severely, and proved our superiority to them', proudly cites the local
historian, blending geological details of the rock with the tale of a
'tribe' being thrown from the top. A more sophisticated tourist operation would obliterate that immediately.

But, if their haphazard efforts make country towns eccentric to the
global tourist economy, they also suggest a general difficulty in constructing guides to the Present, or theories of the tourist homing
instinct. It isn't just that they are obdurately *there*, waiting in ambush
like the suburbs on the edge of the metropolis, with their own de-
clarations of reality. It's rather that even in the smallest places, where
the production of space involves a limited number of 'conflictual
programs and contractual proximities', in de Certeau's phrase, the
operative *simultaneity* of programs and proximities makes the effort to
take any one as exemplary (either of the Now, or of a 'domestication'
of history in myth) only one of the more aggressively territorial programs competing to found its place.

Thousands of miles away, Jean Baudrillard writes in *Amérique*: 'Why
go off to decentralize myself in France with the ethnic and the local,
among the scraps and remains of centrality?' He wants to become ex-
centred in the centre of the world. Fair enough. But when he gets
there he finds, like a postmodern mystic, the universe in a Burgerking
crumb—or a Studebaker, or an empty motel. His America is a 'gigantic
hologram . . . all the information contained in each of its elements'.[41]
I do know what he means. Even in an Australian country town—a
vestige of failed decentralisation rather than a residue of centrality—
I can see something of All Australia in the Saddlery, or the becoming-
Burgerking of the old Greek café down the road.

But the point about holograms (like simulacra) is that they volatilise,
rather than re-place, other models of signifying practice (spatial
stories). In fact, a hologram is one of the visual events least able to
admit of relations in contiguity: it is defined (in Baudrillard's description) by an absolute self-containment. It really doesn't recognise the
logic of the *next*—hologram here, cinema next door, painting over
there—which activates spaces in contemporary culture and makes
philosophies of grounding so difficult to sustain. It is a traffic in
negotiable proximities (temporal as well as spatial) between conflicting practices that follows from the decentring of a Renaissance 'perspective' on life—and not the restoration of hierarchy by a controlling
reference point that marginalises the 'rest'.

A motel is a good place in which to consider the question of traffic, precisely because it is consecrated to proximity and circulation. It is neither the car nor the highway nor the house nor the voyage nor the home, but a space of movements between all of them. It punctuates travelling with resting and being-there with action. It represents neither 'arrival' nor 'departure', but operates passages from one to the other in the *metaphorai* of the pause. Motel-time is a syncopation of different speeds in varied degrees of duration.

But it is not an exemplary site—precisely because it only exists transitionally, in any usage, between other possibilities. It provides an operational link not only between practices but between institutions. In countless fictional motels, gangsters, lovers, psychopaths, drifters, and defaulters come to be killed, seized, abandoned, or imprisoned as well as to hide, to escape, to recover—in transit between many kinds of prison, and many attempts at release. So, despite its resonance for highway romance, the motel may always, in the end, affirm the being-there of the place and the modalities of the map—but it creates the possibility of the tour.

■

In recent articles Lawrence Grossberg has used the model of the road-side billboard to pose problems about interpreting events in popular culture and the politics of everyday life.

Billboards, for Grossberg, are 'markers' (neither authentic nor inauthentic) that are there to be driven by. They don't tell us where we are going, but yet they mark, and comprise, boundaries; they are the outside, inside, and limits of the town that they announce and that we are passing through. They advertise, yet we drive past without paying attention to what they say because we already know, or because it doesn't matter. Yet they do tell us what road we are on, and they reaffirm that we are actually moving. They are not there to be interpreted or 'read'; yet they are a space in which many different discourses appear (so they are sites of struggle). But any *individual* billboard is in-different. It is 'neither built upon a radical sense of textual difference, nor does it erase all difference'.[42]

So Grossberg suggests that interpreting the politics and effects of popular culture is less like reading a book than like driving by bill-boards—not because the street is the only reality, but because bill-boards belong simultaneously to the orders of local detail and national structure, and connect to places off the road (factories, gaols, houses). Billboards are also like the bric-à-brac in Centenary Cottage—apparently meaningless 'signposts' which, for all the irrelevance and seeming uselessness of their specific inscriptions, become sites of investment and empowerment (not necessarily benevolent). For Grossberg, such signposts make it possible to continue struggling to *make* a difference, by devising 'mattering maps'.

So if billboards (unlike the motel) are dominated by the operationality of space and the modality of the tour (by 'going' rather than 'seeing')

270

they enable in turn the making of maps, the citing and seeing of places.

This image is all the more useful if we remember that, as well as driving by billboards anywhere, people sometimes stop near particular billboards somewhere—live near them, photograph them, picnic and read books beside them, deface them, or even (near Tenterfield) shoot at them.

For most of the 1980s, the limits of Tenterfield were marked on the three main roads by 'National (The Big Entertainer)' billboards. They ringed the town with images of Peter Allen at the piano, declaring that he 'Still Called Australia Home', and that Tenterfield was the Home of the Tenterfield Saddler. These routine, concentric productions of Place from the figure of Allen (Saddler/Tenterfield/Australia) were in perfect conformity with the older myth of Henry Parkes (Motel/Tenterfield/Australia). In 1987 they were replaced by billboards advertising a nearby natural wonder, Bald Rock (Australia's Largest Granite Rock)—each separately handpainted in the perfect image of its postcard by two women artists from Tenterfield. For a while, at least, these three serialised 'individual' billboards will figure on local mattering maps—not as in-different signposts enabling the making of difference, but as signs (for those to whom it matters) of a difference *made*. That they may revert, in time, to in-difference makes no difference to the spatial story.

■

Once out at the billboards, the tourist could go home to the Henry Parkes Motel, home to her mother's place nearby, or head home on the road to Sydney. Each ending might define a different kind of domesticity: formalist (return to first principles), feminist (return to a place of origin), or postmodernist (Blase admits the transience of her interest in small towns, and reclaims her intellectual mobility). All of these resolutions might be perfectly realistic.

In any case, I can drive away still thinking about Henry Parkes, of whom I've had very little to say. My interest has been in the disjunctions between the rhetorics of movement, displacement, and rapidity in debates about popular culture, and the feminist insistence on recognising place in critiques of everyday life. But, if so, it is because there is a political stake in the awkward relations between them.

The problem for feminism might be summed up by Prato and Trivero's claim in 'The Spectacle of Travel' that transport ceased to be a metaphor of Progress when *mobility* came to characterise everyday life more than the image of 'home and family'. Transport became, instead, 'the primary activity of existence'.[43] Feminism has no need whatsoever to claim home-and-family as its special preserve, but it does imply a certain discretion about proclaiming its present marginalisation.

It's possible to argue, for example, that in Australia (and in many places) the mobility/*domus* distinction is at best historically doubtful.

It is mobility as a *means* of endlessly making prospects (or 'progress') for home-and-family that becomes, for many people, the primary activity of existence. And colonisation may be precisely a mode of movement (as occupation) that transgresses limits and borders. In and after colonialism, the voyage/*domus* distinction loses its oppositional structure—and thus its value for announcing the displacement of one by the other in the 'course' of Human History.

Yet the sort of claim being made by Prato and Trivero does not seek its grounding in historical 'truth'—even the truth of approximation—and thus makes feminist criticism more difficult. It is meant, perhaps, to be a billboard, a marker in a certain landscape. It marks a recognisable trajectory along which it becomes possible not only for some to think their lives as a trip on a road to nowhere (etc), but for others to think home-and-family as a comfortable, 'empowering' vehicle.

So, rather than retreating to the invidious position of trying to contradict a billboard, feminist criticism might make its own. I have two in mind—two textual places that might be transformed by a shuttle between them producing a spatial story.

As individual billboards, they don't tell me anything in particular—not how to read the history of the family, tourism, or Australian politics, and certainly not how to read the relations between political change and the persistent vagrancy of clichés. But together they mark out space for considering convergence and overlap, rather than divergence and distinction, between the rhetoric of mobility and the politics of placement, the mapping of the voyage and the 'metaphorics of *home*'.

One is a quotation from Henry Parkes—self-made man, traveller, family man, Premier, moderniser, philosopher, and Father of Federation—who spoke of the political reforms of the 1860s in these terms:

> *Our business being to colonize the country, there was only one way to do it—by spreading over it all the associations and connections of family life.*[43]

The other is a media anecdote from the *Sydney Morning Herald* last year, entitled 'Great moments in philosophy'.[44] Paul Keating—self-made man, family man, Federal Treasurer, moderniser, philosopher, Deregulationist—refuted accusations that he was using his travelling allowance to purchase antique clocks. Asked why he claimed travel refunds when he lived in Canberra with his home-and-family, he replied on the steps of Parliament House:

> *We are wayfarers on one long road. Mere wayfarers.*

NOTES

Thanks to Joyce Morris, Colin Hood, and Anne Zahalka.

1   Some material in this essay is from a forthcoming book about myths of progress in Australia, which will include a more developed study of the figure of Parkes.

Henry Parkes (1815–96) came with his wife to Australia from Birming-ham as an assisted immigrant in 1838–39. He was a penniless artisan, and, despite several efforts at business in Australia, he spent much of his life on the verge and over the edge of bankruptcy. He was a member of the Birmingham Mechanics' Institute, and was influenced by the early phases of Chartism. As his biographer AW Martin points out (*Henry Parkes*, Melbourne: Melbourne University Press, 1980), the timing of his emigration left him, 'for good, a Birmingham man of 1832 rather than of 1839: a radical, but dedicated to middle and working class co-operation as the key to reform and progress' (p. 17).

During a political career which lasted from 1848 till his death, he was five times Premier of New South Wales, presiding over the implementation of most of the ideals he had arrived with, as well as of a pro-white, pro-Anglican (anti-coloured, anti-Catholic) vision of Australia's destiny. He ended in the 1890s as an arch-conservative, utterly baffled by the Labor Party.

He married three times, and fathered the last of seventeen children at the age of 77.

Needless to say, his 1889 speech did not cause Australian Federation. His reasons for making it seem to have been at least partly opportunistic, and the speech itself had at best a symbolic effect in galvanising public interest in the matter, particularly in NSW.

2   Iain Chambers, *Popular Culture: The Metropolitan Experience*, Methuen, London and New York, 1986, p. 12.

3   Dean MacCannell, *The Tourist: A New Theory of the Leisure Class*, Schocken, New York, 1976.

4   Georges Van den Abbeele, 'Sightseers: The Tourist as Theorist', *Diacritics* 10 (December 1980), p. 13.

5   Robert Venturi, Denise Scott Brown, and Steven Izenour, *Learning from Las Vegas: The Forgotten Symbolism of Architectural Form*, Cambridge, Mass, MIT Press, 1977, pp. 34–5.

6   Daniel Boorstin, *The Image: A Guide to Pseudo-Events in America*, Harper & Row, New York, 1961. See also the critique of Boorstin in MacCannell, op. cit., pp. 102–7.

7   'Places are odd and call for interpretation . . . Pseudo-places entice by their familiarity and call for instant recognition': Paul Fussell, *Abroad: British Literary Travelling Between the Wars*, Oxford University Press, New York and Oxford, 1980, p. 43.

8   Jean Baudrillard, 'The Precession of Simulacra', in *Simulations*, (Semiotext(e), New York, 1983); also in *Art & Text* 11 (Spring 1983), pp. 3–47. Baudrillard makes explicit reference to Boorstin in *La Société de Consommation*, Gallimard, Paris, 1970.

9   Paolo Prato and Gianluca Trivero, 'The Spectacle of Travel', *Australian Journal of Cultural Studies* 3, 2 (December 1985), p. 27.

10 Paul Virilio, 'Véhiculaire', in *Cause Commune, Nomades et Vagabonds*, (UGE 10/18, Paris 1975), p. 52; my translation.

11 Richard Sieburth, 'Sentimental Travelling: On the Road (and Off the Wall) with Laurence Sterne', *Scripsi* 4, 3 (1987), p. 203.

12 In both Paul Virilio's *Esthétique de la Disparition*, Ballard, Paris, 1980 and Jean Baudrillard's *Amérique*, Grasset, Paris, 1986, the traditional connec-tion between the perceptual shifts brought about by cinema and rapid transport is developed in terms of *disappearance*. For Virilio—concerned with movement in the history of militarisation rather than tourism—the

invention of the camera is also associated with the chrono-photographic rifle and the Gatling gun: *Pure War*, Semiotext(e), New York, 1983, pp. 82–3.

13 Paul Virilio, *Vitesse et Politique*, Galilée, Paris, 1977, pp. 18–19. Virilio's term is actually *implantation*. He argues that the strategic implantation of the fixed domicile is more important to the historical formation of bourgeois power than commerce or industrialism.

14 Venturi, Scott Brown, and Izenour, op. cit., pp. 34–5.

15 See Anthony Giddens, *The Constitution of Society*, Polity Press, Cambridge and Oxford, 1984, pp. 122–6. See also MacCannell, op. cit., pp. 91–102.

16 See CMH Clark, *A History of Australia*, vol 5: *The People Make Laws 1888–1915*, Melbourne University Press, Melbourne, 1981; AW Martin, *Henry Parkes: A Biography*, Melbourne University Press, Melbourne, 1980; and, on country towns and myths of progress, Donald Horne, *Money Made Us*, Penguin, Harmondsworth, 1976.

17 John Robertson and Charles Cowper, factional leaders in the NSW parliament. Colonial politics was organised not by a party system but around vying personalities.

18 Van den Abbeele, op. cit., p. 9. Subsequent page references appear in the text in parentheses.

19 MacCannell, op. cit., p. 3. Subsequent page references to this appear in the text in parentheses.

20 This is one of the ways in which a hierarchical distinction between 'travelling' and 'tourism' is frequently maintained. In Jean Baudrillard's *Amérique* (Paris: Grasset, 1986), 'Nothing is more alien to pure travelling than tourism or leisure' (p. 24). For Baudrillard, the tourist, not the traveller, is an archaic figure, still searching for meaning, reason, and reality.

21 Sam Shepard, *Motel Chronicles*, City Lights Books, 1982, San Francisco, p. 102.

22 Neither writer pays much attention to the 'work' of the leisure industry, or considers the problem of domestic labour in relation to either industrial or 'post-industrial' production. Doing so might have made the industrial/post-industrial line more difficult to draw. Instead, domestic labour is simply subsumed, by implication, in the shift from 'work' to 'leisure'.

23 An example of the political complexity of tourism was provided after the military coup in Fiji in May 1987, when efforts at economic protest on behalf of the former government were undermined by the immediate introduction of cut-price air-fares from Australia. It is interesting to wonder to what extent touristic imperviousness to a coup in a nearby country can count as a danger to *Australian* 'integrity'.

24 Biddy Martin and Chandra Talpade Mohanty, 'Feminist Politics: What's Home Got to Do with It?', in Teresa de Lauretis (ed), *Feminist Studies/ Critical Studies*, Indiana University Press, Bloomington, 1986, pp. 193–4.

25 Menie Parkes, *Poems, Printed for Private Circulation* (Sydney, 1867). See AW Martin (ed), *Letters from Menie: Sir Henry Parkes and his Daughter*, Melbourne University Press, Melbourne, 1983.

26 Iain Chambers, 'Maps for the Metropolis: A Possible Guide to the Present', *Cultural Studies* 1, 1 (January 1987), pp. 1–21. Subsequent page references appear in the text in parentheses.

27 Chambers, *Popular Culture*, p. 13.

28 Anne Zahalka, 'The Tourist as Theorist 1: (theory takes a holiday)', *Cultural Studies*, Vol 2 No 1 1988, pp. 17–28.

29 Angus Fletcher, *Allegory: The Theory of a Symbolic Mode*, Cornell University

Press, Ithaca and London, 1964, p. 35. Subsequent page references appear in the text in parentheses.

30 Cited in Donna Haraway, 'A Manifesto for Cyborgs: Science, Technology and Socialist Feminism in the 1980s', *Socialist Review* 80 (1985); reprinted in *Australian Feminist Studies* 4 (Autumn 1987).

31 Regretful notation of the predominantly 'masculine' orientation of popular culture seems to be Iain Chambers's main response to the kind of criticism made some years ago by Angela McRobbie, in 'Settling Accounts with Subcultures' (*Screen Education* 34 (Spring 1980), pp. 37–49). The problem, however, may not be a matter of the objective masculinity of the streets and whether women are or are not getting out there too, so much as it is a problem with the *model* of 'popular culture' being derived (or imposed) from a limited range of experience. For women at windows, see Dick Hebdige, 'The impossible object: towards a sociology of the sublime', *New Formations* 1 (Spring 1987), pp. 47–76.

32 Haraway, op. cit.

33 Frank Moorhouse, *Room Service: Comic Writings of Frank Moorhouse*, Penguin, Harmondsworth, 1985, p. 52.

34 *Tenterfield Star*, 6 December 1882; cited in Norman Crawford, *Tenterfield*, Tenterfield District Historical Society, 1949.

35 Michel de Certeau, *The Practice of Everyday Life*, trans. Steven F Rendall, University of California Press, Berkeley and London, 1984, pp. 117 ff. Subsequent page references appear in the text in parentheses.

36 See Martin and Mohanty, op. cit.

37 De Certeau, op. cit., pp. 118–20. De Certeau borrows the tour/map distinction from Linde and Labov's study of apartment descriptions by New York residents: 'spatial networks as a rite for the study of language and thought', *Language* 51 (1975), pp. 924–39.

38 The motel was in fact built by a couple whose family had known Henry Parkes in his heyday, but well before he was knighted. So the motel is named simply the Henry Parkes, in order to represent appropriately the nature of the family connection.

39 RR Garran, *Prosper the Commonwealth*, Angus & Robertson, Sydney 1985, p. 101.

40 Like many country towns, Tenterfield—faced with decline in agriculture, sensitivity in the timber industry, and closure of the local meatworks— talked in the 1970s about the possibility of its own extinction. Natural and historical 'resources' then began to be mapped for a semiotics of attraction. If the highway brings fewer commercial transports in search of wood and meat, it now brings more urban transients in search of trees, animals, the homes of pioneers. The town adjusted quite successfully, although many residents depend on social security to survive.

41 Baudrillard, *Amérique*, pp. 56, 59.

42 Lawrence Grossberg, 'The In-difference of Television', *Screen* 28 (Spring 1987), pp. 28–45. See also his 'Putting the Pop Back into Postmodernism', in Andrew Ross (ed), *Universal Abandon?* University of Minnesota Press, Minneapolis, forthcoming. Grossberg uses billboards as a way of discussing the gap between 'ideological' and 'affective' maps.

43 Prato and Trivero, op. cit., p. 40.

44 New South Wales Legislative Assembly, 14 August 1866; cited in Stephen Murray-Smith (ed), *The Dictionary of Australian Quotations*, Heinemann, Melbourne, 1984, p. 211.

45 'Stay in Touch', *Sydney Morning Herald*, 30 June 1987.

17
'Cup City': Where nothing ends, nothing happens

LESLEY STERN
PHOTOS BY KEVIN BALLANTINE

See in your mind's eye a body posturing, imagine a posture of anticipation, a posture of arrival. The pose, the posture, the gesture—these
are processes, movements of the body, of bodies in relation to other
bodies; an arena of proxemics, of energy.

Imagine a perfect location.

Look at these images. Two views: a beach of sorts, a cluster of
possibly urban buildings. They could be anywhere, any place, this
beach, these buildings; there is nothing in the photographs to render
the particularity of Place. No landmarks, no familiar iconography, no
human interest. If photographs are inescapably descriptive, as some
would have it, then these are perversely nondescript. They evoke the
ideality of Anywhere or Nowhere. If the photograph is documentation, why do we not instantly recognise these views as the Being of
Place? From one perspective it's because nothing takes place (so more
is happening than just the ellipsis of iconography). There is no obvious
happening, no promise of eventuality, no incipient drama. There is
an erasure of the figurative (in the still photograph drama is always
only incipient, projected as a potential, or a trace, in the spacing of
bodies and things, the rendering of Space into Place).

Yet, even if place is elusive, space figures insistently in both these
views.

The America's Cup, an international yachting competition held in
Fremantle, Western Australia, over the summer of 1986–87, was or-
chestrated, and for the most part presented, as an epic event. It was also
a nationalistic event, since Australia was defending the Cup, wrested
last time round from the Americans, who had long held both the title

* This essay first appeared in a longer form in *Cultural Studies* 2/1, 1988,
pp. 100–16.

and the location for the race. Alan Bond, a local-boy-made-good (read made-millions), was both skipper of the main Australian boat and prime mover of entrepreneurial activities associated with the event. It was an event staged, like many sporting and competitive events, for a particular kind of rendition—'live coverage' (with television as the agency of presence for those not fortunate enough to be participating observers). For more than a year before the happening, media publicity was geared towards a fostering of anticipation—anticipation of suspense, primarily; also, anticipation of Fremantle as a tourist utopia. Fremantle: a venue for street theatre, for the festive conjugality of flamboyant entrepreneurs and discreet aristocrats; Fremantle as a carnivalesque setting where international yachties would walk in step with sunloving and barefooted locals, a setting at once cosmopolitan and cosy, worldly and casual. The ocean was anticipated as both backdrop to this tourist extravaganza and as focus of attention, a screen for the projection of spectacle, excitement, suspense.

There is something shocking, arresting, about this series of photos taken during the Cup.[1] There is not a yacht in sight. These images do not correspond to the Fremantle we had been led to expect, or even the Fremantle we remember from the media, especially television. Not only are there no yachts; there is no colour, and the series suggests an air of languid immobility. There are few people and lots of space. The figures that do appear seem to have been left over from some other photographic event. They are hanging around as though waiting for something to happen. They are watchful (though not of the camera) and awkward in their desultory vigilance. These photos do not invoke spectacle, excitement, suspense.

To turn again to those views where space figures so insistently.

The path to the beach is paved with civilised intention. There is a skinny strip of sea that obtrudes across a fraction of the frame somewhere towards the top. A bit of sand and a few tussocks lurk in the centre. On the horizon, between the sea and the sky—something that looks like a ship. It is not simply the mass of the foreground that affronts the gaze; an expanse of sand would be expansive and picturesque. No, it is the civility inscribed in stone, in stone slabs laid as a margin between the imaginary but obdurate texture of tarmac and the vagaries of sand and wind. For these stones are a testimony to emptiness, to space—a space unfilled by people. If there were bits of litter or footprints, we could read in the emptiness an inscription of presence, a murmuring of desolation. But there is no sense of abandonment here, just the banality of an empty barren space.

A paved courtyard, a space for strolling. A dense layer of shadow covers the ground. Arising out this shadow mass, an edging of buildings, sharp angles and curved awnings, bright clean surfaces, a pristine palm tree. No people and, again, no litter. The sense of intimacy generic to the courtyard scene is both evoked and mocked by the dense triangular slab of space that grounds the composition, by the scrupulosity of cleanliness. Yet there is a detail that perturbs. In a

window we can see a building ladder propped against another window. The depth of focus paradoxically renders this detail obscure. Is it a reflection of a ladder just out of view, or is it a ladder seen through the window, situated in an empty space lurking behind the building's façade? What it does suggest, either way, is an air not of abandonment but of prematurity. It is too soon to look through the window. For what we see pictured here is on one level a familiar transnational style of architecture—a 'West Coast' hybrid or televisual Miami. Yet it is distinctly a Miami without vice. It's a film set not quite ready for the action.

To situate these two photographs as an 'opening' (as the instigation for a sequence) is obviously a loaded manoeuvre. They are unavoidably set up to frame the images that follow, to set the scene. They are bound to restrain, to put into place the mechanisms for reconciling time and space. Yet in the presentation of still photographs (as opposed to film or writing) a contradiction, precisely between time and space, is played out against the impulse to anticipate. If the articulation of time and space (most notably in dreams, but in other forms of narrative too) locates *difference* as much as *continuity*, this is nowhere more evident than in the sequencing of still photographs. It is to possible dislocations that I want to look. And to do so I want to anticipate the projection of two possible scenarios and to suggest a third.

Given the known context of these photographs, it would be possible to read these two images as having a narrative motivation. This reading would be less concerned with the apparently idiosyncratic perspective of the photographer (in comparison with other representations of the Cup—filled with teeming life and streamlined technology) and would read the evocation of empty space as a narrative pretext. Expectation would be inscribed into the space, an expectation that an event (the Cup, the spectating) will take place, that this will effect a filling of the emptiness, a transformation of space into place. This reading prefigures the figurative, for it anticipates action and actants. These images, then, suggest suspense. The second potential scenario is more grounded in metaphor and an impulse to thematisation. This perspective renders these images familiar—not as a particular place, but as the representation of a metaphor. The dead centre, the inland sea, the empty heart, the barren waste that is Australia is read into these images so that they become evocations of a generalised place—*terra nullius*. This reading also transforms space into place but inscribes suspense not as temporal but as immanent.

Holding these two potential scenarios in mind, I want to explore a third. Let me complicate two terms already invoked—space and place—by introducing notions of 'location' and the 'perfect location fallacy'. I borrow the term 'location' from cinematic practice, where it is used to indicate a 'real' environment where filming takes place, as distinct from a studio and the paraphernalia of studio sets. It is used in association with fiction more often than with documentary, for in the latter the environment does not readily present itself as a potential mise en scène.

When Raul Ruiz, the film-maker, was asked 'Why do you make films?' he replied:

le cinéma m'est toujours apparu comme l'expression la plus parfaite de la 'perfect location fallacy' (AN Whitehead). D'après ses principes, il y a toujours une place qui est mieux qu'une autre pour placer un object et il y en a une de parfaite par objet. L'ennui, avec le cinéma, c'est qu'on perd beaucoup de temps à la chercher et que toutes les places, au hasard, ont l'air parfaites.[2]

The perfect location exists only in imagination. Yet it is not non-existent. The traces of desire (for a perfect mise en scène, staging of objects and bodies in a signifying space) are found in the event of filmic images, in the imaginary of fiction. What we have (what we see?) in the event is not an absence of perfection, but traces of dislocation.

Location, in the filmic sense, is not habitually used in the realm of still photography, perhaps because of the force (even if only residual) of documentation. However, in the collision between Ruiz and Ballantine a collusion is generated, and the 'perfect location fallacy' appears as strikingly pertinent to still photography. This collection of photos suggests Fremantle/Perth as a location in at least two, overlapping, senses. First, the photographic process explores and documents another process—the social/historical siting of the Cup in this location. In this filtering of processes, what we see is not the perfect location but traces of the search, an imaging of the perfect location fallacy. Hence, not an absence of crowds, yachts, and so on, but a tracing of dislocation between place and the anticipatory imaging of that place in the hysteria of media hype. Secondly, Fremantle/Perth is deployed as a location for the imaginary of fiction. Because still photographers don't generally go on location hunts with a script under their arm, we might assume they are not motivated by desire for the perfect location. Yet why should we assume that they are not driven by a search for the perfect location as that space where everything falls into place, as that place which is better than any other for situating objects, items, ideas, dreams? In different ways the sea and the factory have provided pretexts for the development of documentary genre photography, yet simultaneously these very genres can be read as projections of the imaginary. So perhaps the concept of location— as both a siting and the potential for a staging, for a mise en scène— is pertinent to all photography. What interests me particularly in these Ballantine photos is the convergence of a desire to site with an impulse to citation.

A beach, a cluster of buildings—empty space. These images (reading to and fro between these and other images in the series) cite the *idea* of location as an arena of the imaginary. In their figuring out of space (and erasure of the figurative) they suggest not so much a particularity of place as a potential for photographic rendering. That potential is evoked in a diffusion between the materiality of the representation and the abstraction. These images evoke the 'perfect location' (for a particular photographic rendition) at the very moment when they inscribe the fallacy of perfection. The series as a whole reminds me of Freud's description of the unconscious as a location where 'nothing ends, nothing happens, nothing is forgotten'. But particularly in these opening images, which set the scene for a photographic staging in which the desire of the photographer (and the viewer) renders space into place, and, more acutely, place into space.

To read these images as a citation of siting is to displace to some extent the 'narrative pretext' reading. The empty space is not loaded with expectation or suspense. However, it would be brashly precipitous to refuse all entertainment of suspense. This series of photographs is located (by this writing, by other media images) and contextualised by an extravagantly rhetorical event. A rhetoric of suspense and anticipation was integral to the production of this event as a contemporary commercial epic. Ballantine's photos deploy their own rhetoric to infiltrate, diffuse, and defuse the rhetoric of the epic.

And what of the metaphoric? Can we fill these images with all the plenitude that the void, the empty heart of Australia, has to offer? The metaphoric is enticing, yet I think the photos resist such a reading in their deflection of the familiar. The image of Australia as an uninhabited and hostile space is an image that exactly renders place into space. As has often been pointed out, it is a white colonial rendering (a whitewash job), an image conceived by urban eyes. Mudrooroo has observed that it is not entirely a reactive image; it is also a perversely imaginative projection:

> Terra Nullius, that heart of emptiness, has always been sought to be filled by the European...by a huge inland sea [a fantasy of early explorers] reflecting what else but the coast of Australia, representing what else but the familiar, especially the British familiar, the island familiar, the sound of the sea, the taste of the sea, the sight of the ocean never far from their senses, until a mind reality must be projected into suitable emptiness.

Further:

> A land people would not have dreamed a sea where none existed, nor would they have pictured all that is land as being a wide dreary beach edging on to the true reality of a sea.[3]

A curiously insular imagination, then, an anachronistically imperial insularity, produces this resonating metaphor (which still multiplies and reverberates in those endless lists disgorged by the ubiquitous postmodern pasticheur).

Mudrooroo's perspective provides an apt framing for the reflective process of Ballantine's series. So we can read the images of people looking out to sea (where nothing appears to happen) and the emptiness of the ocean as projected back into the urban landscape. Thus the photographic event (as opposed to the Cup event) is not

devoid of metaphoric trace, but it is not the predictable metaphor that frames the emptiness. For if these photos conjure Fremantle as an imaginary location they are also and simultaneously (through the process of the series) a documentation of place. Not a documentation of an event (though the event provides a dimension of fictionality), but of a place, perceived as a constellation of traits. There are none of the usual media landmarks—pavement cafés pulsating with cosmopolitan atmosphere, overflowing and convivial pubs, quaintly rejigged buildings, meticulously restored façades. But this is undoubtedly an urban coastal landscape. The landscape is austere, sparse, composed in a gauchely ad hoc manner—but the urban is imprinted in every composition. And, if the images are ghosted by the America's Cup, so too they are haunted by another Fremantle, never pictured as such. Fremantle is a port town: its immediate coast is industrialised, it is historically a place of arrivals and departures, a point of exit and of destination. On the edge of Perth (linked by sprawling suburbia), it is also on the far edge of the continent, facing towards the Indian Ocean rather than the rest of Australia. Perth is nowadays also the home of those who have 'arrived'—the self-made millionaires, the nationalistic sporting tycoons—and of those who are always about to leave (sacrilegiously ungratified by the laid-back lifestyle) in search of a 'real' city.

So people hang around in these photos, never quite arriving or departing, in transit yet poised, in vague expectation of movement, of something happening. They look out to sea and appear to see bugger all. If there are yachts out there, there is no sense of a race, no sense of departure and arrival, nothing happens, nothing ends. If letters always reach their destination, yachts, it would seem, are curiously suspended and imaginary. And yet the Cup, as an event (that takes place through duration), is inscribed in these still photographs in the configuration of urban space. It is not the desert that is imprinted in this space; it is the ocean as location of an imaginary epic event.

An immaculate Norfolk pine is planted dead centre. In the top half of the frame: sky. In the bottom half: paving stones. A discrete slash of ocean separates the elements. Off-centre a second tree, diminished by perspective but in perfect symmetry with the centre. A hard dark shadow is cast jaggedly on the paving stones by a suspended rubbish bin. Is it there as a repository for pine needles which might escape composure and contaminate the unsullied surface? But then is it a real pine tree? Perhaps the set has been cleared, all litter already deposited in the bin; or perhaps the bin is a sign of anticipation, a premonition of untidy tourists. Are we seeing a real location that is like a set, or a set that is preparing for the real?

In the distance, reduced out of proportion, a corporate toy town. Presiding over these miniature buildings, an austere yet menacing sprinkler. An ungainly tree lurches sideways, away from buildings and sprinkler. Is this prehensile watering device located here to nurture the expansive grassy foreground, or to put a damper over the city? Is this an appropriate place for an epic event?

A souvenir kiosk in the middle of nowhere. A prefab, hired, temporary structure; backed on to the foreshore, it faces a clean and empty road. A large litter bin stands waiting. The paving, the road, the litter bin—all testify to an urban location, yet, simultaneously, to a forlorn lack of urbanity. There is a sense of anonymity (Nowhere or Anywhere) evoked by the composition, a sense that persists, pervasive, despite the declaration of place. 'G' day'—an Australian colloquialism, a greeting, a hello—becomes incorporated into a declaration of Western Australian identity/hospitality. Functioning as a slogan of the euphemistic 'hospitality industry', it renders local identity equally euphemistic. It appears, compelled by the force of repetition, in the most inhospitable configurations: in symmetry with other repetitions—sale, sale, sale—and inscribed on T-shirts worn by headless mannequins posing behind glass windows.

The Bond building is underwritten by graffiti: 'Fathers are the danger *not* the stranger'. In the context of a series on the Cup, the paternal might be inflected as the menace of City Fathers, of corporate capital; incest and domestic cannibalism as more immediately threatening than sporting competitors. Cannibalism surfaces elsewhere (where else but on T-shirts?) in a possibly more playful mode—'Dennis Conner Eats Kiwis'. If it is playful, it is only so because the intelligibility of the slogan depends upon a posturing of Siamese twins. Yet, after Arbus (and after the Bond building), how can this posture avoid traces of sinister discomfort?

A solitary woman with her back to the camera holds binoculars to her eyes and looks out to sea. Her body is settled to support the raising of her arms; she is entirely focused on the activity of looking, appears settled in this posture as though she has grown into it, waiting. Although we do not see the binoculars, they are imaginatively present, evoked through gesturality. Similarly, the sea is scarcely present. We can imagine its being there, but what she actually sees is entirely in the realm of the imaginary. The view of the binoculars and the view of the camera do not coincide.

They look in different directions these watchers, shoulders averted, glances crossing. A haphazardly formed group clusters, anticipating an arrival, but from where, and what is it that will happen? They appear to be suspended in transit, perhaps at a bus stop, perhaps awaiting a message from the sky. A woman, rising out of the sea, arrives in an empty space, glances towards an empty chair on the edge of the frame. She clutches a towel to her body as though pausing, shielding herself awkwardly from a hostile view. The same location, but peopled, people coming and going, turning their backs on the ocean. A group of three men, arrested in a moment of confidentiality, of body confidence.

Nothing appears to be happening out there on the ocean. Nothing begins or ends. And yet in the photographic scene nothing (of what is happening out there) is forgotten. If the America's Cup, in the event, turned out to be an impossible vision, impossible as a spectator

sport, the imaginary of the event is imprinted in the photographic space. These hapless spectators see something: instead of yachts they see 'G'day from WA'. They will leave eventually, bereft of photos, documentation of an epic event enacted by a cast of thousands: but they will go bearing souvenirs, memories of the place inscribed on their bodies, on T-shirts which they will wear out.

If the image of an ocean event occurs as an impression imprinted on T-shirts (and in empty space), this process involves both deflection and reduction. While the photographic process evokes generalised reflections upon the 'perfect location fallacy', the elision between spectatorship and tourism, it also documents, in a quite specific way, the relation between space and place and dimension. The siting of Fremantle/Perth involves a perception of the way in which small cities (particularly cities small in population and large in terms of space) project their own identity by reducing everything (starting with litter, with foreign contamination), by an impulse to scale down. So the Bond building finds its reflection in a tacky makeshift kiosk. But, obversely, the photographic process projects the tawdriness of souvenirs back into the site of entrepreneurial pretension.

There is one photograph in the series which shows a group of people, suspenseful, all looking intently in the same direction. The

location is a pub and their necks are craned, their eyes cast upwards. Following their gaze, where do we arrive? An expansive ceiling, the whirr of a fan immobilised rendering atmosphere tactile, an invitation to travel—Air New Zealand—propped in a corner. And in the centre, at the bottom of the frame but close to the ceiling: a television set. There are images there in the small screen, a sense of crowding, of activity. But what are those images? We can only imagine.

NOTES

1 I have made a small selection from the series. Kevin Ballantine made a different (though sometimes overlapping) selection for an exhibition held in Perth in September 1987.
2 *Libération* (May 1987).
3 Mudrooroo, 'A Sea of Dreams; A Rock of Reality; A Land of Travel', unpublished paper.

Further reading

This reading list offers a selective, even an idiosyncratic guide to recent Australian work in cultural studies. The sections correspond to those we have used to order the Reader, but this is mainly for convenience; many entries could equally well be placed under other headings. Since space constraints preclude any effort at comprehensiveness, we have chosen to emphasise influential essays which have not yet been anthologised or which appear in useful collections and journals. Readers interested in particular issues will find additional references in the endnotes to individual essays, and in these important survey texts:

Grossberg, Lawrence, Nelson, Cary and Treichler, Paula (eds), *Cultural Studies*, Routledge, New York, 1992.
Ruthven, Ken (ed.), *Beyond the Disciplines: The New Humanities*, The Australian Academy of the Humanities, Canberra, 1992.
Turner, Graeme, *British Cultural Studies: An Introduction*, Allen & Unwin, Sydney, 1990.

While we do not wish to subsume as 'cultural studies' the distinct fields of Aboriginal Studies and literary multiculturalism, the following texts provide basic reference points for much contemporary critical work on culture in Australia:

Davis, Jack and Hodge, Bob (eds), *Aboriginal Writing Today*, Australian Institute of Aboriginal Studies, Canberra, 1985.
Gunew, Sneja, and Longley, Kateryna O (eds), *Striking Chords: Multicultural Literary Interpretations*, Allen & Unwin, Sydney, 1992.
Narogin, Mudrooroo, *Writing from the Fringe: A Study of Modern Aboriginal Literature*, Hyland House, Melbourne, 1990.

292

FURTHER READING

I REPRESENTATION WARS

Ang, Ien, 'On Not Speaking Chinese', forthcoming in *Migrations of Culture*, Routledge/Comedia, London.
Chakrabarty, Dipesh, 'Postcoloniality and the Artifice of History: Who Speaks for "Indian" Pasts?', *Representations* 37 (Winter 1992), 1–26.
Chakrabarty, Dipesh, 'Subaltern Studies and Critique of History', *Arena* 96 (1991), 105–20.
Creed, Barbara, 'Horror and the Monstrous-Feminine: An Imaginary Abjection', *Screen* 27:1 (1986), 44–70.
During, Simon, 'Postmodernism or Post-Colonialism Today', *Textual Practice* 1:1 (Spring 1987), 32–47.
During, Simon, 'Postcolonalism and Globalization', *Meanjin* 51:2 (1992), 339–53.
Freadman, Anne and Macdonald, Amanda, 'Is this a TV interview or a trial?' in Freadman, A and Macdonald, A, *What is This Thing Called 'Genre'?*, Boombana Publications, Mount Nebo QLD, 1992.
Hamilton, Annette, 'Fear and Desire: Aborigines, Asians and the National Imaginary', *Australian Cultural History* 9 (1990), 14–35.
Hodge, Bob and Mishra, Vijay, *Dark Side of the Dream: Australian Literature and the Postcolonial Mind*, Allen & Unwin, Sydney, 1990.
Jayamanne, Laleen, 'Love Me Tender, Love Me True, Never Let Me Go. . .: A Sri Lankan Reading of Tracey Moffatt's *Night Cries*' in *Feminism and the Politics of Difference*, ed. Anna Yeatman and Sneja Gunew, Allen & Unwin, Sydney, 1993.
Kirby, Vicki, '*Corpus delicti*: the body at the scene of writing' in *Cartographies: Poststructuralism and the Mapping of Bodies and Spaces*, ed. Rosalyn Diprose and Robyn Ferrell, Allen & Unwin, Sydney, 1991.
Lawson, Sylvia, 'Towards Decolonization: Some Problems and Issues for Film History in Australia', *Film Reader* 4 (1979), 63–71.
Martin, Adrian, 'The Night Has a Thousand Eyes', *Cantrills Filmnotes*, 41:2 (1983), 53–68.
Michaels, Eric, *For A Cultural Future: Francis Jupurrurla Makes TV at Yuendumu*, Artspace, Sydney, 1987.
Michaels, Eric, *Unbecoming: An AIDS Diary*, EMPress, Sydney, 1990.
Sophia, Zoë, 'Virtual Corporeality: A Feminist View', *Australian Feminist Studies* 15 (Autumn 1992), 11–24.

II AESTHETICS AND EVERYDAY LIFE

Craik, Jennifer, 'The Azaria Chamberlain Case: A Question of Infanticide', *Australian Journal of Cultural Studies* 4:2 (1987), 123–51.
Grace, Helen, 'Business, pleasure, narrative: The folktale in our times', in *Cartographies: Poststructuralism and the Mapping of Bodies and Spaces* ed. Rosalyn Diprose and Robyn Ferrell, Allen & Unwin, Sydney, 1991.
Grace, Helen, 'One Man's Meat', *Art & Text* 28 (March–May 1988), 38–49.
Hamilton, Annette, 'Beer and Being: the Australian Tourist in Bali' in *Writing Australian Culture: Text, Society and National Identity* ed. Julie Marcus [*Social Analysis* 27], Department of Anthropology, University of Adelaide, 1990.
Hunter, Ian, 'Setting Limits to Culture', *New Formations* 4 (Spring 1988), 103–23.
Hunter, Ian, 'Aesthetics and Cultural Studies' in *Cultural Studies* ed. Grossberg, Nelson and Treichler, op. cit.

293

Johnson, Dianne, 'From Fairy to Witch: imagery and myth in the Azaria case', *Australian Journal of Cultural Studies* 2:2 (1984), 90–107.

Morris, Meaghan, *Ecstasy and Economics: American Essays for John Forbes*, EMPress, Sydney, 1992.

Nightingale, Virginia, 'The Texture of Everyday Life', *Australian Cultural Studies Conference 1990 Proceedings* ed. Deborah Chambers and Hart Cohen, Faculty of Humanities and Social Sciences, University of Western Sydney, 1991, 359–66.

Rowley, Sue, 'Mind Over Matter? Reading the Art/Craft Debate', *West* 1:1 (1989), 3–7.

Sanders, Noel, 'Bondi the Beautiful: The Impossibility of an Aesthetic', *Media Papers* 16, New South Wales Institute of Technology, Sydney, 1982.

III THE USES OF POPULAR CULTURE

Bennett, Tony, 'The Political Rationality of the Museum', *Continuum* 3:1 (1990), 35–52.

Bennett, Tony, 'Marxist Cultural Politics: In Search of "the Popular"', *Australian Journal of Cultural Studies* 1:2 (1983), 2–28.

Brophy, Philip, 'Horrality—the Textuality of Contemporary Horror Films', *Screen* 27:1 (1986), 2–13.

Brophy, Philip, Dermody, Susan, Hebdige, Dick and Muecke, Stephen, *Streetwise Flash Art: Is There A Future For Cultural Studies?*, Power Institute of Fine Arts Occasional Paper 6, Sydney, 1987.

Fiske, John, 'Popular Forces and the Culture of Everyday Life', *Southern Review* 21:3 (1988), 288–306.

Fiske, John, Hodge, Bob and Turner, Graeme, *Myths of Oz: Reading Australian Popular Culture*, Allen & Unwin, Sydney, 1987.

Frow, John, 'Michel de Certeau and the Practice of Representation', *Cultural Studies* 5:1 (1991), 52–60.

Grace, Helen, 'The Mysteries of Manhood', *Intervention* 21/22 [*Flesh*] (1988), 75–83.

Hayward, Philip, 'Desire caught by its tale: the unlikely return of the Merman in Madonna's *Cherish*', *Cultural Studies* 5:1 (1991), 98–106.

Hodge, Bob and Tripp, David, *Children and Television: A Semiotic Approach*, Polity Press, Cambridge, 1986.

King, Noel and Rowse, Tim, '"Typical Aussies": Television and Populism in Australia', *Framework* 22/3 (1983), 37–42.

King, Noel ('"Not To Be An Intellectual": Adrian Martin on Teen Movies') and Martin, Adrian ('Mon Cas'), Teen Movies Debate, *Cinema Papers* 89 (August 1992), 44–48.

McHoul, Alec and O'Regan, Tom, 'Towards A Paralogics of Textual Technologies: Batman, Glasnost and Relativism in Cultural Studies', *Southern Review* 25:1 (1992), 5–26.

Martin, Adrian, 'Time Tunnel', *TV Times: 35 Years of Watching Television in Australia*, ed. Denise Corrigan and David Watson, Museum of Contemporary Art, Sydney, 1991.

Morris, Meaghan, 'Things To Do With Shopping Centres', in *Grafts: Feminist Cultural Criticsm* ed. Susan Sheridan, Verso, London, 1988.

O'Regan, Tom, '*The Man From Snowy River* and Australian Popular Culture' in *An Australian Film Reader* ed. Albert Moran and Tom O'Regan, Currency Press, Sydney, 1985.

Potts, John, *Radio in Australia*, University of NSW Press, Sydney, 1989.
Rowley, Sue, '"My Stories Are My Wealth"—Craft and Narrative Traditions', *Craftwest National*, August 1992, 14–18.
Stratton, Jon, *The Young Ones*, Black Swan Press, Perth, 1992.
Taylor, Paul, 'A Culture of Temporary Culture', *Art & Text* 16 (Summer 1984/85), 94–107.
Tulloch, John and Turner, Graeme (eds), *Australian Television: Programs, Pleasures and Politics*, Allen & Unwin, Sydney, 1989.

IV THE POLITICS OF PUBLICS

Ang, Ien, 'Stalking the Wild Viewer', *Continuum* 4:2 (1991), 19–35.
Bennett, Tony, 'Putting Policy into Cultural Studies' in *Cultural Studies* ed. Grossberg, Nelson and Treichler, op. cit.
Cunningham, Stuart, *Framing Culture: Criticism and Policy in Australia*, Allen & Unwin, Sydney, 1992.
Frow, John, 'Class and Culture: Funding the Arts', *Meanjin* 45:1 (1986), 118–28.
Jacka, Elizabeth, 'Australian Cinema: An Anachronism in the '80s?' in *The Imaginary Industry: Australian Film in the Late '80s* ed. Susan Dermody and Elizabeth Jacka, Australian Film, Television and Radio School, Sydney, 1988.
King, Noel, 'From "Play" to "Players": Stuart Cunningham's *Framing Culture*', *Filmnews* September 1992.
Hartley, John, 'The Real World of Audiences' in *Tele-ology: Studies in Television*, Routledge, London and New York 1992, 199–25.
Mercer, Colin, 'Neverending Stories: The problem of reading in cultural studies', *Australian Journal of Communication* 16 (1989), 125–38.
Miller, Toby, 'Splitting the Citizen', *Continuum* 4:2 (1991), 193–205.
Nightingale, Virginia, 'Media Audiences—Media Products', *Australian Journal of Cultural Studies* 2:1 (1984), 23–35.
O'Ryan, Gabrielle, 'Oh Bondage: Up Yours!', *Continuum* 6:1 (1991), 45–51.
Routt, William, 'Keith Windschuttle's *Media*', *Australian Journal of Cultural Studies* 3:1 (1985), 128–34.

V THE PRACTICE OF PLACE

Benterrak, Krim, Muecke, Stephen and Roe, Paddy, *Reading the Country: Introduction to Nomadology*, Fremantle Arts Centre Press, 1984.
Brophy, Philip, 'A Face Without A Place', *Art & Text* 16 (Summer 1984/85), 68–80.
Foss, Paul, *Island in the Stream: Myths of Place in Australian Culture*, Pluto Press, Sydney, 1988.
Freadman, Anne, 'The Vagabond Arts' in *In the Place of French: Essays in and around French Studies in honour of Michael Spencer*, Boombana Publications, Mt Nebo, Qld, 1992.
Fry, Tony, and Willis, Anne-Marie, 'Criticism Against the Current', *Meanjin* 48:2 (Winter 1989), 223–40.
Gibson, Ross, *South of the West: Postcolonialism and the Narrative Construction of Australia*, Indiana University Press, Bloomington, 1992.
Gunew, Sneja, 'Denaturalizing cultural nationalisms: multicultural readings of "Australia"' in *Nation and Narration* ed. Homi Bhabha, Routledge, London, 1990.

Hartley, John, 'Suburbanality (in Cultural Studies)', *Meanjin* 51:3 (1992), 453–64.

Healy, Chris, '"We Know Your Mob Now": Histories and their Cultures', *Meanjin* 49:3 (1990), 512–23.

Horne, Donald, *Money Made Us*, Penguin, Ringwood, 1976.

Morris, Meaghan, *Great Moments in Social Climbing: King Kong and The Human Fly*, Local Consumption Publications, Sydney, 1992.

Muecke, Stephen, *Textual Spaces: Aboriginality and Cultural Studies*, University of NSW Press, Sydney, 1992.

O'Regan, Tom, 'Towards a High Communication Policy: Assessing Recent Changes within Australian Broadcasting', *Continuum* 2:1 (1988/89), 135–58.

Schaffer, Kay, *Women and the Bush: Forces of Desire in the Australian Cultural Tradition*, Cambridge University Press, 1988.

Stratton, Jon, 'Deconstructing the Territory', *Cultural Studies* 3:1 (1989), 38–57.

Sutton, Peter, 'Aboriginal Art, the Nation State, Suburbia', *Artlink* 12:3 (1992), 6–9.

Taylor, Paul (ed.), 'Special Section: Antipodality', *Art & Text* 6 (1982), 49–88 [includes essays by Paul Foss and Imants Tillers].

Thomas, Martin, 'Making This State Grate: The Pretensions of Darling Harbour', *Art & Text* 29 (June–August 1988), 64–75.